Letters of Sherwood Anderson

Portrait of Sherwood Anderson by Steichen, 1926

Letters of
SHERWOOD ANDERSON

SELECTED AND EDITED WITH AN
INTRODUCTION AND NOTES BY
Howard Mumford Jones
IN ASSOCIATION WITH
Walter B. Rideout

With Illustrations

Little, Brown and Company · *Boston*

To
Eleanor Anderson

Introduction

G. K. Chesterton once remarked that there is no such thing as a novel by Charles Dickens, but only something cut off from the vast and flowing stream of his personality. In the same way one can assert that there is no such thing as a work of fiction by Sherwood Anderson. The novels are autobiographical, the autobiographical books have in them the elements of fiction, the letters read like the first draft of a novel. There are short stories so compact they might become novels, and there are novels that are at best only dilated short stories. Yet this library, at once unified and variegated, has its common denominator. The books represent facets of Sherwood Anderson, that enigmatic and engaging personality whose friends ranged from Gertrude Stein to the stone-worker near Ripshin farm in Virginia, and whose alternating moods of exaltation and despair are as kaleidoscopic as ever Byron's were.

The letters here printed, most of them for the first time, read like a posthumous novel. But they also read like something buttressed and substantiated by whatever Anderson's books had already told us of the writer. Surely there are not many other instances in which a man's letters thus neatly confirm his works, and his works confirm his letters.

A sample paragraph will illustrate this intimate relationship as well as a dozen could do. Anderson writes:

> I have been to Nebraska, where the big engines are tearing the hills to pieces; over the low hills runs the promise of the corn. You wait, dear Brother; I shall bring God home to the sweaty men in the corn rows. My songs shall creep into their hearts and teach them the sacredness of the long aisles of growing things that lead to the throne of the God of men.

This might come from *Dark Laughter*, or from *Many Marriages*, or from a short story, or it might even be a preliminary note for something in *Mid-American Chants*. It appears as a matter of fact in an early letter to Waldo Frank. Of course there are readers who do not like epistolary writing of this sort. It makes them uncomfortable, and they murmur

something about posturing before a mental mirror. But others will remark upon the identity of style in the letters with that in the books.
Either way, favorably or unfavorably, what you get is Sherwood Anderson.

The qualities of this style are evident. It continues throughout this
collection, as if all the letters were written at one time. It is a style that
is supple, conversational, vivid, lyrical, having a touch of artifice, having
also, perhaps, a touch of the amateur, but it is a style that presents us
the author in his habit as he lived. It begins with the first letter and it
extends through the last. The first letter is dated 1916 and was written
when Anderson was forty; and since there are almost five thousand letters in the great Newberry Library collection, it may reasonably be
asked why no earlier letter appears in this collection.

The answer is simple. One day, so to speak, Anderson woke up and
said, "I am a writer." As a writer he was born adult or at any rate as
mature as he was ever to be. There is no good exhuming letters written
by Anderson the businessman, a quite different fellow, and the few letters in the collection about writing and written before 1916 do not say
what is said in the letters here printed.

The myth which pictures Sherwood Anderson walking out of his
office in the midst of dictating a letter is historically false but symboli-
cally true. When he discovered his purpose in life was not money-
making but writing, the discovery was absolute. Of course there was a
period of hesitation, of course there was a shy, awkward, hidden ap-
prentice time, of course there were later agonizing episodes of doubt
or despair. Some of these darker moods are recorded here and some are
recorded in letters not reprinted. Nevertheless, the discovery was final
in the sense that among the saints conversion is final. From the time of
this discovery our writer was a dedicated spirit, a single, if complex
and sometimes divided, personality, which, when it published itself to
the world, by the strength of its insistence upon subjective, personal,
and unconventional values, aroused the hostility of the genteel and the
enthusiasm of youth.

There was in Anderson a combination of simplicity and subtlety that
lies in a recognizable Midwestern tradition. You can see it in his attitude toward New York. In an early letter to Waldo Frank you find the
awe of the child of Middle America before what he conceives to be the
superiority of the East. He returned from a visit to New York, he says,
filled with "odd feelings of reverence and humbleness." One thinks of

Howells's first visit to the enchanted ground of New England. Then, in the cycle of letters to Van Wyck Brooks, you can watch the alternation of moods. The friendship with Brooks develops, there is never any doubt about it, but Anderson's attitude is patently ambivalent. He loves Brooks, he urges Brooks to write him more freely, he counsels Brooks about Mark Twain — and Anderson, with some justice, thought he had the "feel" of Clemens as Brooks had not. But he is also a little afraid of Brooks, whom he thought of as a scholar, a college man, an intellectualist, a sophisticate critic with all literature at his command.

Brooks, then, was somebody to be both loved and placated. By 1930 Anderson was writing of the power that Brooks exercised over his (Anderson's) mind, since, precisely as when Brooks had been writing about Mark Twain, Anderson had obediently thought about Twain, so now, when Brooks is writing about Henry James, Anderson reads James. Then, suddenly, another facet of Anderson appears, the subtle side, in a revealing paragraph guaranteed to raise the hackles of every intellectualist critic in the country. Anderson writes:

> You may be interested to know my reactions to some solid weeks of James reading — the feeling of him as a man who never found anyone to love, who did not dare love. I really can't care much for any character after he gets through with it; he, in short, takes my love away from me too.
>
> I've a fancy — can it be true that he is the novelist of the haters? Oh, the thing infinitely refined and carried far into the field of intellectuality, as skillful haters find out how to do.

One's response to this passage may be one of three kinds, perhaps of more. One may, for example, be instantly confirmed in the opinion that Anderson was a minor writer, of limited range, deserving the oblivion contemporary neglect wants to consign him to. Or one can say that East is East and West is West, and in American literature never the twain shall meet. Or, once past the shock of the thing, one can be struck by Anderson's penetration. I suggest there is some truth in each of these responses.

Certainly Anderson's range was limited. (So, for that matter, was Thackeray's.) Out of his voluminous publications it is at least possible that only *Winesburg, Ohio,* and a handful of the short stories will survive, marvelous as some pages in *Tar,* for example, or in *Dark Laughter* may be. Moreover, his Midwestern qualities determine and limit his work and keep him apart from the world of the *Nation* and the *New*

Republic — those fellows, he thought, were too analytical — and from the aesthetic movement on the Atlantic Coast. Note, in this connection, a late letter to Paul Rosenfeld, in which Anderson finds it necessary to justify, against his aesthetic friend, an interest in the common man. Finally, but more importantly, the insight is really acute. The very phrasing is Jamesian — "Oh, the thing infinitely refined and carried far into the field of intellectuality, as skillful haters find out how to do" may, to all appearances, exist somewhere in James's prefaces or in the fiction. What is more to the point is the truth in Anderson's remark. There is a real sense in which skillful haters do carry the thing refined far into the field of intellectuality, and there is a real sense in which James is the novelist of the haters, as any prolonged study of Jamesian criticism will by-and-by reveal.

Anderson, though he had the subtlety to make this comment, never carried anything to this pitch of intellectual refinement, not merely because his sensitivity was alien to that of James, but also because, whether James is or is not the novelist of the haters, hatred in this degree was omitted from Anderson's make-up. He was capable of indignation, but that is another thing. "I want," he wrote the Copenhavers in 1934, "to write one joyous book before I die . . . not at all sentimentally joyous, but having in it a deeper joy. . . . Isn't there a deeper lesson God wants us to know, and that we, like perverse children — that's what we are, quite hopelessly children — that we will not know?" In contemporary fiction joy has become unfashionable, and love is seldom discussed except when one is discussing Kierkegaard or Dostoevski. But love and joy are central to Sherwood Anderson.

At this point, of course, the mean sensual man sagely wags his head. Love, he will aver in his ribald way, love is, indeed, the word for a novelist who was married four times, whose works were sometimes banned because of their frank sexuality, and whose writing is supposed in part to have prepared the way for Freudian fiction in the United States. The mean sensual man, however cogent he sounds, is, I think, essentially irrelevant. The point at issue is not eroticism but generosity of spirit. Read the letters to young writers in this book. Read the letters in which Anderson expresses his pleasure in discovering a fine personality or a fine work of art. Or read the letters in which Anderson broods over man's inhumanity to man — those, for example, having to do with the Danville strike. His astonishing statement to Paul Kellogg, in a letter of December 14, 1920, that what the country needs is a new

leisure class is at once his protest against the gospel of getting on and
his demand that there be a larger American margin for love and joy.
(One must remember that in 1920 leisure was not yet a problem, but
merely an ideal.)

> I want these men and women to stop me on the road or in the
> city streets and talk with me without feeling that I am keeping
> them from their tasks in some factory or office. . . . I want a body
> of healthy young men and women to agree to quit working, to
> loaf, to refuse to be hurried or try to get on in the world — in
> short, to become intense individualists.

That, he added grimly, is "pretty un-American, and I am afraid the
Americanization Committee of my home town will get after me for
saying it."
Love and joy, however, are commonly by-products, a truth Anderson
recognized only occasionally, as when he wrote Trigant Burrow that

> . . . no man knows himself or can arrive at truth concerning him-
> self except by what seems like indirection. I have a desire to take
> hold of indirection as a tool and use it in an attempt to arrive at
> truth.

Usually, however, he tried to attain these ends by direct assault.
Hence his feverish wanderings over the earth, his incessant beginning
of manuscripts that were never finished, his constant self-examination,
his devouring sense of incompleteness. Two or three times he refers to
himself as a child. Once he admits (to Van Wyck Brooks) that he is the
perpetual adolescent. As such, he says, speaking for his generation, "I
do represent much." One thinks of Fitzgerald.
      In some sense Sherwood Anderson knew himself better than his
critics knew him. He was, indeed, the child, he was, indeed, the perpetual adolescent in the kingdoms of this world. Without debating the
question of who the inhabitants of the kingdom of heaven truly are,
without entering into the vexed problem of whether the eye of the
artist is or is not identical with the eye of the child — I have in mind the
parallel between Anderson's prose and the painting of his time — one
notes the naïveté of his loneliness and of his moments of joy. The latter
were the moments of a child happy in the day. The loneliness is the
grievance of a child who fancies he is not wanted. In saying this I do
not in the least mean to derogate from the genuineness of either the

rapture or the suffering, I am merely trying to particularize his moods.

Take, for example, the letter to Horace Liveright in which he describes *Dark Laughter,* a letter which has all the serious appeal of a child who longs for approval:

> Since you were here, I have been working on it every minute of every day, in fact have kept at it so hard and long that each day when I got through, I was so exhausted I could hardly get up from my desk. . . . You see what I am trying to give you now, Horace, is something of the orchestration of the book. The neuroticism, the hurry and self-consciousness of modern life, and back of it the easy, strange laughter of the blacks. There is your dark, earthy laughter — the Negro, the earth, and the river — that suggests the title.
>
> Bet on this book, Horace, it is going to be there with a bang. I wanted to write you about it again and tell you how I feel about it, but I have been so absorbed in the novel itself, tearing away scaffolding, laying new foundations, putting in joists and doorsills, that I could not think of anything but building the novel.

The very metaphor, though Anderson uses it often, suggests playing house. But note especially how, as with children, the intensity of absorption in the play becomes identified with value. The novel must be good because he has tried so hard.

In such moments Anderson's simplicity — a simplicity well-nigh embarrassing — is naked and evident. But there is another, mystical aspect to Anderson which places him with Whitman, Twain, Van Gogh, and Dostoevski — even with the religious mystics. There are many instances of this spiritualized pantheism in the letters, but perhaps the noblest expression is a long letter of comfort addressed to Burton Emmett in 1933. We also, says Anderson, are a part of something, of some incomprehensible thing, and this incomprehensible thing is "the real inner glory of life." I believe, he writes, "that it is this universal thing, scattered about in many people, a fragment of it here, a fragment there, this thing we call love that we have to keep on trying to tap." The whole letter breathes such nobility, it is impossible to leave it. He says, for instance:

> In others life goes on. When I have no more courage, it may be that the person sitting next to me or walking beside me in the street is full of courage. Why shouldn't I ask for it, take it when

I get it? There is a curious contradiction here. Sometimes when I go like a beggar asking warmth, comfort and love from another, knowing I do not deserve it, I begin living a little in others, and thus I get away from self.

And again:

As for the end, I have often thought that when it comes, there will be a kind of real comfort in the fact that the self will go then. There is some kind of universal thing we will pass into that will in any event give us escape from this disease of self.

This is perfect writing. It has the clean line and lofty economy of style of the great French moralists.

The longing to escape from self, the desire to merge with others and with the universe, is central in Anderson's complex outlook. He insists, paradoxically, upon both the need of individuality and the curse of self-consciousness. His desire to transcend mere egoism runs throughout his correspondence. It is clear, from the letters concerning the Hedgerow Theatre or his own interest in playmaking, that the warmth and intimacy of the theater had special attraction for him. Again, we read that an unfinished novel, *Immaturity*, was to have illustrated this overcoming of the self. It was to have been a book that

. . . oozes out over the whole landscape and should be in the end the kind of book that a man takes to bed with him on bleak winter evenings. . . . The winds and rains come, and the land is black with fertility. Men will be born, infinite men of broad girth and cocky eyes. Escape if you can all the art and intellectual talk.

Inasmuch as Anderson is one of our most expressive commentators on the nature of art, in this context "art and intellectual talk" connotes the false separatism of art from existence he disliked in the New York circles.

What *is* the writer's true self, his dream self or the economic unit that he is? What is the relation of imaginative work to the world of bargain and sale? How much shall an artist sacrifice to the market place? Can an honest man split himself in twain, one half of him creating after his instincts and the other half becoming a literary carpenter at contractor's labor? This theme also runs throughout the correspondence. One finds Anderson in a panic imploring his agent, or a publisher, or a magazine

editor, or a politician to accept a scheme of hack work he outlines, for
which he can get pay; and in a later letter one finds him roundly con-
demning the crassness of this very procedure. It is interesting to watch
him demand support for struggling young artists — the letter to Otto
Kahn is an example — while almost simultaneously he shies away from
other well-meant attempts to subsidize free spirits, fearful that he who
pays the piper eventually calls the tune. If his economic thinking in this
regard was both confused and emotional, who has done any better? The
letters in this respect give us a perfect example of the psychological dislocation of the artist in industrial society, a dislocation the more keenly
felt because Anderson had seen business from the inside and felt a
lack of integrity in it.

Another theme haunting the correspondence seems likewise pertinent
here. Anderson dreamed of, but never wrote, a book about Lincoln. For
him Lincoln transcended self, he expressed the social mysticism of the
Middle West; and though Sandburg, not Anderson, was to write the
work which supremely set forth the Midwestern interpretation of our
secular saint, Anderson was perpetually drawn to him. Note also, in this
connection, a passage in a letter to Paul Rosenfeld, which runs:

> I take these little, ugly factory towns, these big sprawling cities
> into something. I wish it would not sound to[o] silly to say I pour
> a dream over it, consciously, intentionally, for a purpose. I want
> to write beautifully, create beautifully, not outside but in this
> thing in which I am born, in this place where, in the midst of ugly
> towns, cities, Fords, moving pictures, I have always lived, must
> always live.

This was true self-knowledge. Wander as he might, Anderson remained perpetually the troubled Midwesterner, alternately revolting
against industrialism and finding poetry in machines, rejoicing in American productive energy and pitying the joyless workers, believing both
in the mass and in the individual, yet acutely conscious of the limitations in these antithetical concepts. His radicalism was a function of
this need for self-transcendence, and it expressed itself confusedly, as
in the vague, inconclusive symbolism of *Marching Men*. His radicalism
was never essentially economic or political — not once but many times
he repudiated the Communists — for it was always mystical, the radicalism of the poet, the child, and the pragmatist. I think it still has much to
say to the thirst after democracy in our times.

Radicalism in another sense was deep-sunk in Anderson's own nature, and permits us to have from him a fresh view of the nature of the imaginative process itself. The great prefaces by Henry James, prefaces which only Ellen Glasgow's book, *A Certain Measure,* can approach in illumination, are by common consent the most revealing statement in American letters of the way of the writer with his material. Great as these essays are, they are inevitably the expression of a second stage in the creative process — the stage wherein the writer reflects upon what he has done in the perspective of time and tells us of the relation he now sees among intention, craftsmanship, fulfillment, and reception. They show us, they admirably show us, how best to understand the work of art. A very large part of Anderson's discourse in these letters concerns an earlier and more primitive stage in the creative process. He brings us down to a more primary level of the psychology of writing — to writing as obsession, to writing as rhythm, to writing as a function in large degree of a subconscious, certainly of a nonrational, part of the psyche.

Thus of *Marching Men* he tells us that the concept appealed strongly to "my rather primitive nature," that

> . . . the beat and rhythm of the thing would come and go; a thousand outside things would flow in. I worked madly; then I threw the book away. Again and again I came back to it. In the end I had no idea as to whether it was good or bad. I only knew that the thing was out of me . . .

Three or four times he compares literary composition to the experience of pregnancy and deliverance, and also to the poles of maleness and femaleness in life. After *Mid-American Chants* had, as he thought, liberated him from the reproach of "sentimental liberalism," he again insisted upon the primacy of rhythm —

> I want to achieve in it rhythm of words with rhythm of thought. . . . In making this book I have felt no call to responsibility to anything but my own inner sense of what is beautiful in the arrangement of words and ideas . . .

and he distinguished an outward technique from an inward technique, a kind of compulsion to truth:

> One day I found out that when I sat down to write, it was the more difficult to lie. The lie lay before one on the paper. It haunted one at night.

"I have," he said, "a great fear of phrase-making, for words are very tricky things," and "I do not want to make them rattle."

When the thing came off, when the divine afflatus was upon him, the effect was like the effect of vision on the mystic. He always remembered that the writing of "Hands" was such a moment of obsession; later he described another such seizure:

> I have begun working again and yesterday, for the 1st time in months, sat at my desk, here in this little country hotel, for hours with no consciousness of time passing, completely lost, the words and sentences with a fine rhy[th]mic flow, ideas coming like flights of birds, for the time, at least, completely happy. No. Happiness is not the word. To be happy there must be consciousness of self as happy, and in this state there is no self.

The trouble with the creative impulse, he said later, is that

> . . . it tends to lift you up too high into a sort of drunkenness and then drop you down too low. There is an artist lurking in every man. The high spots for the creative man come too seldom.

When they did not come, however they were desired, the result was an almost unbearable desolation. A sequence of letters to Paul Rosenfeld, in 1927, graphically records this spiritual dryness; and another sequence, addressed to his son John, perhaps unique in literature, adjures the son as a beginning artist to avoid some of these sorrows:

> You have to pay dearly for being an imaginative person. Learn to give as little time as possible to self-pity. It is ten times as important to be devoted as it is to succeed. You will be a fool if you think ever that you have succeeded in the arts.

The self, that old enemy, was again the perplexing element in the problem. As he wrote John —

> I presume it is the power of losing self. Self is the grand disease. It is what we are all trying to lose. . . . How people ever lose themselves who are not artists I do not know.

In the end, "perhaps a man has to manufacture his own interest in life."

> A man who is really sensitive has moments that lift him up higher than the average man. He wants to stay up there and can't. Then he begins to feel life is unfair to him. He broods. Self becomes all-important to him.

For the paradox of self was that it was at once the instrument and the obstacle of the artist, who is

> . . . after all, partly a product of his environment. He can do nothing with nature, cannot draw close unless sensitized. If sensitized, everything beats in on him. He does not escape the general tone and mood of the world in any event.

The only solution to the enigma was simplicity; and his complaint against writing as carried on in America was that it was smart. "Eternal lack of force taking itself out in smartness or cleverness and thinking they've done something," he said of some of the more "sophisticated" of his contemporaries. As for theories of art and aesthetics —

> Well, talking about it all is a little like handling a flower. It gets wilted or soiled. One speaks of the matter and then, right away, feels a little stuffy. I can't tell exactly why I think this is true, [yet] the one thing I detest, because it makes me feel detestable, is preaching or being a wise man or seer.

The best thing was to go among living people — human beings, he wrote a librarian, are "my library" — and then, as he said to Dreiser, "when we are simply telling, as we should really always be trying to tell, the simple story of lives, we are doing our best service."

Much could be said of Anderson's feeling for painting, of his incessant wish to unite the two arts in a common vision. But perhaps the best statement of how, in his experience, a work of art comes into being is found in the following passage, again from a letter to John Anderson.

> I used to think that the thing sought by the painter o[r] the sculptor was already in the stone or on the canvas, that something stood between it and the artist. There was what I thought of as the disease of individuality. I don't think this any more. This I have found out: there is in me, as in you, or any working artist, always the danger of a kind of statement. It may be that this only comes because we ourselves, as individuals, get between ourselves and the thing sought. Of course others thrust themselves in there too, but that is not what I am thinking about now. This I have found out from experience, that these floating ideas, always drifting through the mind, if given free play by action, seem to become definite and alive. As the painter might make an infinite number of sketches, often rapidly, but nevertheless making

them, as a writer puts down on paper the same kind of passing things, something does often result. Often a sudden realization of beauty. So in human relationships.

For him, therefore, all doctrine of external form was meaningless. He sought, instead, the under surface, the subconscious meaning of a human situation; and form, as he told Dwight Macdonald in a long and unfortunately somewhat illegible letter, is not something imposed, but is brought to life by the mystery of creation itself. So far as Anderson could explicate it, he tried, in the letter to Mary Chryst Anderson here reprinted, to show at once his debt to Gertrude Stein ("she taught me to recognize the second person in myself, the poet-writing person"), and the mechanism of imaginative work, not mechanical and automatic, yet

. . . all of the more beautiful and clear, the more plangent and radiant writing I have done, has all been done by a kind of secondary personality that at such times takes possession of me.

In the perspective of time it becomes increasingly clear that the generation of the 1920's stood on the watershed that divides the old American literature from the new. The pre-World-War-I tradition, despite notable exceptions, was Apollonian; the generation of Anderson, Dionysiac. The tradition of form, of propriety, of idealism ended, so to speak, with the sinking of the *Lusitania;* the world of subrational psychology, of the mixed genre and the indeterminate work of art — the world, for better or worse, of modern writing — began about the time Sherwood Anderson discovered that he was a writer, but that a writer could go to no school and follow no program. To a surprising degree, therefore, the roots and beginnings of our contemporary notions of literature and of the creative process are to be found in these occasional letters by a man described as "groping," "confused," "immoral," and various other pejorative things by timid or genteel critics. We, for whom Anderson's experimentalism opened paths, are not so likely to condemn experiments or even failures from which we have profited. The letters of Sherwood Anderson stand at the fountainhead of American modernism.

A Note on the Editing

The preparation of a one-volume selection of Sherwood Anderson's letters has presented certain problems and has required of the editors certain decisions. The first problems, of course, were to determine the bases on which selection would be made and then the order in which the chosen letters would be presented. Although the collection in the Newberry Library is so rich that another equally interesting volume might have been assembled on quite different principles, the editors decided to include letters which related significantly to at least one of several major concerns in this correspondence: (1) Anderson's own methods and purposes as a writer and his struggle to become one; (2) his special sense of the place (or lack of place) of the writer in America; (3) the nature and psychology of art, with particular reference to writing; (4) his relationships with other writers and artists. Included also are a number of letters showing his response to various social, economic and political issues of the day. The best method of arrangement appeared to be by simple chronology, but it should be noted that there has been no attempt by the editors to create an epistolary biography of Anderson.

The letters having been selected, the next problem was to prepare an accurate transliteration — one might almost say "translation" — of them. Perhaps half of the five thousand letters in the collection are in typescript, but the other half are written, sometimes with pencil on the cheapest kind of scratch paper, in a scrawl which Anderson himself admitted was often baffling even to close friends. The editors have nevertheless made every effort to present an accurate text. In a few instances where the reading of a word is ambiguous, the probable word, with a question mark preceding it, has been entered in brackets. Wherever possible the text has been obtained from the original letters or from photostats of originals, but occasionally it has been necessary to rely on Anderson's own carbon copies of the originals when these have been the only ones as yet available in the Newberry Library. Any exceptions to these practices are noted in the text itself.

As soon as one has mastered Anderson's boldly illegible script, he will notice that the writer's spelling, quite aside from frequent errors of haste, tends toward the phonetic rather than the traditional. "Definite" consistently appears as "definate," "subtle" as "subtile," "rhythm" as "rythm." Anderson could write "hoards" for "hordes," "analasys" for "analysis," and almost anything for "psychological." Although it is amusing, for example, to see him describe one of his recurrent bodily ills as "cynos" (sinus) trouble, and although such an unintentionally fused expression as "nomantic" — that is, nomadic and romantic — may be psychologically revealing, the editors decided that for the purposes of a one-volume selection the spelling should be normalized. Anyone wishing to draw conclusions about the reasons for Anderson's inability to subdue the vagaries of English spelling should do so only from a close study of all the available materials, and individual misspellings are of considerably less importance than the over-all fact that an important American writer was to this extent outside the formal education patterns of his society.

Anderson's spelling, then, has been standardized, but neither it nor his vocabulary has been bowdlerized. When he used an Anglo-Saxon colloquialism for a bodily function, it has been retained because that was what he wrote. Again, although he habitually wrote "negro" instead of the standard "Negro" of the text, he often used the vulgate term "nigger," which has been allowed to stand in spite of our present revulsion for it. It should be clear from the following letters that Anderson, however dubious might be his conclusions about the "primitivism" of the race, had both love and respect for the American Negro.

Like his spelling, the writer's punctuation is uncertain. Question marks are usually omitted, hyphens or dashes often serve as commas, commas may or may not appear where they should according to the rules in grammar books. In the interest of readability, the punctuation of these letters has likewise been normalized. On the other hand, Anderson's very casual paragraphing has been allowed to stand.

One of the most difficult problems met with by any scholar in dealing with the Anderson letters is the assigning to them of the proper dates and places of composition, for only during the last decade of his life did the writer make it a frequent practice to give his letters headings. Where any part of a heading has been assigned by the editors rather than by Anderson himself, that part has been placed in brackets.

Any date or place which could not be definitely verified is preceded by a question mark. All headings, it should be noted, have been somewhat standardized. Where Anderson's manuscript contained the name and address of the recipient, these have been given, sometimes in shortened form. Where the manuscript had no such address, we have simply stated to whom the letter was written.

The editors would like to acknowledge a great debt to Mrs. Amy Nyholm, cataloguer of the Anderson Collection, for originally establishing the chronology of many of these letters.

Omissions from the text by the editors have been kept at a minimum, although all of Anderson's signatures have been eliminated as unduly repetitious. Moreover, upon advice of counsel, it seemed expedient to delete a few remarks which might incur legal liability. Any omission made in a letter is indicated by the entering of five asterisks at that point. A very few names of persons it has been thought best to leave anonymous; in such cases "X." has always been substituted. A few illustrative diagrams drawn by Anderson have been omitted, because the difficulty of reproducing them in the present text would far outweigh their value as interpretive aids. In several instances clearly unintended repetitions of words by Anderson have been struck out. Any words or parts of words inserted by the editors, except mere spelling corrections, have always been placed in brackets. Postscripts are indicated always by a bracketed P.S. [P.S.] before the first sentence of the postscript, except in the rare instances where Anderson entered a P.S. himself. Occasionally the writer elaborated a remark by a comment in the margin or on the back of a page after completing the original letter. In such cases a single asterisk has been placed at the end of the statement so amplified, and the material which Anderson wished inserted at that point has been reproduced, after another asterisk, at the end of the letter.

Finally, a word on the footnotes. The editors have attempted to keep in mind that while certain persons, places or things may be obvious to the point of absurdity to a literary scholar, they may not be equally so to all readers; hence most such references have been explained upon their first appearance in the text.

The editors wish to express their gratitude to various persons for assistance given them during the preparation of this volume. Their debt to Mrs. Eleanor Anderson, donor of the Sherwood Anderson collection, is expressed in the dedication of the book. To the trustees of the Newberry Library and to the library's director, Mr. Stanley Pargellis, they wish to express thanks for the grant of a Newberry Fellowship which made possible the preparation of the volume. They thank the staff of the Newberry Library, particularly Mr. Pargellis, Mrs. Gertrude Woodward, and Mrs. Amy Nyholm, for their constant co-operation and help. Mrs. Nyholm's day-to-day assistance and wise advice were especially helpful.

To those who have in previous years given up their Sherwood Anderson letters to the collection, the editors are in debt, but they wish also particularly to thank Van Wyck Brooks, Waldo Frank, and Charles H. Funk for making their many letters available directly to the editors. The Library Committee of the Yale University Library graciously granted permission for the use of the three sets of letters: those to Georgia O'Keeffe, those to Gertrude Stein, and those to Alfred Stieglitz. Letters to Gertrude Stein are from the Gertrude Stein Collection, and those to Alfred Stieglitz are from the Alfred Stieglitz Archive of the Yale Collection of American literature.

Among the many who have been good enough to answer specific questions raised by problems in the text are William H. Bond, Van Wyck Brooks, Wallace C. Brown, Ralph Church, Donald G. Gallup, Mr. and Mrs. Roger Sergel, Emily J. Sheppard, Jessie C. Treichler, and Mary Day Winn. The editors also gratefully acknowledge the valuable research assistance of Dr. John Pilkington, Jr.

A final statement of indebtedness is that to Mrs. Jean Rideout, who not only typed the various copies of the manuscript and helped to compile the index, but who, through her advice, her skill as a librarian, and her encouragement, virtually constituted herself a third editor.

A Chronology of Sherwood Anderson's Life and Work

1876   Born in Camden, Ohio, September 13, third child of Irwin Anderson, harnessmaker, and Emma Smith Anderson.

1884   Family settled in Clyde, Ohio, where Sherwood attended public school irregularly, earned nickname of "Jobby" because of performing many odd jobs about town.

1896   Went to Chicago, worked as unskilled laborer.

1898–1899   Infantryman in U. S. Army. Stationed briefly in Cuba after close of Spanish-American War.

1899–1900   Received last year of formal education by attending Wittenberg Academy, Springfield, Ohio.

1900   Became copy writer for advertising firm of Long-Critchfield Company in Chicago.

1904   Married Cornelia Lane of Toledo, Ohio.

1906–1907   President of United Factories, mail-order house, in Cleveland, Ohio.

1907–1912   Headed own business, mail-order paint firm, in Elyria, Ohio. On November 27, 1912 suffered brief nervous breakdown and left his business office — source of legend that he had deliberately feigned insanity in order to walk out of the world of business into the world of art.

1913   Returned to Chicago and the Long-Critchfield Company. Did not finally give up advertising as a means of support until 1922.

1914   Began publishing short stories and literary articles in various "little magazines."

1916   Divorced from Cornelia Lane Anderson, married Tennessee Mitchell, music teacher. *Windy McPherson's Son*, his first published novel.

1917   *Marching Men*, novel.

1918 Lived much of this year in New York, was briefly publicity man for a movie company. *Mid-American Chants*, poems.

1919 *Winesburg, Ohio*, short stories.

1920 Spent winter and spring in Fairhope, Alabama; much attracted to the South. *Poor White*, novel.

1921 With Tennessee and his friend Paul Rosenfeld, took his first European trip, financed by Rosenfeld. Met James Joyce and Gertrude Stein, whose work he much admired. Was first recipient of the *Dial* Award for contribution to American writing. *The Triumph of the Egg*, short stories.

1922 Spent winter in New Orleans, where he became friends with William Faulkner. Closed out his last advertising accounts. Moved to New York.

1923 *Many Marriages*, novel. Took up residence in Reno, Nevada, in order to obtain divorce from Tennessee Mitchell Anderson. *Horses and Men*, short stories.

1924 Divorced Tennessee Mitchell Anderson, married Elizabeth Prall, formerly bookstore manager. Moved to New Orleans. *A Story Teller's Story*, autobiography.

1925 *Dark Laughter*, novel — his only best seller. With proceeds from book and from lecturing bought farm at Troutdale near Marion, Virginia. *The Modern Writer*, published lecture.

1926 Built country house ("Ripshin") on farm; despite travels this was his home for the rest of his life. *Sherwood Anderson's Notebook*, essays and sketches. *Tar: A Midwestern Childhood*, autobiographical narrative. Began second European trip.

1927 Returned, much depressed, from Europe. *A New Testament*, poems. Bought the two weekly newspapers in Marion and edited them for the next two years.

1929 *Hello Towns!*, editorials, essays, sketches from the Marion newspapers. As third marriage began to break up, entered long period of emotional depression.

1930 Through Eleanor Copenhaver, Y.W.C.A. executive, became interested in labor conditions in Southern mills.

1931 Visited mills and factories throughout the South. *Perhaps Women*, long essay.

1932   Engaged briefly in several radical activities. Divorced from
       Elizabeth Prall Anderson. Became interested in writing
       for the theater. *Beyond Desire*, novel.

1933   *Death in the Woods*, short stories. Married Eleanor Copen-
       haver. Traveled about the United States writing articles
       for weekly newsmagazine *Today*. Became an editor of the
       American Spectator.

1934   Continued traveling and writing for *Today*. *No Swank*,
       articles.

1935   *Puzzled America*, articles.

1936   *Kit Brandon*, novel.

1937   *Plays: Winesburg and Others*, plays.

1940   *Home Town*, long sketch.

1941   Started on unofficial good-will tour of South America.
       Died of peritonitis at Colón, Panama Canal Zone, on
       March 8.

1942   *Sherwood Anderson's Memoirs*, posthumously published
       autobiography.

Contents

Illustrations

Letters of Sherwood Anderson

Letters

Chicago, November 6, 1916

Mr. Waldo Frank,[1] *Seven Arts* Magazine, New York

Dear Mr. Frank: I cannot resist the desire to write to you at once and thank you for your intelligent discussion of my book in the initial issue of the *Seven Arts*.[2]

I like particularly your slap at my ending of the novel. What you say is no doubt true. In secret I do not mind telling you that I never knew how to end a novel and am afraid I never will. Always feel as though I were just at the beginning when the thing has to be wound up and put aside.

By the way, it may also be of interest to you to know that I had never heard of Dreiser or Dostoevski when I wrote this book. I met Floyd Dell,[3] the first man interested in writing I had ever known, when I was at work on my third novel,[4] and he introduced me to the work of both these men. This is particularly interesting, as I have been rather widely accused of imitating both of these writers.

What you say about Mark Twain interests me. I have long wondered why he, with Whitman, has not been placed where I have always believed he belonged — among the two or three really great American artists.

[1] Waldo Frank (1889–), novelist, critic and translator. See Book IV of the *Memoirs*.
[2] See Waldo Frank, "Emerging Greatness," *Seven Arts*, I, 73–78 (November, 1916). "My book" is *Windy McPherson's Son* (1916).
The monthly, *Seven Arts*, edited by James Oppenheim, Waldo Frank, and Van Wyck Brooks, was published in New York from November, 1916, through October, 1917, and was devoted to the "newness."
[3] Floyd Dell (1887–), novelist, literary editor of the Chicago *Evening Post*, 1911–1913, and associate editor of the *Masses*, 1914–1917. Concerning Anderson's relation to Dell see *Memoirs*, pp. 234 f.
[4] Presumably *Mary Cochran*. Although this book was never published as a whole, portions of it appeared as the short stories "Unlighted Lamps" and "The Door of the Trap" in *The Triumph of the Egg*.

Mr. Rolland has, in this same issue of *Seven Arts*,[5] said the thing that I would like to try to do:

"This is your first task — diverse personalities that compose your states must dare to express themselves, freely, sincerely, entirely, in art. They must avoid the false quest of originality. They must be careless of form. They must be fearless of opinion."

Come to see me, Mr. Frank, if any wind blows you toward Chicago. Very truly yours

2.   CHICAGO, NOVEMBER 14, 1916

MR. WALDO FRANK, *Seven Arts* MAGAZINE, NEW YORK

My dear Mr. Frank: I sent you a little thing the other day that I believe you will like. Here is a suggestion.

I made last year a series of intensive studies of people of my home town, Clyde, Ohio. In the book I called the town Winesburg, Ohio. Some of the studies you may think pretty raw, and there is a sad note running through them. One or two of them get pretty closely down to ugly things of life. However, I put a good deal into the writing of them, and I believe they, as a whole, come a long step toward achieving what you are asking for in the article you ran in *Seven Arts*.[1]

Some of these things have been used. *Masses* ran a story called "Hands" from this series.[2] Two or three also appeared in a little magazine out here called the *Little Review*.[3] The story called "Queer" you are using in December [4] is one of them.

This thought occurs to me. There are or will be seventeen of these studies. Fifteen are, I believe, completed. If you have the time and the inclination, I might send the lot to you to be looked over.

[5] Romain Rolland, "America and the Arts," translated by Waldo Frank, *Seven Arts*, I, 47–56 (November, 1916).

[1] See Letter 1, note 2.

[2] "Hands," *Masses*, VIII, 1 (March, 1916). This magazine, founded in 1911, was edited by Max Eastman from 1912 until late 1917. Devoted to radicalism in politics and the new freedom in literature, it numbered among its contributors John Reed and Floyd Dell.

[3] Among Anderson's contributions to the *Little Review* only "The Philosopher" [III, 7–9 (June–July, 1916)] was gathered into *Winesburg, Ohio*, though he contributed six other items before that date to this magazine.

The *Little Review*, the creation of Margaret C. Anderson, began publication in Chicago in March, 1914, removed to New York in 1917, and to Paris later, where it expired in 1929.

[4] "Queer," *Seven Arts*, I, 97–108 (December, 1916), was reprinted in the *Winesburg* volume.

It is my own idea that when these studies are published in book form, they will suggest the real environment out of which present-day American youth is coming. Very truly yours

3.   CHICAGO, DECEMBER 14, 1916

MR. WALDO FRANK, *Seven Arts* MAGAZINE, NEW YORK

Dear Mr. Frank: I am glad you liked the story "Mother" [1] and that you are going to publish it. Damn it, I wanted you to like the story about Enoch Robinson [2] and the woman who came into his room and was too big for the room.

There is a story every critic is bound to dislike. I can remember reading it to Floyd Dell, and it made him hopping mad. "It's damn rot," says Floyd. "It does not get anywhere."

"It gets there, but you are not at the station," I replied to Floyd, and I think I was right.

Why do I try to convince you of this story? Well, I want it in print in *Seven Arts*. A writer knows when a story is good, and that story is good.

Sometime when I am in New York, I'll bring that story in, and I'll make you see it.

In the meantime, thanks for the check for "Mother." I have another fine story about the same woman's death. Very truly yours

4.   CHICAGO, JANUARY 2, 1917

MR. WALDO FRANK, *Seven Arts* MAGAZINE, NEW YORK

My dear Frank: You are as bad as myself, and I have been unable to make a complete translation of your longhand letter. I take it, however, that you step on my toes for yowling about money. Presume you are right about that, but Lord, man, I would like to smell money.

I am not a hack writer in the sense that I have to depend on what I write for bread and butter, but I pay the price just the same. Eight hours a day I have paid, working as an advertising writer these last five years, while trying to save nerve force and courage enough to admit other writing. It has cost me dearly in fine moods destroyed, rare projects gone wrong because of lack of strength to get on with them, and all that sort of thing.

---

[1] "Mother," *Seven Arts*, I, 452–462 (March, 1917), reprinted in *Winesburg, Ohio*, and the basis for the play *Winesburg*.

[2] See "Loneliness" in *Winesburg, Ohio*.

But why should I tell you of my woes? It is an old tale in the literary world. I will, of course, abide by what you can pay.

At the same time I do reserve the right to point out that you are not taking real venturesome things in the magazine and that you edit only a little more closely than the ordinary magazine editor.

However, I am coming to New York the last of this month or the first of next. I will quarrel with you personally then.

Where are you to be found?

Do you go daily to the office of the magazine? Very truly yours

[P.S.] Am looking eagerly forward to seeing your book.[1]

5.   CHICAGO, JANUARY 10, 1917

MR. WALDO FRANK, *Seven Arts* MAGAZINE, NEW YORK

My dear Frank: Just the trouble with me, Frank, is that I do not want to write you about your book. I want to walk and talk with you for hours and hours. I want to know many little subtle things you know and that I do not know, and I want to tell you things, make you feel things concerning life and writing that I have felt and that you have not felt.

We are so different. Something very rank and vulgar in me is lacking in you. We both need growth, but in what different directions.

I have a boyhood friend. He is like you. There is something intense about his nature. Life caught him in its meshes, and he has become rich. New York has hurt him terribly. He has become sordid, cynical.

You haven't. The arts have saved you. That is apparent in your book. It has meant the same to me as knowing and associating with you would mean.

Oh, so often I want to shake you. To cry, "Let go, let go." And so often I just plain admire you.

There is something reeking and vulgar about life you haven't got at. Why? Have you been in rooms too much? Have you been doing too much thinking?

I ask these questions, and then I remember my friend whom I have so loved and who by intensifying his native bent has become rich and cynical.

And you have escaped that. In the midst of all our terrible American

---

[1] Frank's first novel, *The Unwelcome Man,* was published in January, 1917. On January 8, Frank wrote Anderson that he had mailed a copy to him.

trick of specializing, you have remained alive to a thousand things and willing to open your mind and your soul to all of us. You haven't shut yourself off from us as you so well might.

I got all this from your book. I like you and what you have done. I just want you to "let go" more. When I see you, I'll try to make clearer what I mean. We will talk of it.

And how I do thank you for this chance you have given me of knowing you better. The book is a fine piece of work. Very truly yours

6. [CHICAGO, BEFORE FEBRUARY 26, 1917]

TO WALDO FRANK

Dear Frank: I put off calling you up until the evening when we left town and then could not find your house number in the telephone book. Let me take advantage of this chance to tell you how much seeing you and Oppenheim[1] and Brooks[2] made my visit to New York notable. Your clean, wholesome outlook, your generosity in praise, and your willingness to listen to my provincial, Western point of view warmed my heart.

And then the evening at your house and the joy we had in the company of yourself and Mrs. Frank. It was all good. It rested and gave me new courage.

I came home from New York with an odd feeling of reverence and humbleness. Perhaps it would do me no good to talk to you fellows too often. I should talk too much, but this was good for me. I hope I did not take too much of your time.

I am a little puzzled concerning the monthly articles.[3] This occurs to me. I have written a series of ten or twelve papers about writing. Could you not publish them without using my name? Say simply, "By a Western novelist," and let it go at that?

My notion is that I do not want to embarrass you by having you use my name too often, and I want you to publish stories by me.

Then also I would achieve by this a certain freedom. I could stretch my legs better.

Read them over and talk to Oppenheim and Brooks. See what they

[1] James Oppenheim (1882–1932), poet, editor of *Seven Arts*.
[2] Van Wyck Brooks (1886–), biographer and literary critic, then on the editorial staff of *Seven Arts*.
[3] See "From Chicago," *Seven Arts*, II, 41–59 (May, 1917) — all that appeared of the proposed series.

say. I am sending you three of the kind of things I mean. With sincere regards

[P.S.] What could you pay for 'em? Eh?

7.   [?Chicago, ?March, 1917]

To Waldo Frank

[No salutation] All night, after I read your letter, I kept thinking of you and was puzzled and confounded. I know the road I took long ago, but when I try to think of talking to anyone with any notion that what is good for me will be good for them, I draw back.

Primarily the difficulty with all of us is that, being Americans, we in some way got a wrong start in life. The notion of success in affairs, in love, in our daily life is so ingrained that it is almost impossible to shake it off.

You perhaps do not know that I was married and the father of three children, that I had to undertake the delicate and difficult task of breaking up that marriage [1] and of trying to win the real love of that woman out of marriage and outside the difficulties and complications of sex.

For myself I found it necessary to disregard all of the smart conclusions of the men of my time and set up gods. I found it necessary to my continued existence to utterly and finally embrace failure, the one terrible, hard thing for an American to do.

That was the year, Frank, that I went into the Ozark Mountains. I took the woman and the children with me. I lived in a separate cabin on a hillside, and together the woman and I went through poverty, hatred of each other, and all the terrible things that can come from such a situation.

It is odd now to think that it was misunderstanding that brought us through. She came to the conclusion that I was not mentally sound. That awoke the mother instinct in her. We began to make progress.

No story I will ever write will touch that story, and that is one of the keenest pleasures of life to me, that I lived something beyond any power of mine to write of it.

There are certain definite things I came to out of that — the ability to be brutal with women, the conclusion that for me there must always be my own place, some hole in the wall into which I could crawl to

---

[1] Sherwood and Cornelia Lane Anderson were married in May, 1904, and divorced in the summer of 1916. His three children — Robert, John, and Marion ("Mimi") — were by this first marriage.

pray and be alone and to catch and hold my own note out of the jar and jangle of noises.

You know, there is one thing about Brooks. In some way he keeps hitting on the note that living and feeling is the thing.

Well, aren't you doing that?

It seems to me you are.

I'm damned if I can feel anything but glad for you.

8. [CHICAGO] MARCH 2, 1917

MR. THEODORE DREISER,[1] c/o JOHN LANE COMPANY, NEW YORK

My dear Dreiser: I must personally thank you for your illuminating article in *Seven Arts* magazine.[2] It sets forth as nothing else I have ever read has set forth the complete and terrible fact of the wall in the shadow of which American artists must work.

To many of us here in America the one really hopeful note in our times is your own stout figure pounding at the wall.

Our hats off to you, Captain. Very sincerely yours

9. CHICAGO, MARCH 2, 1917

MR. WALDO FRANK, *Seven Arts* MAGAZINE, NEW YORK

My dear Frank: What you must do is this. I am going to try to achieve three months in the mountains of northern New York State this summer. I want June, July, and August. I will live in a tent on a lake. You must plan to come and spend some time with me there. Of course I've got to rake in some shekels to pull it off, but I'm going to try hard to get away with it.

About the article — I will leave it to you to arrange it. I am sending three more papers and these, with what you have, should give you the material you want.

About signing these things — my attitude is this. If there is no story appearing in the issue in which the article appears, I see no reason why it should not be signed. For the sake of book sales I want to build up my name as fast as I can.

I'm damned, Frank, if I am going to let you pull and haul among my stories, taking the cream at $40 per. It isn't fair, and you know it. I

---

[1] Theodore Dreiser (1871–1945), whose recent books had been published by John Lane.

[2] "Life, Art and America," *Seven Arts*, I, 363–389 (February, 1917).

will send you the stories one at a time, and you accept or reject. Forget the notion that there is no other market for these things. I've got offers on my desk for them now. I believe in *Seven Arts* and want to swim with you, but there is no reason why I should give you this unseemly privilege. You may consider this an overt act, but I'm going to stand on it. Now, damn it, man, behave.

Again I have to thank Brooks for a bully article.[1] Tell that man to keep his vision. He is thundering along the right trail sure as hell.

Oh, but those poems [2] would make you sit up.

Now, lie low, little grey squirrel, you can't see them yet.

Be sure to let me see proofs of the article.

I read one of the poems to an old man who sells shoestrings on Jackson Boulevard Bridge. The bank of the river caved in, a gull fell from the sky, and in the excitement the man swallowed his stock in trade. Love to you all

10.   [?CHICAGO, AFTER MARCH 2, 1917]

TO WALDO FRANK

My dear Frank: You know my West is not like that; in fact, I believe you know that Far West of horses, cattle, and winds better than I do. Really, my land is the corn-growing, industrial Middle West.

And as for the Adirondacks, my place there is not as you have pictured it. There will be a woods and a lake but no people, except when we want to cross the lake to them. Instead there will be black shadows in the woods and the flare of the furnace of an iron foundry at night.

You must definitely plan to be with me the second week in June. After that a Johns Hopkins man will be on the same side of the lake. That week we can have to loaf and think and talk.

I've got in some way a big swinging notion to get to you. It isn't mine. It belongs to waving cornfields and the marching impulses of men that go on, have to go on, in spite of these things that seem to cloud the world.

Oh, hell, this sounds wordy. The thing is essentially not that.

Old chap, you are ill. I know because I have been ill and am so much of the time ill now. Things are drawn all out of proportion. Damn! I

---

[1] Probably either "Toward a National Culture," *Seven Arts*, I, 535–547 (March, 1917), or "The Splinter of Ice," *ibid.*, 270–280 (January, 1917).

[2] At this time Anderson had begun writing the poems or "songs" which were published by John Lane in 1918 as *Mid-American Chants*.

wish it were now that I could lay down my work and go walking and talking with you.

I can't. I have to work like hell to save money for my long summer. You see, I have a family of 3 children that must be fed and cared for while I am away playing and earning nothing.

You wait. We will get at something sure. I have a feeling in my bones that we have a lot for each other.

I have sent you some more songs. Tell me if they sing to you.

The $60 will help. If you want to work in another such an article[1] later, let me know. I have material for it here.

If you can come West any time, come on. Both Tennessee[2] and myself want to play with you. With love

11. [CHICAGO] [?MARCH] 26, 1917

MR. THEODORE DREISER, 165 WEST 10TH STREET, NEW YORK

My dear Dreiser: I thank you very much indeed for your invitation to come and see you, and you may depend upon my doing so the first time I am in New York, as I have long wanted to know you personally. Very sincerely yours

12. [?CHICAGO, ?APRIL, 1917]

TO WALDO FRANK

Dear Waldo: And whatever happens, don't forget the two weeks with me in the mountains in June. Have just got the April *Seven Arts,* but have not read it. I read nothing. Something is waiting in the wind. I write songs and walk in a kind of wonder of unexpressed things.

Wish you had liked my story of the drunken boy.[1] I liked it fine. It was true as hell. I'll stir the pot again soon.

Please don't always apply your reason to these things. They are to my mind fragments that will be more keenly realized in the minds of the reader than you fellows think.

There is a danger that always besets a group of keen fellows like yourself. It is the sort of thing that has happened to the crowd over at

---

[1] See Letter 6, note 3.
[2] Tennessee Mitchell, Anderson's second wife. They were married in August, 1916.

---

[1] See "Drink" in *Winesburg, Ohio.*

the *New Republic.*[2] You become too keen; a madness for analysis takes hold of you.

I would like in an early issue to have you publish a group of my songs. Why not do that in the issue after the printing of the sketches? We might let the stories rest awhile. What do you think?

I saw Sandburg[3] the other night, and we had a long evening together. He liked my songs very much, and I liked him. There is something Scandinavian about him, a suggestion of closed-in icy places. Most of his verses do not sing, but he does. Ben Hecht[4] called him a true poet who could not write poetry.

Well, I do get you now as more or less caught in the mess. I was so a week ago. I will be so again tomorrow.

In a dim way I am trying to feel that the War has meaning, that it is mankind's stupid way of working something out, a terrible house cleaning. I was sick with dread of the thing until the Russian Revolution.[5] That gave me something to cling to. I began to have hope and am still hoping the War has meaning.

Well, you come up in June. I have bought a tent. We will get at a lot of things.

13.   [?CHICAGO, ?MAY, 1917]

TO WALDO FRANK

Dear Waldo: Your scrawl is more atrocious than my own, than which I have been told there is none worse. Well, I dug most of it out after an hour's fine effort. One thing I get clearly, that you are coming for the visit with me. That is bully. We will have leisure to get at things.

I do think you are terribly young in your dissertation on prose and poetry. You see, there is something in you that has not burst into song yet, and you have not found your own song. I have felt it in your prose and in you, the repressed thing. I have wanted life and the sun of days to put you in a great cradle and swing all of your false weariness away.

[2] The *New Republic* had been founded in 1914, under the leadership of Herbert E. Croly, as a liberal weekly.
[3] Carl Sandburg (1878–), poet, whose *Chicago Poems* had appeared in 1916.
[4] Ben Hecht (1894–), journalist and author, then associated with the Chicago *Daily News.* On Anderson's relations with Hecht, see *Memoirs,* Book III.
[5] The "Kerensky Revolution" of March, 1917.

The songs sing to me. They have carried me far. I am only sorry that *Seven Arts* does not want them, because it is the only place I at this moment know for them.[1]

Honestly, old chap, can't you imagine the sweat coming on the brow of God when men set forth upon this analysis of song? I used to have for my dreams a thing I called the Sonnet God, a great face towered in the sky, more gigantic than the hills. In his two hands my god held the little round ball called the earth. He blew upon it and watched. Fire, death, and destruction ran over the land. The god smiled. In his smile was all of sadness and of truth.

In my own way, you see, Brother, I have hung onto the face of my god. I would like you to see it in your dreams. It would stop on your lips forever these pronouncements about song and prose. It is all devilish young and untrue like your unhappiness.

Well, I do wish you had freedom, and so also do I wish I had it. I shall probably have to write advertisements of oil well stocks to get money to publish my songs, but there is a kind of gigantic song in that if you can see it.

I have been to Nebraska, where the big engines are tearing the fields to pieces; over the low hills runs the promise of the corn. You wait, dear Brother; I shall bring God home to the sweaty men in the corn rows. My songs shall creep into their hearts and teach them the sacredness of the long aisles of growing things that lead to the throne of the God of men. Be ashamed of yourself, Brother, for preaching at me.

Early in June the tent will be set up, the waters of the lake shall lap on our shores, in the black hills fires will spring up where the iron mines lie, and we shall talk of the lands west of Chicago. Then I shall sing you my songs as the good old men sang. We shall sing and talk as old men talked before magazines and checks for stories came to corrupt their minds.

Don't be won aside from your purpose to come.

[P.S.] The $20 will help.

---

[1] *Seven Arts* published two of the songs: the poem introducing "From Chicago" (reprinted as "Chicago" in *Mid-American Chants*), and "Mid-American Prayer," *Seven Arts*, II, 190–192 (June, 1917).

14.   [CHICAGO, ?MAY, 1917]

To WALDO FRANK

Dear Brother: [1] I was raised, you see, in a family of five strong-jawed boys, and always among us there was a philosophy of blows. We aimed to hit to hurt. When one got an idea, he had to fight for it.

All the time I see you cannot really believe in my impulse toward writing. You intellectualize it, but you do not carry it into your point of view.

Now, you see, I am nearly forty-one. I have had 20 years of the intense grind of modern industrial life. I have carried that through, made industry feed and clothe me and mine, and in the last 5 or 6 years I have in addition written 5 or 6 big books. Much of the prose experiment you talk about has been made by me.

Do you not understand, can you not see that I mean no slur on you when I say that the approval or disapproval of any man must mean but a small thing to me?

One of the things a man has to learn is to fight most bitterly the influence of those who love him.

I say that the gods sweat, and they do when any man lays down the law regarding the possibilities of an art. I say that your pronouncement that prose and not song is my road should make the gods sweat.

Do you not see that with the weight of my weariness on me I am training true when I attempt the swift, sure flight of song?

And anyway, what of it? I am singing to the stout but often weary heart of Sherwood Anderson. I have opened the door of failure a thousand times. I know that road. It doesn't frighten me. In *Marching Men* [2] I said that there was already a song of labor and of industry, an iron song, rhythmic and terrible. Don't quarrel with me if it suits my humor to let much go to hell while I try for a while to catch something of the song of men, machines, and the ground.

And plan to come to me at camp in June.

[1] Often, as in subsequent letters, Anderson used this form of address toward Waldo Frank.
[2] Published in September, 1917.

15. [MERRILL, NEW YORK, AUGUST 27, 1917]

TO WALDO FRANK

Dear Brother: I was afraid something had gone wrong with you and am relieved to find you are not yet in jail. It is beyond doubt the thing to do, and the best men of our times should land there.

It is an odd, perverse thing, but it is nevertheless right that American artists should have prayed for war or anything else that would break up the ugly commercialism of our times, and it is right also that now that we are in war we should go to jail rather than take part in the ugly thing.

As I have loafed and danced and waited in the sun up here this summer, a peculiar thing has taken place in me. My mind has run back and back to the time when men tended sheep and lived a noma[d]ic life on hillsides and by little talking streams. I have become less and less the thinker and more the thing of earth and the winds. When I awake at night and the wind is howling, my first thought is that the gods are at play in the hills here. My new book, starting with life on a big farm in Ohio, will have something of that flavor in its earlier chapters. There is a delightful old man, Joseph Bentley [1] by name, who is full of old Bible thoughts and impulses.

As to the effect of the War on your work and mine, that is something we have in some way got to meet. Perhaps it is the test.

In me always (living as I have among men) there has been the sense of a persistent outcry of little distracting voices. Now it is as though the voices had begun to shout madly and meaninglessly. We will have to write and think and try to believe in beauty and innocence in the midst of the most terrible clutter.

Burrow [2] has been a sharp disappointment to me. Put to the test he proved to have no gift of companionship. The man wanted to reform, to remake me; his attitude was like Dell's. Tell me why men constantly get the impression that I am a thing to be molded.

About the Frenchman's letter. [3] Wait until you get back into town and then send it to me in Chicago.

Of course I do not know what the War has done to the business

[1] Joseph became Jesse Bentley in "Godliness" in *Winesburg, Ohio.*

[2] Trigant Burrow (1875–1950), physician and psychoanalyst, whom Anderson had first met in the summer of 1916.

[3] Anderson had sent Frank a "fine letter" which he had received from someone in Paris, requesting that Frank tell him the man's name. See Letter 18.

where I am employed. I may be without a job when I get back and, if I am, may come to New York. I will write you about that when I get back to Chicago next week.

My regards to Miss Margaret [4] and much love to you. Tennessee is staying on here for a few weeks. You will have a bound copy of *Marching Men* when you get back into town.

16.   [CHICAGO, ?SEPTEMBER, 1917]

To WALDO FRANK

Dear old Waldo: I can't tell you how bully it was of you to write and let me know about yourself. As the days went and I heard nothing from you, I was terribly afraid there had been some bad result from the operation.

The roar and rattle of things go on here. Troops march through the streets. Men who come in from Western towns say that the war spirit is growing.

Still one hears constantly the underground cry for peace that will grow when things tighten up. I still believe that this Middle West has not let itself be led into the spirit of hatred the newspapers are trying so hard to build up.

As for me, well, I came home alone, Tennessee having stayed for a while longer in the hills, and I have been steadily at work. The background for the new book [1] has been laid in, and five chapters are written. I more and more taste the flavor of my people in it.

And isn't this steady work a relief? The imagination stiffens and takes hold. The war of present and perplexing things slips a little away.

As for *Marching Men*, well, you will never know with what interest I have waited for your reaction to the book. As I told you one day, I wrote it in the midst of the big readjustment in my own life. It was a theme that appealed strongly to my rather primitive nature. The beat and rhythm of the thing would come and go; a thousand outside things would flow in. I worked madly; then I threw the book away. Again and again I came back to it. In the end I had no idea as to whether it was good or bad. I only knew that the thing was out of me and I could turn to something else.

[4] Mrs. Waldo Frank.

---

[1] This book, entitled *Immaturity,* was not published.

It is strange that in discussing the dangers to *Seven Arts* we never thought of the possibility of her ladyship running away with the moneybags.[1] That is bad, but maybe it is good too. Perhaps a magazine, like a person, has to meet these blows and survive to be worth a damn. Anyway the big thing is you are getting well. You will go on keeping your head up and working. If *Seven Arts* dies, that is not like the smashing blow it would be to have something stop the flow of your courage.

Now that you can sit up and stir a bit, let me know from time to time about your progress. Get well. That's the first job.

17.   [CHICAGO, SEPTEMBER, 1917]

TO WALDO FRANK

Dear Brother: I have been taking a hard run at the new novel and have finished the first book, five chapters, so that I am pleased with it. I came back in such good physical condition that I should be able to swing right along with it.

It is, however, difficult. The theme is intense and the distractions continuous. I write in restaurants, in my office between interviews with men, and while I am not writing advertisements. It is too early to hear from *Marching Men,* and so I know nothing about whether it will go or not. The poems published in *Poetry* [1] created some stir out here, and everyone abused me. Nevertheless I shall put them into a book. One of the newspapermen made a ten-shot. Do you remember the line, "See the corn. How it aches"? [2] He called me the chiropodist poet. I would publish the verses for one reason if for no other. It will give a rare opportunity to those who desire to flay me.

In a few days I will get into my own quarters and will begin to work in the evening. You must write me often about your condition in the meantime. I want to see you back on your feet.

[1] Mrs. A. K. Rankine, who had subsidized *Seven Arts,* withdrew her financial support because of the magazine's outspoken opposition to American participation in World War I. With the issue of October, 1917, the magazine ceased publication.

---

[1] "Mid-American Songs," *Poetry,* X, 281–291 (September, 1917). *Poetry* was founded in Chicago in 1912 by Harriet Monroe and was for a time the chief organ of the poetry "Renaissance."

[2] The conclusion to the first line of "A Visit." This portion of the line was changed when the poem was reprinted in *Mid-American Chants.*

18.   [CHICAGO, BEFORE OCTOBER 29, 1917]

To WALDO FRANK

Dear Waldo: Your news is a shock to me, but was not unexpected.
There was something about the man, a sort of subconscious businessman air, that I was sure would make teamwork in the end impossible.

Well, that dream is gone, and things are tightening everywhere.
Seven Arts had a chance. Something of the kind still has a real chance
in America. Of course, this new failure will make it harder to get money
to launch another thing of the kind. I am terribly sorry for you and
Brooks, two men I have been able to unreservedly admire.

You see, Waldo, there is one thing I know — it is the commercial
element in life. All these years I have walked with it. I still walk
with it. It is like anything else. Men are not wholly that but part, but
with us in America it is deep-seated. The desire for gain that does not
belong to us, gain in money or fame, goes far. We are success wor-
shipers.

And you should know the thing too. The Jews, you know so well,
have it, but in their case it is offset by a passionate something that is
racial. When it gets into our cold Anglo-Saxon veins, it is terrible.

Keep me posted about your return to health and your plans. Will you
set out for another job, or will you rest and write?

Have just been through a bad week. Last night I felt so unclean that
I spent hours walking by the lake and praying. There is a man, whose
business amounts to a great deal, that I am able to influence and keep
with the house. He is one of the reasons the house pays me a salary.
This man comes here twice a year and gets on a debauch. Others go
with him, but when he becomes unmanageable, I am called on. Last
night I had to go and take him away from a gang of gamblers and
sporting women. The semidramatic incident, the profanity, the effort
of the perverted women to hold him against my influence — it was all
quite sickening.

You may be sure I would like to quit it all, to try to live and think
away from it, but I can't. It may go on always with me. I have to face
that, and I have faith that it is better than cheap writing anyway.

But, Brother, it is beastly unclean. Some days I find myself in such a
state that I can only pray dumbly. Those whom I love seem terribly far
away, and I am ashamed to go near them or write them for fear some
of the filth in which I have been working will carry to them.

Picture by Sue de Lorenzi

Sherwood Anderson at Chateaugay Lake, Merrill, N.Y., 1916

Lots of love and good cheer to you. The game is young.

[P.S.] Look up the letter from [the] Paris man, sent you at *Seven Arts*. Send it back. I want to write him.

19. [CHICAGO, AFTER OCTOBER 29, 1917]

To WALDO FRANK

Dear Brother: I am drunk with the inclination to write. Such times come to me. I have to keep away from people, because every person I see is a big story. I have written a story called "The Net"[1] that is a marvel. It is one of the best things I have done.

You are wrong about the songs. Your argument that I will make more progress by bringing out the novels is all right, but don't you see that I must snap my finger at the world? That must remain a part of my creed. If a road leads to destruction, one must take it as a sporting proposition.

Every day I think of you with the Draft hanging over your head and you trying to get on with the book. Take it quiet and easy if you can. Go for a walk and look at people. Remember that in the vast hordes we are just minute figures. Nothing matters but the long swing of things.

The songs will perhaps not be printed. I have not heard from Jeff Jones[2] and have a hunch he has lost his nerve. Love to Margaret

[The following is apparently a long postscript]

There are certain days when one seems to have the strength of some gigantic and prehistoric monster. It has been so with me today. I worked for hours and then went to walk in the smoky street. A storm swept over the city. Against a black sky the hard snow, half hail, was driven furiously. The people hurried shivering along. I wanted to embrace them all, men and women. It seemed to me that within my old shell was room for them all, that there a fire burned at which they could all warm themselves.

All day my mind has reached out and out. I have thought of everyone and everything. Minute little happenings in the lives of many people have been revealed to me. Today, had I a dozen hands, I could write a dozen tales, strange, wonderful tales, all at one time.

[1] Not published.

[2] Jefferson Jones, New York manager of the John Lane Company, the English publishing house which had brought out both *Windy McPherson's Son* and *Marching Men* in New York and London.

One wears himself away at such times. I did not try to work, but walked and walk[ed]. A storm swept in from the lake, and the rolling, tumbling waters answered something in me and quieted me. Such times cannot last, but they are glorious. They are the reward of holding firm against the daily, dreary commonplaceness of everyday life. When they come, it is revealed again how truly and really life is worth while.

20.   [?CLEVELAND, ?NOVEMBER, 1917]

To KARL ANDERSON [1]

Dear Karl: It was good of you to tell me of your feeling about *Marching Men*. As you must know, it is very amusing to me to see our American intellectuals taking me so seriously. They seem puzzled and disconcerted. I have many a private giggle over it all.

The songs have brought the herds down on me. They offer just that opportunity for snappy satirical comment that delights the soul of the newspaper editorial and paragraph writer. If Lane [2] does not lose his nerve, I shall publish a book of them under the title *Mid-American Chants*. It will probably make me the most abused man in the country.

It is of course all amateurish, Karl, but I am and I hope will remain that. I dare say your own experience has been like my own. I came among artists hoping to find brotherhood there, but there isn't much of it. As it is in painting, so it is among writers. Fundamentally most of our American writing men are graceful and facile fanner[s] [3] and whores altogether. If one did not laugh at them, he would go mad. The artisan and the mechanic talks with fair intelligence of his tools. The average professional intellectual talks, of course, like a silly, puzzled child.

I know you are painting like the very devil, for I have seen some things of yours that made me gasp. Such a riot of finely splashed color and new bigness in it. I do congratulate you on such work. Love to Helen [4]

---

[1] Karl Anderson (1874–), painter, was Sherwood's brother and the oldest of the Anderson children. See Books I and II of the *Memoirs*.

[2] John Lane, the English publisher.

[3] That is, unscrupulous men.

[4] Mrs. Karl Anderson.

21.   [CHICAGO, BEFORE NOVEMBER 7, 1917]

TO WALDO FRANK

Dear Brother: Your letter [is] here, and you will see that I wanted to hear from you, as I had already written today. I like the idea of leaving it to your own mood to come whenever you are ready. The room here is waiting for you. To the east, some three blocks, is the lake and to the west the great West Side with its hordes of people. You shall write at your book all morning, and in the late afternoon we will walk together. Then in the evening we can both walk or play with someone.

I am a great child, Waldo. You see, for all those years I worked away in the midst of laborers and businessmen and knew no artists. I had some sort of general notion that someday I should come into acquaintanceship with men at work in the arts and find them fine, generous, openhanded, ready to understand that although my art might be a poor, blundering thing, my impulses were O.K.

And then when my first book was published, an odd thing happened. People I had long known and who had looked upon me with indifferent tolerance or even friendliness praised me openly, but in secret did things to hurt me.

There has been a good deal of this sort of thing, and I haven't understood it. It has made me a little draw back into my shell. It has opened up to me the fact that men in the arts can be very small and petty. The thing had a sobering effect upon me.

And then there has been something else. I have always thought of myself as peculiarly wind-blown, a man approaching the bucolic in my nature. You know how I have had the notion that nothing from my pen should be published that could not be read aloud in the presence of a cornfield.

And many people have written me of what they call the "morbidity" of my work. It has been puzzling and confusing. I have stood like a beast pestered by flies and by the hot sun, turning my head here and there and having many disquieting little thoughts.

You see, I am not a sophisticated fellow in the sense you are. It is easy to catch me off my guard. It has been done.

And so I began a little to wonder about you also. I didn't give a damn if you found my work unworthy and said so. That's a cinch.

I've no notion of myself as a finished artist. God knows, I may stumble about the place all my life and get nowhere in particular.

And then along comes your letter. In it is the note I have always found in you. Fine generosity to a brother worker. No slobber. Courageous words of good cheer.

Here is an odd thing that may interest you. It may prove to you that I am corrupt. It almost seems to me so and keeps me grinning as I go along the street.

Currie of the Curtis crowd [1] wanted me to do some country town stories for them. I dismissed the idea, said I couldn't write to order, etc.

But the damned cuss got an idea into my head. I was a good deal tired and blue and began doing some small-town stories in a semilight vein for my own amusement. They fairly dance along, and I grin all the time as I write. The idea I have is whimsical and tremendously amusing. In spite of myself I may do just what the cuss wants and make a little money.

Oh, I'm glad you are working. It will be hard at times to hold against the universal depression, and you will have days when you can't work. At such times sit down and talk with me for an hour. I'm your brother to the end of the road, and I know that you have in you both bigness and a delicacy of handling of words I'll always want but won't envy you.

[P.S.] Love to Margaret.

Going to Kentucky tonight.

22.   [?CHICAGO, ?AFTER NOVEMBER 7, 1917]

To WALDO FRANK

Dear Brother: Your letter telling of things astir with you. I get the picture. You withdraw into a little close place, and the flame burns in you. When you are exhausted, you go forth and face life. It is dull, abjective, concerned with little things. Always the million empty voices shouting of nothing.

It is an odd thing how that shrillness got into America. My work takes me up and down the land a good deal. We have no forests out here, but there are tremendous open spaces with white farmhouses dim in the far distance.

Through Ohio, Indiana, Michigan, and Wisconsin were formerly

[1] On this matter see James Schevill, *Sherwood Anderson: His Life and Work*, University of Denver Press, 1951, pp. 38–39, and *Memoirs*, pp. 264 f.

forests. The men walked all day under great trees, followed by the women. They were cutting the timber away, making a place for our towns and cities.

For myself I can't see why we do not get more quiet into our lives out of just the contemplation of the things they did and from walking in the open places.

The mystery has to be solved. In some way we have got to come to an understanding of the cause of the shrillness and emptiness of our times.

Now, you see, here in the West there is an effort being made, but there is much silliness. We get here also young writers gathering in groups and chattering in a quite terrible way. On Michigan Avenue in Chicago young men and women strut along, striving to imitate the manner of the Parisian. They go into places and drink coffee and cocktails. They talk of art. They have notions, or seem to have, that they achieve something by a manner of walking or dressing. They get ahold of ideas regarding the shades of things. One of them to whom I talked actually spoke of "The Politics of Poetry." Do not be too much amused. The thing I am told exists and has its effect on the molding of opinion. It is infinitely silly, but is a part of the shrillness of the times.

A curious notion comes often to me. Is it not likely that when the country was new and men were often alone in the fields and forests, they got a sense of bigness outside themselves that has now in some way been lost? I don't mean the conventional religious thing that is still prevalent and that is nowadays being retailed to the people by the most up-to-date commercial methods, but something else. The people, I fancy, had a savagery superior to our own. Mystery whispered in the grass, played in the branches of trees overhead, was caught up and blown across the horizon line in clouds of dust at evening on the prairies.

I am old enough to remember tales that strengthen my belief in a deep, semi-religious influence that was formerly at work among our people. The flavor of it hangs over the best work of Mark Twain. That's what makes it so moving and valuable. I can remember old fellows in my home town speaking feelingly of an evening spent on the big, empty plains. It has taken the shrillness out of them. They had learned the trick of quiet. It affected their whole lives. It made them significant.

One can say that the coming of industrialism has brought about the present-day emptiness and shrillness of the arts, and there must be something in the saying, but, Lord, man, can art be superseded by the clatter of the machinery in a shoe factory? The prairies are still here. The Mississippi flows southward to the sea. It is but a step from the heart of the Loop district of Chicago to the shores of Lake Michigan.

I suspect that the thing needed is quite simple — a real desire on the part of a few people to shake off the success disease, to really get over our American mania for "getting on." It has got to be pretty deep-seated if it gets us anywhere.

Why is the desire for success so deep-seated? I have wondered. Is it because we are neither urban or rural that we have neither the crude sincerity of the Russians or the finished gesture at art and life of the Frenchmen?

As for *Marching Men*, it don't matter. I know what I tried to do. In any event, if the thing I wanted is at all there, it will take time to grow and mature in the minds of others. That is what is happening to your book.[1] The sincere thing you put into it is beginning to be felt.

I'm grinning now. I take to myself a wide sense of leisure. I'm going to have my own way about the book on which I am at work if it never gets itself finished. We die and rot away, and the author of forty volumes would make no better fertilizer for the corn.

Don't let them crowd you, Brother. You don't have to do the job, and I don't have to do it. When we are dead, a million fools will survive us.

Every day that you work well is a good day. I know that, and I want good days for you, that's what I want.

23.   [?MANSFIELD, OHIO, BEFORE NOVEMBER 18, 1917]

To WALDO FRANK

[No salutation] To be sure you are right, Brother, and the vital thing is to strive to go ahead. The difficulties are immeasurably great. I cannot believe that there is anything approaching national thought anywhere. In the catastrophe[1] that has come upon the world all of the more subtle and delicately adjusted impulses and aspirations of

[1] *The Unwelcome Man* (1917).

[1] World War I.

peoples have been lost sight of. It is good to see you willing to try to swim ahead in this uncertain sea.

As for myself, you know something of what I have dreamed. At my best I am like a great mother bird flying over this broad Mississippi Valley, seeing its towns and its broad fields and peoples and brooding over some vague dream of a song arising, of gods coming here to dwell with my people. At my worst I am a petty writer not big enough for the task I have set myself.

It is needless to say how much your letters have meant to me. Like yourself I cannot understand the competitive spirit among writers. We are all so inadequate in the face of the thing to be done; life among us is so brief and so hurried that to pause and snarl at each other is unspeakably dull.

Well, you don't do it, and thank God for you. Your brotherly affection and understanding is the biggest thing I've struck since I became known as a writer. For that alone it was worth while publishing. My love to you

24.   [CHICAGO, ?AFTER NOVEMBER 18, 1917]

TO WALDO FRANK

Dear Waldo: Out from under a mess. A fool woman came to town intent on going to bed of [sic] me. Where do they get that queer little diseased gleam in their eye when they have that notion? I climbed a tree. Then I ran along the treetops, leaping with hands and feet. I threw nuts down at her and cracked her head.

Tennessee is unspeakably bully in such a situation. She does not become the wife. What she does is to walk blithely along and pay no attention. Then when I have hit the lady with a large coconut and the milk streams down into her eyes, she winks.

I am hugging myself over the naïve, gaudy splendor o[f] *Immaturity*. It oozes out over the whole landscape and should be in the end the kind of book that a man takes to bed with him on bleak winter evenings. It will ramble and stroll and stop to loaf and chatter about the most absurd and unexpected things in the world. It will get nowhere, ain't going nowhere. The sharp-minded, definite, cocksure people are destined to hate it.

It is of course blithering folly for any of us who are aiming to have any fun out of writing to expect recognition or give a damn about it.

What does it amount to anyway? Perhaps silly women mouthing over you. The real writer who got recognition in the country now would be like a bush pissed on by a long procession of dogs. I have my own way of getting recognition. I recognize myself. I have got me a lot of gaudy little feathers, red and green and purple, and I wear them in my hat. That is like putting your finger to your nose in the midst of a desolate place.

I have a chance to go to New York, but think I will stick to my stinking town. I am in a way part and parcel of the muddle out here. The stink of the stockyards is in my clothes.

Brother, I can only think of one thing to beg of you. Keep a swagger. Spit in the eye of the greasy world. Do be of good cheer. The winds and rains come, and the land is black with fertility. Men will be born, infinite men of broad girth and cocky eyes. Escape if you can all the art and intellectual talk. Go wide and free like a good-gaited colt.

Don't I preach like a new Billy Sunday? [1] Damn your eyes, you have that effect on me. I have an irritating and noisy desire to run up behind you and shout and sing and whoop.

The world may be a rotten place, but it can't be rotten for those who can occasionally drink from the golden bowl. My Harry Livermore [2] lay at night in a room that looked down into the Chicago Loop district. An electric sign over a retail store blinked all night. He thought his room a marvelous place, because a god looked in, cocked his eye, and winked. The god and I know infinite things, Harry concluded.

You're bound to get well, Waldo. Someday you will go walk with me over hills and past a thousand fields. What of books? What of artists living or dead? The dust of days will be in our hair.

Do give my love to Margaret, and take for yourself the love of both Tennessee and myself. Incidentally, a million unheard-of people will yet have moments of love and fervor because of work you will do.

Later. After many grim efforts I have unwound your letter. Word by word I fought my way through. You have the wors[t] scrawl in the world.

Don't know whether I can get to New York this winter or not. I'll

---

[1] The Reverend William Ashley Sunday (1863–1935), evangelist and prohibitionist.
[2] A character in *Immaturity*.

try. Do wish I could see Margaret and have the talk with her. I would abuse you roundly.

Remember, the latchstring hangs out here. Come out, either or both of you, any time. Why not tell Margaret to write to me?

25.   [?Chicago, after December 7, 1917]

To Waldo Frank

Dear Brother: I wonder if you know General Grant, great, big, odd child; strange that he should have been a fighter. He was like a field. Nothing jarred him. He had a simple, childlike receipt for meeting life. "I am terribly afraid," he said, "but the other fellow is afraid too."

There is the wisdom of the ages in that simple comment.

As an antidote to the War I now read history. Histories of Poland, Russia, Austria, Italy, France. One gets a sense of the long line of events. The present sinks into nothingness.

Do you know Twain's *Captain Stormfield's Visit to Heaven?* [1] The captain of the ship he met out in space threw, if I remember to quote correctly, a "kazark" of coal on the fire. The captain naïvely explained that a "kazark" was an amount of coal equal to just 26 worlds like ours.

What matter Kenton, Fiske, Jones, etc.? [2]

When you think of them, be Rabelaisian. Fart at the moon. I have seen two of them and know the quality of their minds. The Bobby Jones I don't know and have no hunger.

My *Immaturity* will not be the book you expected. It has gone insane; a really delicious, garrulous, heavy, lame fellow with shaggy eyebrows is writing. If he is successful, as I pray the Chicago smoke gods he will be, the whole world will be puzzled to know what he is talking about. Perhaps you, if the current sets your way, will someday

---

[1] In Mark Twain's *Extract from Captain Stormfield's Visit to Heaven* (1909), the Captain unwisely races his meteor against a comet. The captain of the comet easily wins by heaving overboard his cargo of "eighteen hundred thousand billion quintillions of kazarks," and Captain Stormfield explains that a "kazark" is "exactly the bulk of a *hundred and sixty-nine worlds like ours!*" Quite typically, Anderson misses the details but gets the point.

[2] Edna Kenton (b. 1876), short-story writer and contributor of popular literary articles to magazines like the *Bookman* and the *Ladies' Home Journal;* Harrison Grey Fiske (1861–1942), dramatic critic, director, and playwright; though the name does not seem relevant in this context, possibly Robert Edmond Jones (1887–), scenic designer, whose setting for *The Man Who Married a Dumb Wife,* produced in 1915, made theater history.

hug the shaggy, awkward advertising man for a baked bean concern, who is writing the book, to your heart. If you do not, someone, sometime will.

God help us all.

Let's shake off the culture and the odd toy minds. If I had money and didn't have to write little advertisements, I would come and get you.

The world has a wart on its nose.

In the night the winds come down out of Medicine Hat.

They play in dead cornfields.

In the cold and the night the gods burrow deep in the ground.

There is a stretch of land in the West over which a man may walk 30 days seeing nothing but cornfields. I have a picture. In the midst of that vast open space, exposed to the winds that tramp the world, Edna Kenton and Harrison Grey Fiske are talking of art.

See the moon. Isn't the night delightful?

26.   [CHICAGO, LATE DECEMBER, 1917]

To WALDO FRANK

Dear Brother: I have come to think of the muddle of life as a necessary thing and all direct effort at corrective measures as rather absurd. Perhaps the muddle is a fertilizing thing like the stable manure thrown on the fields.

What happens to so many of us is this. We see the muddle so clearly that we come to think of ourselves as not a part of it. Forgetting our own muddle, we begin to bark and scold at the world.

Do you remember how that element finally crept into the *Seven Arts?* We were all impatient with the *New Republic* because of its blatant preaching at the world.

Then in *Seven Arts* the same thing began. It was as though we had said: "Now you see here, the *New Republic* is not wrong in scolding. It does not scold well enough. Let my voice be heard."

Anyway in the beginning when *Seven Arts* was a project, J. O.[1] wrote to me. "Please be good," I wrote back. "Don't start another magazine to scold at us."

Dear Brother. Isn't there something not aristocratic, just a bit crude, about expecting the world to think clearly and act beautifully? Per-

[1] James Oppenheim.

haps one has to grow old before he can realize the great truth that life can only be beautiful at odd moments and in quite unexpected ways.

I find myself compelled to turn to little playful things. The night is cold and bleak. Unlovely people hurry along unlovely streets. I creep into my room and pull the blinds. I light my candle. The flame dances and throws grotesque shapes on the wall. In the midst of my roaring, ugly city there is a hush, imagined. I am an old priest in an old place. I am a firm believer in the gods.

There is a blessed flavor about understanding people. Tennessee is one of them. She has bought me a little feather to wear in my hat. She has bought me a golden yellow scarf. Tomorrow she will buy me socks all splashed with purple and yellow crystals.

You see, Brother, all this is absurd, but with the feather, the scarf, and the socks I venture out into a drab, warworn world. Not they with the sorrow and the deep grief, but little old me with my splashes of color have the true light on life. For the moment and in a quite child-like way I have restored truth in the midst of ugliness.

You see, dear fellow, how and why I keep at you. You have been so much to the schools. I want to restore to you something of the old semi-barbaric thing that I know well is in your blood. It is the only thing will carry you through the weight of what is ahead for you as you work further and deeper into the things your nature will tempt you to undertake.

Perhaps I am heartless. Everyone who knows me well says so. If the future of mankind depended on my writing a sane, true book concerning life, and I were really tempted to go walk instead where evening shadows play on grey, smoke-begrimed old houses, I would go.

The world might burn in hell for all of me. I love a few people. Time is long. Innumerable wars have been fought and will be fought. You are my brother. I care most to have great moments come to you. Luck for 1918

27.   [CHICAGO, EARLY 1918]

TO WALDO FRANK

Dear Brother: The West, and particularly Chicago, has become a sort of fetish to many Eastern men. They are, I suppose, a little weary of their own smartness, got out of group life and out of the fact that

New York as a city seems to have become a definite thing with a style of its own. Mencken [1] and such fellows must get a little tired of their own smartness. They are a little like weary gamblers whose money is gone, rattling words in a dice box.

Chicago is simply formless. You know what that means — jazz bands; weariness; dreary stretches of dull, middle-class houses; [?d]umb, badly organized labor; rattling, stinking streetcars; utter shiftlessness.

One isn't beset by a little body of opinions, because there is no opinion. It is a place to work, because in work is a man's only salvation.

You really can work here. My room on a little side street is a secluded hole. I am away all day. There is a big table by a window and candles. I will be able to come at the middle of the day and walk with you. In the evening we can again take long walks.

What a flourisher you have become. If I am to be a mother, I shall spank you. You tell me that you are always surprised at a baby's coming out where we go in and then add two terrible sentences: "That[']s not obscene. If you don't like it you can go to hell."

Waldo, you talk like Floyd Dell. Do you not feel spanked?

The days are not long enough. I am working steadily. I want to talk with you before the magazine [2] starts. Give me the chance.

Surely you have no business to be ill. I do it myself at times, but always feel silly. It's a rotten habit.

Come any time. Come soon.

28.   [CHICAGO, ?EARLY APRIL, 1918]

To VAN WYCK BROOKS

Dear Brooks: I am glad you are going to get at Twain.[1] It is absurd that he should have been translated as an artist by a man like Howells [2] or that fellow Paine.[3] There is something about him no one has got

[1] H. L. Mencken (1880–) was editing The Smart Set from 1914 to 1923, together with George Jean Nathan.

[2] Early in 1918, Van Wyck Brooks, Randolph Bourne, Paul Rosenfeld, and Frank were making plans for a successor to Seven Arts, but no financial backer could be found for the magazine, which did not appear.

[1] Van Wyck Brooks's The Ordeal of Mark Twain appeared in 1920.

[2] William Dean Howells (1837–1920), American novelist and man of letters, published My Mark Twain in 1910.

[3] Albert Bigelow Paine wrote the authorized three-volume biography of Twain (1912).

hold of. He belonged out here in the Middle West and was only incidentally a writer.

I've a notion that after Twain passed under the influence of Howells and others of the East he began to think of himself as a writer and lost something of his innocence. Should not one go to *Huck Finn* for the real man, working out of a real people?

Several years ago I tried to write a story concerning Twain. It never got to anything, but I have a copy of the attempt in my desk. There is a character in the story, the old cheese maker from Indiana, that I will sometime make the central figure in a real story. He is Twain's type of man.

It is odd what literary connections one makes. In my own mind I have always coupled Mark Twain with George Borrow.[4] I get the same quality of honesty in them, the same wholesome disregard of literary precedent.

Lane's have decided to go ahead with my cornfield songs. I call them Mid-American chants. Then I am going to publish the Winesburg tales, some two dozen of them, in a book under the title *Winesburg*. When I came to look at my novel *Mary Cochran,* written several years ago, it didn't suit me. I shall hold it back for more work.

One has to realize that, although there is truth in the Winesburg things, there is another big story to be done. We are no longer the old America. Those are tales of farming people. We've got a new people now. We are a growing, shifting, changing thing. Our life in our factory towns intensifies. It becomes at the same time more ugly and more intense.

God damn it, Brooks, I wish my books would sell for one reason. I want to quit working for a living and go wander for five years in our towns. I want to be a factory hand again and wander from place to place. I want my frame to unbend from the desk and to go look and listen to this new thing.

My songs are going to be widely abused and perhaps rightly. I'm a poor enough singer. But there is a song here, and it has been muffed. Masters might get it, but he has too keen a quality of hate.

It makes me ill when I think how little I get done and the years hurrying along, but I suppose we all know that sickness. I would like you to know I appreciate you[r] interest in my efforts. The fact that

[4] The English novelist (1803–1881), author of *Lavengro* and *The Romany Rye,* was one of Anderson's favorite authors.

you are interested is one of the bright spots. The quality of your mind I have always thought one of the really bully things of my generation.

I'll get to New York again sometime. When I do, I hope to see and talk with you.

[P.S.] I'll send you the Twain thing to read if I can find it for the sake of the cheese maker.

29.   [CHICAGO, EARLY APRIL, 1918]

To VAN WYCK BROOKS

My dear Brooks: Your letter has stirred up a world of thought in me. It isn't Twain I'm thinking of, but the profound truth of some of your own observations.

As far as Twain is concerned, we have to remember the influences about him. Remember how he came into literature — the crude buffoon of the early days in the mining camp, the terrible cheap and second-rate humor of much of *Innocents Abroad*. It seems to me that when he began he addressed an audience that gets a big laugh out of the braying of a jackass, and without a doubt Mark often brayed at them. He knew that later. There was tenderness and subtlety in Mark when he grew older.

You get the picture of him, Brooks — the river man who could write going East and getting in with that New England crowd, the fellows from barren hills and barren towns. The best he got out of the bunch was Howells, and Howells did Twain no good.

There's another point, Brooks. I can't help wishing Twain hadn't married such a good woman. There was such a universal inclination to tame the man — to save his soul, as it were. Left alone, I fancy Mark might have been willing to throw his soul overboard and then — ye gods, what a fellow he might have been, what poetry might have come from him.

The big point is: it seems to me that this salvation of the soul business gets under everybody's skin. With artists it takes the form of being concerned with their reputation as writers. A struggle constantly goes on. Call the poet a poet and he is no longer the poet. You see what I mean.

There is a fellow like Waldo, for example. He writes me long letters. His days are often made happy or miserable according to whether or not he is writing well.

Is it so important? What stardust we are. What does it matter?

The point is that I catch Waldo so often striving to say things in an unusual way. It makes me cringe. I want to beat him with my fists.

I pick on Waldo as an example because I love him and I know he feels deeply. He should write with a swing — weeping, praying, and crying to the gods on paper instead of making sentences as he so often does.

Well, now, you see I'm coming around. The cultural fellows got hold of Mark. They couldn't hold him. He was too big and too strong. He brushed their hands aside.

But their words got into his mind. In the effort to get out beyond that he became a pessimist.

Now, Brooks, you know a man cannot be a pessimist who lives near a brook or a cornfield. When the brook chatters or at night when the moon comes up and the wind plays in the corn, a man hears the whispering of the gods.

Mark got to that once — when he wrote *Huck Finn*. He forgot Howells and the good wife and everyone. Again he was the half-savage, tender, god-worshiping, believing boy. He had proud, conscious innocence.

I believe he wrote that book in a little hut on a hill on his farm. It poured out of him. I fancy that at night he came down from his hill stepping like a king, a splendid playboy playing with rivers and men, riding on the Mississippi, on the broad river that is the great artery flowing out of the heart of the land.

Well, Brooks, I'm alone in a boat on that stream sometimes. The rhythm and swing of it is in some of my songs that are to be published next month. It sometimes gets into some of the Winesburg things. I'll ride it some more, perhaps. It depends on whether or not I can avoid taking myself serious[ly]. Whom the gods wish to destroy they first make drunk with the notion of being a writer.

Waldo is coming out to spend a month with me.

Wish I could see you sometime this summer. I'll be in the East for a month or more in June or July. Why couldn't you come to the mountains and have a few days' walk with me?

30.   [?CHICAGO, ?LATE APRIL, 1918]

To VAN WYCK BROOKS

Brooks: I cannot resist the temptation to write you a letter induced by a talk Waldo and I had last evening. In [?sum]. The talk drifted to

Mark Twain and your attitude toward him. Something Waldo said gave me the notion that your digging into his work had made you a little ill — that you had seen, perhaps too clearly, his dreadful vulgarity and cheapness.

Of course your book cannot be written in a cheerful spirit. In facing Twain's life you face a tragedy. How could the man mean what he does to us if it were not a tragedy? Had the man succeeded in breaking through, he would not have been a part of us. Can't you take it that way?

America a land of children, broken off from the culture of the world. Twain there, a part of that. Then the coming of industrialism. The putting of the child into the factory.

Mark Twain was a factory child. I am that. I can, however, stand off and look at him. When it would be second-rate and unmanly to weep concerning myself, I can think of him. For his very failure I love him. He was maimed, hurt, broken. In some way he got caught up by the dreadful cheap smartness, the shrillness that was a part of the life of the country, that is still its dominant note.

I don't want you to get off Twain. I want your mind on it. Please do not lose courage, do not be frightened away by the muck and ugliness of it.

For the Americans of the future there can be no escape. They have got to, in some way, face themselves. Your book about the man they love and in a dumb way understand will help mightily. I do want you to write that book.

31.   [CHICAGO, BEFORE MAY 21, 1918]

To WALDO FRANK

[No Salutation] This morning I came downtown thinking of your letter and of you writing furiously away. My thoughts about you were very pleasant. You have made a deeper impression on me than you realize.

Last evening I read for the first time in the book you left for me, the Englishman's life of Lincoln.[1] It will be mighty well for America when it begins to appreciate such studies of its big figures. I have a desire to send the book to a dozen people, but cannot afford it.

You will understand the drift of my thoughts when I say that the

---

[1] Lord Charnwood, *Abraham Lincoln* (1916).

book might in many respects be a study of me. There is in my heart no presumptuousness when I say that. There is brought out very clearly the tendency in the Western American man to go loose and cheap at time[s], to rise to exalted occasion, to be alternately sad and heavily merry.

In the light of the book I see what Brooks meant when he suggested that I did not take letters seriously enough. I do not. He is right.

But both you and Brooks are more civilized than myself. Much that is in me wavering and uncertain is in you fixed and real.

At the same time I am more closely allied to the soil than either of you can ever be. I did not read you my story of the boy who had been digging potatoes in a field with his father. The boy had a fever later in his bed and crept into a room where his father was praying on the floor. The soles of his father's feet were black. The boy picked up a wooden neck-yoke of the sort used for hitching oxen and wanted to kill his father, because he wanted the house to be quiet.

There must be things of that kind compressed and forced into the minds of boys raised in poverty in the West in the midst of woods and fields and in the midst also of that most terrible of all vulgarities, loose thinking and living, [which] the boy feels has become a part of himself [and which] you will never have as an inherent part of yourself.

As for Brooks, I say frankly I love the man and am not afraid of his judgment of me and my work. He will perhaps be more fair than yourself in not having in him any warmth of affection for me. I do feel in him a solid and direct stab at truth that I respect all the more because the things he says hit so often and so closely at me.

It is something big for him, raised in the atmosphere of scholarship,[2] to have seen through the loud talk, the noise, and the fog and to have comprehended so clearly the tragedy of America. Do not be mistaken, Waldo; Brook's way of thinking is very clear and will carry far.

I do hope you will not think me imp[ertin]ent when I suggest that you do not think too much and too hard concerning America. It will flow into you imperceptibly and graft itself on to what you have.

What you have is well express[ed] in your remarks about Hecht. Your mind is peculiarly clear and lucid. It goes deeply into the souls of people and motives. It means more to me that you love and respect me than it would mean for Brooks to have such a feeling concerning

[2] Van Wyck Brooks graduated from Harvard College in 1908 and was instructor in English at Stanford University, 1911–1913.

me, but Brooks does in some ways see more clearly. His attitude must be and remain toward me somewhat like that of Charnwood's toward Lincoln. Your own will, because of your different nature, be more close and warm and more [determined] to see worth in me that is too often not there.

To return to my thoughts concerning you. If you go on as you are going, looking closely into lives and thinking of lives, the country will bring itself into you through the medium of lives. Is that not the better, the real way?

I express this because I think it important for you not to run out too much. Partly your illness is due to that. You do grip and clutch at the moon somewhat and wear yourself out so.

If you will believe me, and it is hard for me to say, the fact of your affection means to me something of the same thing that Tennessee's affection means. I have a feeling sometime[s], in view of the affections that have been given me, that I am like a crude woodsman that has been received into the affection of princes.

Remember, Waldo, that this Chicago atmosphere has this element you do not perhaps clearly get. The enervating looseness of thinking that was here in Lincoln's time is still with us, but is made more intense and vulgar by the coming of industrialism. That Brooks sees and understands more clearly than yourself. Do not be annoyed at me for saying so.

My chants will fall flat and go unnoticed. They perhaps deserve it, but they deserve something better also. I suspect Brooks of being reluctant about telling me how little he respects them.

My affection for you will always be haltingly expressed. It is, however, a permanent thing and will survive as long as I live. My love to your Margaret

32.   [CHICAGO, MAY 23, 1918]

To VAN WYCK BROOKS

Dear Brooks: I cannot resist an impulse I have to write to you again concerning your book, *America's Coming-of-Age*. Are there any others of your books in which you also develop the theme you have here taken hold of so firmly?

The amazing thing to me about your mind, Brooks, is that you see so clearly what I did not suppose any man with a background such as I had thought of you as having could see.

I have myself understood the trenchant sadness of Lincoln, the rather childlike pessimis[m] of Twain, the half-sullen and dogmatic insistence on the part of Dreiser on the fight with Puritanism and Whitman's windy insistence on America. I thought I understood these things, because I have lived in such a barren place, felt myself so futile, because I have really always felt a lack of strength to continue struggling in a vacuum and looked forward hopelessly to the time when some quirk of the mind would lead me to adopt finally some grotesque sectional attitude and spend myself uselessly on that.

When I talked to Waldo out here, I felt in him a sense of background I have never had. I wondered if he knew the utter lack of background. It means so very much that you know, and of course he must know also.

One works in an oddly futile way. This year, because I have been very tired after ten years of trying to stay among the men about me, to be part and parcel of them, and at the same time to buil[d] something a little permanent at odd moments.

One cannot surrender to the cheaper inclination in writing, to win perhaps the secondary approval of an ass like Mencken as his reward.

But then one gets this queer sense of carving a stone that will presently be cast into a stagnant sea, into the Sargasso Sea as you suggest.

I am very sure, after reading this book, that you must be sad also, that you also must feel deeply the futility of things.

What I want to ask you is why you do not sympathize with me in such expressions as my essay "An Apology for Crudity"[1] or my *Chants?* Where do I hit wrong?

In the chants I reached into my own personal muttering, half insane and disordered, and tried to take out of them a little something ordered. You should see how I clutched at the ordered cornfield[s], insisted on them to myself, took them as about the only thing I could see.

I haven't the right to expect much from such muttering[s], but I have the right to expect that, having written this book I have just read, you would know what I was at.

Forgive me if I sink to the triviality of explanation. Your mind has won my honest respect. I do not so much seek your approval as I do your brotherhood.

---

[1] Published in the *Dial*, LXIII, 437–438 (November, 1917).

May I say that for me yours is the first, the only, note in American criticism that I have ever thought worth a damn. It is really and deeply understanding.

[P.S.] Do try to form the habit of writing me some of your thoughts occasionally. It is lonely out here.

33.   [CHICAGO, ?MAY 31, 1918]

To WALDO FRANK

Waldo: I send you a note from Brooks. Read it and send it back. You will often find yourself able to be of use to me by telling me things to read, sending me odds and ends of your thoughts.

You must come to realize that I do not think as clearly or well as either you or Brooks. Your visit and things you said still come back and are slowly digested in my mind. I am what much of my writing, if you will view it honestly, must suggest, a stupid thing working out of a stupid time and people. Keep your door open for me. I suggest it without humbleness.

34.   [CHICAGO, MAY 31, 1918]

To VAN WYCK BROOKS

Dear Brooks: I know of course what you mean, and it is because you have the clear-sightedness to see that you are of such very great value. American writers have a trick of doing something it is difficult at first to understand. They harden, ripen out of time. Your notion of the stony field has significance. In such a field corn would come too soon to tassel. It would turn yellow and produce no grain.

You can see for yourself how our cities produce that peculiarly shallow effect. Dell goes that way, Mencken, Hackett,[1] and our newspapermen out here are peculiarly so. Waldo can tell you of them.

It is probably true that the reason our men who are of importance — Lincoln, Whitman, Twain, Dreiser, etc. — all begin when they are almost old men is that they have to spend so much of their lives putting down roots. The strength goes into that. We have, you see, Lincoln producing a few notable utterances, Whitman some clean stuff out of much windiness, Twain *Huck Finn,* Dreiser *Sister Carrie,* etc.

---

[1] Francis Hackett (1883–), biographer and novelist, was literary editor of the Chicago *Evening Post,* 1906–1911, and associate editor of the *New Republic,* 1914–1922.

Oddly enough, you are the first man I have seen stoutly at it trying to take the stones out of the field, to give the roots a chance.

If you could get at Twain sympathetically and show how and why he failed, it would be lifting a great stone. He now, you see, is just about to be accepted by the smart alecks as the great man. We shall be clubbed with his failures and the cheap things he did. His bad work will be glorified, as it has been by Howells and others.

As for myself, I think there is soil for the raising of a crop if the stones can be taken away.

I do not know L. M.[2] and have no pull to him, lonely as I sometimes am. I get the notion fixed in my mind that his successes have been founded on hatred. A burning hatred arose in him and galvanized his lackadaisical talent into something sharp and real. Then the fire went away and left the man empty. This is all a theory. I do not know the fellow.

Your attitude toward my own efforts is generous and helpful. What I am trying to say to you in all this letter writing is aside from that but connected with it too.

Any work accomplished is a thing already half dead. It may concern others, but it cannot deeply concern the workman. He has to look ahead to new difficulties, to wading through new times of disillusionment and weariness.

In my own place here, in the distracted crowds and in the midst of distracting things I have often lived on little protective saying[s] muttered to myself. "Do not lose the fine edge of your contempt," I say to myself. Other such smart sayings come to my lips. I find myself living on them.

Of the newer men I have met you and Waldo give me something else. What friendship you give strengthens. It is a thing that cuts across the darkness and the mist.

I could not be hurt by any criticism of my efforts coming from either of you. I would like to have you both feel brotherhood for me and give me as much as you can out of your thoughts.

Is it not probably true that men like L. M. lose their grip because they do not stay among workers? They cannot stand the brusqueness and hardness with which men speak who have much to do. They go among idlers where soft, meaningless flattery takes the place of truth.

[2] Edgar Lee Masters.

Well, if you see things in me, give me your friendship as Waldo has done. Let me see your mind at work as often as you can.

I go back to your figure of the stony field. Corn is planted there. You go about trying to cultivate, throwing stones aside. Much of the corn will be destroyed. That may be my fate. It matters so damn little.

What would matter is that one should grow into a yellow, rare, ripe thing, that one should quit striving to put down roots. You get the sense of what I drive at.

[P.S.] I take the liberty of sending your note on to Frank. I will get and read the book you mention.

35.   CHICAGO, JUNE 7, 1918

To VAN WYCK BROOKS

Dear Brooks: If I can fix one thought in your mind, I will feel more free in approaching you. When I write to men like you and Frank, I do it to cut the fog of my own loneliness. If I can make you feel that no letter of mine demands answering, I shall feel more freedom.

I have had an experience lately that will be of interest to you. I got suddenly an impulse to read everything I could get hold of on Lincoln. Waldo stirred up the impulse in me by giving me Charnwood's life. I read others.

I am wondering if you might not profitably go to Lincoln for a greater understanding of Twain and Whitman. There is something, a quality there, common to the three men. In Lincoln it is perhaps more out in front of you.

I got a sense of three very honest boys brought suddenly to face the complex and intricate world. There is a stare in their eyes. They are puzzled and confused. You will be inclined to think Whitman the greater man perhaps. He came closer to understanding. He lacked Lincoln's very great honesty of soul.

Twain's way lies somewhere between the road taken by the other two men.

I am struck with the thought that I would like to have you believe that Twain's cheapness was not really a part of him. It was a thing out of the civilization in which he lived that crept [in] and invaded him.

Lincoln let it creep in less, because he was less warm and human. He did not love and hate. In a simple, solid way he stuck to abstract principles. He squares up to those principles. That's what makes him seem so big.

There is a kind of unconscious dodging in that. The country girl who died — I mean Ann[1] — left Lincoln a thing to love that wasn't living and about. He could reach out his hand to that shadowy thing when he was lonely. It was all very fine for the making of the big, stony thing that stood up sometimes before the world.

Twain got more deeply into the complex matter of living. He was more like you and me, facing more nearly our kind of problems.

Here I am going to confess something to you. Whitman does not mean as much to me as do the other two. There is somewhere a pretense about him, even trickiness. When I was a boy and another boy caught me fairly doing some second-rate thing, I was supposed to do what we called "acknowledge the corn."

Lincoln wouldn't have done the second-rate thing.

Twain would and would have acknowledged the corn.

Whitman wouldn't have owned up.

Well, there you are. I am putting Whitman below whe[re] he stands in my mind.

It is unfair. It springs from a growing desire I have to sell you Twain.

36.   CHICAGO, DECEMBER 28, 1918

To KARL ANDERSON

Dear Karl: I keep thinking about our talk. For a good many years I did not appreciate you as an artist. I thought you were too far away from life, were not coarse enough. I used to ache to have your things put roots into the ground.

Two or three years ago I saw something of yours that startled me. I began to sense out your impulses. Now I do not think you were at fault before that. I think I was at fault.

There is something very much alike in you and myself. The nature of our lives has brought about what seems to be a difference. I have had to live with people and deal with people. It has made me understand that I must never listen to what people say, but must try to go deeper into their motives.

In reality I haven't much intellect, and I don't believe you have.

[1] Ann Rutledge was the daughter of Lincoln's landlord in New Salem, Illinois.

What we have got to do is to feel into things. To do that we only need to learn from people that what they say and think isn't of very much importance.

It is stupid of me to say it, because you know it as well as myself, but I can't help saying that I wish you could see both more and less of people. Can't you brush the matter of expense aside and take a room in town and keep it all thru the year? It would cost you perhaps $6 per week. It would be a place to which to escape.

The room should be utterly your own, and your ordinary, everyday life should not be brought into it. You must have, as all men of your kind are bound to have, periods of feeling very ineffective. It is a sign that the time has come for you to run away. You should always keep a place to which to run, your own place, where you can pray and work and think your own thoughts.

Do pardon me for what may seem an impertinence. It is a matter of technique of living. I have found the idea invaluable to myself. I do wish you would try it.

37.   ON TRAIN IN KENTUCKY [?LATE DECEMBER, 1918]

To VAN WYCK BROOKS

Dear Brooks: Beside[s] my own recurring thoughts of you I keep crossing your trail from time to time. The other day I went into a hospital to see the wife[1] of a Chicago judge who is Tennessee's friend and who has been ill for a long time. She was reading your *Letters and Leadership*[2] and said at once your mind had helped her understand the difficulties of American writing as nothing else had.

"I have so often not seen what you were driving at, everything you wrote seemed so incomplete. Now I see that you stand on nothing," she said. I sen[t] over to her your *America's Coming-of-Age.*[3]

In a book store I saw a Jew named Larson[4] who is a friend of yours. We talked of you. It was his notion you were almost too prolific, wrote too easily.

I hadn't that angle on you. "I thought he was painfully careful, almost to the point of being constipated sometimes," I said.

We discussed the matter but a few minutes. I liked the looks of

---

[1] Mrs. Harriet W. Walker, wife of Judge Charles Morehead Walker.
[2] Published in 1918.
[3] Published in 1915.
[4] A misspelling, according to Van Wyck Brooks, for Max Lippitt Larkin.

him and didn't want to dispute, and then I felt that he might, as well as not, be right and I wrong. "Everything you say shows you don't know Brooks," he declared, and I took his word for it.

I have been reading *The Education of Henry Adams* [5] and feel tremendously its importance as a piece of American writing. New England can scarcely go further than that. It must be, in its way, very complete. We do, I am sure, both live and die rather better in the Middle West. Nothing about us is as yet so completely and racially tired.

When you get at your Mark Twain (I suppose you already have) you must do a chapter on the American going East into that tired, thin New England atmosphere and being conquered by its feminine force.

I came West with my new book, *Poor White*,[6] about laid by, as we out here say of the corn crop in early October. It is in shocks and stood up in the field. The husking is yet to do. I will not attempt it for a time, as the proof on *Winesburg* should be along most any time.

When I left New York, Waldo and I were rather at sixes and sevens. When his new book [7] was finished, he did not show it to me, but I secretly saw it at Paul's [8] and thought it very badly overwritten and wordy. He got, it seemed to me, into a particularly bad period, and one heard more talk of great men than usual. He is so solid and the fineness of his nature has been such a blessing to us all that I felt cheap in always having in the back of my mind that reservation about him — I mean the necessity of always saying to oneself, "He doesn't mean anything when he always goes on about great men."

One afternoon I blurted it all out. It made a breach that kept closing and opening during the few weeks I remained with him. It will come right in the end I am sure.

I am back at the old place in the advertising office. The moving picture dependence became impossible.[9] That isn't my road out.

Back here I almost feel able to say that I don't care if I never travel again. The place between mountain and mountain I call Mid-America is my land. Good or bad, it's all I'll ever have.

[5] Published in 1918 after a private printing in 1907.

[6] Published November, 1920.

[7] *The Art of the Vieux Colombier*, 1918.

[8] Paul Rosenfeld (1840–1946), proponent of modernism in the arts; musical critic, editor, and friend of S.A. See *Memoirs*, p. 313.

[9] Anderson was in the office of the Taylor-Critchfield Company, which became Critchfield and Company, the advertising agency. In the autumn of 1918 he had worked briefly in New York as a publicity man for a movie company.

What I want now is to see a magazine started here in the heart of America. I want you fellows from the coast to come here. We have always been going to you. I want it changed if possible.

It isn't impossible I will get money for the purpose. I have two or three leads that may lead to money. I shall try it out thoroughly.

Do write me the news of yourself. Give my love to Mrs. Brooks. If I were at home, Tennessee would want me to wish you a happy year.

38.   [CHICAGO, ?JANUARY, 1919]

To TRIGANT BURROW

Dear Brother: I called your attention to a story I wanted you to see and that was to appear in *Little Review*. Later I withdrew the story. The *Little Review* got too dreadfully inartistic and bad. I can't stand appearing there any more, and there is no place else to appear. There never has been a time in America when the literary artist was so completely stranded high and dry. Politically-minded men have outlets of a kind. For example, I think the *New Republic* covers its field very well indeed, and there is in addition the *Dial*[1] and the *Nation*,[2] both very good things.

With the death of *Seven Arts*, however, the door was closed to anything like subtlety in writing in the country. You and I know that the big story here is the story of repression, of the strange and almost universal insanity of society. The story does not need to be an unpleasant one to right-minded men and women, but it must be boldly and subtly told and make its audience slowly.

That means an endowed magazine devoted solely to good writing, and who is to put up the money for it?

The *New Republic* and *Dial* got money,[3] but then the thing they wanted to do was so much more obvious. Everyone knows that materially the modern state is a mess. Who knows to what depths modern

---

[1] The *Dial* (1880–1929) was founded and published in Chicago as a fortnightly. In 1916 Martyn Johnson took it over, shortly thereafter George Bernard Donlin became editor, and the magazine became the organ of the "newness." It removed to New York late in 1918.

[2] Under Oswald Garrison Villard, editor from 1918 to 1933, the *Nation* ceased to be the conservative critical organ it had been in the days of Paul Elmer More, editor from 1909 to 1914.

[3] The *New Republic* in the period was partially subsidized, and in its later phases the *Dial* was largely the possession of Scofield Thayer and Dr. J. S. Watson, Jr.

prose writing has sunk, and who gives a damn? The outlook is, you see, discouraging.

I have had to come back to my grind here. It means working in an office eight hours a day at work in which I have no interest. Much of my energy is exhausted in that and in the effort to keep my outlook on life sweet and clear. Most of our artists give themselves up to protest and become in the end embittered and shrill. It is fortunate, however, that I have the constitution of an animal. I still rebound quickly and do manage to creep off into the world of the imagination.

Proof is read for my next book, *Winesburg, Ohio,* and it has gone to press. I expect it will be published in March.[4] The new book,[5] a novel, stands still for the present. It wants two or three weeks' steady writing yet and then a week or two for cutting to shape. I wonder how and where I am to get the time for that.

I may be wrong, you know, Brother, but it seems to me that I am now ripe to do something, and I hate to see the years and the days go by in the writing of advertisements for somebody's canned tomatoes or in long days of consulting with some fellow as to how he can sell his make of ready-made clothes instead of the other fellow. I want to go up and down the great valley here seeing the towns and the people and writing of the[m] as I do not believe they have been written of.

Well, you see how it is. The modern system will pay me five thousand a year for writing the canned tomato advertisements. It doesn't want the other, or rather it thinks it doesn't want them.

From time to time I am tempted to go to some rich, dissatisfied man or woman and see if she won't give me the five thousand a year to do the other thing. However, when I think of it, I grow timid. It seems so like begging, and yet, you see, I would so like to do something real, and I know I have it in me to do something real.

I suppose my wanting to start a magazine is just a subterfuge. I don't really want to read manuscripts. I want to write. That's all I do want to do.

Well, I have poured myself out. It is because I have always thought you had a real comprehension of the realities of life. The quarrel[6] we once had didn't go very deep with me. I think you understand that.

[4] *Winesburg, Ohio* was published in May, 1919.
[5] *Poor White.*
[6] Possibly a reference to the conversations of the two men in the summer of 1917 when Anderson denied the therapeutic value of psychoanalysis.

It was good of you and Rosenberg to send me the book.[7] It a little puzzles me. I am unforgivably stupid in the matter of economic thought of any kind. I suppose it is because in the economy of things I haven't had time to think in that direction. In secret I suppose I have a desire not to have you become interested in reforms. It seem[s] to me that the more subtle thing is more in your line. There are plenty of reformers, but who has understanding of just life itself? With love and good wishes

39.   [?CHICAGO, MARCH 31, 1919]

TO VAN WYCK BROOKS

Dear Brother Brooks: I am so glad to hear from you that I gladly forgive you the long silence. The winter has slipped away for me. I went through *Poor White* for the first writing and then put it away to ripen a bit. In the meantime I am doing some experiments.

First, a new book of tales[1] made up of some already written and others that are on the fire.

Second, a purely insane, experimental thing I call *A New Testament*.[2] It is an attempt to express, largely by indirection, the purely fanciful side of a man's life, the odds and ends of thought, the little pockets of thoughts and emotions that are so seldom touched.

I've a fancy this last experiment would make your hair stand on end. It is infinitely more difficult than the chants.

Why do I insist on looking upon you as the apostle of clearness? For some reason you stand in my mind as the representative of all that is best in what is orthodox and certain.

I am myself as uncertain as a weathercock. It seems to me that anything approaching accomplishment grows wearisome.

I want constantly to push out into experimental fields. "What can be done in prose that has not been done?" I keep asking myself.

And so I constantly set out on new roads.

What is gained? — perhaps nothing but a little colorful strength in

---

[7] A volume on English Guild Socialism, probably G. D. H. Cole's *Self-Government in Industry* (1917).

[1] Anderson's next collection of short stories, *The Triumph of the Egg*, appeared in November, 1921.

[2] The prose poems under this general title were not published in book form until 1927, but a number of them were given magazine publication from 1919 on, chiefly in the *Little Review* and the *Double-Dealer*.

my everyday writing. I push on, knowing that no one will perhaps care in the least for these experiments into which I put so much emotion[al] force.

It is at least the adventure. How I wish I could sit with you for a[n] hour and talk of what I mean.

About Twain. I have still the hunch. Do not look too much to him for an explanation of what is not understandable in him. Think of him as a boy whipped and blown about by the winds of his times.

Look to his times, to the men and the emotions of his times. He wanted very much to be respectable. I wonder if there wasn't a touch of the inferiority complex in him. That would explain much.

He never gave himself to a great or a deep emotion, didn't dare, didn't trust himself. Whitman must have seemed a monster to him.

He stood on the doorstep of New England. It's a ridiculous notion, but it's a fact. Twain with hat in hand and an apologetic air on New England's doorstep.

Good luck to you and Mrs. Brooks. I could write many pages and not say what I would like to you.

40. CHICAGO [?SUMMER, 1919]

To WALDO FRANK

Dear Mike and Jim and Ezra Bean and Waldo: What a letter. What a singer you sometimes are in prose.

I don't wonder you write me handsome words, words dressed in velvet and fine linen. It is entirely right that you should do so.

I am a charming person these days. I write advertisements and go about, walking up and down, but no one is quite onto me or sure of me. I am walking at the edge of a new fancy, at the outer edge of the bowl of life. To the casual eye I am on these days just a fat-cheeked man in a brown coat and a very yellow necktie. In reality I am no such thing. I am a river running down through a valley. I am a princely man with a broken leg. I am one who sits on the roofs of tall buildings in Chicago and sees sheep nibbling grass beside a brook in the state of Missouri.

It is useless for me to try to tell you what a gaudy creature I am. There are no words made for the purpose. O you maker of words, go into the forest of languages and cut for me new words.

I mean, you will see, to convey to you the impression that I am a little dog walking in a fog and putting my cold nose against people's legs.

What I want to get across is that I will not tell you what I am doing. I admire and love you, but I will tell you nothing of my occupation. I have been busy forgetting you and Margaret in order that I may the more vividly remember you tomorrow or next week or next month.

If you knew what I was up to, you would declare me a spider weaving a web with which to choke myself.

I have conceived of you as a big man with thick fingers who is building a fence about a field on a farm to fence in me and Mississippi and Memphis, Tenn. I like you all O.K., because you wink as you work. What do you care? Shut up, man. The fence building is as important as what I am doing. These are gaudy days. If you do not hear from me for some time, bear in mind that I am a prairie dog and am busy hiding corn in a hole in a field. Love to Margaret

41.   226 SOUTH LaSALLE STREET, CHICAGO, SEPTEMBER 15 [1919]

To TRIGANT BURROW

Dear Brother Burrow: Have you read my new book, *Winesburg?* The book has been getting rather remarkable recognition even from those who have fought me before. In another year it will no doubt get publication in France and perhaps in other European countries.

Naturally I am very anxious to continue my work as a writer, but the truth is that I am rapidly approaching the time when I shall have to give it up. It begins to look as though, having made myself this tool of expression by infinite labor, I shall have to put it aside.

The situation with me is one you will readily understand. For twenty years I have carried a double load, making my living as a writer of advertisements and trying always to steal as much time as possible for this other work. Unfortunately I have not made much money, a living only as I have gone along. Now I begin to tire. For weeks and months at a time now I find that the reserve of energy I have always had is gone. The long hours of work in an office every day begins to take the strength I need for my writing.

As you no doubt know, there is no money to be got by writing the sort of books I write. A copy of such a book is read by ten people to every one who purchases it. The result is that the author gets little.

In facing what I face now — that is to say, the possibility that I will have to give up the fight — my mind gropes about trying to see some way out. Surely I am willing to live in the very simplest way to accomplish what I want, but I do need some assured income every year. I have three children who have to be supported. In all I need from twenty-five hundred to three thousand a year to live.

Do you think there is any chance at all of my interesting some man or woman of money to back me to this extent in trying to do my work? I know nothing of such things, but do know that money is constantly being invested in schools, magazines, young singers, in a thousand things of the sort.

It seems to me that I have proven my ability as a writer. I know of no other man in the country who has got such recognition as has come to me. Yet I make no money, and it is evident that the only source of income I might expect to open to me, the magazine field, will not open. The editors of such magazines write me personal letters congratulating me on the fine work I am doing, but laugh at the idea of printing my stuff. It is all very perplexing and disconcerting.

It may be possible that the idea of striving to interest some man or woman with money is equally futile. It is a difficult matter to approach. I surely do not know how to do it. Do you think there is a possibility in that direction?

What I want you will understand. The development of my mind and my skill as a workman has brought me to the place where I naturally want to do more and more delicate and subtle work. I want time to go about among people. I want something of leisure to develop in leisure my impressions of life. Having made myself an artist by infinite labor, I want to lead the life and do the work of an artist and not have to spend my days writing stupid advertisements.

Surely I have that right. Surely I am not to[o] self-pushing in setting up the claim I do here. Is there any hope at all that someone might be found who would sympathize with my desires enough to help me achieve them?

To tell you the truth, I know of no reason why anyone should do this; that is to say, I know of no reason from their point of view. I may be after all but a man grasping at straws. What do you think about it? Very truly yours

[P.S.] I have lost your Baltimore address.

42.   [?CHICAGO, ?OCTOBER, 1919]

To TRIGANT BURROW

Dear Brother: Here is a notion that can't fail to interest you. I am proposing to write a book to be called *Industrial Vistas*.[1] It is to be the autobiography of a man's secondary self, of the queer, unnamed fancies that float through his brain, the things that appear to have no connection with actualities.

In me, and, I fancy, in most men, odd, detached fancies are born, blossom, sometimes like flowers, sometimes like evil-seeming weeds, then appear to pass.

My notion is that no man knows himself or can arrive at truth concerning himself except by what seems like indirection. I have a desire to take hold of indirection as a tool and use it in an attempt to arrive at truth.

Industrial Vistas, you see, because it is written out of the jangle and ugliness of industrial life.

By my plan and by indirection, you see, I hope to make an odd, insane-seeming man emerge into actuality.

I want your own knowledge of indirection to do this thing, but perhaps I will get it. A surprising number of hints you have given me in the past have come into fruition. They have led me along paths I hope to try to follow in this new attempt.

I'll be glad to show you later, when it is a little accomplished, what specifically I mean.

Once you said something regarding the making of an analysis of America. My own notion is that perhaps that can best be achieved by the autobiography of the fanciful life of an individual.

We'll see. It is going to be a subtle and intricate experiment.

43.   [?DECEMBER, 1919]

To WALDO FRANK

Dear Brother: I am writing to you from the train. There are a thousand things to be said. In a sense I have gone through a kind of revolution since I came to New York.

One thing I have found out. I cannot continue to live the life I have lived as a businessman. In a sense I have been like one living in a damp, dark cellar ever since I went back into business after my

[1] Not published.

few months of freedom in New York last year. To think straight at all I had to get temporarily out of it. In New York I did.

Several things happened. I saw the O'Keeffe things and the Stieglitz[1] things. I went into a gallery and saw some paintings of Renoir. I found out again the old lesson that one cannot muddy oneself and be clean.

I shall have to get out of business at once, within a month perhaps. I know nothing of how it can be done. I only know it must be done. If it cannot be done, I shall get out anyway and suffer what loss of friendship and what ugly hatred is necessary. Children like mine do not come of a breed that starves.

It was really delicious that the blow aimed at you by *New Republic*[2] should have miscarried in such a complete way. Nothing could be better evidence of the worth & power of your book. You will not, of course, answer in any way, but laugh and go straight on with your work.

I saw Cannan,[3] a fine fellow, somewhat difficult and maybe thin. I shall, I hope, see more of him at the end of this month when he will be in Chicago. Margaret seemed very well and was lovely.

You will be amused when you get the full story of Thayer[4] & the *Dial*. Poor man, he intended to be such a nice, rich man, a true English gentleman, bringing culture to America. It was vicious to step on his toes. I wired Sandburg to charge a minimum of $25 per page for poems. For my stories I shall get $200, or they will be sent free to someone else. If you send them a story and they want to print it, please stand out for that price. Will you write & ask Booth[5] to do the same?

One has to meet this sort of thing on these terms. All Thayer has is money, & if he does not surrender the money, he is N.G. to anyone. Will you also write something of the sort to Brooks? I feel like a labor leader, but if you have ever been in the presence of Thayer's interior decorator's soul, you'll understand, old Brother.

---

[1] Georgia O'Keeffe (1887–), painter, and Alfred Stieglitz (1864–1946), photographer. They were married in 1924. The famous "Little Galleries of the Photo Secession" in New York, generally known as "291," were devoted to exhibitions of advanced and modern work.

[2] See F(rancis) H(ackett), "Mr. Frank's America," *New Republic*, XXI, 122–123 (December 24, 1919).

[3] Gilbert Cannan (1884–), English novelist.

[4] Scofield Thayer, the "angel" of the *Dial* in its later phase.

[5] Fred Booth, a New York writer, friend of Frank and Anderson.

Emerson [6] has not come through for me, but please do not say anything to him until I have seen you or we have talked more in some way.

I am much better in my mind than I have been for a year.

44.   CHICAGO [?DECEMBER 17, 1919]

TO HART CRANE [1]

My dear Hart Crane: Well, I shall see and have a talk with you somewhere some of these days. Now, no doubt, the candy business [2] drives you as some other form of the same mix-up does me. I am hoping to go to New York for a few days between Christmas and New Year's. There are many things I must do there. I would plan to spend a day at Cleveland, but am afraid I shall not have time. Paul Rosenfeld is coming here from New York to see me Monday. Do you know him?

Yesterday I had a long letter from Van Wyck Brooks, who is in California. His new book, *The Ordeal of Mark Twain,* is written and is in the publisher's hands. Doran is to bring it out, I believe, in January. It should be a remarkably fine piece of work. Brooks has not Frank's flame in criticism, but he has a remarkable mind. In a way I respect it more than any other mind in America.

In a way I like the structure and mood of the *Testament* thing better then anything I have found. In it I hope to express much of the vague, intangible hunger that constantly besets me, as it must you. One doesn't hunger to defeat the materialism of the world about. One hungers to find brothers buried away beneath all this roaring modern insanity of life.

You in Akron, another man in California, a fellow like Fred Booth, shivering in some cold room in New York.

The land is indeed vast. In an odd way groups defeat growth. We must remain like seeds planted near each other in a field. No voice any of us may raise will quite carry across the spaces.

It is odd how the fact of your being in a love affair vivifies you. My

---

[6] John Emerson (1874–), actor and playwright, who married Anita Loos in 1919. He and Anderson had been boyhood friends in Clyde. See *Memoirs,* pp. 110, 113–119.

[1] Hart Crane (1899–1932), poet, author of *White Buildings* (1926) and *The Bridge* (1930). Anderson and Crane corresponded frequently during the next few years.

[2] Crane was working for his father, a manufacturer of candy in Cleveland.

mind shall play with your figure at odd moments, you hungering and being defeated and arising all the time to new days.

In the *Testament* I want to send the voices of my own mind out to the hidden voices in others, to do what can't be done perhaps.

Write me whenever the mood hits you. I am uncertain and jerky about letters, but nevertheless I do write them, and they are the nearest approach we can have to knowing each other better now.

45. [?CHICAGO, ?LATE DECEMBER, 1919]

TO VAN WYCK BROOKS

Dear Brooks: I've been thinking about your letter of the other day and my answer that didn't say what I wanted it to say. Your not writing letters doesn't bother me. I have no special feeling about it at all.

I would in some way like you to know how I feel in another respect.

I dare say your book, when it comes, will not have the passionate flaming thing in it that Waldo's book [1] often has. But, Brooks, you must realize what an inciter to flame in others you are.

I have a hunch you are doomed to be a man whose voice will not be heard by many here for a long time, but you should realize what it means to those who do hear it.

When in speaking of *Winesburg* you used the word "adolescence," you struck more nearly than you know on the whole note of me. I am immature, will live and die immature. A quite terrible confession that would be if I did not represent so much.

I am conscious I do represent much, and often I feel like a very small boy in the presence of your mind and of Waldo's too.

What is true of me is true of Sandburg, but we are different. He is submerged in adolescence. I am in it and of it, but I look out. Give Sandburg a mind, and you perhaps destroy him. I don't know whether that would be true of me or not.

Be sure of this, Brooks. No matter how much you may seem to yourself to work in isolation, it is not true. Your voice always comes clear to me and will to some others. You have been the bearer of a lamp that has illuminated many a dark place for me.

Nothing that is going to happen next year will mean as much to me as getting my hand on your new book.[2]

[1] Waldo Frank, *Our America* (1919).
[2] *The Ordeal of Mark Twain* (1920).

You, Waldo, and me — could three men be more unlike? How truly I love you two men.

[P.S.] I think of my *Testament* as a passionate attempt to get poetry into the thing you have expressed time and again and that you and Waldo have together made me a little conscious of. I want to have it be a distillation. God knows how far I shall succeed.

46.   FAIRHOPE, ALABAMA, MAY 15 [1920]

TO VAN WYCK BROOKS

Dear Brother: It was a big moment for me when I got your note and found you liked *Poor White*. When the novel was finished some weeks ago, I said to Tennessee: "There is one man's mind I would like to have on that book. It's Brooks'." I thought of sending it on and asking you to read it, but know yours is a busy life and hadn't the nerve. Then Huebsch[1] did it for me, and now I have what I want. The gods are good to me. I am also happy about two other things — that your book is at last on the way to me and that you saw what I wanted someone to see in the *Dial* story, "The Triumph of the Egg."[2] To my mind it was one of the very best things I had ever done, but when I showed it to Paul and Waldo, they did not seem much impressed. O[h], Brooks, if you but knew what your own clear, fine mind has meant to me these last two or three years. Well, there's no use trying to tell you.

It has been a wonderful time for me here these three months. In the first place, I persuaded Tennessee to be utterly reckless, chuck her job and income, and run off here with me. That has worked out. She is getting well and is happier than I have ever seen her. What a tremendous thing life is. For several years she has been a tired woman. Here she rested and then suddenly began to play. There are great quantities of red, yellow, and blue clay here, very fine and plastic. Tennessee suddenly began working in it, and already she does really remarkable things. What new joy in life that approach towards beauty coming in a definite form out of herself has given her. [I] go about whispering to myself, "She is going to be well. She is going to be

---

[1] B. W. Huebsch, characteristic publisher of the 1920's, who merged in 1925 with the Viking Press. Subsequent letters illustrate Anderson's relations with him.

[2] *Dial*, LXVIII, 295–304 (March, 1920). Reprinted as "The Egg" in *The Triumph of the Egg*.

well." O[h], for a world of people not tired. What things would come out of them.

Waldo has been for a long time silent. Knowing nothing, I still feel I do know there is something the matter. I am sure it is about the novel, *The Dark Mother.*[3] It is not getting across with people who have read it and away down underneath has not got across with him, but he is fighting that thought, insisting. Is my hunch at all correct? If it is, I am unspeakably sorry. I love Waldo very deeply, and the deep-seated desire in him to be a great man hurts me at times like an open wound.

We will be leaving here in about a week, and after that address me at c/o Critchfield & Company, 10th Floor, Brooks Bldg., Chicago. I hope to be in New York for a short stay early in June and trust I shall see you then. There are many things I want to talk to you about. Have begun a rollicking, Rabelaisian book called *Many Marriages,*[4] a thing I have long hungered to do. It will take marvelous good health and spirits to carry the thing off, but I may never be in better shape to begin it.

Also I am painting and doing my own kind of poetry. The two things are much alike in me — mystic, vague impulses. There is a painter here who looks at my things, shakes his head, and goes home and takes Epsom salts. It is perhaps the best way to take the two sides of me.

Tennessee sends love to you. Please bear our love to Mrs. Brooks. Is there any chance I may sell serial rights for *Poor White* to *Freeman* or *Dial?* It would give me some more freedom if I could achieve some money in this way. With love

47. FAIRHOPE, ALABAMA [?MAY 21, 1920]

To WALDO FRANK

Dear Brother: How good it was to get your letter. Everything you say I have had a sense of, but it was good again to hear your voice. It has been, I know, a hard six months for you; across the mountains and streams that have separated us I have felt that keenly. Now and then there came a doubt. Had I said something that rang unpleasantly in your ears? Had some action of mine cut the cord that binds us? Such thoughts did not linger.

[3] Frank's novel was published in this year.
[4] Published in February, 1923.

For me it has been a golden time — long days of work, of walking under towering trees, in golden canyons, muttering to myself, adventuring on new roads of thoughts, finding a new and strange world in color and form that calls to me and that may eventually make me a painter, the problems I have faced so long for the time far off. Here I have lived as the gods live. In these times I have at times cut all costs down to $5 or $6 per week. I have swum naked in deep, dark pools, seen the great, white beaches of the Gulf of Mexico, got young and strong, talked with gods, been on the blood-red roads of this country when tropical storms came up from the south and trees leaped out of the ground. What golden days. May the gods who have guided me sleep at night in azure beds.

What can I say about your news that is not news? There is only this, gained from my own suffering at such a time. It is given only to the few to know how to open doors and close them again. Can you believe that no word can explain, that when the hour strikes, one must be terribly brief, one must not talk to friends or to the one that has been and still is dear? One must go as a wind goes off through the forest. It is the only way. That can be my only word to you. It is to me the essence of what I have learned, the good medicine of the Indian.

I am sorry if the novel [1] bothers you, but will not preach my preachment about that. There is only this — you do not have to finish the novel for them at any time. No man can command you. You have already given immeasurably more than you have received from the men and women of your time.

For myself it pleases my fancy to think of giving up all serious thought of writing and in the future only do it for fun to please myself. There is to me a deep impulse to paint. By disregarding all roads taken by other painters I have seen, I have already found out some things. We will talk at length of that when I see you.

I leave here in three days and go to New Orleans. After two or three days there I go to Kentucky. Then to [New York] [2] and Chicago for perhaps two weeks. If my money hold[s] out, I will come to New York and should get there about the middle of June. I want to see you, Paul, Brooks, and others.

It will be impossible for me to go off this summer. The strings

---

[1] *The Dark Mother* was published by Frank in the fall of 1920.
[2] Text reads: Kentucky.

of that other life of mine have been cut for a long time. Now they must for a time be patched up again.

Tennessee mentions that she wrote you and ask[ed] for some information about the professional analysts of the East. She wanted the information for a Chicago friend of hers. Will you send it? Address her c/o me, at Critchfield & Co., 10th Floor, Brooks Bldg., Chicago. She is almost well and declares I have given her the golden days of her life these last two months. Her own plans for the summer are uncertain, but for June she will go to Ephraim with Mrs. Walker,[3] the Judge, Mrs. Walker's husband, having just died and been buried.

As you see, the days ahead hang uncertain in the air. I can know little until I get to Chicago and mend the broken strings of my economic life. My novel[4] has gone to Huebsch, and he has given it to Brooks to read. I have a glowing letter from him.

Whatever you do for the summer we must plan to spend some time together in the summer or early fall. Perhaps we could walk together down through some harvest land in September or October. Will I not see you in June? With all my love to you

48. ON TRAIN BOUND NORTH, CHICAGO TO EPHRAIM, WISCONSIN [?EARLY JULY, 1920]

TO JEROME AND LUCILE BLUM [1]

Dear Jerry and Lucile: Got your good letter from the jumping-off place. It was hell to be in New York and you two gone. The town was empty. "To hell with it," I said and got out. Went up into Connecticut for a few days and then hit west for Chicago. Now I am going north to Tennessee.

You and Lucile were the two people we most wanted down there in Alabama. After I got down there alone in January, I went color mad, a thing that had never happened to me before. Went North to get Tennessee and colors. There was a Chase[2] pupil down there in town, had a class. Went once and stayed 15 minutes. Then I knew that was no go and got up and lit out. Later I tried sitting before things and painting, but that wasn't the thing. Then I just went into

[3] Mrs. Harriet W. Walker, whose husband, Judge Charles Morehead Walker, died on May 13, 1920.
[4] *Poor White.*

[1] Jerome Blum (1884–), Chicago-born painter, and his wife.
[2] Possibly William Merritt Chase (1849–1916), painter and teacher of painters.

a room that had a window facing the sea and painted as a nigger would sing. It was a tremendous experience, quite sharply different from writing, although in the end that is where my painting may count most, to give more color and a sweeter roll to the old boat I call my prose.

Anyway, that's when my mind turned to you two (damn this jerky train). I kept sensing new things, was like a kid in a strange, wonderful country. Couldn't talk to the Chase man, although on fishing or just fooling around he was a prince.

Well, I got about a dozen things done I wanted you two to see. I'm glad you're off there[3] for your sake and damn sorry for my own.

My own program is laid out. I'm going back to Alabama this winter and paint and write. If necessary, I'll be an unfaithful husband to Tennessee and run off into the woods with a black wench. I'm going after the American nigger. He's got something absolutely lovely that's never been touched.

In New York I got my new novel into the printer's hands. I'm deep in a new one I call *Many Marriages*. There is an idea of a new novel form floating about in me, something looser, more real, more true. I want to go after that.

Saw Margaret and Jane[4] in New York, W. Frank, Paul Rosenfeld, Griffin Barry,[5] L. Cary,[6] Karl Anderson, Brooks and several others. Barry had just come from Russia. He thinks the new government there is going to be more intensely industrial than any other, everybody at it. I've a notion [we're] all going to wake up someday [to] find revolution accomplished and the artist in a worse hole than ever. God help us when we must submit our work to committees of workingmen, eh?

The new novel, out in October, will, I hope, build up the country about Winesburg, sweep Winesburg into the modern industrial life, show what made it an Akron, Ohio.

Well, *Many Marriages* will have no purpose on God's sweet, green earth.

[3] The Blums had sailed to spend a year in Tahiti.

[4] Margaret C. Anderson and Jane Heap. From 1922 to 1929 Miss Heap helped edit the *Little Review*.

[5] An American newspaperman, at this time a foreign correspondent for the London *Daily Herald*.

[6] Lucian Cary (1886–), journalist and writer.

You will be glad to know that the *Mercure de France* is out with an article [7] saying *Winesburg* is the most important book published in any country since the Armistice.

Tennessee is sweeping the cobwebs out of a little house a[t] Green Bay. I'll be with her tonight and hope to stay right there with her for the next two months. Then next winter, by some hook or crook, by stealing, begging or murder, I'm going to get money enough to take me back to Alabam' and my niggers.

Love to you and to Lucile from both of us. When a mood comes, sit down and write us from that far place.

[P.S.] Until Sep[tember] 1, Ephraim, Wis. Later c/o Critchfield & Company, Brooks Bldg., Chicago.

49. [EPHRAIM, WISCONSIN, BEFORE AUGUST 22, 1920]

To VAN WYCK BROOKS

Dear Brooks: There are two reasons why *Freeman* can't use such things as "The Man in the Brown Coat." [1] First, because it isn't any good. That reason don't go. It is. Second, because *Freeman* is a political magazine. *New Republic, Nation, Freeman.* None of them give a damn for literature really. They seem to feel that creative writing has nothing to do with revolution. They want to put a new sort of government in at Washington. Well, the *Freeman* permits you. [2] That's a long step.

There remains *Little Review* and *Dial* as voices for what artistic urge there may be in the country. The gods protect and nourish us. Scattered, immature, undignified, pretentious, asinine things. I don't look at *Little Review* at all. I throw such things as "[The] Man in the Brown Coat" into it.

Have just looked at the last *Dial*. It's spoiled eggs. ***** — a lot of other half-bake[d] stuff — no editing — no purpose — hell!

I don't know why I should swear to you about all this; most of the time I don't think about it but go on working. It did hurt, though, when I found you also rather taking *Winesburg*, for example, as a sex book. It got under my hide a bit. I'm usually thick-skinned.

---

[7] See Vincent O'Sullivan, "Précisions sur la littérature américaine," *Mercure de France*, CXXXVI, 535–540 (December 1, 1919).

[1] This prose poem was published in the *Little Review*, VII, 18–21 (January–March, 1921).

[2] Brooks was contributing a weekly literary column to the *Freeman*.

To me it seems a little as though one were permitted to talk abstractly of things, to use scientific terms regarding them, in the new dispensation, but when one attempts to dip down into the living stuff, the same old formula holds. A really beautiful story like "Hands," for example, is — well, nasty. God help us! Dozens of men have told me privately they knew Wing Biddlebaum. I tried to present him sympathetically — taboo.

I get so much force and reality in your *Ordeal*. I read it over and over like a Bible or Shakespeare's sonnets. Twain is dead; he paid the price of caving in, but —

I wonder if I make you feel what I'm talking about. In the first place, I wish you could know how much I have loved, do love, your mind. I've frankly banked on it more than the mind of any other American. Am I right in my secret belief that you, down at bottom, believe me, in my reactions to life — well, not nice? Can I — have I the privilege of cornering your mind so?

I've settled down to a quiet new novel, a tale of country life in Ohio.[3] It has marched steadily along, a living tale, I believe, full of winds and barnyards and people. I paint too quite a lot. Your *Ordeal* has struck deep. It sets people talking and wondering.

[P.S.] Does Twain's formula — "Freedom and the other precious things" — still hold?

What a God-damn letter. Well, it's off my chest. It's glorious to have a few more months out of doors steadily at work.

50.   [EPHRAIM, WISCONSIN, BEFORE AUGUST 22, 1920]

TO WALDO FRANK

Dear Brother: Have been ill for several days, one of those absurd illnesses that come after too prolonged and too intensive work. For a time life does not go on. One is a tree, or he is not even that. At such times all those you love might die, a fire burn your house, a horse kick you on the balls — it would make no difference. You blink like an old owl. All your senses are passive. You wait, wait, wait for the machinery of your imagination to set itself going again.

You may remember — more than likely you do not — a tale I began

---

[3] This novel, tentatively entitled *Ohio Pagans,* was not completed. See the following letter.

a year or two ago, about a boy, grandson of a Welsh poet, named Twm o'r Nant.[1] The boy's name was Tom Edwards.

I took that yarn up again, and it is expanding into a novel of country people and their efforts to find God, a tale of barnyards and fields and the back yards of village house[s], ice cutters on a bay, etc. It is absorption in it has floored me temporarily. I'll recover in a day or two.

There is an odd and interesting cycle. One is so utterly absorbed outside himself and then sweeps about like a boat coming into the wind. For a time he is himself the very center of life.

Such time[s] are the beginnings of illnesses.

In me lately these ill times are centered around resentment that so many people insist on seeing me as one absorbed only in sex. I grow furious at what I feel, for the time, is the stupidity of people.

I read Brooks' book[2] and was filled with admiration. Then I grew angry. I became brother (in imagination) to Twain, saw just how impossible it was for Brooks to really see the man.

That made me angry, and I wrote an angry letter to Brooks. I accused him of escaping out of Puritanism by the trick of the psychologist, of having no real sympathy for any living effort to lift the veil from morality. What I suppose I said was, "How easy to slaughter the artist Twain now he is safely dead."

You see how nasty that was. It grew out of resentment of something he said, the inference being that many of my stories, such stories as "Hands," were indecent. I had heard he said something of the sort. It made me furious. And then I wrote the letter and was utterly ashamed of having done so. "Why cannot I be more manly?" I ask myself day and night.

You see I am in no mood to understand why any man should love me. I love you, yes, and Brooks and the other men who are doing good work and who are alive, but I ask myself, "When will I, in a weak moment, write some other man such a letter as I wrote Brooks?"

I have a keen feeling of the distraction & uncertainty of your summer. Am I right?

For a few days I'll fish and walk and try to get the swing back into

---

[1] See the opening paragraphs of the story "An Ohio Pagan" in *Horses and Men.* This story and "'Unused'" in the same volume are the published portions of the novel described in the following paragraph.

[2] *The Ordeal of Mark Twain.*

my writing hand. The cloud of weariness and distraction will pass. There are so many books I need to write, pictures I need to paint. I shall keep at painting. It is a doorway out of much that is disordered in myself.

Believe me, I do love you and your spirit. That is why I try to tell you what a shattered, disordered thing your letter finds me.

51.   [EPHRAIM, WISCONSIN, AUGUST 22, 1920]

TO VAN WYCK BROOKS

Dear Van Wyck: A clear, beautiful Sunday morning. What a stir I made within myself by writing you that letter. It was written at a time when the engine that is myself was running wildly, grinding no grain.

Someone had told me that your attitude toward my work was that i[t] was not sound, wholesome. In myself, in my right mind, I should have paid no attention. It happened I was spiritually very tired.

There came, and still come, odd, hurtful reaction[s] from some things I write. A woman I have once know[n], strange men and women I have never seen write me queer, abusive letters. "Why do you wallow in ugly lies about life?" they ask. I have got a dozen such letters in a week.

I put them aside, the thought of them aside. There were certain minds. I did not expect of them [that] they approve what I do. I did expect they would feel sure I was going on at my work honestly, with an intent of spiritual integrity.

You must know, must have felt how much I counted on your mind there.

The slipshod gossip that you had another attitude, joined [to] these others in the wallowing theory, would, had I not been spiritually weary, have made no impression on my mind. I did harbor it a little and am ashamed. After I had written you the letter, I awoke at night sick with shame. I couldn't work because of it.

I won't say I won't do the same again. When I'm tired I'm no good, a yellow dog sometimes.

As for your not knowing sometimes what I'm driving at, I don't always myself. God knows, too many of my things don't fully register.

Perhaps I don't care enough. I feel myself often an instrument to adventure in flights along strange paths. Why should you ever, under any circumstances, feel any obligation to say anything about my work — to approve of it, I mean?

A nasty, tired building up of substantiating proofs that the gossip I had heard was true must have gone on within me.

O brother Brooks, please forget my silly letter.

There are lots of sweeter, finer things I can quarrel with you about at the Pittsburgh meeting. I could quarrel with you indefinitely as to the value of the whole lot of political-minded magazines.

I am writing a new book I'm sure you are going to love. It really does, I feel, get hold of a man and woman in American life intimately, intensely. Am I not a lucky dog to have this time to work undisturbed? If my damned books would only sell a little better. Is the *Ordeal* going to sell? I want that book to sell for other reason[s] than your own interest. I wish to God I could make all Americans read it.

52.   [?CHICAGO, ?NOVEMBER, 1920]

To HART CRANE

Dear Crane: I have your fine letter about *Poor White,* and naturally I am pleased to hear from you that it hit you. When a man publishes a book, there are so many stupid things said that he declares he'll never do it again. The praise is almost always worse than the criticism, but you know how to take a story naturally and simply and how to react naturally and simply. It does one good.

Do keep pressed up against the wall and don't sink into resignation. I imagine revolution doesn't accomplish much, but constant irritation with ugliness is necessary. I may go East in January.

53.   PALOS PARK, ILLINOIS, NOVEMBER 12 [1920]

To JEROME AND LUCILE BLUM

Dear Jerry and Lucile: I got your letter yesterday, and it was a delight to me. I could see Jerry trotting along the street in his loincloth, although, as I've never been to the South Seas, I transferred the scene to a rainy day in a Middle Western town in America. At that, the transference didn't make the picture the less delightful.

Well, our little house in the country is all fixed up, and it is charming. It is only a box, about the size of your downstairs at Mt. Kisco.[1] I practically stay out here, and Tennessee comes for about 3 days a

---
[1] In Westchester County, New York.

week. From my windows I look out on oak forests, and they are charming now. Yesterday was our first wintry day, with flurries of snow and a raw, cold north wind.

I wrote my publisher to send you *Winesburg* some weeks ago, and I suppose it is on the way. Also I have ordered sent you the new novel, *Poor White,* and that will be on the way.

I've got my water colors hung [2] in Chicago now, and there is a good deal of discussion as to whether I am insane, decadent, or a new note. You know what bosh would be talked. Well, I stay away from the place. Looks as though I would be right here for the winter, as my only source of income, a little business graft I still hold on to, is cut to almost nothing; but I've got coal and wood and a good-sized Sears, Roebuck order on my pantry shelves, so I'm not worried.

Seems the country is gone to the bow-wows businessly speaking. It's just the reaction from the riot of high prices and profiteering, I suppose. Don't know nor care much.

Mencken was out with rather fulsome praise of *Poor White,*[3] and Huebsch says he's going to push it; so maybe when you blow this way, I'll have money enough to go to Alabama with you. If I haven't, I'll steal it.

Who do you reckon is going to motor out from Chicago to see me this afternoon — Theda Bara,[4] the vampire queen. Seems she admires my stuff and sent word she wanted to come. All I need now is a visit from Charlie Chaplin.

Tennessee is pretty well, but the trouble with her now is this. Down in Alabama she got some beautiful clay in her hands and turned out some remarkable character heads. The result is she doesn't want to be an honest working woman any more, but has the same disease that has caught the rest of us. She wants to sit under a fig tree by a green sea and have beautiful blacks bring her clay to be modeled. Ask Lucile. I suppose a woman artist would want black male slaves. Anyway, the poor woman went and married me and is stuck to make her own living, and it's hell. She really has something smashing, I believe, in the clay thing.

Aren't we all a lot of damn fools? There you are, and someday you'll

[2] A one-man show of some twenty of Anderson's abstract paintings was held at the Radical Bookshop.

[3] In *Smart Set* for December, 1920.

[4] Theda Bara (1890–), famous "vamp" of the silent movies, starred in "Salome," "A Fool There Was," and other pictures. See *Memoirs,* pp. 313–314.

get the itch to come out. You'll get to imagining yourself listening to beautiful talk, dining with beautiful people, finding love and comradeship among your own kind.

Then you'll come back here and find the same moneygrubbing asses, the same sentimental fools you left. Why don't we all who want to do things live in the South Seas or in China or on a river in the interior of Alabama among the blacks?

We get, I fancy, a notion we want to see our things register, which they won't much if they are really beautiful. The Lord made us fools. How shall we escape, O Lord?

I'm gathering myself together for a new book, but can't say yet whether it will be a book of short tales or a long novel. The novel is half completed, the tales half told. The tales will no doubt win.

Wish I could come in the evening sometime and read to you from my *New Testament.*[5] It's the best thing I've ever done, but it is done for quiet, meditative people living among beautiful savages.

What I want to know, Jerry, is this: how does Lucile stack up in a loincloth? With love to you both

54. [?CHICAGO, BEFORE NOVEMBER 29, 1920]

To PAUL ROSENFELD

Dear Paul: I feel more a human being this morning and want to try to add a word about the Waldo article.[1] Do you really feel it essential to write it at all? After reading this article, I have quite sharply the feeling that you are a little too close to the man and his problem to write of it.

After all, we must realize that the outside world, readers of the *Dial,* etc., have no special interest in the family in 79th Street.[2] From all I can gather, Waldo's book[3] has made little or no impression, at least out here. I hear no one speak of it.

You see, I have just published a book myself, and that always means for me a period of mental illness. One is building a house which he does build with love. On a certain day he opens the door and going into the street invites the people to enter. In spite of himself he does,

---

[5] *A New Testament* was published in book form in 1927, but articles and poems under this title appeared in various magazines beginning in 1919.

[1] Rosenfeld had sent his article, "The Novels of Waldo Frank," to Anderson prior to its publication in the January, 1921, issue of the *Dial.*

[2] Frank's residence at that time.

[3] *The Dark Mother.*

in some vague, foolish way, expect all the people to come joyously, to understand against what difficulties he has struggled.

They don't a[t] all. Most of them are engaged in house-building enterprises of their own. One finds that in spite of native good sense he has been dreaming of some impossible brotherhood of understanding.

I know, Paul, that much of your article was fine, but in spite of myself I felt a little too much elaboration of the man's weakness. There was revenge in it. I am sure the article defeats its own ends.

Tell me if you think so after rereading it. Also tell me if you do not believe, in spite of all the assertions he may make, that Waldo is really realizing his own failure in the book. I can't say less and defend in my own mind the sense of brotherhood I feel toward both you and Waldo.

55.   [CHICAGO] DECEMBER 14, 1920

MR. PAUL U. KELLOGG, c/o THE *Survey*, NEW YORK

Dear Mr. Kellogg: I am afraid I can have nothing very intelligent to say on the subject on which you want me to write,[1] but I'll say what I feel, and then you can use it if it has any value. If you do not find it usable, I'll not be offended.

Here goes.

When I look within myself and ask myself what I most want to see come to life in America, I have to answer, "A leisure class." That, I take it, is pretty un-American, and I am afraid the Americanization Committee of my home town will get after me for saying it.

You see, people, not things, interest the novelist, and I am afraid it has come to the place with me that I care nothing at all about who owns the factories, what wages men get, where their children go to school.

I am not oblivious to the fact that these things are important and that many very vital things have to be done before men in general may have more leisure. However, and although I am filled with admiration for what is being accomplished for struggling men and women and for underfed children, I am not satisfied. I want my leisure class, and I want it now. I want men and women who, at any physical cost to themselves and others, will refuse to continue to work as we understand the word work.

---

[1] In a letter dated December 9, 1920, Paul U. Kellogg, one of the editors of the *Survey*, requested Anderson to contribute to a proposed symposium on what must be done to make this a livable world.

You will understand what I am driving at. When all the world is crying out for more production at less cost and when the workers are striving for a greater share in industrial management, I want some of the best blood of the country to quit work (in the old sense) entirely.

What I suppose I am asking for is a surplus of energy that doesn't have to farm farms, tend machines in factories, or buy or sell anything. I want these men and women to stop me on the road or in the city streets and talk with me without feeling that I am keeping them from their tasks in some factory or office. I want to hear less about the future splendid physical growth of towns, factories, or farms and more about trees, dogs, race horses, and people.

It is my notion that if we can in America by some method, fair or foul, create a leisure class, something surprising may come out of it. Such men and women are bound to begin looking about and asking questions. They will wonder why every other person met on the streets is tired or nervous. When they have had time to look about a little and have bottled up within themselves some surplus energy that need not be expended in making anything at all to feed, clothe, or house other people, most anything in the world may happen. It is even conceivable that under the influence of such people and with some such surplus energy loose among us, we may begin to do some of the things that now seem entirely out of our reach. We may begin to make towns, houses, books, pictures, gardens, even cities that have beauty and meaning.

And so you see I want a body of healthy young men and women to agree to quit working, to loaf, to refuse to be hurried or try to get on in the world — in short, to become intense individualists. Something of the kind must happen if we are ever to bring color and a flair into our modern life. Naturally I believe that the growth of such a class would do more than anything else to make this a better world to live in.

56.   [CHICAGO, DECEMBER 24, 1920] DAY BEFORE CHRISTMAS

TO JEROME AND LUCILE BLUM

Dear Jerry and Lucile: What a contrast to your place. Yesterday it rained, but in the night, last night, it turned cold and a heavy snow fell. The country is lovely. All day I have been writing, and now I'm on the train going to town. That's the reason for the pad. Shall have Christmas with the kids.

Jerry['s] gift, in the way it was given and all, was about the finest and sweetest thing I've ever had happen to me. I'll take it, old brother, and, when the work I have in hand is done, will go on a bat with it.

Have been depressed. Always am after I publish a new book. (By the way, the publisher started a copy on the road to you.) There is something about my writing that arouses the animosity of a certain kind of people. Why they read them I don't know. They do and then write me unbelievable vile letters. They come into my place and crap on the floor. I am called abominable names. It passes after a month or two. There must be something that gets under people's hides, makes them sore. Perhaps it is my treatment of the sex thing.

About the matter of the American Negro. There is something big there that hasn't been touched, perhaps hasn't been seen much. It wants some staying with and should be tackled by people who are not out after immediate recognition by the public of what they are after.

My notion is that the American Negro is a thing apart from the Negro in Africa or anywhere else. It is a subject race, and yet a strange thing has happened. One isn't long in the Southern states without realizing that the land, the rivers, even the cities belong to the blacks and that all the whites are outsiders there. Perhaps that's what makes the Southern white so unnecessarily vain and casually brutal. It is the brutality of the small man who by a trick has got the better of the bigger thing.

You see, I've a notion that the black is really powerful — "The Terrible Meek."

It is next to impossible to live in Alabama in the summer. My notion would be that you come back here and spend, say, May in Palos Park. It will be beautiful here then. If you haven't any summer plans, perhaps we could all go up north somewhere. You would want, maybe, to be in New York in the fall, and that's the time of year I really skirmish around and try to pry a little money out of a reluctant commercial world. Then off to Alabama in late Jan. or early Feb.

During the first whirl at it down there we might not get any nearer the thing than to sense it.

I want to write, not about the American Negro, but out of him, the way Jerry painted that thing of Masefield.[1]

---

[1] Blum's painting "John Masefield" was exhibited at his one-man show in New York in 1929.

It was that thing set me off on the notion that Jerry would see and get at what I sense in the American Negro. My feeling has survived the first hot flush. It stays. To my mind there is a thing to be done as big as any of the great masters ever tackled.

The Negro race in America is something. The reformers are trying to make them race conscious, fight for their rights and all that. It's silly.

On the other hand, the Southern Negro is truly naïve. A Negro woman o[f] real beauty with colors in her skin that would drive you mad believes some asinine white middle-class woman more beautiful because she is white.

What a thing to make that woman realize in paint, in poetry, that her beauty is a living thing. Well, we'll have a chance to talk of it. It isn't a job that can be rushed at. Maybe it's a life job for all of us if we want to really tackle it. I guess the only way we'd know would be by going down there.

Love to you both. Tennessee sends love too. Hope *Poor White* will be coming along and that you'll both get something out of it. I'm doing some honest to God tales just now, best I've ever done.

57. [?CHICAGO, LATE DECEMBER, 1920]

To PAUL ROSENFELD

Dear Paul: I'm wondering about Lawrence. Have not read far into *Women in Love*,[1] but it seems to me I feel that so sophisticated a manner is in some way indicative of spiritual weariness. Have you felt that in his later things?

It is a terrific struggle he has gone through. What courage and fortitude he has shown.

When one has become sufficiently weary, the next thing is to invent a manner, a point of view. One is not relaxed, does not receive freely impressions of life.

I do not mean this has actually happened to Lawrence. I wonder if he has not been touched by it.

Waldo's book was very tired. He did try something wearily.

It will be very hard for the men of this generation to escape weariness. Living in the Middle West, feeling compelled to produce creative work, wanting to be great men, being editor of a column in a semi-

[1] D. H. Lawrence's novel was published "for subscribers only" in 1920 in New York, and for general sale by T. Seltzer in 1922.

political weekly, living in New York, the complications of sex — we are all trying a little to penetrate one's self.

Weariness has a thousand hands that can be laid upon one's shoulder. Sometimes you express it. I know I often do.

Someday, with me, it will take the form of having to escape out of these Middle-Western towns for good. In the back of my mind I am always vaguely planning on that.

In some way one must remain alive, working toward life, not death.

I am going to work now. Am glad I am going to see you this winter.

58.   [PALOS PARK, ILLINOIS] MARCH 4 [1921]

To HART CRANE

Dear Hart Crane: I was in Cleveland for a few hours one evening last week and tried to find you in the telephone book but without success. The last address I had was Washington; so I supposed you must be there. I went in to see Richard Laukhuff [1] and had a visit with him. Then I went to see a newspaper man I used to know. Later Laukhuff and O'Neil, the Playhouse man,[2] came to the train to see me off. What a damn shame I didn't see you. The trip was unexpected, and I rushed off.

I did not make the trip East, because a friend asked me to go to Paris and London in May, and I decided to do it. With that in view I had to save every possible cent; so I have stayed here in my house in the wood.

There seems to be a good deal of talk of *Poor White,* but it doesn't really sell much. I suppose *Main Street,*[3] for example, has sold more in one week than *Poor White* altogether.

I'm glad you've found Dostoevski. Had I know[n] you had not read him, I should have been shouting at you long ago.

It is delightful that you should also have picked the two books I care for most, *Karamazov* and *Possessed.*[4] There is nothing like *Karamazov* anywhere else in literature — a bible. You will like *The Idiot* and the prison tales [5] too. However, one doesn't like this man, one

---

[1] Richard Laukhuff was the proprietor of a Cleveland bookshop.
[2] Raymond O'Neil was at this time associated with the Cleveland Playhouse.
[3] Sinclair Lewis's novel had been published in 1920.
[4] *The Brothers Karamazov* and *The Possessed.*
[5] *Letters from a Dead House.*

loves him. I have always felt him as the one writer I could go down on my knees to.

Your poem[6] seems to me something fine not realized quite in you yet. I predict it will come through again and come through more completely and better realized.

The last line[s] of the second and third verse[s] do not seem to me a part of the same impulse as the others — something intellectualized. Am I right?

I'm so damned sorry I missed you.

59.   CHICAGO [MARCH 10, 1921]

To PAUL ROSENFELD

Dear Paul: I will be sending you along the passport with my income tax receipt and all the other signatures, pictures, scrolls, etc., needed to get out of the country, by registered mail today or tomorrow.[1]

The new book I have decided to call *The Triumph of the Egg*. It will contain about eight or ten short stories, the long story "Out of Nowhere into Nothing," and another long story[2] I haven't yet given a title to.

I think you are mistaken about the title to the story "Out of Nowhere, etc.", but about the other points you make against it I don't know. I shall read it over again and think about it when I am in better shape.

It has in many ways been a rotten winter for me, but at last I seem on the trail of what has been the matter with me. I have had no real pep for months, and every day's work tired me out so I have gone about most of the winter as glum as hell. Now the doctors tell me my system has been filled with poison for all these months because of infected antrums. They seem right, as the few treatments I have taken are making me feel more a man.

I wonder about your strictures regarding form. Is it inevitable that the matter of form become uppermost in the critic's mind? Must he always have that ground to stand on? Your article on Cyril Scott[3]

---

[6] "Black Tambourine," collected in *White Buildings*. See Letter 60.

[1] On January 20, 1921, Paul Rosenfeld telegraphed Anderson asking him to go to Europe with Rosenfeld on May 17, all expenses paid.

[2] "Out of Nowhere into Nothing" appeared in the *Dial* in August and September, 1921. The other "long story" may be "Unlighted Lamps," printed in *Smart Set*, July, 1921.

[3] Paul Rosenfeld, "Cyril Scott: A Portrait of the English Modernist Composer," *Vanity Fair*, XVI, 46, 88 (March, 1921).

set me thinking. To be sure, I had no quarrel with much you said about him, but it did seem to me I objected a little to the ground on which you stood when you fired some of your shots at him.

Hackett [4] always attacks me by saying my sense of form is atrocious, and it may be true. However, he also commends me for getting a certain large, loose sense of life. I often wonder, if I wrapped my packages up more neatly, if the same large, loose sense of life could be attained.

This has been an amusing year. Neither *Poor White* [n]or *Winesburg* were selling much until W. L. George [5] and later Sinclair Lewis began talking about me. Now they do sell, not hugely, but surprisingly well for me. In other words, I find people taking these two fellows' word on me as an artist. The gods must be amused. Lists of names float through the papers. I am at various times grouped with Fitzgerald of *This Side [of] Paradise*,[6] Webster,[7] William Allen White,[8] Dell,[9] Lewis, E. P. Roe [10] and others.

In the matter of form, Paul, I have much to say to you that we shall have an opportunity to say this summer. One thing I would like you to know is this: as far as I am concerned, I can accept no standard I have ever seen as to form. What I most want is to be and remain always an experimenter, an adventurer. If America could have the foolish thing sometimes spoken of as "Artistic Maturity" through me, then America could go to the devil.

I am not so foolish as to think of this statement as in any way a challenge to you and your point of view; it is rather an assurance to you that the praise I may have had this year does for the most part seem utterly foolish to me.

I am sorry about Waldo and his attitude. While I am not sure I can in any way change that attitude, I do want to talk of the whole matter with hi[m] and am looking forward to the opportunity to do so.

[4] Francis Hackett.

[5] W. L. George (1882–1926), novelist, whose *A Bed of Roses* (1911) was an "emancipated" treatment of prostitution.

[6] Published 1920.

[7] Henry Kitchell Webster (1875–1932), who published *Real Life* in 1921.

[8] William Allen White (1868–1944), novelist, editor of the *Emporia Gazette* after 1895.

[9] Floyd Dell published *The Briary Bush* in 1921.

[10] Edward Payson Roe (1838–1888), author of *Barriers Burned Away* (1872), *Opening a Chestnut Burr* (1874), and other sentimental novels.

What I fancy will happen is this: that he may in the end come to see the justice of all you said about his work, but will never quite forgive you for having said it.

The prospect of this summer with the three of us together stirs me deeply every time I think of it. Tennessee is a much stronger person physically than she has been since I have known her and will be a great companion. I am glad you are going to know from longer association a certain thing about her that makes her often almost too decent to be a woman at all.

I have said little. I have much to say. Anyway please do not feel guilty if you let fifty of my letters go unanswered. With love

[P.S.] Will you please send me soon Waldo's address?

It is very characteristic of our Chicago life that I should not know Alfeo Faggi.[11] That is the way things are done out here.

I scurried around to the News [12] to find out about Sandburg's illness, but found he had gone to California on a lecture tour. As a matter of fact, he is at this moment playing with moving picture beauties out there. I think he is making some money lecturing and has somewhat changed his point of view regarding the capitalistic system.

60.   CHICAGO, APRIL 2 [1921]

To HART CRANE

Dear Hart Crane: It seems to me that your poem [1] has now real charm and meaning.

Still, I wonder if the American Negro is quite lost in mid-air between Africa and our stupid selves. Sometimes I think he alone is not lost. I don't know.

Doesn't one have to be careful here? A figurative impulse comes that has beauty as a figure. Perhaps that is enough, but I have never found it to be enough for me. I've seen a good deal of American black men this last year, and I'm going to see more, to paint them perhaps, to learn something from them in any event.

Still I don't quarrel with your conception. It may be the true one, and you've got beauty into the singing of it. Remember only that the

[11] A Chicago sculptor about whose work Rosenfeld had written Anderson enthusiastically.

[12] The Chicago Daily News, on which Carl Sandburg was then serving as an editorial writer and moving picture reviewer.

[1] "Black Tambourine."

black man above all men knows song physical. The tambourine cuts small figure with him.

Wish I might see Sommer [2] and you, but I'll hardly get to C[leveland] before I leave.

The gods be with you.

61.   PALOS PARK, ILLINOIS, OCTOBER 12, 1921

TO TRIGANT BURROW

Dear Trigant: Far from its being the unusual undertaking, as you seem to think, I should say your book [1] would be a very good publisher's risk. I shall write to Huebsch about it at once.

Let me say a few things to you about him. He really at bottom, I suspect, doesn't know what a good book is or how to sell books, but he is a fine fellow; and at any rate you wouldn't have to, with him, go through the wearisome business of having some smart publisher tell you what to do to make your book sell. There is somewhere hidden away in Benny a real altruistic streak. In practice it takes itself out in radicalism. As you know, he is also publisher of the *Freeman*.[2] Besides which he is a single-taxer, a Socialist, and I'm not sure what else.

As you know, my own books do not sell much, but I suppose a smart publisher could sell twice as many; at least several have come to me with the proposition that they would undertake to do something like that if I would only come to them. I've stuck to Ben because my years as a businessman cured me so effectually of any desire to make money that there is almost a satisfaction in some of Ben's inefficiencies as a publisher. You will know what I mean by that.

As to the reading of the book, I should like to have it read by such men as Van Wyck Brooks and Paul Rosenfeld. They are both men whose opinion Ben would look upon as more valuable than that of professional Freudians, and they would, I am sure, both be entirely in sympathy with your point of view. I shall wait until I hear from you again before doing anything, but if it is agreeable, I will then

2 William Sommer (1867–1949), painter living in Cleveland, friend of Crane.

1 Apparently *The Social Basis of Consciousness,* eventually published in 1927 by Harcourt, Brace.

2 A political and cultural weekly, published in New York from 1920 to 1924 by B. W. Huebsch.

write Ben and at the same time suggest the names of these men as the right readers and also write them.

It is a peculiar thing that the coming of a man to your present point of view really does something to make the air of America taste better. Already, I believe, there is living in the country a real brotherhood of such men, but sometimes I'm so afraid it isn't true that I hardly dare mention the matter. The commercial aspect of thing[s] is really more deeply seated in all of us than we quite dare allow ourselves to realize. I constantly myself have men come to me, men who I think love me too, and say: "Now, Anderson, you could write a novel or a play that would make money. Why don't you do it and thus make money enough to be a free man? Afterward you could of course do your real work."

One is, you see, to make a mess on the very floor of the temple wherein he worships.

I remember last year to have written you a horrid letter because you were at that time interested in some kind of social movement in England and very kindly sent me a book on the subject. You see, I believe that the artist must come before all the others, the remakers of the social state; and always when such men as yourself who have at bottom the artist's point of view are carried aside from it by any movement of any kind for the present betterment of society, I am a bit sore and ugly.

In this connection something Paul said to me this summer has left a deep impression. He suggested that after all the only thing the present generation of men in America could expect to do is to make with their bodies and spirits a kind of fertilizing element in our soil.

There is one thing more I do want to say. There is something in your letter, a kind of humbleness, that I don't like from you now. You are, to my mind, a man coming into his kingdom. There are rich years ahead for you. No man in America ever really becomes anything until after forty, as the rest of his life is spent working his way through a fog. I did it in business; you did it as a professional doctor. I suppose I want pride in you now as a thing to set up alongside that dearly-bought humbleness. In the morning now you can get out of bed facing yourself. You can breathe. You are really a prince come to his kingdom, and it doesn't matter that no one knows it. Am I wrong if I want my brothers to be proud men too? All my love to you

62. PALOS PARK, ILLINOIS, OCTOBER 19, 1921

To GILBERT SELDES [1]

Dear Gilbert Seldes: I am wiring you today saying I shall be glad to accept the *Dial* Prize [2] and in addition want to say to you, to Mr. Thayer, and to Mr. Watson [3] and the others there that I am very proud and happy that you have found my work worthy this offer.

As you no doubt know, I am compelled to make most of my living outside writing and have in other years been fortunate in being able to do the job and still leave myself free a great deal of the time. This year and because of the general business depression I am making practically nothing, and this money coming to me at just this time would give me freedom to do work I very much want to do.

I speak of this because, had I an income this year from any other source, I might feel guilty about accepting the money when some other man or woman might need it more.

As to the other side of the question, there is no other source in America from which such an offer could come that would give me a fraction of the satisfaction I shall get from having it come from the *Dial*.

Naturally I shall be glad to say nothing at all of the matter to any-one until you are ready to make the announcement yourself.

The offer has made me very happy. I hope it will not make me too unbearably chesty.

At present I am at work on a long novel, but as soon as it is off my mind, I have some things I want to send for your consideration. Sincerely yours

63. PALOS PARK, ILLINOIS [AFTER OCTOBER 24, 1921]

To PAUL ROSENFELD

Dear Paul: It was good to hear from you. I have been in the country almost continuously since I got home, and whenever I have gone to

---

[1] Gilbert Seldes (1893–), associate and managing editor of the *Dial*, 1920–1923.
[2] In June, 1921, the *Dial* announced that on January first of each year it would "acknowledge the service to letters of some one of those who have, during the twelvemonth, contributed to its pages, by the payment to him of two thousand dollars." (*Dial*, LXX, 730–732). Formal announcement of the award to Anderson was made in the January, 1922, number (LXXII, 116–117).
[3] See Letter 38, note 3.

town or whenever Tennessee has come out here, the greeting has been the same. "Have you heard from Paul?" It threatened to become one of those annoying family sayings that no one else understands, but that always makes the members of the family smile.

I'm glad you reminded me of *Windy*. I'll send it Monday from town. Also I'll have what there is of the *Testament* copied and send it at once. There should be more than the one copy anyway.

You understand, of course, Paul, that the *Testament* is a purely experimental thing with me. Many of the things you will now find in it will no doubt eventually be cast out altogether. However, I'm going to send it to you just as it is. In this book I am trying to get at something that I think was very beautifully done in some parts of the Old Testament by the Hebrew poets. That is to say, I want to achieve in it rhythm of words with rhythm of thought. Do I make myself clear? The thing if achieved will be felt rather tha[n] seen or heard, perhaps. You see, as the things are, many of them violate my own conception of what I am after. In making this book I have felt no call to responsibility to anything but my own inner sense of what is beautiful in the arrangement of words and ideas. It is in a way my own Bible. I think in a way you and Brooks and Waldo have always a little misunderstood something in me. Have you ever known well an old priest of the Catholic faith? He will make almost ribald remarks about Mother Church sometimes, but if you take that to mean he hasn't real love and devotion to her, you make a great mistake.

You see, after all I was raised in a different atmosphere than most of you fellows. Among workers, farmers, etc., here in the Middle West it used to be thought almost unwholesome to be outwardly serious about anything. After all, you see, I am a product of the same thing Brooks talks so much about in his Mark Twain.

There was, you see, an outward technique. If a man say anything seriously to another, he must immediately turn it about and make a kind of half joke of it. The serious, not the half-joking thing, was meant. The half-joking thing did, however, answer a purpose. "We must laugh or die" was at bottom the thing felt.

I emphasize this phase of myself to you, Paul, because you, Brooks, and Waldo were all brought up in a different atmosphere. I think your atmosphere was as difficult as my own to penetrate, but it was different. The New Englanders and the Jews have always at least had the privilege of being serious. You see, I put Brooks among the New

Englanders. He may not have been born there,[1] but spiritually he belongs there and has in his make-up the beauty and the inner cold fright of the New Englander. That's what makes it so difficult for me to feel warm and close to him, as I so often do to you and Waldo, although I respect him sometimes more than any other living man. Is all this stupid? However, I will go on and try to get off my chest what I am trying to say. I have in my inner consciousness conceived of what we roughly speak of as the Middle West, and what I have so often called Mid-America, as an empire with its capital in Chicago. When I started writing, my conception wasn't so clear. Then I went only so far as to want health for myself. I was a money-getter, a schemer, a chronic liar. One day I found out that when I sat down to write, it was more difficult to lie. The lie lay before one on the paper. It haunted one at night.

Then, you see, I knew no writers, no artists. Everything was very much mixed up. When I began to know writers and painters, I couldn't abide the way most of them talked. They were also doing the American trick. They were putting it over.

You see, I had by this time got up out of the ranks of laborers and lived among businessmen, had them for my friends. I went to conferences, lunched with these men. They were always talking so earnestly and seriously about nothing. The nothingness back of the spirit of their lives led to sex-mussiness. Brooks, I believe, once called me "the phallic Chekhov." I really do not believe I have a sex-obsession, as has so often been said. I do not want to have, surely. When I want to flatter myself, at least, I tell myself that I want only not to lose the sense of life as it is, here, now, in the land and among the people among whom I live.

Please believe, Paul, that I am writing all this to you not having your article in mind, but rather in mind you as my friend, as a man I love.

Let me go on. You will see in *Windy* and in *Marching Men* the effects of a reaction from businessmen back to my former associates, the workers. I believe now it was a false reaction and carried with it something else. It is the thing Mencken calls "sentimental liberalism." For a time I did dream of a new world to come out of some revolutionary movement that would spring up out of the mass of people.

That went. A break came. You will see it in *Mid-American Chants*.

[1] Brooks was born in Plainfield, New Jersey.

What happened was something like this. A new conception came. Will you read now the first of the New Testaments. "In a purely subconscious way I am a patriot. I live in a wide valley of cornfields and men and towns and strange, jangling sounds, and in spite of the curious perversion of life here, I have a feeling that the great basin of the Mississippi River, where I have always lived and moved about, is one day to be the seat of the culture of the universe."

Now you understand, Paul, something in me. There is acceptance in that. I take these little, ugly factory towns, these big, sprawling cities into something. I wish it would not sound to[o] silly to say I pour a dream over it, consciously, intentionally, for a purpose. I want to write beautifully, create beautifully, not outside but in this thing in which I am born, in this place where, in the midst of ugly towns, cities, Fords, moving pictures, I have always lived, must always live. I do not want, Paul, even those old monks at Chartres, building their cathedral, to be at bottom any purer than myself.

There are infinite difficulties. You with your quick, warm nature will perhaps never quite understand my slowness or the slowness of men like Sandburg. I am stupid. You will never believe how stupid. There is something almost of the Negro in me there.

This leads to misunderstandings, too. There are men, like Jones[2] of the Chicago *Post*, who, having no doubt at some time heard me say something derogative to smart men and smartness, have got the idea fixed in their heads that I am without respect for old things, old beauty. Jones, for example, is always harping on the idea that I do not believe in reading the work of the old masters of my craft and that I am no respecter of words, am afraid of words. I do not blame Jones. If he has such a notion, it is because of something I have myself said.

I have had a great fear of phrase-making. Words, as you know, Paul, are very tricky things. Look, for example, how that man Mencken can rattle words like dice in a box. Our Ben Hecht, here in Chicago, has naturally the same talent, but I happen to know he isn't particularly proud of it, not at bottom.

Being, as I have said, slow in my nature, I do have to come to words slowly. I do not want to make them rattle. And well enough I know that you, Waldo, Brooks might do in a flash what I will never be able

[2] Llewellyn Jones (1884–), literary editor of the Chicago *Evening Post*, 1914–1932.

to do. You may get to heights I can never reach. That isn't quite the point. I'm not competitive. I want, if I can, to save myself.

And now, you see, this brings me to the point of all this. Granted I am slow and stupid. Now, at this time, in America, culture is not a part of our lives out here in Mid-America. We are all, businessmen, workers, farmers, town, city and country dwellers, a little ashamed of trying for beauty. We are imprisoned. There is a wall about us. You will see, as you get into the spirit of the *New Testament,* how that wall has become a symbol of life to me. More men than you and I will ever know have become embittered and ugly in America, Paul. The flush-looking, hearty, go-with-a-slam-bang businessmen and others, what we have come to think of as the up-and-going American, are not so up-and-going. They are little children. Immaturity is the note of the age, and immaturity is a wall too.

And so in my inner self I have accepted my own Mid-America as a walled-in place. There are walls everywhere, about individuals, about groups. The houses are mussy. People die inside the walls without ever having seen the light. I want the houses cleaned, the doorsteps washed, the walls broken away. That can't happen in my time. Culture is a slow growth. How silly to think you won't understand all this, that you haven't understood from the first. Sometimes, however, you, Brooks, Waldo, all the men I love and respect seem so far away. I say stupid things, act stupidly. I grow afraid too.

You see, all I want is to have such men as you know at bottom that I love what you love — that is enough. Artists have to be strangers to the body of the people now in Chicago, in Ohio, in all this empire of Mid-America. I just don't want any of you fellows who are real, who love beauty and who understand more than I ever will, to be fooled by my crudeness or to be led to believe that I am not, in my own way, trying to live in the old tradition of artists. And that's all of that. "Thank God," you'll probably say.

You will know how I feel about the *Dial* matter. They had told me something about it, gave me to understand I would probably be the man, etc. After all, the *Dial* is the one thing we have. They are sincerely trying for something the rest of us are after also. How could I be anything but pleased and flattered? Also the money will be a big help this year. I've got so I am not particularly well in this damp, cold climate during the winter months, and there are times when certain physical facts make it impossible for me to work. I have continuous colds, and that poisons my body so that both body and mind are stupid.

I'll probably run away somewhere. There is so much work I want to do.

Today the rain falls dismally, and winter is close at hand. I'll probably come to New York later, not for a dinner, but because I would like to see some of you fellows, will be getting hungry for the sight of you.

At least O'Neil [3] won't be able to wear tights on the streets this kind of weather. I'll probably be safe until spring. At bottom, perhaps, I should fear you more than he anyway. Anyway Tennessee will want me to send her love. She would probably make it more direct if you would occasionally write to her. With love

[P.S.] Oh, by the way, I am offering the *Dial* some of the Testaments.[4] Don't know whether they will want them or not.

64. [?PALOS PARK, ILLINOIS, BEFORE NOVEMBER 22, 1921]

To BEN HUEBSCH

[No salutation] Now that you have taken over the publishing rights of the novels *Windy McPherson's Son* and *Marching Men* and the book called *Mid-American Chants*, I am taking this opportunity to send you some changes I would like to see made in the text of *Windy*.[1]

Regarding this book and the impulses back of it I have also something to say to you and thru you to its readers.

The book was written under rather trying circumstances, and all the later part of it represents too much my own floundering about in life.

That in itself would not, to my mind, make the book untrue or formless.

But there is another and a great weakness. At the time the book was written, circumstances and a false conception of what is due the reader of a novel led me into something like trickery in writing.

Consider the circumstances. There was I, a manufacturer in an

[3] Raymond O'Neil, producer and playwright, who in 1922 dramatized Anderson's short story "The Egg." In the letter to which this is an answer Rosenfeld had jokingly warned Anderson that if O'Neil ever appeared in tights Tennessee would probably desert her husband for the playwright.
[4] The *Dial* did not publish these.

[1] A revised edition of *Windy McPherson's Son* was published by Huebsch in 1921.

industrial city in Ohio. I had reached near to the middle station in life and was unfitted for my place in i[t]. My own nature was in revolt against money-making as an end in life, and the history of Sam McPherson is the history of such a revolt.

But I am afraid I had come to novel writing through novel reading. I could not leave Sam in my reader's hands having achieved nothing but money and weariness.

Therefore my mind reached back into childhood. In a new generation of Americans the impossible was perhaps to be achieved. Having laid on the reader's doorstep a basket containing some three children picked up during one of Sam's period[s] of debauchery in the city of S[t.] Louis, Sam and I both tiptoed out of the book.

Now the simple fact is that when I come to the rereading of *Windy*, I have no stomach for repeating that performance. The crudities of the book, the occasionally terrible sentences, the minor faults I am willing to let stand. They are the faults of a badly educated man struggling to tell a story to his own people in his own way. But in this new printing of the book I want to take those three children back to their mother in S[t.] Louis and to leave Sam facing what he and every American must face, the fact that it is hardly fair to

[Unfinished]

65.   [CHICAGO] NOVEMBER 28, 1921

MR. LEWIS GALANTIÈRE,[1] 33, RUE JEAN GOUJON, PARIS

My dear Lewis: A friend of mine and a very delightful man, Ernest Hemingway, and his wife are leaving for Paris. They will sail December 8th and go to [the] Hotel Jacob, at least temporarily. Hemingway is a young fellow of extraordinary talent and, I believe, will get somewhere. He has been a quite wonderful newspaper man, but has practically given up newspaper work for the last year. Recently he got an assignment to do European letters for some Toronto newspaper[2] for whom he formerly worked, and this is giving him the opportunity he has wanted, to live in Europe for a time. I have talked to him a great deal about you and have given him your address. I trust you

---

[1] Lewis Galantière (1895–), Chicago writer, attached to the International Chamber of Commerce in Paris, 1920–1927.
[2] The Toronto *Star*.

will be on the lookout for him at the Hotel Jacob along about the 20th or 21st of December. He is not like Stearns, and his wife is charming. They will settle down to live in Paris, and [I] am sure you will find them great playmates. As I understand it, they will not have much money, so that they will probably want to live over in the Latin Quarter. However, Hemingway can himself find quarters after he gets there, and the Hotel Jacob will do temporarily.

I am very sorry about X., but not at all surprised. Your experience with him is a universal experience, and I suspect there is nothing to do but to be brutal and stop loaning him money and save your own peace of mind.

I note that you would like to see Hecht's book; [3] so I am going to send it to you or will ask Hemingway to bring it. You can form your own opinions after you see it.

About Burton,[4] surely you haven't got the impression you seem to have in your letter from anything I have said. It may be, as you suggest, that too much bad whiskey and chattering has interfered with his work. If it has, I have no way of knowing about it. My own understand[ing] was that he held up his book because, in thinking it over, there were things he sincerely wanted to change in it. If this is true, surely one cannot do anything but respect him for that.

I am glad to hear about Pierre [5] and think it very strange that he has not heard from Paul. I am going to New York in two or three weeks and will ask Paul about it. By the way, if you want to write Paul, his address is 77 Irving Place, New York.

I dare say the *Triumph* [6] will reach you ahead of this letter. It gives [sic] the most inspired, thoughtful, well-written reviews of anything I have yet put out.

As the big announcement of the "DIAL of WARD" [sic] will be made on the first, and as this letter will not reach you before that time, I will betray no secret in telling you that it is to be made to me.

I want to thank you again, Lewis, for the kind interest you have taken in helping Madame Gay [7] with the translation, but when it

---

[3] Ben Hecht's *Erik Dorn* (1921).

[4] Burton Rascoe (1892–), literary editor, New York *Tribune*, 1922–1924.

[5] Not now identifiable.

[6] *The Triumph of the Egg* (1921).

[7] Marguerite Gay, contributor to the *Mercure de France*, became Anderson's French translator. He was introduced to her by letter from Galantière.

comes to that, there is no way in the world I will be able to repay you for the many beautiful things you have done for me.

With love, Yours very sincerely

66.   CHICAGO [DECEMBER, 1921]

To PAUL ROSENFELD

Dear Paul: The article [1] is very beautiful, Paul, and in it I feel a hammering on and a breaking-down of walls between us, too. I have always wanted from you and two or three others just this understanding, not of what is accomplished, but of the thing aimed at.

For a long time I thought the structure of your own life so different from my own that you would not see the road I was trying to follow, and now you have put your foot on it so firmly and surely. Your article makes me feel as I felt when you, Tennessee, and I walked out into the open space fronting the Louvre and as you and I sat on the bench before Chartres.

And one of the most lovely things in it is your recognition of my immense debt to the man Brooks. When you said that, my heart jumped with joy. I have been so sore at him so often, but deep down in me I have always loved him so really. When I began first to read him in *Seven Arts*, his voice was as a great shout saying: "You are on the right road. You may never get to the sacred city, but you have put your feet on the right road."

And other subtle things I did not know you knew — the escape from the dominance of women and children, the eternal begging of the question, the waiting for life to be lived by someone else to come after you.

I have said these things to myself on my prayer rug, but did not know you battled with them too and were walking through the same grey fog.

It is very beautiful and gives me the warmest feeling of living comradeship I've ever had.

We will be in New York Sunday or Monday, and you may be sure we will be there with you on the thirtieth. Tennessee is going to stay until the 1st, and I will stay longer. I'm thinking of sneaking off to the niggers for a month or six weeks. With love

[1] Rosenfeld's article was published as "Sherwood Anderson" in *Dial*, LXXII, 29–42 (January, 1922).

67.   Chicago, December 3, 1921

Miss Gertrude Stein,[1] 27, rue de Fleurus, Paris

Dear Miss Stein: I am writing this note to make you acquainted with my friend Ernest Hemingway, who with Mrs. Hemingway is going to Paris to live, and will ask him to drop it in the mails when he arrives there.

Mr. Hemingway is an American writer instinctively in touch with everything worth-while going on here, and I know you will find Mr. and Mrs. Hemingway delightful people to know.

They will be, temporarily, at the Hotel Jacob, rue Jacob.[2] Sincerely [P.S.] Did you get my note about the introduction?[3] Love to Marsden Hartley.[4]

68.   Chicago, December 13, 1921

To Lucile Cox [1]

Dear Lucile Cox: I'm glad you told me of the outcome of the trip to California and am more glad than I can tell you for your understanding of the difficulty of Ivor's present situation.

Of course I knew, from the few minutes talk I had with him, that his outlook on writing was utterly corrupt, but he can't be blamed for that. The man has probably never had life and its purposes dignified by putting it in any other terms than money and success.

What he is is probably something like this: a young man who has in him the making of an artist and at the same time a man who doesn't even know what an artist is. He came into my office and talked of writing a book as though it were a matter like going out and getting an advertising contract. Ye gods! Does he think there are no men who haven't minds and hearts above such cheapness? I wish he could know personally, as I have, some of these men who are the big selling successes and get big prices for stories in the *Saturday Evening*

---

[1] Gertrude Stein (1874–1946), expatriate and experimental writer.

[2] This has been changed, apparently by Hemingway, to read: "They will be at 74 Rue de Cardinal Lemoine."

[3] Miss Stein had requested Anderson to write an introduction to her forthcoming book, *Geography and Plays* (1922).

[4] The American painter (1877–1943).

---

[1] At one time a secretary of Anderson's.

Post. I'd like him to know what cheap, vain, slick, oily men they are with their second-rate successes.

Can't you get the man to read a few things? Get him to read, if you can, Waldo Frank's *Our America* and Van Wyck Brooks' *Letters and Leadership* and *America's Coming-of-Age.*[2]

One thing is sure. If he has in him the making of an artist, the fact that this California trip has fallen through is the best thing in the world. He might have written some second-class bunk about Chinese gods or something of that kind and had a cheap newspaper success. Then he never would have had a chance to see the light.

What I hope now is that he will realize that anything worth-while has to be come at by long, patient effort. He doesn't need to worry. There are plenty of cheap, flashy men. The fact that he hasn't ground out another second-rate book won't hurt. The world will lose nothing.

Of course, all America is losing tremendously all the time, because there isn't anyone to tell these young men, who might possibly be artists, that they are on the wrong road, that they should learn some humbleness and most of all learn to face themselves.

It will be interesting now to watch this man. Will he go to work to educate himself, to find out what the few real artists in America are talking about, and let writing go until he has found out a little about life; or will he flop back into business and try to find there the quick, cheap, flashy success a man can get by making a lot of money by some form of trickiness — in other words, is the artist in him big enough and strong enough to begin standing on its own feet one of these days?

I am glad you are able to keep your place at Gunther's. Sincerely

69.   708 ROYAL STREET, NEW ORLEANS [?FEBRUARY, 1922]

TO GERTRUDE STEIN

My dear Gertrude Stein: I was delighted to get your letter of today and to hear that arrangements are made for the publication of the book.[1]

I was afraid you might have changed your mind about having me write the introduction, and had you done so, I should have been quite

[2] *Our America* (1919); *Letters and Leadership* (1918); *America's Coming-of-Age* (1915).

[1] *Geography and Plays,* Boston, The Four Seas Company, 1922. This contains Anderson's introduction.

upset. It's a literary job I'd rather do than any other I know of. I'll get at it very soon and send it along.

Someone told me you were off Americans, that you had become bored with them, and that frightened me too. "I'll bet she'll put me in with the rest of the mess and chuck us all," I thought.

In the January *Dial* Paul Rosenfeld had an article on my own work in which he spoke of the influence on myself of first coming across one of your books at the time they [were] raising such a guffaw over here. I'd like you to see the article, but haven't it here.

I came down here about a month ago and am living in the old French Creole Quarter, the most civilized place I've found in America, and have been writing like a man gone mad ever since I got off the train.

You will hear from me with the introduction very soon. Your sincere admirer

70. [NEW YORK, AUGUST 21, 1922]

TO KARL ANDERSON

Dear Karl: There has been recently a revival of interest in the work of Gertrude Stein. She has written and is to publish a new book for which I have written, at her request, an introduction. I speak of this, Karl, because of an annoying thing that appeared in the *New York Tribune* here yesterday.

In the introduction I spoke of your having first called my attention to Miss Stein and of a conversation we had about her work. One day last week I was lunching with Mr. Edmund Wilson, editor of *Vanity Fair*.[1] Rascoe of the *Tribune* was at the table. Wilson and I had a conversation about Miss Stein. Yesterday in the *Tribune* I saw what was supposed to be a reporting of this conversation.[2] In the introduction spoken of above I had said or had made you say, "It gives words an odd, new personal flavor, doesn't it?" To my astonishment and [*sic*] in the *Tribune* there was this: "My brother came into my room laughing his head off about a book called *Tender Buttons*[3] by Gertrude

---

[1] Edmund Wilson (1895–), the literary critic, was managing editor of *Vanity Fair*, 1920–1921.

[2] See Burton Rascoe's column, "A Bookman's Day Book," in the *New York Tribune*, August 20, 1922, Section V ("Weekly Review of the Arts"), p. 4. Rascoe dates the lunch as having taken place on August 9.

[3] Published in 1915.

Stein." This is particularly annoying because, as a matter of fact, you did introduce me to Gertrude Stein's work, and I afterward got a good deal out of it. And here I am made to appear to represent you as a somewhat boorish gentleman, as this fool says, "laughing your head off." I am sorry, Karl. It is a part of the price you pay for having a scribbling brother.

I am sending you the new Clive Bell book,[4] as I think you will enjoy it. Hoped you would come in to see me when you went through town. Am at work. With love

71.   [NEW YORK, LATE AUGUST, 1922]

To KARL ANDERSON

Dear Brother: I knew, of course, that you would dismiss from your mind the silly business in the *Tribune,* but my attitude toward it had to be somewhat different. What I suppose the fool wanted was someone to laugh at Stein. In my article[1] about her I had explained that I came to her through you. He just sacrificed you to make a Roman holiday for his asinine newspaper column. I haven't settled with him for the trick yet, but am laying for him.

I suppose you must know, Karl, that I have come to love you more than almost any other human being I know, and I do want you to know how much I admire your work and your attitude toward your work.

As for myself, I have been a stormy cuss and perhaps am still that. In the first place, I had myself almost come to middle life before I really sensed out what I wanted to do. I was full of ugly, fighting resentments for what life had done to me.

As for Clive Bell's notion of significant form. I think the man is very helpful in many ways, but he does rather lay down too many laws. The question remains: What is significant? Is the thing that is significant to you significant to me?

It is rather a large order, this one of his, trying to define art within the channels of his own reactions. Men have always been trying to do it. No one has done it yet.

As for Stein, I do not think her too important. I do think she had an

―――――――

[4] *Since Cézanne* (1922).

[1] "Four American Impressions," *New Republic,* XXXII, 171–173 (October 11, 1922).

important thing to do, not for the public, but for the artist who happens to work with words as his materials.

It has happened that since I have been here I have been working like a crazy man. Have, since you left, written five short stories and a long poem. The result is that I have been nowhere and have seen few people.

Have about made up my mind that I am through with the advertising business. By spending a little more time on the ground I can easily pick up at least a simple living and will not have to write silly nonsense about breakfast foods.

I am rather set just now on developing in myself a satirical vein that I have never worked. Satire, delicately handled, can be a quite tremendous thing. I have done a thing which is to appear later in *Vanity Fair*, a satire on the new movement in the arts,[2] and have also done a long satire on the small businessman.[3]

The thing has to be handled with entire sympathy, and any taint of patronage would ruin it. But there are so many lovely things to touch off.

I think I do myself, Karl, rather think that the swing of the pendulum has begun. The material age has had its say and has said nothing. What we all are now is partly due to life itself in the time in which we happen to have lived. You and I will not live into an age that may come out of the growing disgust with life's emptiness, that is to say, an age when the spirit may again breathe and live. Dear Karl, if you feel yourself wounded, are we not all just that? I know of no man whom one can approach, through the people about him, and get a sharper impression of inner love of life. Well, after all, that terribly abused word "love" is at the bottom of all the decay. When men do not dare love, they cannot live, and the men of our day did not dare love either God or their fellow men. You have dared to love beauty all your life, and please remember that no man knows himself, or do his contemporaries ever know how much of the love he had to give has found form in his work.

It has happened that I have rather had my bellyful of men who think always, "Am I a bigger man than Jones? What can I do to appear

[2] Anderson published nothing in *Vanity Fair* between "Pages from a New Testament" (October, 1922) and "Aching Breasts and Snow-White Hearts" (January, 1926). Neither is a satire on the new movement in the arts.

[3] "Ohio: I'll Say We've Done Well" appeared in the *Nation*, CXV, 146–148 (August 9, 1922).

bigger?" Which makes the dignity of your own attitude rather fine to me.

I do wish you did not have to paint portraits, just as I have wished for years not to write any more advertisements. Once I could work eight hours a day at it without the psy[ch]ic injury to myself that now comes with doing it eight hours a year.

I suspect that if you are physically ill now, it will pass when the last of that bunch of portraits is done, and I hope, when you get through, you will be able to take a real playtime. Why don't you run off over to Paris, if only for a few weeks or months, this fall? I'm almost tempted to say I will go along. If I had a little more money, I would.

About Jamie.[4] He did a lot of actual work. Wish you would let me pay for it, but I will take the check and talk it over with you when you come back. Won't you write or wire me c/o B. W. Huebsch, 14 Mount Morris Park West, when you are coming through?

72.   [?NEW YORK, ?JANUARY, 1923]

To JEROME AND LUCILE BLUM

Dear Jerry & Lucile: If our being there meant something to you, think what it meant to me and to Elizabeth.[1] In town a fellow has to go about so, so, walking along — don't stumble. There aren't many people dare love other people, even a little. People shiver along, quarrel, say nasty things, then go home and pray to God.

"God, forgive me my sins. Let me die, God, and go up to heaven to sit on a golden throne!"

I'm not ready yet to work, as I thought I was. The story I want to get at is pretty rich. I'll walk about and wait awhile. Perhaps I'll run away for a week or two to where I know no one very well or not at all.

One gets the relations of things that way — fellows going along, eating, chewing gum, smoking. Women seeking lovers, making eyes at people. It's so with a storyteller, perhaps just so with painters and sculptors too. There is an overtone, what it all means to something outside people.

One remembers always little thing[s], a walk on a dark, windy road at night, down below in the shadows an old wooden pump handle creaking.

[4] Probably Karl Anderson's son, James.

[1] Elizabeth Prall, who became Anderson's third wife in April, 1924.

The gods and the mystery in that as well as anything, I suppose.

I went into the Victor place and heard a dozen or more Negro records, but couldn't bring myself to buy any of them. I'd heard the niggers sing on [the] river and in the woods. I couldn't send the damn things to friends who are artists.

Something happens to a nigger when he gets up in front of a house to sing. He isn't a conscious artist. He's a bird.

Luck comes along. A magazine has paid $750 for the story about the jealous husband.[2] It's odd. Since I've been here, I've got more for two stories than I ever got for all the stories I've written these years.

There'll be a howl. I've sold out, I suppose. It doesn't matter. My bread and butter struggle is probably at an end. There'll be another and more intense kind of struggle with all the things I want to do.

I sure love you both.

[P.S.] Jerry, do, if you can, drop T[ennessee] an occasional line. She is out in the cold rather, and I can't manage it now.

73. [NEW YORK, JANUARY, 1923]

To PETER OCHREMENKO [1]

[No salutation] I yesterday received your letter telling me that you are translating my *Triumph of the Egg* and that you are interested in seeing my other books, and to tell you the truth I am highly pleased and flattered and will do everything I can to help you.

You must understand that my first and natural anxiety is that the translation shall carry, as far as is humanly possible, the spirit of the tales. For that I must trust God and you, as I do not read Russian. Please bear in mind these things. Do not try to follow my text slavishly. If these tales touch you, try to carry the same feeling over to your Russian readers.

You must, of course, realize, in reading my tales, that I am very deeply indebted to your Russian writers, and I shall be very happy if I can repay the debt a little by giving aesthetic pleasure to Russian readers or can make your Russian people understand more fully the life among us in America.

[2] Presumably "The Man's Story," *Dial*, LXXV, 247–264 (September, 1923). Collected in *Horses and Men*.

[1] Russian translator then working for the All-Russian State Publishing Company.

As an introduction to the work I would think the thing you have by Mr. Lawrence Gilman [2] would be very fine, but I am sending you also an article by Mr. Paul Rosenfeld [3] which goes more deeply into the thing I have been driving at.

Tomorrow I shall see my publisher, Mr. B. W. Huebsch, 116 West 13th Street, New York, and shall have him send you the rest of my books, of which there are three novels, two books of tales, and a book of poetry. Another novel, to be called *Many Marriages,* will be published by Huebsch in February this year, and this will be sent as soon as it is published here. This is the novel now being published serially in *Dial.* The two articles concerning my work by Mr. Rosenfeld and Robert Lovett [4] also appeared in the *Dial* at the time last year when I was awarded the *Dial* Prize for my contributions to American literature.

As regards the pictures, I will try to find a photograph and a print to send on to you.

I suppose the general feeling of my work must represent a reaction going on here from the industrial note of our civilization. I myself was a manufacturer of the Middle West and at one time promised myself that I could grow rich. The thought made me ill within myself, but as I had no formal education and had in fact but a few years before risen into the middle and prosperous class from the ranks of labor, I did not know where to turn.

I began writing and wrote three novels which I afterward threw away. Then I wrote *Windy McPherson's Son* and *Marching Men,* which were accepted first by a publishing house [5] in London, England. They were, however, published at the same time in America and had some little success here.

However, I myself felt they were influenced by my notion of writing got from novel reading rather than my own reactions to life. I was in an unhappy state about my writing and my life. My business failed. I went to Chicago and became a writer of advertisements to make a living.

[2] Apparently this refers to Lawrence Gilman's review of *The Triumph of the Egg* as "an American masterwork." *North American Review,* CCXV, 412–416 (March, 1922).

[3] See Letter 66, note 1.

[4] "The Promise of Sherwood Anderson," *Dial,* LXXII, 79–83 (January, 1922), a review of *Horses and Men.*

[5] John Lane Company.

Out of that black period came the book of poetry, *Mid-American Chants,* and that led to what I think is a more authentic expression. With the publication of *Winesburg* I felt I had really begun to write out of the repressed, muddled life about me. The book, followed by *Poor White* and last year by *The Triumph,* [which] you have, gave me artistic recognition in America, France, England, and Germany. The books are now being translated into French and German.

However, they have had no popular success and have brought me little or no money, but that doesn't matter too greatly. One eats and sleeps and is no longer engaged in buying and selling. Life goes more happily. The recognition I have had from the world of artists here and in Europe is also sweet.

May I say that, until I found the Russian writers of prose, your Tolstoy, Dostoevski, Turgenev, Chekhov, I had never found a prose that satisfied me. In America we have had a bad tradition, got from the English and the French. To our tales that are popular in our magazines one goes for very clever plots, all sorts of trickery and juggling. The natural result is that human life becomes secondary, of no importance. The plot does not grow out of the natural drama resulting from the tangle of human relations, whereas in your Russian writers one feels life everywhere, in every page.

I remember how, as a boy, I heard of Russia as a strange, cruel land in which — one got the notion — well, you see, it was a land in which most of the people spent their lives down in dark mines. A few tall figures in beards and wearing expensive fur coats strode about. Everyone carried a whip with which to beat others.

I had this picture, and then I came to your writers. A door opened. I saw at last that the art of prose writing might spring into life directly out of an impulse of sympathy and understanding with the man beside you.

Is it not possible that your people think of us Americans also as giants going about jingling dollars, piling up great heaps of dollars in the streets? One day last year a young Russian who lives in Chicago now walked with me in one of the crowded, noisy streets there. "It does not want a new land and a new people here. It wants Dostoevski or a Tolstoy to come into this street and see things with their eyes," he said.

We are a mixed people, all races thrown together. Our cities are ugly. We have not come to such an understanding of each other as might come readily if we were all one people, but we Americans are men and women too.

If my tales or novels make you feel that, I shall be glad. Very sincerely yours

74.   [RENO, NEVADA, ?FEBRUARY, 1923]

TO JEROME BLUM

Dear Jerry: You and Lucile have been over the mountains; so there wouldn't be anything exciting to you in my telling you how they made me feel or what the vast green desert made me feel.

I'm drifting about now, looking at people, sitting still a good deal. There isn't much to say for myself. I'll get me a quiet little hole after [a]while and settle down to do a lot of work I want to do — that is to say, I guess I will.

It's spring where I am now, with warm days. I'm sitting at this very minute by a small river where it jumps over a waterfall, and it's warm and nice without my overcoat, although I can see plenty of heavy snowdrifts up in the mountains. I've never been in a mountain country before. It excites me.

Everything here excites me too much; it's the clear, rarefied air, I suppose. I have to tear myself away from my desk, and I'm not ready to work yet. I will be pretty soon, I think.

Of course, I'm as lonely as a coyote, at nights particularly. In the daytime I just lie low, look, and listen.

Dear Jerry, I think of you a lot and the last little walk we had together. There is so little one man can do for another. What is to be said? What is to be done?

It might even be that you have already done better things than anyone else, felt deeper. No one would quite know. Perhaps you would. That is, I suppose, the only test.

I know I do not want New York and the neurotics any more for a long, long time. I've got some seeds in me, and if they'll sprout, I'll grow a little fruit along.

There's too much pissing on the soil in the East just now. The uric acid kills the roots of things I think.

Also I've had too much prominence. It isn't any good. It's bunk.

A man's one happiness is in his craft, for me the white sheets on which to write words that may have a tang to them and color to them.

That and the flesh of life through a loved one one isn't afraid to love. We're a scared crew, Jerry. You know that and I know it.

My love to you and dear Lucile.

75. [RENO, SPRING, 1923]

To GERTRUDE STEIN

Dear Friend: Got your note yesterday and just recently have been thinking about you a good deal. You see, in this book [1] on which I am at work I am trying to make a kind of picture of the artist's life in the midst of present-day American life. It has been a job. So much to discard. Have never thrown away so much stuff. I want to make it a sort of tale, you see, not a preachment.

Also I have to find out, if I can, what really affected the fellow. There isn't any doubt about you there. It was a vital day for me when I stumbled upon you.

But also there was and is something else. There was not only your work, but also your room in the house there in Paris. That was something special too. I mean the effect on myself. You would be surprised to know just how altogether American I found you.

You see, dear friend, I believe in this damn mixed-up country of ours. In an odd way I'm in love with it. And you get into it, in my sense of it, quite tremendously.

I've been checking over things and people that have meant most. You, Jane Heap, Dreiser, Paul Rosenfeld, Van Wyck Brooks, Alfred Stieglitz. That about nails the list. It is a list that would make Jane sputter with wrath perhaps. She is an arbitrary one, that same Jane.

What I have to figure is just the people who have given me fine moments. I've an idea that's what counts most.

Well you'll see the book someday. I'm glad Jane is going to publish the "Valentine." [2] I like it, because it always stirs me and is full of sharp criticism too.

Am sitting right here in a desert as big as God until I get this book done and a divorce. Then I'll shift to something else, and I hope some of these days my shifting will bring me to your door again. With love

---

[1] Tentatively entitled *Straws*, but published as *A Story Teller's Story* (1924).
[2] Gertrude Stein, "Idem The Same — A Valentine to Sherwood Anderson," *Little Review*, IX, 5–9 (Spring, 1923).

76.   [RENO, MAY 9, 1923]

To GERTRUDE STEIN

Dear Gertrude Stein: Your letter found me out yesterday. Am still out in the Far West, in the desert country, and I surely did think I had written you recently. There must be a letter, somewhere, on the road to you.

I got the book,[1] with the charming "Valentine," about two weeks ago. Someone forwarded it.

And now I have this letter of yours about the book.[2]

Do you know, I think it the most clear-headed criticism I've had and that you have its weaknesses and good points about rightly sized up. It's a job, for an American, with the damned Anglo-Saxon blood in him, to become quite impersonal, but I've a hope I'm going toward it.

I cut out of New York about the time your book and my own were published and did not see the comments on either.

I felt like work and wanted to work and did not want to be thinking much about the job done, for good or evil.

Then I got out here and the painting impulse got me, and I've been fairly swimming.

For one thing I'm doing a quite frankly autobiographical book.[3] That may take something of the tendency to be too much interested in self out of me, unload it, as it were.

Then I am getting a book of tales, call it *Horses and Men,*[4] ready for book publication this fall. There are, I fancy, some good things in it.

I am dead set on getting to Paris next year and do hope I shall make it and that you will be there. If you aren't, I'll look you up where you are.

I believe I'm getting some things in painting. I get up early, write in the morning, tear around for two or three hours, and then settle down to paint. It excites me, even more than writing; it's such a holy gamble, for me, anyway.

[1] Presumably *Geography and Plays,* which had appeared in the previous December.

[2] *Many Marriages.* Gertrude Stein's letter, here referred to, contains an extended commentary on this novel.

[3] *A Story Teller's Story.*

[4] Published in November, 1923.

I've a long novel at work in me, but I shall not get to that until next fall or winter.

Am delighted you are working. I fancy what you are doing means more to more people than you know. With love

77. [?RENO, MAY 18, 1923]

To ALFRED STIEGLITZ

My dear Stieglitz: The package got to me today, the 18th, and it was a wonderful package to open. The two things of your own do for me just what I wanted — clear, sensitive, the lovely sensual feel for the surface before you. I swim in them as in some wondrous sea.

The turgid head of Anderson I hadn't seen, even in reproduction. It is surely a great piece of work. In that one thing you make me respect myself. That is the man who has done anything good Anderson has ever done.

The two others are in a way terrible but wonderful to have about. They are to me the man disintegrated, gone to pieces, fallen down before the ugliness in himself and others. I'll look at them on certain days, when I dare perhaps.

It is a visit of yourself and your spirit, feeling you here where I am trying to work now. God bless you.

I wish I could have my O'Keeffe, but someday I will. I'm going to have a house someday.

You have done a lovely thing for me. With love

78. [RENO, MAY 31, 1923]

To KARL ANDERSON

Dear Karl: I am sorry to hear of Melissa's [1] illness and hope it turns out to be but a passing matter. And your own freedom this summer — I thought you had rather got into shape for a year of freedom to go to Europe, travel, or something of the sort.

I don't know about the country out here. The mood of it is elusive — color, form, and all. I am in a high panlike valley or plain, nearly 5,000 ft. up but surrounded on all sides by a rim of still higher mountains. The light is clear and the air thin, but for that very reason everything, form and color, changes with the rapidity of a breath blown on a windowpane.

[1] Karl Anderson's first child.

Yesterday, May 30, for example, I drove far up into an upper pine country (I have a secondhand Dodge roadster to get about in) and while I got in an upper grassy valley amid the pines, a snow storm came on and I drove down, snow banked on the shield, to a warm rain below.

One feels terrifically energetic here and then, suddenly, quite exhausted. I have been engaged on two books, one now completed and sent off to the publisher for fall publication, a book of tales to be called *Horses and Men*. Then I am doing a long book called *Straws,* half narrative of experiences with men and women, half dissertation on life, and amid all this a good deal of pure fancy, in short, pure lying. It's rather fun.

I have painted some ten or twelve things, but have only got one or two so far that get the true spirit of this country. I've a notion you might have done something with it. It wants a light, facile hand, a kind of strange upper fairyland of changing form and color. The South with the Negro and slower, more lusty rhythm of life is more to my own rather heavy hand, I fancy. Time and again I have fairly wept tears trying to get the feeling of a line of hills, strangely suggestive, and then have gone back to reinforce my impression, and what I saw at first wasn't there at all any more.

As regards the law,[2] it was beaten in the New York legislature, I think. I know little about it. My policy is, I'm afraid, pretty much to write what I feel like and let the fighters stay on the battle line. *Many Marriages* sold well, and I have assurance of a year's living ahead. No artist dare ask more. I let the bourgeois worry about right and wrong, morals, respectability, and money in the bank. My plan shouldn't work, but it does, so I ride along. I believe a bookseller at Boston got arrested and fined $200 for selling my last book in Boston, where it was outlawed by some local purity law, but then he no doubt was getting $5 or $10 a copy. The distiller must make his beverage, I presume, and not worry about an occasional caught bootlegger.

I go into San Francisco occasionally, and on the whole life is sweet

[2] The publication by Thomas Seltzer of D. H. Lawrence's *Women in Love* (1922) set off another contest over censorship in New York State. The Walker bill for the repeal of the law censoring motion pictures was defeated in the Assembly on May 3, 1923, but on the same day the "Clean Books Bill," favored by advocates of stricter censorship, was defeated in the Senate. *Many Marriages* occasioned a letter by W. McAdoo on censorship addressed to Mr. Justice Ford. See *New York Times,* March 15, 1923.

here. I'll shake off the heavy, rather gloomy hand of T[ennessee], I presume, and then Elizabeth and I may go live in Europe. I would like to take the children over there.

As for immediate plans, next winter I rather hope to be in the South again. It may be Mexico. Am sorry you did not find yourself able to drift this way.

79. [RENO, JUNE 30, 1923]

To ALFRED STIEGLITZ

Dear Alfred Stieglitz: Where will one find another such as you, to take the trouble to write me when you are so tired and distraught? I imagine these things begin to happen after a time, people on whom one has depended begin to disappear, the place begins to seem empty. But, dear man, you do so make the world a living place for so many people. I imagine only a few have really got to know you. It takes time and a kind of power in oneself to know another just as it does to get anywhere in one of the crafts. There are little distracting things not understood in oneself and the other. As for myself, I freely admit that I have often been stupid about you, and it was only last year that I came to know and really value you.

One day I was going to the country, and as I sat in the train, I suddenly began to weep bitterly and had to turn my face away from the people in the car for shame of my apparent[ly] causeless grief. However, I was not unhappy. It was just that I had at last realized fully what your life had come to mean to me. In our age, you know, there is much to distract from the faithful devotion to cleanliness and health in one's attitude toward the crafts, and it takes time to realize what the quality has meant in you. I really think, man, you have registered more deeply than you know on Marin,[1] O'Keeffe, Rosenfeld, myself and others. I myself was helped to an understand[ing] of you and your life by just a chance remark dropped by Marin. It illuminated and made clear a whole side of your nature I had not understood.

My new book *Horses and Men* [2] is in press and, I hope, will turn out to be a real book of tales. There are some new ventures in it that have, I believe, real significance. In the meantime I get along into this semi-autobiographical thing on which I am at work. It is thoughts, notions,

[1] John Marin (1872–), whose work was often exhibited at "291."
[2] Published by Huebsch, November 24, 1923.

and tales all thrown together. The central notion is that one's fanciful life is of as much significance as one's real flesh-and-blood life and that one cannot tell where the one cuts off and the other begins. This thing I have thought has as much physical existence as the stupid physical act I yesterday did. In fact, so strongly has the purely fanciful lived in me that I cannot tell after a time which of my acts had physical reality and which did not. It makes me in one sense a great liar, but, as I said in the *Testament,* "It is only by lying to the limit one can come at truth."

I was a good deal disconcerted last year when I saw you in the Galleries doing a thing I thought might well kill you if you did not let up, and now I am glad enough to think of you up there at that quiet place with O'Keeffe. And whatever blows the actuality of life may deal you, I think you may well know that no other man of our day is so deeply loved. You have kept the old faith that gets so lost and faint, but that always has some man like yourself to make it real again to the younger ones. At any rate, you may know that this feeling I have come to have for you is no sudden thing, but a slow, sure growth.

It is dear of you to want me to have the things of your[s], and I want to have them. I get them out every day and look at them, and they are symbols to me of you and the real morality of you. They are living things to me, and I suppose that is what every artist wants — to leave thus living traces of the fine thing in himself for other craftsmen to see and understand a little.

Bless you, man. I hope the summer will bring peace and rest, and naturally I hope after a time you will begin working again, as of course you will.

Do you know the letter Petrarch wrote to Boccaccio when Boccaccio was foolish enough to write to Petrarch and suggest that he, Petrarch, was tired and had better not try to work any more? [3] It is the answer.

My love to O'Keeffe. I have one little painting you and she may like a little — no more. With love

80.   [Reno, July 1, 1923]

To Lucile Blum

My dear Lucile: It is the morning of July 1st. I went over [to] the Overland Hotel and found your letter. It had been there several days

[3] See *A Story Teller's Story,* p. 289.

perhaps. They neglected to send it to my present address, 33 E. Liberty St. We had cold weather here until 10 days ago; now it is dry and hot.

For 25 days we have had running races every day, and I haunt the tracks. Horses and Negroes seem to be the two things in America that give me the most ascetic [*sic*] pleasure. A flat-nosed, tobacco-chewing man is leading a thoroughbred. In the horse what a noble bearing. No lousy inferiority complex here. The small, graceful head is thrown back. The legs are clean and hard, the breast strong. All the flesh of the body quivers with desire to run. We pay something, dear woman, for our silly minds, don't we, always wanting to be great, not daring to just run the cards out and let her ride?

There is an amazing good library here, and I read as I haven't for years. Tried to paint, but got only one clean, fine thing out of about 20. Think my nerves were pretty much shattered when I came, and I hadn't enough energy for writing and painting both.

Many Marriages did pretty well, but the dealers got scared of it. You know I had a little flare of success last year. Think it is over. The magazines are scared of me again. Aside from the financial thing it's better so.

If I have luck here and get what I'm after, E.[1] & I will probably go South in the fall, probably to Mobile or New Orleans. I do want to try to paint a little, but there is this book to finish and a novel eating at me. I'm going to pretty much stay away from Chicago and New York. Whether I'm any good or not, what I want is to work. The eternal quibbling about the purposes of art, its drift, etc., gets on my nerves, knocks me flat.

Maybe you and Jerry will both come back to the American Negro in the end. The plan of putting the Negro on the stage, making him paint, sing, etc., etc., is all nonsense. What he has to give is rather noble, but is physical, like the running horse or dog. I'm pretty sure of that.

The thing here for the painter is very elusive, but there is something here too. Golden color, a light, fleeting thing. If the deserts and mountains ever produce artist[s], they will be telling of delicate, half mystic fairy tales. The same influences that produced Egyptian art perhaps, but pretty foreign to an American. There should really be old ascetic monks in the holes in the mountains at the desert's edge. A strange land. Someday I'll tell you two more about it.

[1] I.e., Elizabeth.

The Indians are something too, rather better in their decay than the Anglo-Saxon[s] in their victory.

E. is well. She makes me always happy to be in her presence. I love her as I have no one else. It is rather odd how little influence any of my other women have had on me.

Think I'm going to get well, less afraid. I won't do what I want. God, I want a lot, in work, but I'm going to keep at it, keep going after it.

We'll meet again. Jerry will get into his swing, and so will you. It's hell for us Americans to get some sense, isn't it? All my love

81.   [RENO, BEFORE JULY 30, 1923]

TO VAN WYCK BROOKS

Dear Van Wyck: I think also that "I'm a Fool" is a piece of work that holds water, but do you not think its wide acceptance is largely due to the fact that it is a story of immaturity and poses no problem? After all, isn't it, say, Mark Twain at his best, the *Huckleberry Finn* Mark Twain?

In the same book there is a story, "There She Is — She Is Taking Her Bath," I would like you to read.[1] And then the story called "The Man Who Became a Woman" and "The Man's Story."

One doesn't want to go on always with the childlike feeling for surface, not just that. I suppose this is my quarrel with you, which isn't a quarrel because I love you and you have done so much for me, cleared so many paths for me. I mean, I presume, that I do not want you to like best of my things the things easiest to like.

I am happy that you are working again and that Paul is working. For a long time after I came out here, I was uncomfortable about him, feeling that he was not at work and was disturbed for some reason. Then at last the beast wrote me and reported himself at work and all right.

You have a kind of power over my mind, Van Wyck, of making me think of what you are thinking, and so I got James[2] on my mind after you got to work at him. You may be interested to know my reactions to some solid weeks of James reading — the feeling of him as a man who never found anyone to love, who did not dare love. I really can't care much for any character after he gets through with it; he, in short, takes my love from me too.

---

[1] In the form in which it was finally published, *Horses and Men* ("the same book") contained all of the stories named in these two paragraphs except this one.
[2] Brooks's "Henry James: The First Phase," a portion of his later book, *The Pilgrimage of Henry James* (1925), had appeared in the May issue of the *Dial.*

I've a fancy — can it be true that he is the novelist of the haters? O[h], the thing infinitely refined and carried far into the field of intellectuality, as skillful haters find out how to do.

It is, you see, but a notion, but I thought it might interest you.

I am enthusiastic about Paul's theme — *The Port of New York;* [3] the title is inspired.

Your garden does sound inviting. When will I be where I may talk now and then with the few men who give me most?

I'm working steadily on the book *Straws* and have a new novel [4] stirring and alive in me. I hope strongly I shall be able to get into it this fall and winter.

My regards to Mrs. Brooks. If you get a chance, please insult Paul now and then because he does not write to me oftener.

82.   [RENO, JULY 30, 1923]

TO VAN WYCK BROOKS

Dear Van Wyck: After all, Van Wyck, the danger is not imminent.[1] The book is one that spreads out and out. I have to confine it. Get and keep it within a channel if I can.

Do I not know there has always been some of my work you do not like? But how could it be otherwise? I dare say if you and I were to see each other more closely, become really personally acquainted, which we never have quite, there would remain a difficulty.

As for myself, Van Wyck, I have seen so much of ugly, meaningless, drifting men that I have come to love the men I feel definitely at work; and when you write me of your feeling of being crowded inside, I am made happy by your letter. The feeling spreads a sense of richness, of fecundity over my consciousness of you just now, and I like that.

I want to settle down really and make myself a home somewhere soon, but Westport [2] has its difficulties. Cost, for one thing. You see, I can live more economically any number of other places. I have to consider that.

There are a lot of thing[s] I would like to talk with you about —

[3] Rosenfeld's *Port of New York*, a collection of critical essays on contemporary writers and artists, was published in 1924.

[4] *The Golden Circle,* which Anderson worked on during the spring of 1924 but never finished.

[1] In a previous letter Anderson had asked Brooks to read *Straws* when it was finished.

[2] At this time Karl Anderson, Paul Rosenfeld, and Brooks were living in Westport, Connecticut.

the attitude of the artist, for one thing. In your *Twain* you came so near getting what I felt about the man, but you did miss an essential thing, some way.

Do you know I had, Van Wyck, a feeling that it was just the artist in Twain you in some way resented? There was somewhat the sense of a just judge trying a criminal, rather than the sympathetic friend or lover.

Can we understand at all, ever, where we do not love?

Perhaps all that struggling side of James you will feel more fully. He is more of your own world, isn't he? Twain was more of my world.

You see, in my book — which, after all, I think I shall not call *Straws*, but *A Modernist Notebook* — I am frankly daring to proclaim myself the American Man.

I mean by that to take all into myself if I can — the salesmen, businessmen, foxy fellows, laborers, all among whom I have lived. I do get the feeling that I, in a peculiar way and because of the accident of my position in letters, am a kind of composite essence of it all.

And actually there are days when people by thousands drift in and out of me. On a recent day here when I walked in the streets, this actual physical feeling of being completely *en rapport* with every man, woman, and child along a street wherein I walked became so intense that I had to go hide myself, to rest a little.

I speak of this because, when the feeling has leaked over into expression in my work, you have so often said you didn't understand what I was talking about.

I want you to understand more than I can say.

And, God knows, I don't say this as an apology for what is not fully [?functional] in my work. No one can be more conscious of the failure of the greater part of it than I am.

But I do want you, Van Wyck, to feel for James and his difficulties; give yourself wholly to James. I can't help asking that you do it more fully than you did when you wrote of Twain. With love

83.   [?RENO, AUGUST 4, 1923]

To GEORGIA O'KEEFFE

Dear Georgi[a] O'Keeffe: I got your letter yesterday and a very fine one from Alfred a few days ago. Well enough I know what you must have felt this year, seeing the man so many of us love wearing himself out. Sometimes when I saw him and you at your own show and how he so patiently worked with the stupid people who came in, it weari[?ed] me and made me half ill.

Surely I know I haven't any of his patience and would in many cases have kicked out of the room people I saw him working with so patiently. There is one person I shall always remember, just the figure of heavy, pompous stupidity standing on his two heavy legs like a bull, and before him the small, tired, intense figure of Stieglitz trying to tell that man something of his own delicately fine feeling about the artist's work.

I wanted to cry and wanted to swear, and I couldn't bear looking at the sight, so went away. There was something in it of the whole story of the artist and his life. Ye gods!

And later the body of that sensitive man shattered by pain. I am afraid I knew it would happen.

I am at this book, the one about which I wrote Alfred the other day. I want to dedicate it to him when it is published, if I may. The truth is I owe something I'll hardly be able to repay to you both.

I rather fancied you might like *Many Marriages*. Perhaps I'm getting a little better hold of the longer form. That is what I have wanted. To get the longer form well in hand and then pour the tale into it as wine in a vessel. We'll see. It's job enough, God knows, to keep me at work the rest of my life.

Some of the book of tales to be published this fall Alfred will like, as he and I share our passion for race horses. I would like him to read, when they come, "I'm a Fool" and "The Man Who Became a Woman."

As for this book in hand, it's still on the knees of the gods, delicately balanced there between good and bad, perhaps. I should really have something to say. Stieglitz, Paul, Brooks, Frank, so many others have as a kind of gift so much I have struggled for, am still struggling for. I don't so much want to tell of anything accomplished as I want to tell the tale of a journey toward understanding of whatever may be beautiful and fine in life, my own life and other lives.

And I hope you are working. Love to you both

84. [RENO, AUGUST 6, 1923]

To ALFRED STIEGLITZ

Dear Alfred Stieglitz: What a nut I am, not being more clear. The book I want to dedicate to you is not the *Horses and Men* book,[1] but

---

[1] *Horses and Men* was dedicated to Theodore Dreiser.

the book on which I am now at work [2] and that belongs to you much more fully.

In this book I am trying to tell, as plainly and clearly as I can, the story of a man — myself — who found out just about what you have outlined in your letter today.

You see, dear man, I have been a long time finding out just that people are really innocent, and it may be that much more than you know of what I have found out has come to me because of a growing awareness of you. Since I have known you, your figure has been standing all the time a little more and more clear.

You see, the book in question (I may call it *A Modernist Notebook*) is an attempt at a man's story of his adventures with men. The man is puzzled. There is no definite leadership for him.

What he knows after a time is that, while a man may become aware of the innocence of people in general, he cannot quite love that innocence itself. It does not reach far enough. One wants comrades, grown men such as I have come to feel you, and Paul [3] too.

We have together the love of horses. In my own boyhood I went to them, lived with them, was groom to running and trotting horses, now I know, because they were the most beautiful things about me.

But it did not suffice. Will not suffice. The horse is the horse, and we are men.

And it is just because I feel that way I waited for this book as being your book, most essentially. I should have made it clearer. You see, *Horses and Men* is the book of another year, put behind me now, but just coming toward others in the form of a book.

While this book is just forming now, and forming at a time when I am most aware of you.

I believe I have selected the right book to bear your name on the title page, because I believe it will have in it the most of you in me.

85.   [?RENO, AFTER AUGUST 21, 1923]

To MARY AUSTIN [1]

Dear Mary Austin: Perhaps I had to be for a time out in the West before I could know the people and things you write about. I shall look

---

[2] *A Story Teller's Story* was dedicated to Alfred Stieglitz.
[3] Paul Rosenfeld.

[1] Mary Austin (1868–1934), American writer on primitive peoples.

up *American Rhythm* [2] the next time I am in some place where the book may be had. I may see you before I leave the West, but when that may be I do not know.

I like particularly your own writing about wandering people, and there was one thing of yours called "The Field" [3] I loved very much.

Do not be annoyed that I have been so long finding you out, will you? I am such a long time finding anything out.

Jacques Copeau [4] and several others have tried to get me interested in writing drama, but whenever I go to the theater, I shudder at the notion. I've a fancy myself that anything I have to give can be given as a tale teller as well as any other way. God knows, I have yet enough to learn about that.

I am sorry you have been ill. Have been myself recovering from nerves. They go along more steadily now. You may be sure I shall write you when I have got my hands on *The American Rhythm*.

May I thank both Mabel Luhan [5] and yourself for the invitation to come in and see you? I may, one of these days, be wandering past. Sincerely

86.   [RENO, SEPTEMBER, 1923]

To FERDINAND AND CLARA SCHEVILL [1]

Dear Ferdinand & Clara: I did write you a letter some weeks ago and wonder you did not get it. It has been an odd year for me. First, I was, as you know, quite shattered. I worked, but rather desperately. At any rate, I had managed at last to be honest in an unhappy position, but such virtue gives but little consolation.

I came west to Nevada, hoping to be able to get a divorce out here. I shall hope to do that. If it is done and when it is done, I shall go for a time to the coast.

The mountains and deserts have done much for me. It is a long ways

[2] *The American Rhythm* by Mary Austin was published in 1923.

[3] Presumably a reference to "My Neighbour's Field" in *The Land of Little Rain,* Boston, 1903.

[4] Jacques Copeau (1878–), French critic, actor, manager, and producer, who brought his Vieux Columbier Théâtre to New York in 1917–1918. In 1924 he announced his "retirement," but in 1926 he was back in harness.

[5] Mabel Dodge Luhan (1879–), who married Antonio Luhan in 1923 and lived in Taos, New Mexico.

[1] Professor Ferdinand Schevill (1868–) of the History Department, University of Chicago, and Mrs. Schevill (Clara), devoted friends of Anderson.

from those I love, a long ways from those who are interested in what interests me, from music, painting, good talk.

The deserts are themselves, as you perhaps know, altogether lovely. Often enough I wish myself quite uncivilized, a Piute or a Washoe. I'm not, however. Civilization has taken too deep a hold on me.

I want something, naturally, that you two have, man and woman love that is also comradeship. When I saw you that afternoon in New York, fresh from that boat, God, how much I loved you both, what you were as individuals, what you were together. God bless you.

As for work, I have tried to do this book, big (physically), on the position of the literary artist in American life. It is outside my field, but I did want to have a kind [of] say. There is a chance I may say something that will mean something to some younger Sherwood Anderson, someday.

There is a book of tales to be published next month called *Horses and Men.* You may like some of them.

As for this present book on which I work now, it has been rewritten several times. The physical labor has been tremendous. Never did I tear up so much.

I've a fancy that the intellectuals are in for their inning. Perhaps I shall be pushed aside. Well, it doesn't too much matter. There is plenty of work to do at any rate and not too much time in which to do it.

I'm pretty well, rather fat. I spend a good many hours every day out of doors. And I love you both.

87.   [RENO, EARLY OCTOBER, 1923]

To VAN WYCK BROOKS

Dear Brooks: When, sometime ago, I ask[ed] you to take a look at this new book of mine, I did not realize what a whale it was going to be. There are almost 150,000 words of it, and I could not ask you to wade through any such pile. You have enough on your hands as things stand, and an unfinished book waiting. I should so much rather have you spend your time writing so that I may later read. I'll send it along to Otto Liveright,[1] who is to show it to Harper's. They may want a part of it for the magazine.[2]

The book has you in it with many others. It contains no criticism of

[1] Anderson's New York literary agent.
[2] *A Story Teller's Story* was not published in *Harper's.*

you, but expresses the regret of a Middle Western workman that you seemed unwilling or unable to respond to his hunger for more intimate contact, as fellow workman, with some of the more cultured men of the East.

As for the woman's article in *Dial*,[3] I did not in any way connect you with it and did not take her quotation of you as intended to suggest you had said that particular thing of me. I do know, of course, that you have been out of sympathy with some of my work that has meant most to me and that after some years I still think first-rate work, but I can't very well blame you for that.

I might quarrel with such a statement as applied to Lawrence [4] if I had you here to state at length my point of view, which is that no man can be bogged in immaturity who has done as much good work as Mr. Lawrence.

My dear Brooks, isn't there at least a chance that the fear of emotional response to life may be as much a sign of immaturity as anything else? It does seem so to me.

I really think the article in *Dial* was ill-natured and ill-mannered and largely made up of the fragments of ill-natured things that have been said of me ever since I began working. What puzzles me is the *Dial*. The article is so evidently incompetent. Lord, I could have written so much sharper and cleaner criticism of myself. What the *Dial* is up to I can't quite make out. They give me their Prize and buy my novel and publish it, and then seem to devote themselves to a kind of apology to the public for me.

Of course, I want more than anything else freedom for you or any other workman who really wants to work. It has been an odd year for me. I have been more or less separated from all the workmen I know except Stieglitz, who has written me often and some very beautiful and helpful letters this year. Poor man, he has had a year of suffering, a part of the time being unable to lift his arms because of pain.

I myself have had an unhappy year. I think often that a good many people, perhaps you, dear Brooks, among them, think of me as a mere reckless adventurer, but I have been up to something with my life and work. I am not a mere rudderless ship, and now and then I do make a port.

[3] See Alyse Gregory, "Sherwood Anderson," *Dial*, LXXV, 242–246 (September, 1923).
[4] D. H. Lawrence, the English novelist.

Well, I do know that you have and always have had much to give me, and I've got some of it. I'll be glad of more. There are not many sincere workmen in the country, and in New York in particular there is so often just a superficial slinging of some smart saying at the head of a man, when understanding or the inclination to try to understand fails. But you know these things as well as I do and, I dare say, have suffered from them as much. It is a part of the artist's life, and I escape a good deal by not seeing the more ill-natured and superficial slings.

For me, anyway, work looms ahead, plenty of it. I really do begin to see a great many of my own failings and shortcomings as a workman and am at least trying all the time to shake them off.

And I'll be glad when I can be again where I can see and talk to men whose aims are somewhat like my own.

The book is done for better or worse and will be going off to Liveright, I think, sometime next week. With love

88.   [RENO, AFTER OCTOBER 15, 1923]

To ROGER SERGEL [1]

Dear Roger L. Sergel: Thank you much for your fine generous letter, and thank Mrs. Sergel for me. She is the first, I think, who has spoken well of that poem,[2] and her praise touches me deeply.

I am glad you particularly liked "The Egg." It is to my mind about my best shot. I like "Untold Lie" in *Winesburg* and "Out of Nowhere in[to] Nothing" in *Triumph* next best. I hope you will like my new book of tales half as much as I liked your fine novel. Have you done many short tales? There is a little more chance of selling them to magazines than there used to be, and if you are always needing money, as I am, that means something.

Have this year written a long book called *A Story Teller's Story* that Harper's may publish a part of in the magazine. I fancy you will find it rather fun.

Do not know when I shall come East, but hope someday I may see and talk with both you and Mrs. Sergel.

[1] Roger Sergel, at this time an assistant professor of English at the University of Pittsburgh and later head of The Dramatic Publishing Company in Chicago, became one of Anderson's closest friends. For his novel, *Arlie Gelston*, see Letter 90, note 1.

[2] In a letter from Roger Sergel, October 15, 1923, Mrs. Sergel is cited as saying the closing passage of "The Man with a Trumpet" (in *The Triumph of the Egg*) was the noblest in modern poetry.

Are you on another novel? Sincerely

[P.S.] If you have any short thing you want to sell, I suggest you get into touch with

> Otto Liveright
> 2 West 43rd St.
> New York

He has done well for me as an agent.

89.   [RENO, NOVEMBER 11, 1923]

To ALFRED STIEGLITZ

Dear Alfred Stieglitz: I am sure you will find another copy of the book at your brother's house in New York. Am glad you like "Man Who Became a Woman." Perhaps O'Keeffe will not. I remember once she told [me] she was afraid of "niggers."

The fall weather here too is glorious. Cold mountain nights followed by clear, warm days. There is a strange place here where hot water bubbled up out of the ground. Back of it deep gullies penetrate into the mountains and pine trees grow. The soil is white like chalk, then an intense yellow, then fiery red or green. From the mouth of such a small canyon one can see over vast stretches of sagebush desert to other mountains in the distance. There will be one line (5 miles long perhaps) and not a break in it. The eye follows it with a kind of intense inner satisfaction. You or O'Keeffe would get something from it, make it live. I've tried, but can't seem to catch it.

The colors change constantly even as you look at them. Well, O'Keeffe knows. She has lived in such a country.

I keep working. After the long book was finished and went off, I got off a short tale, then another that did not fun[c]tion and had to be put aside. Now I am at work on a third, longer one.

One misse[s] most here the graciousness of life, a half hour's walk and talk with Paul, coming in to see you two. Went to a dinner party the other night. Such food. Here I have had trout, sage hen, quail, venison, wild goose, wild duck — such food.

And the Basque shepherds hereabout have wine.

But I presume one forgets how unsophisticated, childlike, crude, life remains outside an artist class. Talk of food, of hunting, anecdotes. No real talk at all. One wonders how life goes on and on, men and women not caring much for anything in particular.

A nice letter from Paul yesterday. As happens sometimes when I publish a new book, strange, lonely, defeated people write to me. They want — love, I fancy. "You will understand my need," they say.

It opens wide fields. One can't come close to so many. You know, I fancy. One has to save some strength for work, hoping that out of it a little beauty and meaning may come. One can't be a preacher or an evangelist.

How long I shall be here yet I don't know. I'm pretty happy but deuced lonely sometimes for the men and women I love and admire. Love to you both

90.   [RENO, DECEMBER, 1923]

To ROGER SERGEL

Dear Roger Sergel: Have been reading *Arlie* [1] again and with growing admiration of the job you have done. It is very finely done.

When I first read the ms., I hurried to get off a letter to Ben Huebsch asking certain impertinent questions. "How old is this man?" "Has he money?" Etc.

Personally and physically I am a very strong man. I know a little of what an artist among us has to face — misunderstanding often enough, most of all the patronage of inferior men.

I couldn't help hope you had money and, by that token, liberty and leisure. Well, you have an understanding wife and your children. That is much. I also have three children, but cannot live where they are. I see them but two or three times a year.

I want so much for you the quiet leisure that would enable you to develop your talent. You aren't going to get it, I'm afraid.

Now I rather think — in America, at least — survival and development is largely a matter of nerve force, of survival. It may always have been so everywhere. God only knows.

At any rate, you do not face what Dreiser did. Now I think it true that no man can do good work among us without its being known. A small body, at least, of intelligent criticism does grow up. One has to remember that Dreiser waited ten years after *Sister Carrie* before he began to get recognition from Hackett, Dell, Mencken, and others.

I have myself a notion that prose writing can't go on just stating. It has to become more sensually aware of life, color, sound, form. There

---

[1] *Arlie Gelston*, a novel by Sergel, published by Huebsch in November, 1923.

must be flame and play too; the fabric, the feel of surfaces must be consciously sought after.

You pleased me, I think, most of all by liking *Many Marriages*. It was an attempt at a rather gaudy, colorful play with the material and in so many places was taken too realistically. You will know what I mean.

At any rate, Sergel, you have now *Arlie* as a sound piece of work to stand upon. It will be more and more, as time goes on and as the immediate quibbling that comes dies away, a foundation to yourself and a fort from which you may sally forth.

Indeed I would like to see you both at Pittsburgh or in any other possible place, but now all my plans are vague.

Do not take your leisure, but when you are in the mood, do write me of your thoughts and impulses.

91.   [RENO, DECEMBER 7, 1923]

To ALFRED STIEGLITZ AND GEORGIA O'KEEFFE

Dear People: Now you are back in town. Yesterday I got Alfred's letter about the storm and the snow over everything and the barn in the still night.

I have been in a state — horrible depression. It comes on sometimes like a disease. What is it? One knows that when work is put out, little spiteful things will be said here and there. One tries to close the ears, go along, but there are always people who write spiteful letters too.

I went off on a long automobile ride with four men — a marvelous country — long, sweeping valleys, 30, 40, 50 miles across and the air so clear you could see trees and now and then a horseman moving on the far side.

The men went to see about buying a mine, and we stopped at Goldfield, a place famous for fights, gambling, prostitutes, herded like cattle into what was called a bullpen. There the ore taken out was so rich that the miner often concealed $500, $1,000, or even $1,500 in his pockets and dinner pail when he came from work. Downtown he went to drink and gamble it away or spend it in the terrible women places. The wealth seemed inexhaustible.

And then "bang," the veins in the mines faulted, were lost. Recently half the town has burned down.

Men wander about, bearded old fellows, hoping for another such glorious, riotous outpouring of gold. I found men from my own home town, from New York, London, who had been there 30 or 40 years waiting. They do not dig, they wait.

We came back through a marvelous mountain country. What color, forms.

With companionship, other artists, one might dream on in such a place, happy for a lifetime.

The men in the car thought mostly of gold, talked of gold. They relaxed out of that into rather unclean talk, whiskey, rank cigars.

One lives so much in an imaginative world, imagined people, crude often enough, but with tender realities in them too; then one is shocked, hurt by the immaturity, the bad-boyishness of men. Why will they not let themselves see the beauty in things about, in one's own work sometimes, too? Each man is afraid of his neighbor, outdoes him in vulgarity to seem manly.

I know all in advance, always, but each time come out of my fanciful world hopeful, seeking comrades. My book[s], I think, go out seeking comrades for me.

Seems to me I have lost any sense I ever had of competitiveness. I shall do little enough, and there is much to do.

I work asking myself questions, challenging. Then the impulse to work comes again, and I am happy. Only so many of the finer, more beautiful people seem pretty far away now.

And if you but knew how grateful I am that you write, telling me of your own fine moments. Love to you both

[P.S.] Please do not kill yourself with work.

92.   [RENO, ?DECEMBER 16, 1923]

To FERDINAND SCHEVILL

Dear Man: I am using this child's copy paper because I find myself on Sunday morning in the provoking position of a scribbler short of paper and the stores closed. Still I want to write on things other than I had to write you yesterday. Perhaps the rest of my days I shall have to keep in touch with you by letter. I shall likely never live in Chicago again.

Naturally your interest in my craft touches me deeply. I am so made, Ferdinand, that I should have gone insane long since but for this devotion. For it I have sacrificed a lot, life with my own children, perhaps in the end the respect of that great body of people, simple and good, much of my work has offended.

It goes deep, the whole import of such an attitude as I have taken, into the structure of a man's life. To such a man as myself, who can only grow in expression, some of the expression is bound to miss fire.

One learns so slowly. Will the true balance come in the end? Perhaps not. What I may always be hungering for is the perfect artist who cannot exist.

One of the deep things I am sure T[ennessee] never realized was the harm in our relation to each other. Can you understand my saying, without my feeling her to blame, that these months away from her have done more to make me feel less assertive, combative, egotistical than I ever felt in her presence? Can you conceive of this being true and at the same time of my effect upon her being equally bad?

I feel, and more so now than ever, like one just coming to the foot of the hill one is to try to climb. I think it was that very reticent Joseph Conrad — who, I am afraid, would have little use for me, but for whom I have much use — who said that the writer only lived after he began writing,[1] and by that method of reckoning I am but 10 years old.

I think I wanted and have wanted to talk to you a little about *Many Marriages*. Perhaps it was boyish, an attempt at a kind of flaming going toward the flesh. My groundwork I perhaps laid too bare; time will tell. What I wanted was that a certain cold purity in the prose balance the nakedness. In some natures the balance was struck, but I am bound to say that in many, many more nothing came but revulsion. Perhaps people were unprepared for the Latin thing in me.

However, I do dare always to think that I must grow in work, that literally I only grow in work. Perhaps the bare truth is that T[ennessee] was sacrificed to that by some inner voice that said over and over, "Do it, do it."

Perhaps I shall be more and more isolated by all this. I want love. That you and Clara can manage to love me means more than you can know.

[1] See Conrad's *A Personal Record,* Harper and Brothers, 1912, p. 174: ". . . A writer is no older than his first published book. . . ."

93.   [RENO, ?DECEMBER 18, 1923]

To ROGER SERGEL

Dear Sergel: Please do not feel the necessity of writing when you might be scribbling. I want to answer your letter at once, but do not want you to feel you "owe me a letter." I write at once because I like to talk of our common craft. Here I get few or no literary reactions. It is pretty much, I fancy, all of America before there was any cultural bloom at all. Now the thing one needs in order to live and work here exists. Such a note as this one from you is the living expression of the thing needed.

As to the social implication of a story, my own mind simply does not work in that channel. My friend Paul Rosenfeld once said I had a deficient social sense. Like yourself I think storytelling worth-while in itself, for the sake just of storytelling, and one of the things that got me cleverly and beautifully.

That is workmanship. One can, I think, take for granted the fact that the storyteller knows the story he is trying to tell. Does he make me feel what he felt? That is surely the test.

I remember one evening sitting with a lot of men in the Coffee House in New York — we had all been drinking, carousing — rather cheap actresses, magazine illustrators, popular painters, popular novelists. A pretty bad lot in general, sold out and all that, but suddenly I found myself saying to myself, "These are my people." *

Don't you rather think, Sergel, the quality that makes people aware of "social implication" is and should be implicit in good work?

For example, I think of the man at B. F. Goodrich.[1] He is right and wrong both to think of the artist as unaware. Fancy a man's trying to give his work "social implication." I think that is just what some men, say Waldo Frank, does [sic], and it does something wholly bad to his work.

You see, when your Arlie[2] went downtown, rode about on streetcars, saw the movie man and had him up to her rooming house, I followed just her, felt with her, the distracted, lonely, puzzled something in her.

Of course it had social implication. What beautiful reality touched to life by an artist's fancy has not?

---

[1] In Sergel's letter, to which this is a reply, Sergel refers to "Pierce, a physiologist and author of texts, now with the B. F. Goodrich Co. in Akron, O."
[2] In *Arlie Gelston.*

The literary crowd in New York — you will come to know them someday — Wilson, Rascoe, Heywood Broun,[3] and the other rather superficial men — not mean — book-made men.

Then there are the Jews — Gilbert Seldes, Paul Rosenfeld, Alfred Stieglitz — intense men, not sour, very fine, in contrast to the men like Frank who have — they seem unable to get rid of it — something of the Jewish prophet spirit in them, preachers really and by just that much corrupt.

As for Huebsch, one of the most sincere, lovable men I have ever known, God bless him. Behind the door I would whisper you that I do not think too much of his artistic perception. He's a queer kind, has ideas, etc. You see, he's a single-taxer or something of the sort, makes bad puns, tells you at length how his one child said "go[o] goo," will occasionally bring out the damnedest dullest thing imaginable and declare it an artistic masterpiece; and all the time you grow more and more to love and respect him and to realize you would rather have him as your publisher selling 5,000 than some of the damned smart young men of the publishing world "putting you over" to the tune of 25,000.

There are other men and women there — Lawrence Gilman, Mary Colum,[4] I could name a half dozen — real people. You must live there someday for a time.

Between ourselves, I shall in the end live in New Orleans, a really lovely, leisurely American city. I hope to have a house there, near the harbor mouth, and have every day the joy of the ships and the niggers.

Harper's have rejected my big book for magazine publication and that knocks me out $3,000. It meant a tight year, but I'll slide along.

What I am glad to know about you is just that physical resiliency in you. Really I think, in large part, it comes to that now, the physical and nerve force to last until the inevitable resistance to a new force, such as you are, breaks down a little.

I used to tell myself years ago that it was a race between exhaustion of nerve force and the coming of a little leisure, not to be compelled to press.

God grant you may be on the right side of that. It is all I can ask for you, and my only notion in writing you as I did was a desire that you

---

[3] Heywood Broun (1888–1939) newspaper columnist and writer, on the staff of the New York *World* 1921–1928.

[4] Mrs. Padraic Colum, philosopher and critic, member of the staff of Columbia University.

learn, sooner than I did, not to be made too sore by the vast stupidity you will inevitably have to meet.

I guess you're safe. Your note has made me feel oddly happy for you. A good Christmas to you and Mrs. Sergel and the children.

* The implication of which being that I feel the need of the peculiar quality that marks the artist, value it more, even when corrupt, than I do the scientifically exact turn of mind, for the artist.

94.   [?RENO, AFTER DECEMBER 25, 1923]

To ROGER SERGEL

Dear Roger Sergel: I've a sort of notion that we haven't much kick coming, really. Lately I have been looking over some of the earlier American writing, such books as *The Hoosier Schoolmaster*,[1] much of Bret Harte, and a lot of Twain, Howells, etc. It seems pretty childlike in the light of more modern stuff, ugly approaches to human being, brutal humor without delicacy.

I've a notion also that all an artist dare ask is that there be other artists living and working in his medium in his time. This year I have had you and the Negro Toomer[2] added to my list of realities. I think that makes it a pretty rich year.

I am older, in years, but I am sure that it has meant something in your work that Dreiser was here before you. Toomer, I am sure, can do a real book younger in his life because I have worked here.

I spent all those years floundering about. No approach I found satisfied me. Like other Americans, from the beginning, I had to go abroad. I was perhaps 35 years old when I first found the Russian prose writers. One day I picked up Turgenev's *Annals of a Sportsman*. I remember how my hands trembled as I read the book. I raced through the pages like a drunken man.

Afterward in Tolstoy, Dostoevski I found the same thing. I did not want to write like these men. The truth is I found in them the love of human life, tenderness, a lack of the eternal preaching and smart-aleckness so characteristic of much Western writing, nearly all of it, in fact.

Artists had become respectable men; there was no daring, no taking

[1] Published in 1871 by Edward Eggleston (1837–1902).
[2] According to *Negro Literature in America* (1950) Jean Toomer was born in Washington, D. C., 1894.

on their shoulders the strange sins of others because the same sins were theirs. It was as though all English and French prose craftsmen were a little ashamed of their craft.

What I have felt all the time is that every new workman is something added and that every new man will help also to make it possible for future artists here to begin working at 25 instead of 35 or 40. There will be a greater stretch of room for individual development in the craft.

To be sure, the country is spread out; men at work do not see each other. We all have these times of feeling lost in a huge empty place. The novel on which I am now at work is really an attempt to express that feeling in a man.

I myself am a mad letter writer. Often when I go to my desk in the morning, I write 3, 4, 6 letters, to one of my sons, to a friend, to anyone. That came also from lack of contact through many years. In Chicago I used often to sit all day writing letters, sending them out sometimes, sometimes tearing them up. It was, I fancy, but an attempt to reach out of the narrowness and bleakness of my life to other artists, imagined when they did not to my knowledge exist.

My first attempt to come a little closer to Dreiser was a failure. The same thing on him used in *Horses and Men*, when published years ago in *Little Review*,[3] made him mad. The blessed old horse had just fallen in love with a new woman perhaps, and it made him mad that I called him old, which he was, I fancy, always. Sandburg isn't much better. He is a silent, didactic old warrior who always seems to want to knock someone down — really sweet and sound at bottom though.

The rest of them in Chicago, except Ben Hecht [4] now and then when he isn't being a smarty, are just talking. The smartiness will perhaps defeat Ben. It may have already.

As for the Farrar type, they are funny — will bully you if they can, lick your hand if you don't watch out. With them it's a lack of force really, and they know it. Sometimes they make you want to cry. Read Edmund Wilson in the last *Vanity Fair*.[5] You can't dislike such men when you see them.

[3] "Dreiser," *Little Review*, III, 5–6 (April, 1916); in *Horses and Men*, pp. xi–xii, slightly altered.

[4] Ben Hecht was connected with the *Chicago Literary Times* until 1925, and published *1001 Afternoons in Chicago* in 1923.

[5] Edmund Wilson, "Wanted: A City of the Spirit: Reflections upon the Spiritual Problems Which Confront the Younger Generation in America," *Vanity Fair*, XXI, 63, 94 (January, 1924).

God knows, you can't live and talk with them either.

Paul Rosenfeld and old Alfred Stieglitz are sweet and sound Jews.

To tell the truth, I've found a lot of men. Don't ask too much, Sergel. The staleness exists, the flatness. Often enough it gets into a man and infects him like a disease. It is a disease, I think, crawling fear of what? Life, I fancy.

Eternal lack of force taking itself out in smartness or cleverness and thinking they've done something. One doesn't need to give a damn. Perhaps it's good. Anything is better than the childlike faith in sentimental nonsense of a generation ago. New men coming on who have force will discard [it] quicker.

I handed Mrs. Sergel's article [6] to a keen friend. When she read it, a look of delight came over her face. She said nothing of whether or not I deserved such fine praise. All she talked about was what a really fine person the writer was. She had it in her head the writer was a man. "How good it is to know there are as nice people as that in the world," she said.

What I really feel badly about is that your book didn't sell for the simple reason that it would have given you more leisure to write me. Huebsch kept me posted. I knew it wasn't going. What I want above all is that you do not let that depress you. Sincerely

95.   [?BERKELEY, CALIFORNIA, JANUARY 10, 1924]

To THEODORE DREISER

Dear Dreiser: I was damned glad for your letter. In reality I doubt if you know what you have meant to a lot of other writing men in America. When I wrote the thing in *Horses and Men* and the introduction to *Free*,[1] I had a strong feeling of fear afterwards. "Perhaps," I thought, "he won't like it."

It is difficult and delicate business, this writing of another man you so much admire.

Are you quite settled in New York? I shall be in the West until May or June. If you are going back to the West before that, let me know so that I may call on you. As ever

[6] Mrs. Sergel had reviewed *Horses and Men* in a book review column which she conducted in the Fargo (North Dakota) *Forum.*

[1] Dreiser's *Free and Other Stories,* first published in 1918, was reissued in the Modern Library with Anderson's introduction that same year.

96.   [RENO, NEVADA, ?FEBRUARY 22, 1924]

TO PAUL ROSENFELD

Dear Paul: How long it seems since there has been word from you.
Do you work steadily? I hope so.

About a month ago I had an attack of flu and later a relapse that has
kept me from work for a month. Perhaps the life here, its lack of anything to feed upon, its going on so much longer than was necessary, has
got my nerves a little worn too.

I have worked some. The thing[1] in February *Mercury* was done out
here and is a part of my book *The Story Teller's Story*. Also *Century*[2]
bought a fragment.

I go along storing something up, I think. Perhaps my whole outlook
has to open a little in response to a kind of opening out of my inner
life, having the woman in it, wanting her there.

I try to have patience, although sometimes the time left of my full
vigor seems short for what I want to do.

Now it is a novel I want to call *The Golden Circle*.

And then I want to do a Lincoln.[3] That has been a buried treasured
dream, and I begin a little to scrawl on it. Do not say much of it to
others. It may not come off.

During my time here I have soaked myself in every scrap of Lincoln
I could come by.

The thing projected is not a life, but an attempt to make felt the final
opening out of that strange, grotesque, sweet man.

I think you and I have talked before of the need of great themes.
Lincoln is that. Always I have felt him, dreamed him, thought of
him.

I would like to do my bit at the idea of the perpetuation of such a
theme, at which artists of other generations might try too. He did, I am
sure, at the last, mature, come into being. I want to tell the story of his
doing that if it is possible.

Do read the story in *Mercury*. Perhaps you will not remember the

---

[1] "Caught," in *American Mercury*, I, 165–176 (February, 1924) — the "Epi-
logue" to *A Story Teller's Story*.

[2] "When I Left Business for Literature" appeared in the *Century*, CVII, 489–
496 (August, 1924), and forms pp. 298–312 of *A Story Teller's Story*.

[3] Anderson never completed his projected book on Lincoln. His "Lincoln Fragment" was finally published in Paul Rosenfeld's *The Sherwood Anderson Reader*
(1947).

afternoon when you, Brooks, and I went to Kenneth Miller [*sic*] [4] and later to a little restaurant, and anyway there was no reason either of you should have known of my own desolation during those hours. Perhaps I got it from Miller, something fine and at the same time cheap in him.

Anyway the tale in *Mercury* got in some way born into definite shape in me that afternoon and was written out here.

I had the chance to write in O'Keeffe's catalog and was really brokenhearted that the chance came when I was ill and dull. With love

97.   [RENO, EARLY MARCH, 1924]

To ROBERT MORSS LOVETT [1]

Dear Robert Lovett: Your review of *Horses and Men* in *Dial* has stirred up in me anew a desire I have long had to write you a note. It would be infinitely nicer if I could talk to you.

As for the review, I have no quarrel with it of course. You have always been wholeheartedly generous with me.

However, you have written several reviews and articles after books of mine, and in all of them I have thought there was — in minor, but to me important directions — a misunderstanding of what I had aimed at and sometimes, it seemed to me, achieved.

You make a point, which you have made before, of my having sacrificed intelligence to the emotional. Is that quite sound? Can emotional surrender to a theme get anywhere without guiding intelligence?

Add to this your stricture about my taking people who "are mussed up."

Dear friend, do you really know anyone who is not mussed up?*

Naturally I prefer, in life and in art, drawing close to rather sensitive people. Can a man be at all sensitive to life and be quite clear and unriled?

It would seem to me a kind of stupidity to be so.

And does not the very point you make — that one person chose a particular story as having been my best, while another is untouched by that story and deeply by another — imply that the writer of all these various tales has used his head also?

[4] Presumably Kenneth Hayes Miller (1876–), painter and etcher, with a studio on East 14th Street, New York.

[1] Robert Morss Lovett (1870–), long a member of the Department of English of the University of Chicago, literary critic and novelist.

You see, I am puzzled by you, frankly.

The wide divergence of opinions you have heard are, of course, even more apparent to me. Ferdinand [2] and Paul Rosenfeld (two widely different types of men, I think) were both deeply moved by "An Ohio Pagan" in this book, a tale that apparently left you untouched.

You do also take for granted the failure of the novels. That seems strange to me. Both *Poor White* and *Many Marriages* seemed to me to do what I wanted them to do. One does not go from the novel to the short tale for any reason but that some themes offer themselves for long, involved treatment, others for direct, simple treatment.

You see, I am not quarreling with you, dear man. I am interested to develop from you, someday, an amplification of what is only formula, if it can be found written out in a form that will answer for such men as myself.

P.S. Perhaps after all our difference is one of technical formula. Perhaps you do have a formula on which you may depend. I wish I had. Your saying definitely that the novels are "failures" does imply, doesn't it, that you know they are?

And yet how deeply they have touched many people, how completely they have sometimes seemed to answer.

Not often, I grant you.

I certainly do not wish to be impertinent, dear Lovett, but I wish also the definite implied [*sic*] in any [ms. torn] article I have seen of yours. Perhaps I shall have to wait until some day when I can walk and talk with you. Sincerely

* Perhaps the word "mussed" is too strong. I mean to imply that the general mess reacts on the lives of all sensitive people. That I try to make the implication of my tales.

98.   BERKELEY, CALIFORNIA, APRIL 25, 1924

To JEROME BLUM

Dear Jerry: What I suppose I feel about this matter we have talked about on several occasions — that is, as to just being a man, going along, looking at things, not trying to be a big artist or any such thing. Well, talking about it all is a little like handling a flower. It gets wilted and soiled. One speaks of the matter and then, right away, feels a little

[2] Ferdinand Schevill.

stuffy. I can't tell exactly why I think this is true. Perhaps it is simply because I am too unsure of myself. I'm rather afraid to do it.

When you are in love with a woman, you find yourself unable to speak of her directly. When you want to speak of her to your friend, you adopt subterfuges. "She was a Chinese girl I knew once. I saw her once when I was in San Francisco." To speak of her directly is impossible. One cannot say: "Her name is Mary. She lives in Q Street."

That is why I think now you find me a little inclined to dodge. You have got nearer my inner works than most people. I'll tell you that. Isn't that about all I can tell you?

The one thing I detest, because it makes me feel detestable, is preaching or being wise man or seer.

The whole secret lies in the fact that it is also my problem to be "just the man, walking along, seeing, smelling." Could it not be that the more fool reputation a man gets the harder the job?

99.   [BERKELEY, CALIFORNIA, APRIL 28, 1924]

To ALFRED STIEGLITZ

Dear Stieglitz: A peculiarly emotional evening, in which you were a part. An etcher and his wife, together with a painter and his wife, to dinner at Elizabeth's sister's.[1] The etcher's wife a devoted admirer of your work. I think you have met her, a Mrs. Partridge, a fine, simple, clean person.

I got out your things for her, also a little thing Maurer[2] recently sent.

Then it started, as it so often does.

One can't blame the etcher and painter, men who have gone patiently along learning dogma, but they get hurt, and something gets all jangled up inside. They usually try to convince themselves that the moderns are all a lot of fakers who have put something over and suddenly grown rich.

One doesn't know quite what to say, seeing the inner struggle of these people. Often I see the same thing going on in writers.

For the most part I go softly along by out-of-the-way paths and try to just look on, but when the painters I know are concerned, when you are concerned, I spit out.

---

[1] Elizabeth Prall's sister, Dorothea, was the wife of Max Radin, professor of law at the University of California.

[2] Alfred Maurer (1868–1932), American painter.

Then I'm sorry. It's too easy. I keep thinking of the etcher lying awake in his bed later (he went away with a white face).

Elizabeth cried after she got upstairs, because people could be so easily hurt and could be so deeply hurt by beauty as by ugliness.

I suppose you have got moved into a new place. Are you both well?

I put my novel aside and went into my Abraham Lincoln. Of course, I am not trying to write a biography of him. What I did was to read everything I could find about him, got as nearly as I could the structure of his story from the facts. Now I am frankly going to make my own story, am doing that.

He gets close to me, always has, but I want him on my own terms, as I understand such a man, having come from the same kind of background.

I've a notion it will be a book, in the end.

Love and health to you both.

[P.S.] Elizabeth and I got married,[3] but you know that.

I feel like a man recovering from a long illness, every day more ready for work now.

100.   2597 BERKELEY, CALIFORNIA [?MAY 24, 1924]

To ROGER SERGEL

Dear Sergel: I think one of the strangest things I feel is the necessity of keeping alive some personal touch with a few men about the country who have not grown too weary. New York this year has seemed strange to me. Even Alfred Stieglitz writes of death,[1] and others of the cheapness of existence. Perhaps my touch has been too much with older men. The sense of life slips easily out of the grasp of Americans apparently.

All of which but to say that my desire to keep touch with you is that I feel you alive. One likes this feeling of other men at work in other places. I like the figure of you walking in the path along the hill at the edge of Pittsburgh and noting the kind of terrain and beauty of the black river bottoms and the smoke lying there — like the thought of dreams and impulses surging up in you.

[3] On April 5, 1924.

---

[1] In a letter dated May 21, 1924.

The desire to write surges up, but often you are too tired or distracted with other things to quite follow out your impulses.

However, you keep on and slowly things get done. It is the way things go with all of us. On the whole I think we are pretty lucky. People are immature, but on the whole not unkindly. To be sure, in New York, where the competition in surface smartness is pretty keen, it all gets pretty cheap and nasty often enough.

Out here in California I get the same sense of the whole thing missed by painters and artists that I got in the desert. An etcher came to see me, bringing his etchings, a very skillful craftsman with his eye on Whistler.

As though Jimmy Whistler immersed in his London & Paris had anything to do with these warm hills, rolling sensuous hills, full of milk. Some of them almost give a man an erection they are so voluptuously beautiful.

And all the dead-tired Indians and feeble, half-sick neurotics, calling themselves artists stumbling about on them. Lord, it's a revelation.

I'll do the Lincoln book pretty slowly, as I want to really get something if I can. It means finding out all I can about what the men around [him] — Seward, Hill Lamon, Herndon, the rest — thought, and then discarding the most of it.

My notion is that when he died and that second-rate man Chase said flamboyantly, "Now he belongs to the ages," he really did say a truth, in the sense that he is our heroic figure.

It would be nice if each age wrote books about him showing the reaction of each age to such a man.

I could talk to you days about painting, might even get you started painting. I do it. It does something, I'm sure, to the sense for prose surfaces too. However, I mustn't start. I'd be writing pages and pages more. A good summer of work to you.

By the way, and quite without anyone's knowing, could you find out if the *Phantasmus*[2] crowd really has money? My summer plans rather hang on my getting my money in from them. Have you any friend in the know there who could find out for me? They will be owing me about $3,000. It's a rather vital matter to me, but I don't want them to know I have fears or doubts. My best regards to Mrs. Sergel

[2] A "little magazine" edited in Pittsburgh, May–July/August, 1924, by J. J. Edmonds. It was to have serialized *A Story Teller's Story*, but collapsed for lack of financial support. See the following letters.

101.

To ALFRED STIEGLITZ

Dear Stieglitz: Got your letter sent here and the one to Berkeley. Things have been moving rapidly. In the first place, I found out that it was too late to withdraw the book[1] from Huebsch. It was already, unknown to me, in type. In a way I was glad.

The truth is that Huebsch at any rate is not vulgar, and as a man I admire him. The others, hearing I was free, wrote and wired me. Good offers were made.

But about it all, in some way, a kind of unctuous greasiness. If you and O'Keeffe were here and could see the letters, you would understand. Most publishers, like most dealers, are rotten really. It makes me realize what you have meant to the painters — someone to take them to the public in a clean way.

I came to New Orleans by way of Chicago, and Huebsch met me there. He showed me stuff, Lordy! The great thing, it seems, that book-dealers and others could not swallow from me was *Many Marriages*. Huebsch has had his troubles too.

Do you remember how for a long time O'Keeffe hated to have people see her things? They were intimate and beautiful, like beautiful children. The greasy, vulgar people, the thought of such people coming into contact with her work, made her feel ill.

Most of the publishers are like that. And they put it all on such high grounds — artistic merit, etc.

As though they knew anything or cared anything for artistic merit. They take that way to ask you, demand, that you pander.

Lecturing I can do. While the people do not buy my books, I am in some odd way a figure in their minds. I stand for something. They wonder vaguely what it is. They will, I believe, crowd to hear me talk.

And I shall talk well and straight. I'll give them something worthwhile for their money. I shall not go around, recite a few poems, sing a few songs, read a story. I'll tell them what men like you have been up to all their lives. I'll have a chance to tell them of real painters and real writers. In two months, perhaps, I shall be able to earn enough to work the rest of the year.

That's my program.

[1] *A Story Teller's Story.*

I'm sorry to hear about O'Keeffe, that she is not very well. Man, take care of yourself. She needs you, as we all do. And I know you'll make her rest and sleep. Make her take quantities of milk and eggs.

Did I tell you of the lecture at [the] University of California? Although my books had not sold much out there, 1,500 people came to hear me talk. They could not all get into the hall; so I had to give the lecture twice in one afternoon. Over 300 people waited 1½ hours for me in a nearby hall.

People feel no obligation to buy books. It isn't their fault. Art seems cheap to them, because almost always it is cheap. They need to be told about books like Paul's.[2] People stick any kind of stuff together between covers and throw it at them.

After I left San Francisco, my boy, Bob, was taken sick. He had beat his way out there to be with me, and the burning desert dust irritated his throat. It became infected. Now he is out there with Elizabeth nursing him. It is rotten luck, but on the other hand it leaves them together, and the boy will grow to love her as anyone must who is near her.

New Orleans is marvelous, as ever — niggers, laughter, easy swinging bodies, ships. It suits me. I'll have your things here and up soon and hope soon to have my O'Keeffe. When you go back to town in the fall.

102.   New Orleans [August, 1924]

To Karl Anderson

Dear Karl: We are settled in the old quarter of New Orleans, and my oldest boy, Bob, is here. It is hot, but like an old horse I feel better, can go better in the heat. The proofs of my *A Story Teller's Story* are all in, and I am deep in a long, complex novel.[1] It has been pouring out of me 2,000 to 4,000 words a day. In truth it is a kind of fantasy of modern life — the War, sex reactions in America, artists, labor, factories. Am trying to make them all dance to slow music.

I still think you would get something as a painter down here. You should plan to come — loaf, look at the niggers, the ships, the lovely old city.

Had some rotten luck this summer. *Horses and Men* did not sell

[2] *Port of New York,* published by Harcourt, Brace in 1924.

[1] *Dark Laughter* (1925).

much. Then the people [2] who bought the serial rights to *A Story Teller's Story* could not pay for it.

Result, I shall probably have to go on the lecture platform for a while this winter. It will take less time than going back to business.

In the end probably I shall have some European income with Swedish, Russian, French, German, and Japanese translations going on.

Don't know about *A Story Teller's Story*, whether I got what I went after or not. I didn't try to set down obvious facts, only tried to get the spirit of something. It will be published in October.

Hope Helen and the children are well. Bob says Cornelia and Mimi were at your place this summer. Love to all

103.   [NEW ORLEANS, ?AUGUST 3, 1924]

To ALFRED STIEGLITZ

Dear Stieglitz: I have been on a grand bat, am still on it. Put aside the Lincoln thing and made several starts at a novel. Suddenly, a week ago Sunday, I really got into it. Since then I've been dead and blind to everything else. I am calling it a "fantasy" rather than a novel. No realism in it. An attempt to catch the spirit of things now. The War, after the War, the puzzle of things, weariness of people, laughter, Europe.

It has danced so far. Often 3 or 4,000 words a day, writing until I could not sit at the desk any more and all my body trembling.

I get here what I always have got — the slow, lazy laugh of the niggers, the niggers' bodies in a slow dance, at work, walking.

In the morning I am up at 7 and down to a coffee shop near the river. Sailors drifting in from a night's drunk — bleary-eyed old nigger women with their pipe-stem legs — dirt, good rich coffee — niggers with market baskets on their heads — old, fat Italian white men before little shops.

Heat. The sun coming up in a mustard-colored sky. Driving rains that come, swirl over a dozen streets of the city, and two minutes after, no sign.

I working. Lazy in body. The brain and the fancy at work. As I sit at my desk, often the paper under my arm wet, from the arm's leakage.

Easy to me all this. Restful to me. Everything seems far away. Much fuss about nothing. I get to smile like a nigger, laugh like a nigger. Plenty of time. Don't hurry.

[2] The owners of *Phantasmus*.

And yet the ink flows and flows. Will it all turn out rot or will it be something?

I'll know in a month or two.

Will be in New York sometime during the summer. Is Georgia better, working? Are you working? Love to you both

104.   [NEW ORLEANS, ?AUGUST 10, 1924]

To PAUL ROSENFELD

Dear Paul: I have been reading again in *Port of New York*. Whenever I am in any creative work, I go to your work and draw from it something I need. I wonder if you have been discouraged that it has not been more warmly received. It seems to me clear, warm writing, feeling, thinking. Nothing else I touch feeds me more directly.

I have put away the Lincoln thing. Whether or not I can ever do it I don't quite know. There was something wrong with the man, and unlike Brooks I cannot feed myself on other men's failures.[1] Perhaps Lincoln was too far from my own time, impulses, feeling.

My mind has wanted a greater immediacy, more right-nowness.

And so I have plunged into a novel of American life now. I call it a "fantasy" and want in it the War, new sex-consciousness, niggers — a slow, fantastic dance of sounds and thoughts, if I can get it.

Financially I've been up against it, and I must choose between going back into advertising or trying the lecture thing. My books won't sell. *Many Marriages* sold — for nasty reasons, I'm afraid; *Horses and Men*, hardly at all.

Then the new magazine, *Phantasmus*, after big talk, turned out to have no money, and I didn't get paid.

I trim sails, that's all. Not quite such gaudy socks, scarfs, etc., perhaps. I'll try to say something in the lectures anyway, if they want me.

The new book flows like a real river, so far. It should dance, a little crazily — bags of corn in the moonlight, niggers, a man and woman at the center of it. I'm at it hard anyway, and the days have joy in them. I've an idea there are fields ahead in which I haven't tried walking before.

I hope you are all right, Paul, and that you are working. Stieglitz sends good letters. When you get back to America, let me know. I'll no doubt see you in the fall. With love

[1] Van Wyck Brooks published *The Ordeal of Mark Twain* in 1920 and *The Pilgrimage of Henry James* in 1925.

105. [NEW ORLEANS, EARLY SEPTEMBER, 1924]

To ROGER SERGEL

Dear Sergel: The temptation was really too strong. After all, I've always written about that life, the Lincoln life. I may come back to it later, but I have wanted a fling at something else, have wanted to write, once at least, of more sophisticated life.

The impulse has been calling to me for a long time.

My notion is that the War[1] broke something — American isolation, perhaps. Something has begun to pour in here. I feel it, unconscious, in my own seventeen-year-old son.

Perhaps the test is coming now. Can Americans step a little beyond, say, 17 years of age and not get rotten inside in the process?

That's the theme of my novel. I think I'll call it *The Lovers.* A lot of it is written, but there is more to write, the best part of it, the hardest part, too.

I'm sorry to put you to all the trouble about the fool lecture thing. I'll have some, anyway. Am going to charge $100 and expenses or $150 and pay my own.

And I do think Mrs. Sergel is wrong not to give Ben[2] a crack at her book. Your book was no loss. Some of these days, when you have written a few more, that book will sell.

Elizabeth is very busy. She is not satisfied doing nothing, so is opening a shop here. She hopes it will give her an income of her own.

Wish you could come down here for a while this winter. Anyway I'll hope to see you in Pittsburgh. My best to you both

106. [NEW ORLEANS, AFTER NOVEMBER 22, 1924]

To HORACE LIVERIGHT[1]

Dear Horace: I have not wired you, because it will take nothing less than a letter to tell you how matters are with me, and I will have to answer your letter to you as a person rather than as a businessman and publisher. Last year when I was up against [it] and wanted a decent offer from someone, you made it to me without hesitation.

---

[1] That is, World War I.
[2] Ben Huebsch.

---

[1] Horace Liveright (1886–1933), founder and head of the publishing firm of Boni and Liveright. See *Memoirs,* pp. 351 f.

Otto [2] is one of my valued friends and has surely done a lot for me. I want to make everything as clear as I can. It may be you will feel I'm a fool.

The truth is I would just find it too hard and uncomfortable for me to make a change. When I started to do it last year, I felt like a dog. I wanted to do it and at the same time didn't want to. While the negotiations were on, I felt like hell. I know, Horace, that all you say is probably correct. It takes an organization to place books, and if they aren't placed, they won't be sold. The number of people who will go out of their way to get books when they must be ordered from a distance or who will wait until a dealer gets them in is small and always will be. All of these things I know and have known for a long time. Why, they haven't got *A Story Teller's Story* in the bookstore down here yet. I[t] probably never will sell much.

On the other hand, Horace, I got out of business some years ago. Things like sticking to old friends have really got bigger to me than anything else. While Ben never has sold my books much, he has been very, very fine with me in other ways. There never has been any lack of moral support. He published me and gave me his support when no one else much wanted me.

Now, I think that had I come to you in the first place, you would have done much the same thing, and I guess that I would have stuck to you in the same way. Last year Otto and I had some bad luck together, and I know it didn't in the least make any difference in our feeling toward each other.

At the same time, Horace, I think it is fine of you to want to give me this chance. There is no question of your not doing the right thing by Ben. It was me who opened the ball with you, but, really, I guess in doing so I wasn't quite myself. I got scared about money matters, had been going through somewhat the same tangle [3] poor Otto has been in this year. Usually I'm not much scared about making a living. I do it always after a fashion. And from now on I am likely to do more and, I hope, better work than I have done before.

What I dislike most about writing you and telling you just how I feel is that I hate not to make it seem necessary for you to run down to New Orleans. It's a great town really, and you would like it. Why don't you come anyway?

[2] Otto Liveright.
[3] The financial collapse of *Phantasmus*. See Letter 107.

Konrad [4] and I had a great visit. He's one nice chap and about the best company I know of. Most writers, you know, are awful sticks to talk with, but Konrad keeps the ball rolling all the time. I got three of his books this morning. I'm glad. With all my best regards

107. [NEW ORLEANS, ?DECEMBER, 1924]

To PAUL ROSENFELD

Dear Paul: I'm so glad to write to you, and when you are gloomy too. I'm utterly gloomy myself, always am when I have published a book. It lasts sometimes two or three months. Also I am gloomy about the finished novel. It is on a shelf in my workshop. I started another and another and put them both aside.

I hated to write to you when I was in such a state; I've bellyached to you so much in the past. And then I was self-conscious. It seemed to me that the last letter I wrote you, about Waldo, the Jews etc., etc., was terrible — stuffy, all that. I felt as you say you often feel about Alyse, only I wanted to cut my own throat. As a matter of fact, I have no cause for complaint about the book. I believe sales are not much yet and may never be great, but such an outpouring of fine letters from fine people. At first I sometimes got several in one mail. What is my great handicap is really the dealers. I am known as a dangerous man, and dealers will not stock me. I think *Many Marriages* did it. The whole mood is one out of which I have quite passed now, but the public does not know that. It seems to them that when they come toward me I do something terrible. There is a kind of fright in their eyes. I could tell you many strange tales of it. That, in reality, is the reason people are afraid to engage me as lecturer. They fear I will piss against the leg of the man who is introducing me or bring on the stage a lady and do her violence there to promote the higher life — something like that. I can't make out whether they want me to do some such violence or are really afraid I will.

I fancy I should be subsidized as an institution, but then, Paul, there are so many needing to be cared for. I must manage in some way to do my own walking. Will get back on my feet in time.

What is really puzzling is that I feel that the publication of *A Story Teller's Story* marked a period for me. I have been so much a naked

[4] Konrad Bercovici (1882–), author of books about the gypsies, who wrote from New York on November 22 of this year saying he was sending three of these books to Anderson.

man walking through the streets after all. Now I begin to want clothes. I have come to care only for working people, Negroes, etc., and very fine sophisticated people, and the more sophisticated people perhaps will not have me. Shall I be forced to become the voice of laborers, Negroes, etc.? Already in some directions I am being called that. The labor papers reproduce my stuff. It all makes me laugh.

As for you, dear Paul, you are terrible, letting me go sometimes for months and then giving me hell suddenly when I have not written for three weeks, but you also are one I have to have. I can't well get on without you, and when I do not write, I go about having imaginary conversations with you. I'm a mystic. Your house is my house. I don't think you can shut me out.

It is more so with you than with Stieglitz, because perhaps we are more one kind of thing. To him I can talk always, because I feel him above me, in a quieter place. And he is to marry. What a pretty gesture for them both. I like it immensely.

I shall be impatient to see your book. Now, for the time being, I shall write only short things. If I am to wear clothes, there will need be time for selection. It would be sad, wouldn't it, if the public had seen the last of me, if always in the future I went about quite clothed and respectable? Let the young go naked. The days are cold. I want my clothes now.

I am sure you will get the nuances of what I mean.

And I shall be seeing you in the late January. May I give Elizabeth's brother [1] a note to you, or may I ask you to call on him while he is in New York? He is something and is going to be there for a few days about the Christmas time.

For God's sake do not get cheerful before I do.

108.   [NEW ORLEANS, DECEMBER 22, 1924]

To DAVID KARSNER

Dear Karsner: I managed to write you a letter yesterday saying what I did not mean. I only meant that your book made one feel so intensely the lack of subtlety of feeling in Debs.[1]

It frightened me a little. And then at the back of the book when

---

[1] David Prall (1886–1940), brother of Elizabeth Prall and professor of philosophy at Harvard University. He was assistant professor at the University of California, 1921–1930.

[1] Eugene V. Debs, the Socialist leader. David Karsner's *Debs: His Authorized Life and Letters* was published by Boni and Liveright in 1919.

you published some of his letters. Was there a determined sort of sweetness, a little cloying?

Something hidden so far, far away, as in Ford.[2] That only I meant.*

In you I felt a sense of something else that has become so precious to me when so much has been mucked in sloppiness. I mean the tightening up, the determination, if possible, to cut in a bit closer to real truth.

The fact that working men have been robbed is something.

But it isn't the money robbery that counts most, I think.

Where we are all most robbed is in the dreadful decay of taste, the separation of men from the sense of tools and materials.

I get no sense in your book that Debs sensed that, felt it as hurtful. The book frightened me in its apparent utter ignoring on the part of this leader of men of what seems to me the most vital thing to men.

There might still be salvation for the soul of a Ford if he had at all any sense or desire for beauty in the products of his huge shop.

Your book gave me the dreadful feeling of Debs as in some way equally lacking.

The matter is between us two. I would not want, if it were possible, to in any way hurt such a man by saying any such thing that might reach him.

He seems in your book very, very old. You do not seem so.

* The scene — the ex-owner of houses of prostitution and Debs — the meeting. A wonderful picture. Tell me why I feel the ex-keeper of prostitutes was more honest, came off best in the scene.

I want to know why.

109.   [NEW ORLEANS, EARLY MARCH, 1925]

To GERTRUDE STEIN

Dear Gertrude Stein: I am back at home — 540 B St. Peter Street,[1] New Orleans — back with the niggers, the ships, the old houses, the rich, often rank Southern smells I love.

Am working again, the pen flying. I lectured, I saw people — Stieglitz, Rosenfeld, Jane (for just a moment),[2] that woman who had

[2] Henry Ford, the manufacturer. In the letter to Karsner written on the previous day Anderson had said that Debs and Ford showed similar limitations when "talking of the arts."

[1] In the French Quarter.

[2] Jane Heap, presumably.

the letter from you about raising money for the Marne house,[3] McBride,[4] a lot of people you knew.

I am to write the blurb for the cover of Hemingway's book.[5] I liked his stories, all of them.

Made a little money and often an ass of myself. Am trying to raise money to buy a house of my own. Never had my own roof over me. I want a place now, near the Mississippi, near the niggers.

I'll lecture, spit over the top of boxcars, do anything to get it but make love to ladies I do not fancy.

I'll get it some way. Have got to do that before I can think of Paris again, but I think often, often of you. Lots of love

110.   NEW ORLEANS, MARCH 5, 1925

To JOHN EMERSON AND ANITA LOOS

Dear John & Nita: We got back to New Orleans Monday evening, the 3rd, and I am already at work. First of all I am going to try to do the book with which my head is now full, and then I am going to make a try at the play.

Elizabeth came to [Chicago] [1] to meet me, and I spoke at some large Jewish synagogue on the South Side. Then to the State University at Urbana.

After that to the old city of Natchez, a charming, sleepy place of about fifteen thousand and much quieter than Clyde. It sits on a high bluff above the Mississippi and in the old days of the River was a great place. Now it has pretty much died. People, however, live there in their grand old houses with great lawns and stables, and seem happy and contented.

We wanted to take a packet down the river from Natchez, but a characteristic Southern thing happened. The boat was advertised in the newspaper to leave on Wednesday, but really leaves on Monday; so we missed it. I asked the boat agent about it. "Well," he said, "it did leave on Wednesdays when we put that advertisement in the papers,

---

[3] Gertrude Stein was at this time interested in a project to buy a house on the Marne River for a friend of hers (Miss Mildred Aldrich) to serve as a memorial to the friend after death. Since she wrote to many women about the project, this person cannot now be identified.

[4] Possibly Robert M. McBride, the New York publisher.

[5] Hemingway's *In Our Time* was published in the United States in 1925 by Boni and Liveright after an initial Paris publication in the previous year.

---

[1] The text reads "New York."

but after [a] while it got to leaving on Monday, and we ain't never changed the advertisement at all."

John, I can't tell you all the trip to New York has meant to me. It came just at the right time. I could not have afforded it but for your own great generosity, but I needed it and got more out of it than I can ever tell you. Perhaps I'll be able to show you in the next year or two by a more direct and objective handling of my work. I think you know that when an American stays away too long from New York something happens to him. Perhaps he becomes a little provincial, a little dead and afraid. You see it in poor little Weeks Hall, a really fine man with, at bottom, a better painter's mind and feeling than almost anyone I know, but so frightened and twisted by life that he can't do anything really healthy.

With the work in sight to do now, with the assurance that I can get the lectures I want next winter, and with the feeling of being alive and a part of what is going on that has come with again getting into contact with people like you and Nita who are really in the game of life and living all the time, I ought to go for a while now.

Of course, John, I can't say for sure, but I've a hunch both you and Nita are going to like Elizabeth when you get to know her. Wish you could come down here this spring. If anything happens you don't go to Europe, why don't you? We have plenty of room for you in the apartment, and you would both love the town. Just now and for the next month it will be lovely. Spring is coming fast, the river is filled with shipping, and the whole place is charming.

The whole memory of my trip to New York is one that fills me with life just to think of, and I, of course, never think of it without thinking of your own generosity. Surely, man, it will be fine to be friends some-day when I have money enough of my own to meet you halfway in that too. Anyway, I love you both, and I hope it won't be long before I can see you both down here. Sincerely

111.   [NEW ORLEANS, ?MARCH 11, 1925]

To ETTIE STETTHEIMER

Dear Ettie Stettheimer: I read *Love Days* [1] on the train going out to Chicago, later on the train going South, and finally in the little town

---

[1] [Ettie Stettheimer], *Love Days*, by Henrie Waste, New York, Knopf, 1923. Miss Stettheimer had published *Philosophy* (1917) under her pseudonym; and in "Archives of Philosophy," Science Press, under her own name, in 1907 *The Will to Believe* (a translation of her German dissertation, 1903).

of Natchez on the river. Elizabeth (Mrs. Anderson) came to Chicago to meet me, and she also read it.

Sometimes it seemed to me one of the finest books I had ever read, and then again it faded away to nothing for me. The people were all so far away, so strange to me. Suzanne I liked often, and then again she did not exist for me. At the last, with the consumptive doctor, I did not get her at all, nor could I get him, his charm and meaning.

All the time I had the feeling that the book might teach me a lot about women, if I could only get it.

No one, however, seemed to quite work from the springs of life that move and impel me along. Most people I have known were both more mean and more noble.

But then these people moved so [?easily] through the mechanism of life. They all seemed to have money, for one thing, and most of the people I have known had no money or had made it. People who have made their own money never, I fancy, lose consciousness of it and are always vulgarized.

The book absorbed me; it carried me very completely into the lives of the people you wrote about, only when I had finished, I felt that I had been among strangers and really did not feel that any of the people, had I known them in the flesh, would have got into my own life in any real way. I would have seen them as I see rare fabrics in a Fifth Ave. shop, knowing they are too rare and costly for me. My fingers ache to touch them, because my fingers are always aching and itching to touch things, but not as they want to touch other things — the flanks of a running horse, blades of corn, the bodies of young trees.

It comes down to my being perhaps infinitely more primitive than any of your people could ever have been. I would feel more at home spending an evening in a cabin with an old Georgia Negress and looking at her hands than I ever would have felt with Suzanne. With love

112.   New Orleans, March 21, 1925

Mr. George Sylvester Viereck,[1] 93 Fifth Avenue, New York

My dear George Viereck: I do not believe that any organized plan for endowing men of talent would really work. The struggle for bread

---

[1] George Sylvester Viereck (1884–) was then editing the *American Monthly,* formerly the *Fatherland.*

and butter is, I am afraid, inevitable. When an individual who has money gives some of it to his friend, who has talent but no money, that is another matter.

The whole difficulty about giving anyone money lies with the giver. It is a difficult thing to do, and few can do it really well. Badly done it hurts more than it helps.

I think I can speak in this matter in a fairly sane way. I myself have no money and am often broke. Naturally I want the leisure money would bring. Often I go into some city where money is being poured out like water, and I grow temporarily furious, thinking of the quiet leisure money might buy for some fellow like myself.

But my general notion is that the man of talent has to take his chances with everyone else, play the game as it lies.

I have set out on a certain road, knowing very well that what I want to do will not bring me much money. If I were to spend my energy in another direction, I might get money aplenty.

Very well. I plan to get something money will not buy. It evens up fairly well.

When you start giving away money, you have to pick the man or men who are to receive it. That is no easy task. It surely cannot be done wholesale.

Men and women may, however, do it for each other as individuals, and that seems to me the only healthy way in which it can be done.

How are you to expect the millionaire to find the man of talents before it is too late and he has worn himself out?

Is he to send out a search party or a detective? What would a search party bring in? Not the real man of talent, you may be sure of that. They would be likely to find the man who protested the loudest, not the best workman at all. I am, Yours very truly

113.   New Orleans, March 25, 1925

Mr. O. K. Liveright, 2 West 43rd Street, New York

My dear Liveright: I want to give you, as nearly as I can, an outline of how the "Childhood" book [1] lies in my mind so that you may tell Miss Lane [2] about it.

---

[1] *Tar: A Midwest Childhood* was published by Boni and Liveright in 1926.

[2] Gertrude B. Lane, of the editorial staff of the *Woman's Home Companion.* Segments of *Tar* began appearing in that magazine in June, 1926.

I am enclosing the first of the tales, and as I plan the book, all of the tales should stand quite by themselves, each having its own flavor and dramatic interest.

There should be a dozen or more of them, but I believe Miss Lane only wants to use some forty thousand words. As the book falls naturally into this form, she can therefore use the tales that strike her as best for her purpose.

The whole book should be written this summer.

The next tale will concern a fire in a small Ohio town at night, a fire that half consumes the town. As the fire fighting apparatus is meager, all the men and women of the town rush out to help.

The child is left in charge of his sister, and there are two babies asleep in a bed downstairs.

When the others are all gone, the sister also goes, leaving the responsibility of the children with the boy of seven.

The fire is raging in another part of the town. The drama of the tale lies in the child's fear of going away through the dark streets to see the great wonder and the growing sense in him that something is expected of him.

What is expected is that he shall stay in the house with the babies.

He leaves, however, and makes his way to the fire. There he finds another child of his own age wandering alone. Fear and wonder draw them together. It is the child's first taste of friendship.

He forgets all about the babies at home, and the mother comes home and finds them awake and crying, all the three older children gone.

On the next day the sister is punished, the smaller child escaping because of his age. The tale will end on the mixed feelings in the child, joy that he has escaped punishment, has seen the wonder of the fire and has made a friend, and a queer guilty feeling that he has in some way sold out his sister.

Several other tales lie quite clearly in my mind, but will have to be worked up in order.

The boy's first days at school.

A tale of the child's first fight with another boy.

The tale of his escape from the house when he had measles and going off to the county fair to creep under the fence and infect half the town.

What I want chiefly to give you and Miss Lane now is a feeling of the tone of the tales. They should be gentle and whimsical and yet with plenty of dramatic force to carry the reader forward. I am, Yours very truly

114. NEW ORLEANS, APRIL 18, 1925

MR. HORACE LIVERIGHT, 61 WEST 48TH STREET, NEW YORK

Dear Horace Liveright: I got your wire last night and [am] sending off my answer at once.

Dear man, I can't exactly write a blurb for my own novel. If it were someone else's novel I liked one-half as much, I could sure sling words about it. All I am afraid is I would say too many good things about it and give away the fact that I am not nearly as modest as I should be. I would so like to pose as a gentlemanly, modest chap and am so afraid I am nothing of the kind.

By the way, I had a telegram from Otto this morning, telling me that the *Woman's Home Companion* have bought the "Childhood" book, which won't do us any harm, I think, as they have a tremendous circulation, something like 2,000,000; and the announcement that they are going to publish this book next summer will, I presume, be made this fall.

To return to the novel, what I will do is to try to write you a letter from which your own publicity man can get what he wants for his own blurb. He should be able to say things I can't very well say.

What I think now is that the novel should be called *Dark Laughter* rather than *Deep Laughter*. The word "Deep" is a little too pretentious. When you read the novel, which I hope you will be able to do early in June, you will agree with me that *Dark Laughter* just fits it, and it should be a corking title. I am sure you will like it.

This whole novel was written in a heat last fall. I went through the whole thing in about two months and have never been so absorbed in a job before. It is the story of the present day, of postwar life in America now and in particular of postwar life in the Middle West.

The three central figures of the book are a young man who has come home from the World War to find his father dead and himself at the head of a large manufacturing plant in the Ohio River Valley in the town of Old Harbor, Indiana. In France he has married a young woman, the daughter of a prominent Chicago lawyer, whose brother and fiancé were both killed in the war. Her marriage with the young manufacturer was the result of war fever and emotionalism brought on by conditions in Paris just after the war.

These people are living in the Indiana town, facing the Ohio River, after the war and have no children. To them comes a man of thirty-four, disillusioned by [a] bad marriage and seeking the romance of life by going backward over his boyhood trail. After they meet, the story intensifies and becomes a struggle for the love of the woman.

The book has in it many strange side lights. Its setting embraces the Middle West, the Ohio River Valley, the Mississippi River, and New Orleans. In it there are lazy, dancing Negroes, a description of the Quat'z' Arts Ball in Paris shortly after the Armistice, and an intense love story. I believe the book is even more intense than *Many Marriages,* but is even broader and has a greater swing to it. It is going to be by far the best novel I have written.

After I had finished writing it last fall, I put it away and have not looked at it since. I knew that it needed pruning and cutting, that there were sags and holes in it that needed filling in, and that the whole swing of it was not carried through. I was simply waiting to get just right on it before going back and cleaning up the job. Shortly after our talk I went back into it again. Since you were here, I have been working on it every minute of every day, in fact have kept at it so hard and long that each day when I got through, I was so exhausted I could hardly get up from my desk. All this is not because I have had any sense of hurry about it. In the first place I believe it is largely because a certain weight has been lifted off my shoulders for the time being, of which you know, and also because the big broad sweep of the story got me hard. If I were physically able, I would work on it day and night, and because I am convinced that it is going to be a ripping novel. It walks and sings. I want the regular Mississippi and Ohio River swing to it with the perfume of corn, cotton, summer nights and the strangeness of life.

Back of all this the mysterious, detached laughter of the blacks.

You see what I am trying to give you now, Horace, is something of the orchestration of the book. The neuroticism, the hurry and self-consciousness of modern life, and back of it the easy, strange laughter of the blacks. There is your dark, earthy laughter — the Negro, the earth, and the river — that suggests the title.

Bet on this book, Horace, it is going to be there with a bang. I wanted to write you about it again and tell you how I feel about it, but I have been so absorbed in the novel itself, tearing away scaffolding, laying new foundations, putting in joists and doorsills, that I could not think of anything but building the novel. And now, Horace, I am going back into it again, and I am praying the gods that this spell of wholehearted work won't break until I can turn the book over to you a complete thing. Do a little praying of the same sort yourself.

The book won't be exactly mild, my dear Horace, and it may stir up the dry bones some, but I do not believe that there is anything in it that is suppressible. It is the kind of book that just now ought to arouse a lot of interest.

Keep your thumb on your ear, and when you go to bed at night, say a little prayer that it is going to be as good as I think it is going to be. Yours very truly

115. New Orleans, May 6, 1925

Mr. Horace Liveright, 61 West 48th Street, New York

Dear Horace Liveright: I am in receipt of your letter and check, and thank you very much indeed.

A fair copy of the novel is now being made, and as soon as it is completed, I will go over it again and send it along.

Went up the river for a week on a little passenger boat and just got back.

I have in the back of my mind something that may develop within the next year or two and seems to me to have immense possibilities. I don't believe anyone has ever done a book on the Mississippi River, and I am going to begin to gather data and see what I can find. There is a tremendous story in the early history of the river, the wild, reckless days on the river of the '40's, the tremendous part it took in the Civil War, and afterwards its decline. The whole story is full of strange romance and interest and excitement, and I would like tremendously to get it all. I am going to keep it in mind and see what I can gather in data to help me get what I want. Don't you think it might be made quite a tremendous book? It certainly is big enough in its sweep. Think it over and one of these days write me something about it, but don't talk to many people about it, as I want the plum for myself if I can get together the material I want. This is, of course, something that would take two or three years to develop, but I believe is mighty well worth working on.

With most sincere regards to yourself and Mrs. Liveright and to Tommy Smith.[1] Yours truly

116.   NEW ORLEANS, JUNE 20, 1925

To ALFRED STIEGLITZ

Dear Stieglitz: A hot, still morning. Last year it was both hot and dry. This year we have tropical rains almost daily. You sit working and the water runs off your back.

Outside the window people going along under the cathedral walls. Sunday there was a religious procession, the archbishop, a fine, grey-haired old actor, going along under a golden canopy, the host pressed to his lips, boys swinging incense, little girls in white scattering roses in his path.

I'm not much worried about my work improving or going off. What I want is to do work that will please me a little. If I can do that, I'll be happy enough.

Wish I had money. If I had, I swear I'd never publish again during my life. There isn't enough intelligent criticism to count much. Things swing back and forth by the dictates of fashions.

The public lies far outside consciousness of what is going on among artists. The public is both more stupid and purer, better at bottom perhaps.

Being down here makes me feel isolated, which may be good for me. And that's enough of me.

I'm just simply glad you are out of New York and in that quiet place.

Paul seems away over on the far side [of] the world someway.

As for Lawrence,[1] when he tells a story, he is fine; when he lays down his principles, I think him a pretentious fool. He dreams of being the great, dark animal. It is, after all, a neurotic wish. To me his whole book[2] lacked reserve, good feeling, delicacy.

Wish I could sit with you while I say just what I think.

My love to Paul and Georgia. A good summer to you all.

---

[1] T[homas] R. Smith of the editorial department of Boni and Liveright.

[1] D. H. Lawrence.
[2] *Studies in Classic American Literature.* The American edition was published in 1923.

117.   [SUGAR GROVE,[1] VIRGINIA, AUGUST 14, 1925]

TO ALFRED STIEGLITZ

Dear Stieglitz: I am going back to New Orleans today, largely because E[lizabeth] had to be there just now and I don't much fancy being where she is not. Have averaged about two thousand words a day for a month, so am rather finely drawn. I think it is full of good spots. It's a childhood thing, horses, cows, fields of corn, the threshers at work, orchards in the late afternoon, country people, etc., etc.

The mountain people are sweet. No books, little false education, real humbleness. It does so beat talking to pretentious half-artists. We may try to acquire a few acres and a cabin. Hills everywhere with cold springs trickling out of them, forests yet. People live in isolated cabins far apart. Everyone wants you to come in, to drink moonshine, to eat, to spend the night.

A thousand people gather from many miles about for what they call a "foot washing," a religious symbol of humbleness. They take fried chicken, corn whiskey. Many of the preachers can't read. I don't see that they preach any worse — if someone has to preach.

It's sweet to see the rains over the hills, hear the sounds at night. It may be that as we get older we draw closer to nature. The cabin where I go to write (it costs me nothing) is a deserted one in a big cornfield on top of a mountain. Cowbells in the distance, the soft whisper of the corn. It all fits my theme.

I start lecturing Oct. 12th — a big schedule. Not many years of that, I hope. I hope to get out of debt, however. Love to you all

118.   NEW ORLEANS, AUGUST 17, 1925

MR. PHIL STONE,[1] c/o JAMES STONE & SONS, OXFORD, MISSISSIPPI

My dear Phil Stone: I had a letter from Mr. Liveright, who said that two of his readers were enthusiastic about Bill's novel,[2] the third reader not so enthusiastic. He was to read it himself and decide. I have a hunch he will take it.

---

[1] A "post-hamlet" in Smyth County, Virginia, several miles south of Marion.

[1] Phil Stone of the law firm of James Stone and Sons, Oxford, Mississippi.
[2] William Faulkner's *Soldiers' Pay*, which was published by Boni and Liveright in 1926.

I am very sure, however, that Bill's novel neither wants or needs an introduction by me. If Mr. Liveright wants me to write a blurb for the outside paper jacket, I'll be glad to do it, as I certainly admire Bill's talent. The jacket serves the purpose wanted without being a part of the book itself.

I'm sorry to have been so long answering your letter. Miss Elizabeth and I were up in Virginia, and I worked so hard at a new book that I let all my mail accumulate. I am beginning to try and clear up now.

With most sincere regards, I am, Very truly yours

119.   NEW ORLEANS, AUGUST 28, 1925

MR. HORACE LIVERIGHT, c/o BONI AND LIVERIGHT, NEW YORK

Dear Horace: I got your fine telegram yesterday morning. Will be delighted, of course, to inscribe the special edition.[1]

I am glad you are going to publish Faulkner's novel.[2] I have a hunch this man is a comer. Will tell you a lot about him when I see you in late October or November.

I am going lecturing about October 15th. If Mr. Leigh of the Leigh Lecture Bureau has not given you my dates, have somebody in the office get in touch with him so the new novel can be pushed in the towns where I appear. His address is 152 West 78th Street.

Last winter when I lectured at the University of California, a little printer in San Francisco, who does very fine work, wanted to publish my lecture in [a] little book,[3] and I gave him permission. Afterward he went broke, and now I understand the lecture is being published in a little book by Gelber, Lilienthal, Inc., who run a bookstore at 236 Sutter Street, San Francisco. I tell you this so you will know how it came about if this little book appears.

I took the day off yesterday and went up river to read *Dark Laughter*. It excited me and pleased me. I believe the book is O.K. and only hope it will sell. There are one or two little typographical errors that might be caught in another edition. Shall I mark them and send them in? I would like to have copies of the book sent to Gertrude Stein, 27, rue de Fleurus, Paris, to Ernest Hemingway, Paul Rosenfeld, 77 Irving

---

[1] That is, of *Dark Laughter* (1925).
[2] See Letter 118. *Soldiers' Pay*, the first novel by William Faulkner (1897–), had been recommended by Anderson to Liveright for publication.
[3] *The Modern Writer*, San Francisco, The Lantern Press, 1925.

Place, New York, Konrad,[4] Otto [5] and a copy to Madame Margaret
Gay, 20 avenue Rapp, Paris. Madame Gay is my French translator.
With love and good wishes
P.S. I forgot to mention how much I like the drawing at the front and
back of the book. It's corking.

120.   [NEW ORLEANS, SEPTEMBER 13, 1925]

To ALFRED STIEGLITZ

Dear Stieglitz: Such talk is inevitable. There is a class of men who
dream of rising by pulling down someone else. Because the arts are
filled with more sensitive men, we get the best and the worst. More
and more I hope to stay out of the battles. A man lays down his work,
and there it is.

The challenge to oneself is enough, I guess. People have contradicted
themselves so often in regard to my own work that I can trust very few,
perhaps no one.

Lots of days of discouragement. I go toward people so often like a
good-natured dog, wagging my tail. Often the very effort to be friendly
is taken as a challenge of some sort. Human relations are difficult,
God knows, and when we are trying to carry on such relations with
fellow artists — God help the good, the true, and the beautiful. The
men talking in the public prints. So-and-so is first, second, or third
class. What nonsense. Such a lot of twaddle talked always.

I am glad the story carried you. I tried to make it dance along,
jazzed it a little at the first where the theme fitted that mood. I wanted
to give the sense of a dancing, shifting world of facts, moods, thoughts,
impulses.

That's me, anyway. I'm not very stable.

Now I want to get this childhood book done and begin on a book
I shall call *Another Man's House*. Isn't that a corking title? I suspect
I shall not get at it until next summer. A lot of gadding about and
gabbing to do. It will bring in some money, though.

I don't care much what they say of you. I do care that you keep well
and have some good days of work. That goes for Georgia too. Lots of
love

[4] Konrad Bercovici.
[5] Otto Liveright.

121.   NEW ORLEANS, SEPTEMBER 15, 1925

TO GEORGE H. DAUGHERTY [1]

Dear George: I am writing to answer your letter right away on account of *Ulysses.* Sure you may lend it to Morrow,[2] but be sure to impress upon the old cuss the necessity of sending it back. I don't want to lose it.

I think as a matter of prose experiment you will sense what Mr. Joyce was driving at when you read *Dark Laughter.* As I think I told you when you were here, I very frankly took his experiment as a starting place for the prose rhythm of the book. I think you will get it when you read the book. I would be sending you along a copy, but I have not any here, as only a few have come. I will have some more I hope within a week.

I have not, of course, seen any of the reviews of the book, although I have been told that Laurence Stallings has given it a fine send-off in the New York *World.*

My plans for next year are pretty indefinite, but I will tell you about them when I see you.

Also I will be mighty interested to see Morrow's new experiment.[3] He will get something out of that book yet.

Don [4] wrote me and will be here the latter part of this month. I am leaving the first week of October, but Elizabeth will stay on here. I am sure he will not have any difficulty finding a place to live, and I am sure he will get something out of New Orleans. With love

122.   NEW ORLEANS, OCTOBER 2, 1925

MR. JAY L. BRADLEY,[1] SPRINGFIELD, MISSOURI

My dear Mr. Bradley: I have your letter of September 25 and note what you say about the difficulty of getting *A Story Teller's Story* in

[1] George H. Daugherty, fellow worker of Anderson's at the Critchfield advertising agency and one of his lifelong friends.

[2] Marco Morrow, journalist, assistant publisher of the Capper Publications in Topeka, Kansas, 1919–1938. The point is that until December, 1933, the importation of Joyce's novel into the United States was unlawful.

[3] Morrow had submitted a manuscript paralleling *The Spoon River Anthology* to Boni and Liveright.

[4] Donald Wright, advertising writer, friend of Anderson and Daugherty.

[1] In his letter Jay Bradley identifies himself as a fifteen-year-old boy who admires Anderson's work and who wants to know how to become a writer.

Springfield. If the book dealers have not got it, I think they will gladly order it for you. If I had any extra copies here, I would be glad to send you one, but I have none.

I was in Springfield ten or twelve years ago for a day or two after having spent five or six months in the Ozark Mountains, and I remember it as a very charming town.

Now as to your questions — I think the best way for a person, such as yourself, who desires to write, is simply to keep your eyes and ears open and learn as much about the way people live and the impulses back of their actions as you can. Keep on writing all the time and do not be discouraged if you do not write anything very good for a long time.

The question as to what authors to read is a large order, but I would, as far as possible, read old authors whose work has stood the test of time, and read a great deal of history and biography.

Your third question — what is my personal favorite among my own books? — is too much like asking a mother which is her favorite child. They are to me somewhat different from what they are to the public, and I simply can't answer the question.

Your fourth question — what do I think of *Dark Laughter* in comparison with my other books? — will have to meet the same fate. By the time a book is published I am usually busy on a new one and don't think much about my own books after they are written.

I hope these answers will be of use to you, and I certainly appreciate sincerely your interest in my work. Yours very sincerely

123. TOLEDO, OHIO, NOVEMBER 19, 1925

MR. LAURENCE STALLINGS,[1] c/o *World*, NEW YORK

My dear Laurence Stallings: For some time now I have had in mind writing to you concerning a notion I have had in my head, but have hesitated because it seems to me a little presumptuous.

Anyway, here it is. I am wondering, sometime, when you have a little leisure, if you ever do have, if you would look through my stuff with the idea in your mind of finding in it possible dramatic material. Jacques Copeau and several other men on the other side have written me from time to time, saying that they thought there were any number of plays in my stories and books. I do not know whether it is true or

[1] Laurence Stallings (1894–), dramatist and journalist.

not, but I have liked your work as a playwright so much that I am having the nerve to suggest the idea to your mind.

It may seem nonsense to you, but if not, I wish you would write me about it sometime. Just now I am flying around doing a lot of "gabbing" before clubs and universities to get the coin to lift the mortgage on a farm I bought down in Virginia and incidentally to build a house on it. My address, therefore, will be care of the Leigh Lecture Bureau, 24 W. 49th St., New York, until about February 1st. After that I will be at 825 Bourbon St., New Orleans until May first and then at Grant,[2] Virginia, for the summer. With sincere regards

124.   [NEW ORLEANS, DECEMBER 22, 1925]

To ALFRED STIEGLITZ

Dear Alfred: I got both your letters back here at New Orleans, a stack of things. *Poor White* in German,[1] a lovely book, beautifully printed. A letter asking that I let them print *Winesburg* in Czecho-Slovak.

The lecturing affects me strangely. Think I'll never do it again. The tales I could tell you — middle-aged women gone nasty, people quarreling. Youngsters full of life, with clean bodies, fine eyes. The professors tired and frightened.

The nice people going silently away, maybe a common schoolteacher saying something you can never forget.

The trouble is you get to know no one. Faces pass like blown things before a window in a storm.

You are tired, go to your hotel tired. No real functioning with any-one.

Elizabeth seemed the most alive thing in the world, because I could sit with her, walk with her, be with her nights and days.

You can't have relations with people that way, as a touring speaker; it's unfair to them and to you.

I keep thinking of you two —

What will they do?

New York seemed to me more expensive than ever. I thought of you coming from the country — not much money.

Well, you have done something.

---

[2] Near Marion, Virginia, where Anderson was to buy his two newspapers.

[1] Published by Insel-Verlag in 1925.

Am working here at home, have been working as I traveled — a spring book of essays, notes on life, such things as the essay on you in *New Republic* long ago.[2]

It will have a certain fragmentary flow of life in it, I'm sure.

Elizabeth and I go to the Pacific Coast to end the speaking Jan. 1st. Not much more of it.

Now that I've done it, I can't tell.

I'm ashamed and not ashamed. God knows.

The room [3] sounds like you, and Georgia, as I know you, love you. It will work out. God bless you.

125.   NEW ORLEANS, DECEMBER 31, 1925

To ALFRED STIEGLITZ

Dear Alfred: The book of notes is going off to Liveright today, we have our ticket to California and leave day after tomorrow, have had two teeth pulled and two filled, and am pretty tired but glad to have things cleared up.

There is an amusing side to Crowninshield,[1] Mencken and all the others. People who used to quibble about paying $75.00 for an article now want to pay three or four hundred. For the most part I have none for them. The thing in *Vanity Fair* [2] was written several years ago to amuse a woman friend who is in the theatre. Someone dug it up out of their files and sold it to Crowninshield for me. Well, it does not matter. It makes you a little sick when you realize people's attitude toward what they call success, but then I guess we always knew it anyway.

I am going to call the book simply *A Sherwood Anderson Note Book.* It has in it a number of essays about yourself, about writing, about life in America in general, together with a lot of little intimate notes scattered through the book. I hope it may have a healthy, nice tone. I am pretty tired right now, but this is largely due to trying to do so many things in ten days. A few days' rest will set me up.

Will be back here about February 15th and stay until May first, then go up to the little Virginia farm for a long, quiet summer. The worst

[2] "Alfred Stieglitz," *New Republic*, XXXII, 215–217 (October 25, 1922).

[3] Stieglitz and Georgia O'Keeffe had just opened "The Intimate Gallery" in Room 303 of the Anderson Galleries Building at 489 Park Avenue.

[1] Frank Crowninshield, editor of *Vanity Fair*, 1914–1935.

[2] "An Estimate of 'Mr. and Mrs. Philip Wase'" [picture by George Bellows], *Vanity Fair*, XXV, 57 (November, 1925).

thing in this year is the fact that I did not see you or Georgia or did not see the things in Room 303.

I shall be writing you from the West. With love

126.   [NEW ORLEANS, FEBRUARY 22, 1926]

To EARL ANDERSON [1]

Dear Earl: A letter just came from Karl, who had been to see you. You will get well, but [it] is going to be a slow business. I have a proposal to make you I think you may like, but first I will tell you something of myself and the outlines of my life. After all, it may be you know most of it. Let me, therefore, get quickly to the point. In addition to my writing I have had to fool along with the advertising business until about three years ago, but now things are breaking well for me. Both I and Elizabeth, my wife, are pretty sick of people. Last summer we went together up into the mountains of Virginia and while there fell so in love with the country, the mountain people about, the quiet hills and the sunshine that we bought a small farm.

Then luck came along. My last book sold. The farm has but one tiny house on it, but this winter I am having a small cabin built. Next summer we will build another. It is far away from the railroads, in the very midst of the mountains, in a little upland valley. We go there May first. I want you to come up into that country and make a home there where I can be near you. I've missed too much of you now. It's too bad you had to have this sickness for me to find you, but having found you again, I do not want you to get away.

We will go there May first, and we are planning to make it our permanent home. Everything is to be done, a house to build, a garden for vegetables and flowers. You can make your own plans for your own life after you get there, have a cabin of your own, live near us with some farmer, have a room in our house, anyway just so you come. You will need a lot of quiet out of doors, hills and sunshine now. How can I tell you of Elizabeth? I was as mature as I will ever be when I married her and am more in love with her every day. You will love her.

Dear man, I do not want to intrude on your privacy after all these years, but we want you. Please make up your mind to come. When you get better, there will be so much you can help us do there. It can be

---

[1] Earl Anderson, brother of Sherwood, had suffered a paralytic stroke February 16, 1926. See *Memoirs*, pp. 186 f.

Three Anderson Brothers by Karl Anderson

Left to right: Earl, Sherwood, Irwin

a home building for yourself and us too. We are planning to spend the rest of our lives there. Think of nothing now but getting well enough so you can come. That's all I ask now. Need I tell you that I love you and want you? I have wanted you back ever since you disappeared.

127.   [NEW ORLEANS, ?APRIL 18, 1926]

To JOHN ANDERSON

Dear [John]: [1] It's a problem all right. The best thing, I dare say, is first to learn something well so you can always make a living. Bob seems to be catching on at the newspaper business and has had another raise. He is getting a good training by working in a smaller city. As for the scientific fields, any of them require[s] a long schooling and intense application. If you are made for it, nothing could be better. In the long run you will have to come to your own conclusion.

The arts, which probably offer a man more satisfaction, are uncertain. It is difficult to make a living.

If I had my own life to lead over, I presume I would still be a writer, but I am sure I would give my first attention to learning how to do things directly with my hands. Nothing gives quite the satisfaction that doing things brings.

Above all avoid taking the advice of men who have no brains and do not know what they are talking about. Most small businessmen say simply, "Look at me." They fancy that if they have accumulated a little money and have got a position in a small circle, they are competent to give advice to anyone.

Next to occupation is the building up of good taste. That is difficult, slow work. Few achieve it. It means all the difference in the world in the end.

I am constantly amazed at how little painters know about painting, writers about writing, merchants about business, manufacturers about manufacturing. Most men just drift.

There is a kind of shrewdness many men have that enables them to get money. It is the shrewdness of the fox after the chicken. A low order o[f] mentality often goes with it.

Above all I would like you to see many kinds of men at first hand.

---

[1] Although this letter is addressed to "Earl," Sherwood's brother, he clearly meant "John," his second son.

That would help you more than anything. Just how it is to be accomplished I do not know. Perhaps a way may be found.

Anyway, I'll see you this summer. We begin to pack for the country this week. With love, Dad [2]

128.   NEW ORLEANS, APRIL 19, 1926

TO HORACE LIVERIGHT

My dear Horace: I have not written to you for some time. As a matter of fact, I have been working every day until I was all in and have not written to anyone.

As I told you sometime ago, I got through the "Childhood" book some two or three weeks ago and have put it aside to stew. I want to let it lie for a month or two and then take another whirl at it after I get up into the country.

In the meantime I got right into the new novel.[1] As often happens with me, I had to make three or four starts with it. I had the whole theme in my mind, but it is a delicate thing to handle, and I had to get the characters fitted into the theme. Twice after writing several thousand words I had to throw it all away. My people got off the track. I did not understand them well enough. They were not what I wanted. I went off to the country or walked around the streets and waited. At last I think I have a start that will do fine.

The man's name is Talbot Whittingham. The central figures of the novel are this man Whittingham and his wife Katherine — their relations to each other and of Whittingham's relationship with other women. He is a Southern man who lives in the North. I won't go any further into it now, because when this novel comes through, I want it to strike you fresh. I believe there will be in it a lot of things that will get close to you and other modern men too.

I hear splendid reports of the sale of Dreiser's novel.[2] Also somebody on the street the other day told me that they had seen an article in the New York *World* saying that Dreiser had got a big price for the moving picture rights to his novel. All of this is very splendid, if it is true, and I hope it is.

---

[2] Anderson rarely signed a letter to one of his children in this way, usually writing instead "S.A.," "Sherwood," or "Sherwood Anderson."

[1] Tentatively entitled *Talbot Whittingham,* this novel was never completed.
[2] *An American Tragedy* (1925).

I saw in the *New York Times* a very good review of the Faulkner novel.[3] I hope you will have sales enough of this novel to encourage both Faulkner and yourself. I do not like the man personally very much, but I have a hunch on that he is a man who will write the kind of novels that will sell. He is modern enough and not too modern; also he is smart. If I were you, I would do what I could to encourage him to keep at work. If you want to do so, why don't you write him a letter telling him some of the things I have said about him, as it may buck him up, particularly if this first novel does not have much sale? You see what I mean. He may be a little bit like a thoroughbred colt who needs a race or two before he can do his best. He was so nasty to me personally that I don't want to write him myself, but would be glad if you were to do it in this indirect way, as I surely think he is a good prospect.

You wrote me some time ago about the Swedish offer for *Dark Laughter*. I should think that it would be all right to accept their offer of the twenty pounds' advance on royalty, but I do think you are right in suggesting that the royalty be higher.

I have got a hunch that if the matter was approached just right and worked just right, a movie offer could be got for some of my things; however, I suppose you will work that through when the time comes or when you think the opportunity is ripe.

It is hardly likely that I shall get to New York this spring. We are leaving for the farm May first, and if this novel keeps going, I may stay right by it until I get through it for the first writing; however, there is a chance that Mrs. Anderson and I might run up to New York for a week or ten days late in May. I will see how it works out.

I will wire you when we are leaving here so that there does not need to be any interruption in mail. We are going to build us a little farmhouse this spring or this summer and have the farm as headquarters in the future.

I want to take my brother who had the stroke up there as soon as we get a little straight. He is now at Westport with Karl.

I wish I could see and have a visit with you, but above everything else now I want to put this novel through, as I have a hunch that it has the making of a knockout in it. With sincere regards, Yours

[3] William Faulkner's *Soldiers' Pay* was reviewed in the *New York Times*, April 11, 1926.

129.   NEW ORLEANS, APRIL 20, 1926

INTERNATIONAL COMMITTEE FOR POLITICAL PRISONERS, NEW YORK

Gentlemen: I have had two letters from you signed by Mr. Lovett, Mr. Hapgood and Mr. Baldwin,[1] asking me for a letter or essay to be used in a book of essays on the subject of the Italian dictatorship.

I beg you to excuse me for not answering these letters, as I have been deeply absorbed in a book and, to tell the truth, have let all my mail go for some weeks.

I hate, very much, to refuse anything asked by the men who signed these letters, but as a matter of fact I know nothing on the subject, and for me to write on it would be a good deal like my writing on some of the affairs of Mars. I have never been in Italy, have read very little on the subject, and have no political turn of mind. To be frank, I feel entirely incapable of doing anything that would be of any value. With sincere regrets, I am, Yours very truly

130.   [GRANT, VIRGINIA, JULY 12, 1926]

TO ROGER SERGEL

Dear Roger: It may not matter in the long run, that dead, sick feeling as you draw near the end of the novel.

It often happens. A man wants so much, gets so little.

We all, as workmen, are often too conscious. I can't tell what it is.

The object, I think — to empty oneself.

Like making love.

It comes off sometimes, sometimes doesn't.

Just physical love-making, work, isn't enough.

We have to give. What have we to give?

Often it seems nothing.

Paul Rosenfeld is here for a week. We both work every day. He also is into a novel.

We talk some.

It has been fine to have him. He goes today.

I shall show the letter about fireplaces to the old builder. Here, however, they know fireplace-making well. They use nothing else.

The stone walls of the house go up. I want you and Ruth here someday.

[1] Robert Morss Lovett; Norman Hapgood (1868–1937), editor of *Hearst's International Magazine* from 1923 to 1925; Roger Baldwin (1884–), long director of the American Civil Liberties Union.

131. [TROUTDALE,[1] VIRGINIA, ?AUGUST, 1926]

To ROBERT ANDERSON

Dear Bob: I have been thinking of you a good deal lately. I think that with your energy, your quick imagination, and your love of life you are bound in the end to go toward one of the arts.

The natural thing would be for you to become, eventually, a prose writer, a storyteller.

But here, my dear fellow, you will always be under a handicap. The great difficulty will always be that your father is one. They would always club you with that.

When I am dead, the sons of bitches will begin to heap laurels on me.

You would have to be almost superhuman not, in the end, to hate me.

However, I think there is a way out, and also I think it may be a way that finally may come natural to you.

As you know, I have never touched the stage. Why not begin giving your mind and imagination to that?

It is, of course, a long road, but any road in the arts is long. I think you might begin consciously to let yourself think and feel in that way. You are a natural dramatist with a quick imagination. Let your imagination, at odd moments, begin to play within a confined place, casting people in there, letting them in imagination play within that confined place.

And then too, Bob, I think that for us, of our tribe, it is almost necessary to have a moral balance.

There is and can be no moral balance like the long difficulty of an art.

If the idea strikes you, begin. Read what all the old and the modern dramatists have done. It is entirely possible and rather nice to let your will, in part at least, control your fancy.

A man needs a purpose for real health. It is a suggestion. Think about it. With love

132. [?TROUTDALE, VIRGINIA, AUGUST 5, 1926]

To ALFRED STIEGLITZ

Dear Stieglitz: I did some new short stories. *Mercury* is to have one of them in an early number.[1] *Scribner's* bought another, but will not

---

[1] "Telegraph address" of Ripshin farm, but usually given instead of Grant, the "post office address."

[1] Presumably "Death in the Woods," *American Mercury*, IX, 7–13 (September, 1926).

publish until next year.[2] They bought it as one of a series by American writers. There is another, an odd sort of story, ready to send off. Then I agreed to do some articles for *Vanity Fair* if they would let me pick the subjects. I sent in a list. They agreed. I have done two of them.[3] Of the novel I have done about thirty thousand words. So you see how busy I have been.

All this along with watching almost every stone that goes into the house.

I rather like these country workmen. They have not been spoiled yet, take an interest.

Paul talked some of his novel. I did not want to ask him to talk too much. Sometimes it is better for a man not to talk of his work. It sounded living to me. His whole visit was a delight to us. He thinks, no doubt, I've changed. I dare say I have. Life does things to a man, as you know. Paul talked a good deal of your year, all you had accomplished. What is going to happen to a lot of people when you can no longer do it, God only knows.

You will be interested in knowing that I am trying to get into the novel a feeling of the automobile as a tool for expression. I mean the running of an automobile. Don't try to do too much, man. Wish to God I could see what you and Georgie are doing.

There is a grand old print of Maud S.[4] over the mantel of my workroom, in full speed, flattened. Why in hell weren't we both horsemen? We'd have had such fun sitting by the stable door evenings talking.

My two boys are here. They would take a book. I'll tell you of them someday.

133.   GRANT, VIRGINIA, AUGUST 19, 1926

To EARL ANDERSON

Dear Earl: Something to say. Every thought going through my head is something to say.

---

[2] "Another Wife," *Scribner's*, LXXX, 587–594 (December, 1926).

[3] The two articles immediately printed were "The Far West," *Vanity Fair*, XXVII, 39–40, 104 (January, 1927), and "Prohibition," *ibid.*, 68, 96 (February, 1927).

[4] Famous American trotter, who in the 1880's set several speed records for the mile.

Why did we let ourselves become detached?

But wait.

I have thought and thought of what you said of Mother. I think men who marry sometimes transfer to their wives the feeling you had in mind.

It may be that the artist who does not function tends to destroy the materials they [sic] touch; women who are not loved have to pass on the seeds of destruction to their children.

Few enough men or women can love. It is the ultimate test.

Men think they seek passion in women. They seek a deep passion, the passion of life itself.

No man can live alone. It may be a man can live in another man. I think so.

After I left you, I had to go to New York to see some men. Two rich men who had mistresses took them with me to dine. The women thought they had been hurt because they had given their bodies for a price.

The real hurt was that none of them knew love.

Too much to say. Karl and Irve [1] are here. Karl is going to try a portrait of me. Irve is much better. His wife is a brick, not like Helen. I think she must give him more than he knows.

Few people know anything. The walls of the house are almost up. As soon as I can, I will send you a snapshot of it.

I have found a way to pray, inside. I pray in every little odd moment you may grow well enough to come here and be with me next year. With love

134.   [TROUTDALE, VIRGINIA, ?LATE AUGUST, 1926]

[NIGHT LETTER] THE VIKING PRESS, NEW YORK

The Time of Man [1] SEEMS TO ME A WONDERFUL PERFORMANCE STOP VERY CLEAR FINE AND ALTOGETHER CHARMING STOP THE PROSE IS ENTIRELY INDIVIDUAL STOP RESTRAINT BACKGROUND STOP LIKE THINGS GROWING

---

[1] Irwin Anderson, younger brother to Karl and Sherwood, who was named after the father. See *Memoirs*, pp. 24, 51.

---

[1] *The Time of Man*, a novel by Elizabeth Madox Roberts (1886–1941) was published in 1926 by the Viking Press.

SUDDENLY ON RICH LAND STOP ELIZABETH MADOX ROBERTS SHOULD DO A
GREAT DEAL OF VERY BEAUTIFUL WORK STOP CONGRATULATIONS TO HER
AND YOU

135.   [TROUTDALE, VIRGINIA, LATE AUGUST, 1926]

To ROGER SERGEL

Dear Roger: Elizabeth and I were out in the hills today in such a
rain as seems to sweep the whole world clean. Torrents coming down
out of cornfields, the roads rivers.

We have about got a house. Our debt on it, all told, may be $4,000,
a stone house with a barn & a tenant house, also a cabin for me.

It has been a queer summer, & I have thought often of you. Was
thinking of you and Ruth today in the rain and wanting to write you.
I want you both to read *The Time of Man* by a new woman writer
(Huebsch). It is a gorgeous, a beautiful book.

We came home, & there was your letter.

Dear man. How many times have I gone through that story and must
yet go. Only last week me creeping to Elizabeth, tears in my eyes, saying [all] I had ever written was nothing, declaring I would never write
anything really decent.

A man plows on and then dies. God knows about it all. This summer I have destroyed 30[,000] to 40,000 words of a novel twice.

Rubbish piled up. The real flaw always eluding a man.

Then when it is almost hopeless, a bit comes.

This year I undertook too much, a house & a novel too. I want the
house there and paid for if it can be managed. It will cut my living
cost down, down.

Lord, I wish for strength for you, endurance.

These times of discouragement come like a disease. A man never
escapes. Sometimes I think I can feel them in the air, from North,
So[uth], East, West.

Will no one do anything beautifully?

I can't.

Then a man begins again, as you must. What else is there to do?

Whether or not my own novel will come through I don't know.

I only pray. Love to both

136. [TROUTDALE, VIRGINIA, SEPTEMBER, 1926]

To KARL ANDERSON

Dear Karl: I can understand your uncertainty about the painting. It has been an odd summer with me. The big canvas I have tried to do — that is to say, this novel — eludes me. I have, I dare say, written a hundred thousand words that will not do. With me always the great difficulty is getting between the canvas and myself. I mean that I am inclined to intellectualize it too much. The people of the novel want to emerge as individuals aside from myself and what I think they should be, and I have difficulty letting them. It is only when I can do it I get something pure.

The days are grey, and the clouds lie low over the mountains. We are expecting the Connicks [1] from Boston this morning. The red in the plaster worked very well. It is almost all on. The plumbing is also about in, and the ram is working fairly well, so that we have water. As for the wine, I put in the water vent and am letting it stand. Have been drinking out of the extra two gallons we made. It is new yet, of course, but does very well.

After you left, we got a woman from town who turns out to be a jewel. She is the wife of the man Ezra shot, a quiet, capable woman, who has already agreed to be with us next year. Then we have got the young farmer who is to move into this house as soon as we are out. He is a capable man.

Any day now the leaves should begin to turn and the nuts to ripen. As yet everything is green. I got the mountain man to make me four kegs of grape wine, made from wild grapes. The other night we set out to take the kegs to him. It was a strange ride over unknown mountain roads, over huge rocks and tree roots. Irve would have died of it, I am afraid. The man is to make the wine for us and keep it until spring.

The woman, Mary, turns out to be a very capable needlewoman. She can also make hooked rugs. I am mighty anxious to have you here painting in this country when [?where] you can live comfortably. Do plan on it for next year.

I will have the money I owe you to send at the end of October, if not before. I think I should pay you interest. Let's plan in the future to be together all we can. Lots of love to you, Helen and the children

[1] Charles J. Connick, designer of stained and leaded glass.

137.   S. S. *Roosevelt* [?December 8, 1926]

To Paul Rosenfeld

Dear Paul: I got the *Dial* and read the piece on New Mexico.[1] Well, of course, it is a difficult thing for the reader to get. How am I to say? So is a good water color by Marin.

It isn't my way, of course, all of these strange, jeweled adjectives. I want my own prose to go like great waves washing the sides of ships, like the Mississippi going down to the sea. It never does, but that is what I want.

You aren't me — more tense, quickly alive, nervous, more modern.

I get a substance, something felt. After reading I couldn't put it into words, no more than you did.

Is that required?

Is that what the writer undertakes to do?

I think he undertakes something more and that you reach for.

The substance comes something like a perfume. It's enough for me.

138.   [?1927]

To William Faulkner

Dear Bill: I'm mighty glad you also have run into the Jackson family,[1] or at least a man who knows something about them. I've been on their trail for a year now and have heard a lot of news about their doings, but haven't met a Jackson yet. What I want specially is to meet Al himself. The whole country around here is full of stories about him. Are they true? I wonder. You know, I am a professional writer, and if I could ever get this Al Jackson's story straight, get a firsthand interview with him with pictures and all, I'd have a gold mine. Wouldn't

---

[1] See "Musical Chronicle" by Paul Rosenfeld, *Dial,* LXXXI, 529–534 (December, 1926).

---

[1] Two undated letters from William Faulkner in the Anderson collection form a nexus of tall tales about the Jackson family. Old man Jackson raised sheep in a swamp, but they tended to turn into alligators from being immersed in the water so much; Elenor slid down a drainpipe at night and eloped with a peddler; and Claude was "kind of bad" after blondes. Proof of their descent from Andrew Jackson lies in the fact that the "congress shoes" on the statue in Jackson Park hide the webbed feet that got him safely through the Battle of New Orleans.

For Faulkner's use of the Al Jackson tale, see *Mosquitoes* (1927), pp. 66–67, 277–281.

wonder if I'd find some big magazine hungry for it. Who wouldn't want to know all about Al Jackson?

I'm sorry you dragged that in about Claude. There was Elenor Jackson too, Al and Claude's sister. I've heard stories about her, not here but over in Mississippi, but if you ever hear any of them, don't tell me. I've always thought of Al as one of the purest and cleanest American men I ever heard of, and I do wish the rest of his family were more like him. He ought to be pure and clean. He's been in the water so much.

But let me tell you how I picked up my own line on the Jacksons. Funny about Al. You meet a man over in Arkansas or Texas or up in Mississippi, and even as far west as Topeka or Denver or, say, in Baltimore, who tells you something about him, and then you go on for days and weeks and months and never meet a man or woman or child who ever heard of Al Jackson's people at all. One day in New York I counted. I met eight hundred and forty-two people between nine twenty-six in the morning and four-eighteen in the afternoon, and not one of them knew a word about Al. I had a boy with me to count.

I first heard of Al and his folks on a train. There was a fellow sitting in the seat beside me, name of Flu Balsam. He used to be a water man himself and claimed he had herded fish under Al for almost two years.

He was a blind kind of man from getting so much water in his eyes, but I never noticed anything special about his legs. He could walk on them all right.

This Flu, it seems, had been herding cows over in Texas, but had lost his horse. He was a nervous, erratic kind of a man with a tin ear got from the kick of a horse, and if he had web feet, like they say so many of the fishherds get, I couldn't notice. He had on congress shoes.

About his losing his horse. It seems he couldn't sleep much nights, and so he traded his horse to an easygoing, restful kind of a Texan, and an expert sleeper, for a night's sleep. The fellow was to come around about seven in the evening to get the horse, and Flu was to get his sleep, and so Flu got the horse out in front of his house early and stood holding him, all ready to rush off to bed, but the fellow didn't show up till almost four in the morning.

And so this Flu Balsam lost his horse and his sleep too and of course couldn't herd cows any more; so he says he went fishherding with Al Jackson. That's what he says. He also said that Al brands all his fish by cutting a notch in their tails. Did you hear anything about that?

But to get back to Al. Here's another I heard. I was in a town over in Alabama and was standing on a station platform, and they had a bull in a crate, shipping him somewhere. I was watching the bull and knocking flies off his nose when a man came up, and we had a talk.

Of course we talked of Al. Nowadays all this country is ringing with stories of Al. He's the biggest man in the fish industry all right.

This new man looked honest enough. Of course he was Southern, but I don't think he was a fishherd himself. You can always tell them by their congress shoes, and his were laced.

What he told me was that he was a traveling man selling congress shoes down here in Louisiana and in all these coast states, and he says about all his trade is among Al's fishherds. He says a fishherd wants to go out into society now and then, same as any other man, or get him a girl or a wife or something, and anything else but congress shoes hurt his feet. On account of having the webs that way, he says.

As I say, he was an honest-looking kind of man with a mustache and a glass eye, and he looked Southern and talked that way too.

What he says and what I started to write you about was for you not [to] get yourself mixed up. He says that Al Jackson's people have nothing at all to do with the Stonewalls or the Andrews, not for me to get that notion into my head, so I didn't.

He says Al Jackson's people were straight slave-running folks. They used to have a boat, he says, and all they did was to run black ivory in.

There was one of them, he said, old Spearhead Jackson, who was a terror. Once he was coming over from Africa with a load of niggers on board, and night was coming on when a Britisher got after him. The Britisher kept closing up and closing up; so this old Spearhead had three niggers brought up and threw them into the sea.

The Britisher stopped, of course, to pick them up, being so humane and not in the business himself, and then he came on again, and so Spearhead had to throw out three more and then two, and just as darkness was coming on, he chucked out six. Fifteen good niggers gone and they worth all of eight hundred dollars apiece. "Do you wonder we hated the British in them days?" the man said who was talking to me. But old Spearhead made his getaway in the dark.

Later and after the war they had him up in the Tchufuncta country shooting what stray niggers he could find floating around loose at two dollars a head. Rather a comedown for him. It may have been up there that you heard about him. A branch of the Jacksons settled somewhere up there.

139. [Paris, ?January, 1927]

To Paul Rosenfeld

Dear Paul: I got your cablegram, God knows. I landed in London sunk. Got to Paris and [had] the flu. Was in bed 10 days.

Everything I have written seems dead stuff. God knows what I am in. I am all right physically, but for the time being am no judge of anything.

The Americans in Paris are terrible. Such a shuffling lot. I am to see Joyce this afternoon. Perhaps he will be alive.

I am none too much alive myself. No sweet, new impulses. My fancy tosses and jumps constantly. I work on a novel for a week, then throw it away. I write a short story. It seems nothing.

Well, I'm too old a bird to think it is all necessarily final for me. I have waded through other long swamps.

All there is about it, dear Paul, is that I can see nothing I am doing as really worth presenting.

I may right myself like an old ship. Now I am in a rowboat in the midst of the sea. I row in one direction thinking I may find a new promised land, then turn about and row in the other direction.

If there is anything I have that seems to me worth while, you shall have it of course. I can't tell now.

Is it just me, or is it a dead time? I am going to see Picasso Sunday.

At last *A Story Teller*, the *Note Book*, *Winesburg* and another book of stories are to be all published in France this year. "A Man Who Became a Woman" & "A Man's Story" were published here — Bernard Faÿ [1] translation — and they seem to have opened this door.

Will be back in America early in March. We will talk then.

God knows, I hope I may be something less rudderless by then.
[P.S.] E[lizabeth] sends greetings.

140. [Troutdale, Virginia, ?April, 1927]

To John Anderson

[No salutation] Something I should have said in my letter yesterday. In relation to painting.

Don't be carried off your feet by anything because it is modern, the latest thing.

---

[1] Bernard Faÿ (1893–), formerly professor at the University of Clermont-Ferrand, who was a specialist in American cultural development.

Go to the Louvre [1] often and spend a good deal of time before the Rembrandts, the Delacroix's.

Learn to draw. Try to make your hand so unconsciously adept that it will put down what you feel without your having to think of your hands.

Then you can think of the thing before you.

Draw things that have some meaning to you. An apple, what does it mean?

The object drawn doesn't matter so much. It's what you feel about it, what it means to you.

A masterpiece could be made of a dish of turnips.

Draw, draw, hundreds of drawing[s].

Try to remain humble. Smartness kills everything.

The object of art is not to make salable pictures. It is to save yourself.

Any cleanness I have in my own life is due to my feeling for words.

The fools who write articles about me think that one morning I suddenly decided to write and began to produce masterpieces.

There is no special trick about writing or painting either. I wrote constantly for 15 years before I produced anything with any solidity to it.

For days, weeks, and months now I can't do it.

You saw me in Paris this winter. I was in a dead, blank time. You have to live through such times all your life.

The thing, of course, is to make yourself alive. Most people remain all of their lives in a stupor.

The point of being an artist is that you may live.

Such things as you suggested in your letter the other day. I said, "Don't do what you would be ashamed to tell me about."

I was wrong.

You can't depend on me. Don't do what you would be ashamed of before a sheet of white paper or a canvas.

The materials have to take the place of God.

About color. Be careful. Go to nature all you can. Instead of paint-shops, other men's palettes, look at the sides of buildings in every light. Learn to observe little thing[s], a red apple lying on a grey cloth.

Trees, trees against [a] hill, everything. I know little enough. It seems to me that if I wanted to learn about color, I would try always

---

[1] John and Marion had accompanied Anderson to Europe and remained for some time in Paris after their father had returned to the United States.

to make a separation. There is a plowed field here before me, below it a meadow, half-decayed cornstalk[s] in the meadow making yellow lines, stumps, sometimes like looking into an ink bottle, sometimes almost blue.

The same in nature is a composition.

You look at it, thinking, "What made up that color?" I have walked over a piece of ground, after seeing it from a distance, trying to see what made the color I saw.

Light makes so much difference.

You won't arrive. It is an endless search.

I write as though you were a man. Well, you must know my heart is set on you.

It isn't your success I want. There is a possibility of your having a decent attitude toward people and work. That alone may make a man of you.

[P.S.] Tell Church [2] that David Prall finally got the Cézanne prints.

Also tell the man at the shop where you go for the Picasso book, or if you have been there, drop him a note — the shop, I mean.

---

141.   [?TROUTDALE, VIRGINIA, ?APRIL, 1927]

To JOHN ANDERSON

Dear John: "Sunday morning and raining." I had just written the above sentence, intending to write you a long letter, when I put the sheet aside and began writing on my book. I have perhaps written 2[,000] or 3,000 words since then. Now I am tired, and my hands are shaky. It is still raining, harder than ever. I shall have to take a drink of moon to write to you at all.

What I want to say is something about the delight that may finally come to you in such moments of work. You may come to get out of canvases what I get out of sheets of paper.

I presume it is the power of losing self. Self is the grand disease. It is what we all are trying to lose.

I think the reason I want you to be an artist, have an artist's viewpoint, is just because such times compensate for so much else.

How people ever lose themselves who are not artists I do not know. Perhaps they, some of them, do it in love.

---

[2] Ralph Church, later professor of aesthetics at Cornell University, was at this time studying at Oxford and making frequent trips to the Continent.

To love a woman and possess her is a good deal. It isn't enough for an eager man.

Power, such as comes with achievement, is something. In the end it becomes a disease. It destroys the man who has it.

In art there is the possibility of an impersonal love. For modern men it is, I think, the only road to God.

I presume that is why, loving you as my son, I want you to be an artist. I don't really give a damn whether you succeed or not.

There is a lot to say, but I am too tired to write.

I will just send this broken fragment off to you.

142.   [TROUTDALE, VIRGINIA, ?APRIL, 1927]

To ROGER SERGEL

Dear Roger Sergel: A confused day. Your note a part of the confusion.

I don't mean of today but of everything.

I can't get excited about Eaton's project.[1] The name, the idea back of the name, repels me.

As though anyone could escape intolerance any more than another impulse. You get to writing, setting something straight, and inside you feel so big.

I'm pretty tired of bigness, big feelings, self-induced.

I went over to Paris, had a success of a sort there.

You haven't come to that yet. I mean feeling yourself established. You get what is called fame.

Sherwood Anderson —

A man's name.

You hearing it around.

Presently a kind of deep sickness.

You writing. You haven't written, because you are so and so and I am so and so.

Just as I read the letter, me sitting by a roadside at evening. A farmer boy hurrying to a house on a distant hillside.

He was going to see his sweetheart. His very walk telling me that.

To tell the truth, I was sick with jealousy at the moment. I wanted to be him, going to a woman [I] had never seen.

---

[1] Geoffrey D. Eaton (1894–), author of *Backfurrow* (1925). The "project" apparently refers to the founding of Eaton's magazine *Plain Talk,* the first number of which appeared in October of this year.

Because I have also been wanting to be fields, trees, horses.

If there is any person, place or thing in this world more important than another.

If you write a successful novel, do you become more important to me?

Would you be more important to your wife, who loves you, to your child?

I get you too making a figure of me, and it hurts.

The world full and full of that nonsense.

Hemingway made a damn fool by it; Joyce, too. I saw it popping in them both.

I am Joyce.

I am Hemingway.

Christ!

Is there nothing more important than that kind of absurd importance, in me and others?

If the arts make men like that, damn and God damn the arts.

You wrote *Arlie Gelston*, didn't you? Well, they didn't proclaim you much.

Who didn't?

Jesus, Maria, who is there to do any proclaiming?

I don't care if you don't write. If you aren't in the mood, why should you?

But not to write because I am Sherwood Anderson, a gigantic mood in some gigantic man that may be destroyed.

It makes me want to shout at you, scream, saying, "Wake up, for Christ['s] sake."

I'll forgive you when you come out of that.

Your woman knows better. Give my love to her.

143.   [TROUTDALE, VIRGINIA, APRIL 29, 1927]

TO PAUL ROSENFELD

My dear Paul: It has been beastly of me not to have written, and I would feel worse about it only that you have been frequently up to the same thing. I remember once, out West, when you went into a simply appalling silence.

Usually I write too many letters. It's a vice I love. I go about having imaginary conversations with you, Stieglitz, strange women seen on the streets who have taken my fancy, historic characters.

As a matter of fact, the dinner was what my little daughter would have called "swell."

I liked the tone of Sergel; Stieglitz and O'Keeffe were in fine form. I of course lost you. The dinner, or lunch, was on your mind. You were away over on the far side of the table.

Well, you see what I mean by lecturing, any damn thing.

I don't want to do anything I don't want to do, never.

I'm afraid my *Testament* [1] won't be all I want it to be.

I've had a bad six months, inside, and may be in for another.

In the first place, it began with money. I did not want any. I wanted to be poor, starve a little.

Then I would grow afraid I would.

There was too much going on. Cornelia Anderson, while rather splendid in many ways, hadn't got hold of the kids. I had to try to get hold of them, learn something of their direction.

I got out of that one boy who has rather swept me off my feet. It's just straight love. He's marvelous just now. That's the one I left in Paris.

I was trying to make a home.

I went to Paris and found myself close to famous. That's just plain sickening. God knows, I hope you escape it. It's sheer nonsense without a spark of meaning.

It might as well have been Jim Tully. [2] Why not?

I wanted to write a novel. It broke and broke.

I came here.

O[h], about the book. I probably won't look at it now.

I'm getting something from nature I never did get before. Every day I wish myself a painter. That's nonsense, of course — dodging some challenge.

For the time I want, if I can, to forget words, as they are in any book.

People, no.

I go about with these farmers. I want to relate people, in a way I never have before, to words. I'm after some tone. It eludes.

I have got too conscious — my little stick of fame, certain pieces set down.

[1] *A New Testament*, published June, 1927.
[2] The American "hobo" novelist, 1891–1947.

I'd like to burn it all.

Some days I just swear inside. A farmer whose field had washed away in a rain said to me, "Take God Almighty up one side and down the other, and he does about as much harm as he does good."

That goes for me, too. I want to be as nice as a horse or a dog, and can't.

I've got energy. God knows, I write enough, feel enough. It's just all a whirlwind yet, though.

I went past an oats field being planted yesterday and thought, "Why in hell can't I grow with the oats in that field?"

I wanted to bury myself in the field and come up green.

I can't shake myself off.

I want to be a boy again without any life lived, and every moment of my life hangs to me like a drag.

I've got to accept it all, use it all.

I keep praying, in an odd sort of way.

Well, you see, this is all about myself. It's the only thing I can think of.

It helps being down here. I'm done with cities. No more Paris, Europe for me ever.

We speak of you, E. [Elizabeth] and I. We both wonder if either of us has told you that a visit from you is a definite, expected part of our summer. You've got to come. E. says it mustn't be for just a week as before. It must be for at least three weeks.

E. will write. She thinks by June the painters, carpenters, etc. will all be gone.

The rhododendrons and laurel will still be blooming then. E. will write. She has a headache today. But save June.

Lucile Swan, that was Mrs. Jerome Blum, but ain't, is coming for the whole summer. She is going to take a house of her own.

She's nice. Quiet. She paints.

We have some gentle saddle horses if you like to ride.

The whole point, what I'm after, is love in words, I guess. I mean in the struggle I'm going through about words.

I'd really like to put some poetry down.

Not calling it that, for God['s] sake.

Well, you'll come, thank God.

144.   [TROUTDALE, VIRGINIA, ?MAY 19, 1927]

To PAUL ROSENFELD

Dear Paul: You say nothing about coming down, but we are taking it as a fact that you will come later in the summer.

It is beginning to be summer now. The corn is up, the very conservative locust trees are putting out leaves, we sleep with all doors and windows open and take shower baths.

If I am getting a little straightened out, I think this time it is Vincent Van Gogh.

Figures of men keep popping up that way. I dare say artists never quit doing things to each other.

And not only artists.

I got suddenly Van Gogh and Gauguin at Arles where Van Gogh cut off his ear for the little prostitute who had asked for it.

Before that Van Gogh in Drenthe.[1]

Just now it seems to me Van Gogh was as near right as a man can be.

I mean only my own efforts to get humanized here. To penetrate into the soil, plowed fields, people in little house[s] in hollows, to shake off, if possible, all smart-aleckness.

This morning I went for a mile walk at six. A house painter had broken into my cellar during my absence, got drunk, and was ashamed to come back to work. I went to get him back.

The shame of the man standing on the porch of his house. His young wife, really like a flower, two children.

The man's relations to me. My relations with him.

Every little thing seems suddenly as important as another.

It is constant, like a river flowing.

My relations with you as difficult and no more difficult than with that workman.

With Elizabeth, with a woman visitor here in the house.

With the woman in the kitchen.

With a man driving a team in the road.

With a field my window faces. I have dared to plant the field to corn. My relations to that.

I own a mare and am thinking of breeding her and raising a colt.

Everything seems suddenly daring, some days even putting my foot down on the ground.

[1] A province in the Netherlands.

We go into the woods and bring out wild flowers, taking them up by the roots, the soil clinging. We bring them here to plant on our creek bank. Some will live, some die.

You get the notion of pain, of death in plants. It gets down into your own being.

It doesn't seem to me, on some days, I ever want to move from one spot.

God knows, a lifetime would be little enough time to live in one valley like this.

The "it" we talk and think about and can't ever quite reach is there all the time.

It comes so very close some times.

For one thing, Paul, it made me pretty sick seeing Hemingway this winter. What seemed to me to have happened to Joyce made me ill.

The Stieglitz controversy about the $6,000 or $600,000 for the Marins.[2]

The Joyce petition [3] to stop the man pirating his damn book. "A man's property must be protected."

I have found myself using the words about my house and fields.

"My property. My horse."

My God, can a man own a white horse standing eating green grass on a sloping hillside?

O[h], well, dear Paul, anyway I am going about, "standing in the need of prayer."

I don't need to be throwing stones into houses.

As you know, we want you to come for long enough time this summer [to] get a feel of the country.

145.   🌲   [TROUTDALE, VIRGINIA, ?MID-AUGUST, 1927]

To STARK YOUNG [1]

My dear Stark: Anyway, Stark, dear, do not worry about the packages. I just wanted to let you know they hadn't shown up, in case they had been sent and lost.

[2] On July 5, 1924, Stieglitz wrote Anderson a long letter denouncing the theory that modern paintings were not worth the prices charged.

[3] On March 23, 1927, in New York James Joyce sued Samuel Roth and the Two Worlds Publishing Company to restrain them from publishing an expurgated edition of *Ulysses*. See *Publishers' Weekly* for April 2, 1917, p. 1416.

[1] Stark Young (1881–), drama critic and author.

About the *New Republic* matter.[2] There is a sense in which the man is right. I mean about the dying condition of the Winesburg S[herwood] A[nderson].

There is too much talk anyway of the sweet, naive S.A. — adolescence, etc.

In general I think this kind of body-punching criticism is a good thing. There is too much softness.

Of course, it made me sick for a day. What hurts, however, is the ugliness — bad workmanship, etc., evident revengeful feeling, so much unconcealed joy in the death.

It was so damned funereal.

You know what would have happened to me had I gone on being the S.A. of *Winesburg*.

A man lives and dies a good many times. You are doing creative work, you know.

However, it isn't this man's business whether or not there is a new and worth-while S.A. coming along. That is up to me.

Anyway, dear man, I'm working at it.

The house is really pretty well done. One or two country men dubbing about in the garden. You'll simply have to come and see it. You know we want you anytime.

Bob is entering the University of Virginia this fall.[3] E. is pretty well. She sends love.

146.   [TROUTDALE, VIRGINIA, SEPTEMBER 28, 1927]

To RALPH CHURCH

Dear Church: I have been intending to write to you for a long time. There has been nothing to say. You were at work. I have worked but little, and what I have done has not been very satisfactory to me. How absurd that you should always hear from me when I am in such a dissatisfied state. It is better not to write.

However, now I am in somewhat of a better temper, having come to a resolution. I have decided that, for my soul's good, I have got to give up the notion of living by writing. This idea that one must

---

[2] Lawrence S. Morris, "Sherwood Anderson: Sick of Words," *New Republic*, LI, 277–279 (August 3, 1927), a review of *A New Testament*.

[3] Robert Anderson attended the University during the academic year 1927–1928.

produce constantly, or starve, is terribly detrimental to any sort of freedom of approach.

All the time I am driven by this demon of necessity. I am a great fool, Church. When I have made some money, I spend it as though it would last forever. For example, my coming to Europe last year was a great folly. I am constantly spending what I have not got to spend.

I have decided that for my own good I have got to begin making my living. An opportunity has apparently offered [itself]. In a neighboring town, Marion, Virginia, a town of about four thousand people, there is a small weekly newspaper. I have an opportunity to buy it. It is earning about six thousand a year.

You know what such papers are. They are filled with local news, deaths, the small affairs of a prosperous small town, half industrial, half a marketing town for a rather rich agricultural section. Even as I write you, I am planning to go to New York to see if I can raise five thousand dollars, the amount necessary to buy the paper. The money and what else I pay for it on notes I shall expect to get back from the paper itself. It is already prosperous and well established. There is a good local printing business and no competition.

I am taking this step for two reasons: first, to free myself from the immediate necessity of living by my pen, and then to get back into closer association with all kinds of people in their everyday lives. I want to free myself from the necessity of professionalism.

Of course it may not work; that is to say, I may not be able to raise the money. In that case I shall probably go back to some city and get a job.

I guess you know that when we were in California, I made an arrangement with Boni & Liveright by which they were to guarantee me a certain amount for a certain number of years. I was afraid of the proposal, but was driven into it by necessity. They have been very nice, but the situation has always been on my nerves. I cannot get over the idea of being at work for them as an employee. When a day or week comes that I do not write satisfactorily, I am beside myself.

Well, you see, I want what writing I do to be incidental, a part of my life, not a profession. I am seeking a profession outside that.

Over here the *Testament*[1] has brought down a furor on my head. It is much the same sort of thing that greeted *Many Marriages*. My death as a writer is being tolled up and down the literary press. The

[1] *A New Testament* (1927).

crapehangers have all been busy. Well, I have been thrown that before. It does not matter much.

However, the other thing does matter. I must earn my living outside
my writing, learn to wait. I cannot possibly do a good book a year. It
may be that what I shall want to write in the future will sell less readily than in the past.

In the meantime I am having apparently a fine German success.

By the way, will you do something for me? When you go into the
book shop of Miss Adri[enne] Monnier, will you explain to her the
great difficulty I have had trying to get published over here an article
on her sister's work? [2] The magazine publishers are such fools. They
sen[d] me wires asking if I will not write for them something about
Mr. Tunney and Dempsey,[3] but when I speak to them of her sister's
work, show the photographs, and speak to them of an article, they
shrug their shoulders. [Our] readers are not interested in needlework,
they say. Art to them means painting or sculpture, nothing else. I have
not despaired of doing something, but would like these good people
to know the situation. I may fail. It is absurd. I haven't the heart to
write and tell them of my ill luck.

Do give my love to your mother, and don't fail to write me of your
own progress.

147.   [TROUTDALE, VIRGINIA, ?OCTOBER, 1927]

To ROGER SERGEL

My dear Roger Sergel: Your letter of late August did me good. Like
yourself, and I dare say all working artists, I get often the feeling that
the bouquet has all gone off the wine. The smart men, it seems, rule.
On all sides nothing but cleverness. I am in despair of ever doing anything myself and hear of others in the same state.

Then, as you suggest, something happens. God knows what it is. The
rhythm (I hate that word, but know of no other to take its place) is
picked up. We go along, sing a bit, dance a little in the moonlight.

In the country sometimes I go about looking at horses and cattle.
They eat grass, make love, work when they have to, bear their young.
I am sick with envy of them.

[2] Marie Monnier had for some years been developing the art of creating pictures in embroidery.

[3] Gene Tunney defeated Jack Dempsey for the world's heavyweight boxing
championship on September 23, 1926. See Letter 154.

As for myself, I also have been in a bad state. Now look at the foolishness of us all. I dare say you mourn sometimes having to go to your foolish classes to make your living.[1] You yearn for leisure. Be careful, man, you may sometime get it.

A little success. There you are. Some money comes in. I have had two years of comparative leisure and look back upon them aghast. "My God, what have I done with them?" The question frightens me.

When I was at work at something other than writing, I had at least the feeling that I was doing something out of necessity. Earning your living gives a certain sense of virtue. It is even good to feel wronged a bit. You know how it is.

And so here am I. No, the book is not done. I do not know when it will be done. I have thrown it aside.

Well, I have come to a resolution. I shall go to work at something other than writing. As you know, formerly I was in the position you are in. I made my living, not by teaching, but by advertising writing. My other writing was incidental. I had not tried to make a slave out of my pen. It could play over the paper.

Then corruption crept in. "Give me leisure," I cried, "and you will see what I shall do." The gods laughed. I got the leisure.

Long days nothing to do. "Write, man." But what shall I write?

I am sitting on a hill in the country or walking in the streets of a town. I am in despair, such despair as you know.

Well, I argue with myself. "But, man, you do not have to write. Live."

But I have come to live by writing. I want beauty and meaning always at my finger tips, and there is no beauty or meaning anywhere in me.

But I am only reviewing a state we are both often in. It is not new to you.

What I sat down to do was merely to give you news of myself. I have got a home now in the country. It is almost paid for. The country is very lovely. It does not cost much to live here.

Well, I am going to a nearby town and go to work. I am at present in negotiation for the purchase of a small town weekly paper.[2] If I secure it, and I hope I shall, I will become a country editor. The paper

---

[1] Sergel was at this time still a member of the English Department of the University of Pittsburgh.

[2] In Marion, Virginia.

can make me a living. I shall live by it and not by my scribbling.

All of this to get something of my own weight off the back of my pen in order that, if the gods are good, it may run a bit more lightly over the paper.

Really, and what a curse to be an artist at all. It is the only way of life. It is at the same time the most terrible way of life. Sweet Jesus. Holy Mary, mother of God, why did you not make me a bricklayer, or a plumber?

I can imagine crawling under houses to fix drains. I look up through a crack in the floor. I see the slender legs of the woman of the house, wish to possess her. My days pass so. I get drunk and go home and beat my wife. On the whole a comparatively good life. At least when I lay my hands to a pipe, I can fix the pipe. You see what I mean. What offended me in your letter of the spring was, as you know, that you addressed me as a kind of great man, one removed from the things that sometimes almost drive you insane. I would not be so removed. O[h] my dear man, work accomplished means so little. It is in the past. What we all want is the glorious and living present.

But enough. If you are to have some leisure next year, why do you not think of coming down into these hills? A little house could be had for two or three dollars a month at least. If you were to come, we could arrange to have a garden planted for you in advance. There are mountain streams, woods, hills, green fields. Think of it during the winter. I know of no place where life can be lived more satisfactorily, if you are working, or where life costs less. Love to Ruth

148.   [MARION, VIRGINIA, DECEMBER, 1927]

To MARCO MORROW [1]

Dear Morrow: To date it seems to us the most satisfactory thing we have done.[2] Please note that absolutely natural editorial "we." I got rather sick of the professional air my position as writer was taking on. It is too much like being a professional lover. It can't be done.

And if I did not want to be in the position of making my living as a writer, what else was I to do? There was the matter of going back into an agency as a copy man. I hate backtracking like that. A big steam-

---

[1] Marco Morrow and Anderson had become friends during 1898 when they were living in the same boardinghouse in Springfield.

[2] At Morrow's request Anderson was sending him a copy of one of the two Marion newspapers, probably of the *Smyth County News*.

ship company offered to send me around the world. I'm sick of running around the world. And it only meant hack writing for them.

Or hack writing for some magazine or publisher. This chance came up. I took it. Here I am. I am sending you an issue.

I rather hope the "What Say?" column may amount to something. People here like it. It might catch on as a thing that could be syndicated and make some dough for me that way.

Many times I think of our talks in the old days. We both wanted to be writers. I got there. You didn't. To tell you the truth, old man, I can't see much difference. I think my next novel will be about that — the man who succeeds and what comes of it.

There is always the chance, and a strong chance, of the separation [from] life of the professional writer. A man becomes famous. I suppose I may say I have done that.

It only means you become a public character, and who wants that? I hold to the opinion that writing should be an incidental part of life, not the leading thing in life. If you acquire fame, people begin putting you outside themselves. You are something special. Who wants to be that?

In a sense this whole thing is a sinking of myself back into life. It is a great sea, this thing we call life, and I like swimming in the sea. I have been in the desert too long.

Oho for the open sea of country journalism. Tell me what you think of the paper, something perhaps I can put right in the paper.

There is the off chance my outside circulation may grow to be something special. We get several every day. Lordy, I wish this were [a] big enough thing for you, George [3] and I to do it together. With love

149.   MARION, VIRGINIA [DECEMBER 19, 1927]

To ALFRED STIEGLITZ AND GEORGIA O'KEEFFE

Friends, citizens, countrymen: That is just the worst of being tied down here. That I can't, now and then, run in on you in the afternoon. There aren't so many it is important to see sometimes.

It is just as Marin says about himself in his letter. I got too damn sick of S.A. He crowded himself in between me and everything, the fathead. In the country I stopped seeing the hills, the streams, the blue

[3] George H. Daugherty.

mists. I swear to God I haven't been a decent citizen in two years. Someone guaranteeing me a living. I attempting to turn out ART. Hell and high water.

Now I am getting up in the morning at six and am at my desk at eight. I do everything. A man wants a little handbill got up for the sale of steers. I write it for him. An old mossback farmer comes in and spends an hour trying to get me to knock off 25 cents on the subscription price of his paper. I enjoy it all and in the moments I catch am writing again. That is what a man lives for.

Lord, I wish I could see the Intimate Gallery [1] and you and Georgia.

Man, you don't want that many papers do you?

Lots of love. I think the papers will amuse you just the same. You make me glad telling me you are in form.

150.   [MARION, VIRGINIA, DECEMBER 22, 1927]

To RALPH CHURCH

Dear Ralph: It is just about a year ago now we were landing in Paris, coming up from the boat so gloomy and cold and finding you at the station.

And then everything getting better. Taking it all in all, it wasn't [a] successful winter. I remained terribly gloomy on the whole.

And now after a year you are married and I am here running two local papers. I did it because I felt it rotten and wrong that I should depend on writing to live. There is so much damned hack work being done. I felt myself drifting toward that. Not that I care so much, only I do want to know what I am doing. I don't like to bunk myself.

Unless I went back to the city, there was nothing I could do to make money. Offers came along. I could have gone with a big city advertising agency — big money. The Cunard Line wanted me to go to the Mediterranean, to write bunk about how happy the rich Americans are, etc., etc.

Then this chance came up. I bought these two papers. As a matter of fact, I bought them on paper. They can, I think, pay their own way out in a few years. I went to work. I'm doing most of the writing myself. As I couldn't afford a reporter, I invented one. I call him Buck Fever, a purely mythical being.

---

[1] See Letter 124, note 3. On January 9, 1928, there was to be an exhibit of forty new paintings by Georgia O'Keeffe; and a John Marin show had occupied it from November 9 to December 11, 1927.

Buck and I do all the writing. E. does the bookkeeping, etc. It's great fun. As a matter of fact, if I have anything in me, my other writing won't suffer. Being busy doesn't hurt any man.

I wish I had had a better chance to know Beth. Some day perhaps I will. We still dream of you coming along here some time.

David's visit was a pure joy. I read a lot of his book.[1] I think it very, very fine stuff. I suppose he'll come across. We tried to talk him into coming back here, letting Europe go.

You must understand running these country weeklies isn't like running dailies. We have no deadline. The papers rather drift out.

Your generous Christmas gift came. It said "Not to be opened until Christmas," but I couldn't resist. I cut right into it. Such grand, gaudy ties. I love them. Bless you.

We closed up the country house and are living at a hotel this winter. It's a little like last winter, only so different. I get up at 6:30, eat, cut out to the office. All sorts of people drift in during the day — old farmers, people wanting a bit of printing, etc. I run about to the county court, everywhere. Then I go back and write.

My own writing sandwiched in. It's healthy for it. Art is a whore. If you pay too much attention to her, she gets upstage.

My getting the papers attracted attention all over America. It seems what I have done half the men in America would like to do. It half seems I have struck thirteen again.

My books keep going big in Germany, and there are to be new Polish, Danish, Swedish, and Dutch translations this year. I'll be writing again if it is in the cards. I've quit worrying about that.

In the meantime E. is well too. We are both leading much healthier and saner lives, being very busy.

I wish this grind over there was over for you. I keep hoping this country may attract you, your mother, and Beth some day. Dave fell for it hard.

The country people like my papers. We got 150 new subscribers in six weeks without asking anyone. The liquor is at least passable. I've in mind, if I ever get this novel off my chest, a serious book. It's hard to tell just what about. I would like to analyze everything. Put it all down. Just what a man feels and why. It may be half if not all philosophic. Wish I could talk of it to you. The chance may come before I get to it.

[1] David Prall's *Study in the Theory of Value* had appeared in 1921. Possibly Anderson read a manuscript copy of *Aesthetic Judgment*, published in 1929.

Give all my love to your mother and tell Mrs. Ralph I count on having the chance to know her someday. E. sends all her love to you all.

151.   [Marion, Virginia, ?late 1927]

To John Anderson

Dear John: It is all ineffectual and vital too. The moment you say life is without significance, you are all wrong; but if you say it is significant, you are just as far wrong.

As I have told you before, I have come here and taken hold of these papers because, having nothing to do but write, I found myself unable to do that.

In the end perhaps a man has to manufacture his own interest in life. A young man thinks he wants fame. I have had that. It amounts to nothing. What does? God knows what except work.

There was a young man in here to talk to me the other day. He was eaten up with contemplation of self. It had grown on him like a disease. I think it is a little like this. A man who is really sensitive has moments that lift him up higher than the average man. He wants to stay up there and can't. Then he begins to feel life is unfair to him. He broods. Self becomes all-important to him. If he is not careful, he will destroy his chances for having other fine moments.

It may be life is only worth while at moments. Perhaps that is all we ought to expect.

152.   [Marion, Virginia] March 26, 1928

Mr. Roger Sergel, 6016 Stony Island Avenue, Chicago

Dear Roger: It is certainly interesting to think of you in Chicago. The address 6016 Stony Island Avenue is almost exactly an address at which I once lived. I am wondering if it isn't the same apartment building, if it is an apartment building. There used to be a lot of low, one-story buildings on Stony Island near 57th Street. Floyd Dell lived there once. That was the first place I ever met any artists or writers. At that time I think I had already written three or four novels, but had never published anything.

I think Jackson Park is one of the loveliest parks in America. How many adventures I have had in that park! How many hours have I spent wandering about in it at night and dreaming!

Did I ever tell you the story of my lost novel? That happened on what is called the Japanese Island in Jackson Park.

I went to Chicago when I was quite a young man. All sorts of love adventures in Jackson Park, a good many of which I have written about.

It is odd to think of you and Ruth living there, facing the same park.

I still think it would be a grand idea, when you get that business [1] thoroughly in your own hands and have got enough of Chicago, to move it to some good small town, like Marion, Virginia. I should think you could do that sort of business just as well in a small place as in a city.

Your friend Buck Fever was just in the office, and I spoke to him about the change of address, but he said it was none of his business; so I will have to do that myself.

The papers seem to be going along all right, and we continue to have a good time with them. All my love to both of you.

And please remember that at some time in the future when you are not so busy, you are going to write me a little piece for the paper.

153.   [MARION, VIRGINIA, AUGUST 15, 1928]

To RALPH CHURCH

Dear Ralph: I have been intending to write for a long time. David has been here. We talked of you a lot. He could stay but two days. We went to the farm and got waterbound by a storm and so stayed the night, very comfortably too.

I guess you know I am editing the two papers here and writing most of them. It fills my life with details, of course. There is just a possibility that next year I may have two books. One may be from my papers.

The other is a fiction attempt. Most of it is unwritten yet. On the whole I am in much better mood than I was while in Paris. I was quite miserable there.

Here I am busy at any rate. The papers will, in time, pay for themselves. At least I will not be beholden to hurry for some book publisher.

There is a kind of interesting experimental thing about it too. I try to give the fancy a little play, create in the town imaginary figures of people and situations.

The climate is good, a lovely country really. David has told you

---

[1] Early in 1928 Sergel took over The Dramatic Publishing Company, which had been founded in Chicago by his uncle.

about that, the hills and valleys and streams. For a long time I have thought it a painter's country. Occasionally I have a passion to paint. I want to throw up writing and paint. I won't, of course. If I had money, perhaps I would.

It might be a more subtle art. But there is no reason why it should be.

David tells me fine things of you, but not such good news of your mother. I had hoped that her wors[t] time had passed. I am sorry I do not know your wife. David is glowing about her too.

John, I presume, still storms away. There's a cloudy one. If there could only be one great storm and then clear weather with him.

D. also tells me you are committed to explain Stein.[1] That's letting you in all right. It's a bit vulgar, I should say, throwing the task off on you. The Stein has her vulgar sides; she's plastered with vulgarity sometimes.

Too anxious to be picked up out of obscurity. She works to keep her disciples warm. Why should anyone need disciples?

At that, a lot done. Well, do give my love to your mother and write sometime.

154.   [?MARION, VIRGINIA, ?1929]

TO CHARLES BOCKLER [1]

Dear Charles: My thoughts have turned to you a lot, these days. My feeling, I think, is half that of a father to a son, ha[lf] pure feeling of companionship, as brother.

It may be you will escape the dark valley I have been in, that I am walking in now. I have had to fight for and defend the artist in myself.

Once Jack Dempsey said a marvelous thing to me. We were both at a photographer's. He walked, in his quick, nervous, half-brutal way, across the room and grasped my shoulders. "Were you ever a fighter?" he said. "You have the shoulders, the frame of a fighter."

"No," I said, and then I thought. "Yes, I am a fighter," I said.

It was just before he fought Tunney. "It is worse winning than losing," he said.

---

[1] Church's "A Note on the Writing of Gertrude Stein" appeared in *transition*, no. 14 (fall, 1928).

[1] Charles Bockler, young New York bank clerk and painter, with whom Anderson had become acquainted in 1928. See Letter 155.

The sense of victory, fought for. You walk over the scene and see the dead and wounded. There are groans, and people weep.

I have hurt so many people, Charles, trying to keep some integrity. Do I dare go on existing? A few tales, told at last. To push something out a little beyond the horizon, no one caring much.

The painter fighting, just for ground on which his easel may stand, the writer for his quiet room, his thoughts, word fitted against word as color.

I take you very close to myself, because I feel in you brotherhood in it, whatever it is.

155.   [MARION, VIRGINIA] JANUARY 26, 1929
MR. OTTO KAHN,[1] 52 WILLIAMS STREET, NEW YORK

Dear Otto Kahn: I am addressing you about a matter in which I am pretty vitally interested and in which I think you may be also interested.

Since I was a boy I have been interested in the art of painting. Perhaps I should have been a painter. I don't know. Often enough after some particularly disappointing experience as a writer I have thought so. I had three brothers who painted. In our house, even when we were children, we talked constantly of painting.

To get to the point, I have never fallen greatly for American painting. To me it has seemed that in most American painting there has been lacking a particular quality tremendously important to the plastic arts. Not many of our painters have much straight sensual joy in life — in fruits, hills, women's bodies, skies, rivers, etc. Most of them, I think, get painting too much up into their heads to ever paint really well.

They haven't even much sensual joy in paint itself, in color as color.

I have within the last year found a young man[2] who has these qualities. He lives in New York and makes his living as a bookkeeper for a big banking house, I think for the City National. He is the son of a small-town banker of North Dakota who went broke by a failure of the wheat crop out there some years ago.

This young man is, I should say, about twenty-eight to thirty years of age. I met him and got acquainted with his work by accident. He goes to work in the bank at five o'clock in the afternoon, after the Stock

---

[1] Otto Kahn (1867–1934), banker, member of Kuhn, Loeb and Company. See Letter 179.
[2] Charles Bockler.

Exchange closes, and works until midnight. In the mornings and afternoons he paints. His wife is a stenographer and works every day.

Some few men have done me the honor to say that I have some instinctive knowledge of painting. To tell the truth, I think I have. This man is a painter. I myself have bought three of his things, and if I could afford it, I would buy more at once.

What I want to do is this: I want to sell to a few of my friends five or six of his paintings at three hundred dollars each to give him a year in the country doing nothing and thinking of nothing but painting. He can live on fifteen hundred dollars a year; as he is frugal and careful and so also is his wife.

As I think you know, I could myself, I believe, put this man across to the public now by beginning to write of his work. I do not want to do that yet. I would like it if he could have several years yet of painting in obscurity.[3] If such a young man should get some fame now, it might set him back for five years. I know something about this, having got some fame myself and knowing something of what it costs. I dare say I would have been a damned sight better writer today if I could have stayed longer in obscurity thinking of nothing but writing.

On the other hand, I do not believe much in the subsidizing of artists. There is a certain fine self-respect left in a man who earns his own way.

What I want to know is this: will you be one of five or six men to pay this young man three hundred dollars for a painting and let me pick the painting for you? If you will, I will guarantee you will never be sorry. I am not taking snap judgment on this man's work. There is real and very lovely sensual joy in his work. When the time comes, and if he stays in the straight, clear painting road he has taken, I am going out on the line for him and his work. I think he has the best chance of any young American painter whose work I have seen. Without consulting him I have taken on myself to try and give him an opportunity to work in this way, and I am doing it, not out of personal feeling for the man, but out of personal feeling for his work.

If you will take my judgment on this man and send me three hundred dollars, I will pick you a painting of his and send it along to you

---

[3] Bockler gave his first exhibition in April, 1929, at the Charcoal Club in Baltimore. For this event Anderson wrote a short "Foreword," saying that he admired the painter's work extremely.

within the next few months. Then I would like to have you hang it up somewhere where you will see it often and where you can, in a sense, live with it. I myself have lived in the presence of some of this man's work for the last few months and have a very decided opinion that he has done more for me and has taught me more about painting than any young man's work I have seen for years. I believe it has in it a lot of what we all want from our young artists and of what we have been waiting for and hoping for in our younger American painters. Sincerely

156.   [?MARION, VIRGINIA, ?FEBRUARY, 1929]

To JOHN ANDERSON

Dear John: The very capacity you have for feeling will inevitably make it burst into a flame occasionally about some woman. My own experience will, I am afraid, be of little help. In the end art is the essential thing, I think.

It is so difficult. The road is so long. Sometimes it is a tremendous easement to center it on some other person.

Women want that, of course. I do not believe that, at bottom, they have the least interest in art. What their lover gives to work they cannot get.

In the end you may prove a great disappointment to women, as I have and as most artists have.

Suddenly you go off. What was all-absorbing is no longer so. It is more terrible for the woman than going to another woman.

You go into something indefinite, into a place where they cannot follow.

I dare say you will have to go through these cycles. Who has escaped them? Read the history of all men who had devotion. In the end perhaps a man can only remain devoted to the intangible. Nature serves the purpose, and woman is sometimes an exquisite manifestation of nature. I would not want you to miss that, but can understand its confusion.

I dare say sometimes you will be disgusted at yourself, as I have been, when you find yourself turning even this fine feeling into work.

You did not give me an address at Madison.[1]

---

[1] John attended the University of Wisconsin during the second semester of the year 1928–1929.

157.   [?MARION, VIRGINIA, ?MARCH, 1929]

To JOHN ANDERSON

Dear John: I think you must do very well if you do no more than to give yourself to the mood of the moment like that. I have so often made a fool of myself and suffered for it afterward. I have gone somewhere in a certain mood and, in the effort to come out of it and join with the others, have gone too far. Evenings when I have talked too much, drunk too much. I have been partially in love with ladies and in the enthusiasm of the moment have led them to think I was ten times as hard hit as I actually was.

You have to pay dearly for being an imaginative person. You see a great deal and feel a great deal, but there is ugliness to see and feel as well as beauty, and in yourself as well as in the others.

I fancy what you have to try to learn is to give as little time as possible to self-pity. That seems to spoil most imaginative men. They are a bit more sensitive than others. They exaggerate the consequences.

As you well know, this is the real reason why the arts may be of help. It is ten times as important to be devoted as it is to succeed. You will be a fool if you think ever that you have succeeded in the arts.

Actually I would take in as many phases of life as I could. Give yourself all you can now to the people about. Let yourself enter into these moods. You have always the danger of letting yourself grow too introspective. Knowing all you can know of the surface of life will not hurt you.

[P.S.] Lots of love.

158.   [MARION, VIRGINIA, ?APRIL, 1929]

To DWIGHT MACDONALD

Dear K.K.: [1] It seems to me that you have got much clear. But a little you do fall into a common error. There is an obligation on the other side too. Again and again I have been attacked for looseness, lack of beauty in my prose, and the one attacking me used,

---

[1] "K.K." is a nickname, apparently, for Dwight Macdonald, then a young writer on the staff of *Time* and later an editor of *Partisan Review*. Although an admirer of Anderson's work, Macdonald had written a letter sharply criticizing the impressionistic prose of *Dark Laughter*.

Since the original of this letter is not now available, the text here printed is by necessity that of an imperfect copy made by an unknown hand. The blank spaces (here represented by dashes) appear in the copy itself.

as the vehicle of attack, prose I would have been ashamed to write.

What I think I want to emphasize by this remark is the difficulty of what you demand.

You want prose clear and flowing like a broad river, and so do I, but I think you should also realize the difficulties of getting at what you want.

I read the two books you recommended to me when we talked in New York, the one by Professor Babbitt [2] and the other by ——.

And here was dull, heavy prose too. Both streams were muddy. A smell of dead vegetation and fish arose from the pages of the book.

In another book, *Port of New York*, by Mr. Paul Rosenfeld, in the essay on Mr. Van Wyck Brooks, for example, you do find living, moving prose. He is saying here beautifully what is to be said about the production of worth-while prose in our country.

I am afraid somewhat that you get [?art] as too separated from life. Cézanne said it was parallel to life. It is the best explanation I have ever hear[d].

And in being separated from life, it has also a life of its own, a thing very little understood.

As regards the movies, you are altogether off the track there. Nothing of permanent value has been produced yet. Your own desire to have something happen has led you astray. There is too much money involved, too much vulgarity.

The point I think I am trying to get at is a delicate one. That the sort of prose of which you speak does not make definite the picture or feeling for you may be your own limitation. As good a painter as Whistler tried to laugh Cézanne out of existence. Everything of Cézanne's was, to use your own words, too loose, "sloppy."

"If I had a ten-year-old boy who could not draw better than that, I would spank him."

The point, I think, is that Cézanne had a better eye than Whistler did. What Whistler took to be bad drawing was really good drawing, in the finest sense.

Why, man, you must realize how young you yourself are. How deeply have you penetrated? There must be in you yet a great deal of the young man's ——.

---

[2] Irving Babbitt (1865–1933), professor of French literature at Harvard and leader of the Neo-Humanist movement. The book referred to may be either *Rousseau and Romanticism* (1919) or *Democracy and Leadership* (1924).

Why, I myself have been ten to fifteen years doing certain short stories of my own. I have walked the streets nights, wrestling with these stories. I tightened a little here, loosened a bit there.

There was, if I may say so, a something wanted you do not even comprehend yet. You are not old enough. You have not been hurt, injured, troubled enough by life. You cannot comprehend yet what does run parallel with life.

Your eye cannot see, your nose smell, your ears hear.

Why, there is this woman or this man, going along the street outside there. Things are happening in this room.

As I sit writing, I am sitting by an old stove in a little shop in Virginia.

What about that stove?

Men and women have come in here and warmed themselves by the stove. They were local merchants, farmers, girls from a college here.

A boy has filled the stove with coal from a neighboring shed a hundred times this winter.

There is a fragment, a fragment of the essence, let us say, of a dozen, two dozen people in that stove as it stands there.

Life is in inanimate things, you see, too. Men and women are touching, touching, touching.

Chairs, beds, hotels, streets of towns, towns themselves.

Cities, countries, forests, hills, and streams.

People hunger to know life that man hasn't touched. They go into primitive forests. The painter Gauguin did that. He failed in so far as he did that.

I am trying to give you in all this a sense of the vast intricate thing out of which what is called art must try to realize itself.

You cannot escape by standing off, being ——, making these little, definite —— of [?yours].

Why, man, what to you now seems loose, sloppy, badly joined together, may tomorrow, before your very eyes, be[g]in to tighten up.

I myself know enough to know that, in the field of painting, in all the plastic arts, for example, I know little or nothing about a work of art until I have seen it many times.

I have to let the thing live in itself a long time before my eyes. It is very fact that a work of art has a life as definite as your wife, your mistress, your friend, your brother.

And just as important too. A Cézanne, a Renoir, a —— has painted a canvas. It has lived a long, long time now. How many thousands of men and women have been born since. There are a hundred thousand men born to live and die who will not be as valuable to the world as one canvas. I myself have written tales that are worth an army of men.

There is one tale of mine — I will not name it — you have never spoken of it. Yes, you did. I remember now. You condemned it.

You will get older presently. Life will hit you hard in many places. Someday that tale will come home to you.

It will be brother to you, friend, lover. In that one tale is more tenderness than in a hundred thousand women.

I am trying to make you see the extreme difficulty of what you want to do. You want to judge, decide. It is all right.

You cannot do it, though, by withdrawing from life.

That in substance is what your friend Babbitt is advising. He is crying out for the safe life, the balanced life.

There is something too ——. The man —— the whole point.

He keeps saying over and over, "There are laws. There are laws. Observe the laws."

Why, indeed there are laws. There are laws all such men as Babbitt will never in this life comprehend. There are laws within the laws, laws that ride over the laws.

Do you think, my dear K. K., that you know how your mother looks, how your sweetheart looks? You are walking in a street. Do you know how the street looks?

You are abroad on a spring morning. What do you smell? How sharply attentive is your sense of smell?

What do you hear, see, feel?

The law of which you are so sure may be breaking to bits before your very eyes. You may not know it.

This thing called form in art. It exists, of course. It is the force that hold[s] the thing of loveliness together.

Often I walk about knowing there is form existent everywhere, in lives, things, in nature too.

It does not become form to me until I comprehend form in it.

There is a little reaching, a straining after the thing, the form. In comprehending it I create it too.

It happens I am an artist, and so this process of creation goes on constantly in me.

It is money[?] often. I grow tired. I grow older.

Often, often, it fails.

I have failed to comprehend the hidden loveliness in a woman too, the worth in a man. Every failure of mine is an insult to my neighbor. I go through life insulting people by my lack of comprehension. They do it to me.

I would like, if I could do it clearly and well, to say something definite to you about the artist's life.

I would like to see growth of that life here. I am writing to you this because you are a young man.

Charles[3] says that as yet, he is quite sure, you have too much regard left for established things. You believe yet that Yale is doing something and Harvard and the University of Chicago.

You believe the great cities are building to some purpose, that wars are fought for a purpose, nations established so.

It is not so, my dear man.

There is no purpose other than the artist's purpose and the purpose of the woman. The artist purposes to bring to life, out of the —— of hidden form in lives, nature, things, the living form as women purpose doing that out of their lovely bodies.

The artist there is your only true male, and for those formed male it is the only life with purpose in it.

If a man does not have the courage to propose to himself to attempt living that life, let him at least be humble before it.

Why, I myself have be[en] accused of being morally a loose man. It is said I have made physical love to many women.

I have made physical love to but few. Any common rake in this town could outdo me at that.

In truth I have made love to whole armies of women.

When I saw you in New York, I said a little to you about the artist's life. I would like to see artists in America become a bit more class-conscious. I would like to see them become men of pride in their bearing.

I would like to see them quit kneeling down before money and middle-class moral standards.

There must come someday real morality here. Towns must be comprehended, lives, fields, rivers, mountains, cities.

[3] Charles Bockler.

Everything is to be comprehended. Life here is loose, unmoral, mean-ingless. We who dare to call ourselves artists are all ————.

The woman who goes to take her lover freely without shame makes me ashamed.

The women are a hundred times as good as we men. They are more moral, finer.

Why do you suppose the women of America have such contempt for American men? They do have it. You know that.

It is because men here do not dare accept the obligations of the artist's life.

They are afraid, and who can be a man while he is afraid?

I would have you understand all this. I would like it if all young men began to understand. My own errors, my looseness, my constant experi-ment —— and failure is the only decent thing about me, man. I would like you to understand that, man.

I would like you to comprehend fully that what is to be got at to make the air sweet, the ground good under the feet, can only be got at by failure, trial, again and again and again failure.

And having comprehended it, I would like young artists to go on the road to [?it]. Toward the thing, not sadly, feeling themselves martyrs, but gaily, proudly, as the lords of life ou[gh]t to go.

159.   [TROUTDALE, VIRGINIA] MAY 23, 1929

MR. FRAZER,[1] CLEVELAND, OHIO

Dear Frazer: Your letter of May 16th stirred me up and gave me a lot of pleasure. It is difficult to write a reply.

I do not think that any of us mind so much our individual inability to reach each other, but at the same time there is something baffling about it.

It seems to me that we are living in an age of peculiar impotence, and, as far as I am concerned, it is only the youngsters with whom I have anything in common. People of my own age seem mostly to have lost ability to go anywhere, to have given up the ghost.

Of course, the idea that there is anything condescending about my working here is all nonsense.

[1] This unidentified admirer of Anderson's work, apparently a traveling sales-man, had written a long letter, signed by his last name, about the ideas suggested to him by a reading of Anderson's *Hello Towns!*, which was published in April, 1929.

I am not after anything for others as much as I am after it for myself, and when I can get nothing more out of it here, I shall leave.

I believe I am looking forward as hopeful[ly] as anyone can to a time when I can really feel man using this new power of which you speak to any satisfactory end, but I really do not feel it yet.

I suppose it is because some of the youngsters feel it that I am so attracted to them, and if you have this feeling, I wish to God you were here this afternoon so you could walk with me and convince me. Sincerely

160.   [MARION, VIRGINIA, JUNE 2, 1929]

TO FERDINAND AND CLARA SCHEVILL

Dear Ferdinand & Clara: I keep thinking about you all the time as rocks of friendship and love.

To tell the truth, I have been this year more dispirited than I ever remember to have been. That made me determined to fight it out with myself, if I could.

My reasoning was that if I could not love a woman for a long time, living with her, when it was so obvious I constantly needed women, I had better try to really live alone.

There was a great temptation to throw everything up and try something new, as I had done so often before — a new place, a new woman, a new book to write, etc.

I have not done it this time, but have hung on here, having my son with me, fighting constantly the impulse to flee, to be near someone, like your two selves, for example, who, thank God, have never given up loving me and always seemed glad to have me about.

I have, however, stayed, in such depression much of the time as I never knew before.

Now I begin to be a little cured, partly by nature, the lovely hills and streams here — it now getting richer than I have ever seen it before — and partly by getting weaned away from myself to again begin thinking of other lives and loving and enjoying people again.

I got Ferdinand's fine letter about the book.[1] It was better, on the whole, than I deserved to have it be. There did in the end, as Ferdinand says, come a kind of unity into it, which I hardly deserved to have happen.

---

[1] *Hello Towns!*

It has been quite misunderstood in some places and very finely understood in others.

I still keep trying to sell the place here and hope I may. It would clear things up fine.

And in any event I hope you can come down this way in the fall or I can get where I can have a little time with you two. With love

161.   [?WASHINGTON, D.C., ?OCTOBER, 1929]

TO JOHN ANDERSON AND CHARLES BOCKLER

Dear John and Charles: There is a ticklish point that I am trying to get at. I have a notion you may arrive at it in various ways. You try this and try that.

What happens to you in the world of painting happens in prose too.

You say, "Everything is in color, in keeping all loose; let form grow out of color."

We say, "Everything is in feeling. Let yourself feel down and down into lives."

It is all right, but there is a kind of insanity in it too. You can't let yourself be quite loose.

As a prose writer, and that is to say, "as a man who pretends to depict human life," I have gone as far, I suppose, as a man can go on the road of feeling. I have wrecked myself time and again.

It is all involved in sex. I think my generation went a little nuts on that, myself with them. We rather centered all feeling in sex.

We got results, did a kind of work, I dare say. I know I have done a few beautiful tales.

You see, there was the resistance of the Puritans. You, Charles, and Kath [1] know about that.

Just because they had power, they were overplayed, given a position of too much importance.

Their power over the minds of men is really gone, I think.

We have got new people growing up who will never know the inhibitions against which we fought.

You see, I am like the painter who, having gone to color and then to color and then to color, turns suddenly again to line, the thing Charles spoke of in his letter.

I have imagined a man who has taken color as sex. Do you see? It is an attempt to return into the pagan world.

[1] Mrs. Charles Bockler, usually called "Kack."

But this isn't a pagan world. It is a world of machines.

When I called what I am trying to do *No God*,[2] I meant only that old gods are dead.

You have to find in some way new centers of relationships. I, for example, have to come, for the time at least, out of a world where I depend on feeling (color) and have to begin again to observe with my eyes, hear with my ears, the definite facts.

It is the same thing you mean when you go back to drawing.

You say to these inner voices, "Be still now for a time."

I imagine our whole lives must be spent in this kind of swing back and forth.

We gather what we can and retire with it, try to let it do something inside of us, to us, like Kack having become impregnated.

Of course it is terribly confusing, working, as we writers must, in lives. But after all, not more confusing than your difficulties. I understand that.

I think the gods are there, but they are far off just now.

The thing about which you spoke was sold to *Scribner's*.[3] I'll send it when printed.

Last week I did a short thing for *Vanity Fair*,[4] almost devoid of color, almost pure drawing. I called it "These Mountaineers," just a description of some people, all my own feeling left out. I think it was good. Love to all

162.   RICHMOND, VIRGINIA [NOVEMBER, 1929]

TO ROBERT ANDERSON

Dear Bob: I am comfortably placed here at the Westmoreland Club, not at all expensive. They put me in a tiny room, but I am moving this afternoon to a large room on the second floor where there is a good-sized room in which to work.

It seems a bit silly of me sometimes, not to be there with you, but this whole thing has done me good.

I think what happened to me was rather strange and amusing.

---

[2] Tentative title for a novel which Anderson never finished and later destroyed. (See Letters 168 and 170.) A subsequent title, *Beyond Desire*, was transferred to the novel which Anderson published in 1932.

[3] Presumably "In a Strange Town," *Scribner's*, LXXXVII, 20–25 (January, 1930).

[4] "These Mountaineers," *Vanity Fair*, XXXIII, 44–45, 94 (January, 1930).

I guess you do not know, and perhaps never will know, the underlying basic difference between your generation and mine. In my generation, as you know — you kids of mine had partly to pay for it — I was a rebel.

Could there be anything more strange than what has happened to me?

I wanted for people, quite frankly, many things my generation did not have. I fought for it in my life and in my work.

Then the War came. The War did more than anything I or my kind could have done to make people face life.

For example, the old battleground was sex. That led naturally to an emphasis on sex. We all saw, everyone saw, the effect of repressions.

I and my kind told the story of repressed life. I have never thought of myself as a profound thinker. I was the storyteller; I took my color from the life about me. You know that for a long time after I began writing I was condemned on all sides. That is pretty much forgotten now. My *Winesburg, Ohio,* was condemned as a sex-server. How strange that notion seems now.

And then came the Great War. Never mind what the War was. It was terrific in its physical aspects — bodies mangled, the young manhood of England, Germany and France blown away or bled white, a great nation like Germany humiliated in the end.

Never mind all that. That is past.

But something else got blown up in that war too: the repressions, the strange fear of sex, the resultant underestimate and overestimate of sex as a force on life got blown up too.

It may be that what happened in the Great War, because of it, was a truer estimate of life. The young men who went into it got, must have got, a profound sense of life's cheapness.

You, my son, did not get into the War. You were too young. You just escaped it. Just the same you are not at all the man you would have been but for the War.

Of course there came other forces at work — the flowering of the industrial age, speeded up, no doubt, by the War.

Thousand[s] of men, everywhere, jerked out of the old individualistic life — plenty of machinery to jerk them out fast, machinery to kill them in masses like cattle — hurled into a new mass life.

The old individualist — the man of the pre-War period, who was a young man then, who got his sharp impressions then (most of us continue all our lives to live in the impressions of youth; the men, the young men who got their sharp impressions of life in the War will probably continue to live in those impressions the rest of their lives) — the old individualist type of man — well, you see where he was.

Why talk of sex repressions now? Apparently there aren't any.

I remember, son, a certain woman who fought long and bitterly for woman's suffrage. The women got what they fought for.

But this particular woman couldn't quit fighting for woman suffrage. She kept right on. One day I was walking with a young woman, and we saw this older woman. As she knew me, she stopped. "What are you doing now?" I asked.

She began again on the rights of women. They had got some things but not enough. The words she was saying would have been glowing words twenty years ago. I shall never forget the puzzled look in the younger woman's eyes. She was a post-War kid. "Rights of women? What the devil is the old girl talking about?" she asked.

Well, you see where I am, son — or at least have been these last five years. I had a world, and it slipped away from me. The War blew up more than the bodies of men, as I have already suggested.

It blew ideas away —

Love

God

Romance.

I am working on a book. I call it *No God*.[1] I could just as well call it *No Love*. It is not without significance that Gauguin is your favorite modern painter while my favorite is Van Gogh. I remember what Gauguin said of love. "If I were to say the word, it would crack the teeth out of my mouth," he said.

As regards this transition, this sweeping change that has come in the whole underlying conceptions of life, it is a profound one.

If I were a bit older, it would not make any difference to me. The old are old.

As a man, as a writer, I had to ask myself which road I wanted to take. I could simply have been old, not to have tried to understand you and your brother and sister.

---

[1] This title was abandoned after Horace Liveright protested in a telegram of November 11, 1929, that the phrase would be misinterpreted.

I fought against you for a long time. Who has cried out more sharply than myself against the coming of industrialism, the death of individualism, the modern world?

Well, I had already told the story of the man crying in the wilderness. I have been going about for four or five years now saying to myself, "To hell with that."

I want to say to you now that I would very likely have lost this little private battle of mine, that concerns no one vitally but myself, but for you kids of mine.

It would have meant kindly tolerance on your part, "The old man's all right." You know, that sort of thing.

In *No God*, the novel on which I am now at work, I am telling the story of a man having his roots in the pre-War life, accepting the present day post-War life.

That is my man's story. He is a man who has had marriage in the old way — memories of it cling to him — and then he comes to accept a woman who is the product of the new world.

No God — No Love — in the old sense. That is what it means.

As for the woman, well, I see her every day on the street. I've a notion that she doesn't want and wouldn't take what men used to give women, calling it love. I hope I am right about her. She is the young female kid of today. She has had sex experience and will have more, when she wants it.

I look at her as my man in the book *No God* looks at her — glad of her, certainly all for her.

Writing about her and of my man's acceptance of her is fun. It is refreshing. It is good for me.

There is certainly plenty of the old pre-War thing in men, the fear of the new life that has constantly to be put down.

163.   [?CHICAGO, DECEMBER, 1929]

To CHARLES BOCKLER

Charles: Katharine [1] wrote me about you and the Van Gogh books.[2] I hope you will keep them a long time. It is an amazing story.

I think that in Renoir and Van Gogh you get the two things of which you once wrote me — the man going toward God and the man going

---

[1] Mrs. Bockler.
[2] *Letters to His Brother, 1872–1886,* two volumes, 1927.

down into earth and finding God there too. Perhaps I think Renoir the healthier man.

The terrible thing about most of the God men is that they seem to identify themselves with God. "I am myself this thing." Van Gogh escaped all that. A terrible humbleness saved him.

A thing apparently Renoir never had at all.

Both sweet men though.

I have been working hard. I hope to see you soon.

A fine Christmas to you.

164.   [CHICAGO, DECEMBER 16, 1929]

To HORACE LIVERIGHT

Dear Horace: I am glad you liked the title, *Beyond Desire*.

It exactly expresses what I am driving at in the book.

I may have made a mistake in coming out here. I came largely because I wanted to get the feel of Chicago back into me. This is, after all, a Chicago novel of the present day.

I may have been spoofing myself and you and Maurice,[1] in saying I had it about done. I did have all the scenes of the book, the people, events, etc., but it did not have any real movement. The music wasn't in it yet.

I think it is coming in all right, but this climate here takes the starch out of me. I caught a hell of a cold as soon as I got here and have been fighting it ever since. If I do not shake it off in a few days, I'll get on a train and go off down South to some little town on the Florida east coast. I guess my money will hold out until I get the book really done. After that I don't care.

I suppose it will not matter if the first twenty-five pages of the book, as you have them there for the dummy, will not be the first twenty-five pages of the real book at all. What difference does that make? The blurb for the catalogue is O.K.

I have had to reshape all of the material. I had to make it click into shape.

I think you know, Horace, that I have to have this book right, not only on account of its chances of success, but also because of myself. I want to whip out of me this sense of defeat I have had.

---

[1] Maurice A. Hanline of Boni and Liveright.

If I shift to Florida where I can be out of doors when I am not working, I will wire you.

I wish I could say definitely that in a week, two weeks, a month, I will be through this job, but I can't. I have to take it as it flows. All I can say is that I will do nothing else, think of nothing else.

165.   [St. Petersburg, Florida, December 28, 1929]

To Ferdinand and Clara Schevill

Dear Ferdinand & Clara: I have got located down here in a room overlooking the sea. It has not been very warm, although for two afternoons now I have been walking about in the sun and even sitting out, clad in an overcoat to be sure.

They say here that the cold is all very unusual, the result of the bitter cold wave all through the Middle West, of which you have had such a dose.

My whole mood has been very silly for a long time. I think I might define it as just plain damn unspeakable gloom. The black dog was on my back all the time I was in Chicago and came right on down here, still comfortably perched on my back. The beast was so heavy on the way down that I remember little of the trip. I did have, I'm afraid, a feeling almost of satisfaction in getting away from Chicago.

There were you and Clara; both of you I love, but I'm damned if I felt I had anything to give. The same with dear little Mimi [1] too.

In this mood, as you may guess, my work does not progress much. I write every day and tear up at night. That is the way I have been going for a long time.

However, no more of this. My kind of men, I guess, just have to go through these times. When they can no longer go through them, they die, I fancy. I won't do that just yet.

The town here is a bright, gay place with plenty of sunshine and always the sense of the sea. I would urge Clara to come on down if it were not that I am such a bum companion now. If she comes, Ferdinand had better come with her. There is a man, at least, who is a man, not a baby.

I have about made up my mind to this — that I shall stay here at least for a few weeks and try to really get ahold of my theme. If I can't do it, I'll probably go to New York and try to get a job.

[1] Anderson's daughter, Marion.

I hardly know what I can do, but do feel I must be at work. I can't go on long just fiddling along like this.

However, I do hope that the sea and the sea air will straighten me out and that I may write more cheerfully after a time.

I love you both, although I am a damn fool. Bless you.

166.   [?1930]

To CHARLES BOCKLER

[No salutation] I think it would be a great mistake to waste any time at all thinking of "form" as form. It is one of the things artists, and most of all half-artists, babble of when their minds are most vacant.

Form is, of course, content. It is nothing else, can be nothing else. A tree has bark, fiber, sap, leaves, limbs, twigs.

It can grow and exist and not grow in the soil of your own being. It is so with women too.

The great thing is to let yourself be the tree, the sky, the earth. Enter into your inheritance. It is difficult and can only happen rarely, as between a man and woman. My meaning is that life is not so separated from art. How often I go away from the presence of talking artists into the street, the field.

What I want is there. If I go in and come out clean, even now and then, in the end these same people who say I have no form will be prattling of the "form" in my work. I'll see you soon.

167.   [ST. PETERSBURG, FLORIDA, ?JANUARY 2, 1930]

To HORACE LIVERIGHT

Dear Horace: Have been wanting to write you for several days, but have written you too often telling why something doesn't come off, etc.

I never will write that novel now. The truth is I have been forcing my pace on it all the time.

I'm going to fool around down here for a month or two and then go up into North Carolina and hang around there. The novel went wrong because I never was honest-to-God behind it. There were some gaudy chapters, but she didn't move.

She didn't move because I'm through with the ordinary problem of middle-class people in love, etc.

I've got an interest, though, and I'm going to go to it, though I'm not going to make promises about delivery. It is working people in the mills, particularly the working people, the poor whites, in the mills in the South. I'm going to build my novel around a little poor white mill girl, what happens to her coming to town, in a strike, etc. It's living stuff whether it will sell or not.

I'm not going to ask for any more money, Horace. I'll earn enough on short stuff to keep going until I get this story written, and say, Horace, let's not make any announcement of it or anything.

The Tennessee thing [1] hit me hard. It had some features I'll tell you about someday.

Wish I had been thoughtful enough to send the ham. Mrs. Ray Flannigan sent it.

168.   [ST. PETERSBURG, MID-JANUARY, 1930]

To FERDINAND AND CLARA SCHEVILL

Dear Ferdinand & Clara: I expect to leave here about Friday of this week and go to North Carolina. I am about fed up on it here. I do swear it is pretty nice — I mean the sea and the sun, etc. — but, by God, man, the people. They are all old, they are diseased, they stumble horribly, they play little games in the park, they are all so rather middle-class.

So I have about decided this is no place for me. If you or Clara or anyone alive whom I love had been here to lie with me on the sand, look at the sea, and talk of something except the Stock Market and the speed of automobiles, I might have stayed until my tired nerves got rested.

I am, however, a bit suspicious about them same nerves. When I am interested in the life about me, they disappear; when I am bored, they come back.

Not to be bored, to find things and people to love, to feel love, to feel life struggling in people. You will not get these things in Florida.

So I am going into North Carolina. I have got into touch with some of the men and women there who are in the labor movement. I am going to join them, hang around them.

Anyway, Ferdinand, you must admit that what is happening to

[1] On December 29, 1929, Tennessee Mitchell Anderson was found dead in her Chicago apartment.

labor in this glorious America of ours is about the most interesting thing that is happening.

Union labor pretty much corrupt, in the hands of corrupt men — suave businessmen themselves they are.

On the other hand, mass production, the speed-up system, efficiency. Labor, men and women, caught somewhere between.

The situation of labor in America I should think is at the lowest ebb it has ever been.

Anyway I have a feeling that somewhere in all this there is a story worthy of the best in a man.

In some way, I don't know why, the other story, of the relationships of men and women, etc., has lost interest for me. I still do wake up occasionally, pretty frequently, lately, with a bone at night.

Well, I look at him — "Elmer," I call him. "Elmer," I say, "you have had enough attention from me."

"Take what is given you, Elmer, and be as quiet as you can," I say. The point is that Elmer and his insistence on being hard is not of prime interest to me any more.

Really, if I belong to anything, I do belong to the defeated people. I have a notion that labor is defeated right now. Pretty soon, if I am not very careful, I will myself be an old man.

I ought to give what is in me, for the rest of my life, to my own people.

That means workers, defeated by Modern America, by the American scheme. I ought to be studying it, trying to understand it, hitting it where I can.

Anyway I am going to try that now. It is what I have in mind. I am going to try at least to put my pen to that, give myself to it.

We'll see how that comes out.

I'll write you when I get located in North Carolina, when I have an address again. Love

169.   [MACON, GEORGIA, JANUARY 26, 1930]

To RALPH CHURCH

Dear Ralph: I have thought often enough of you lately and have wondered how the work was going with you and how you were in general.

As you see, I am drifting. I have my son Bob running the two little newspapers at Marion, Va., and I am just drifting from place to place.

There is a kind of queer intense situation over here — in the South in particular — a lot of labor unrest, industry taking the South as it has the North, etc. and I am interested. I suppose I am an incurable sentimentalist about working people. They seem so much nicer than the rest of us.

And I suppose I am rather through with the man and woman thing, anyway the well-to-do and middle-class man and woman thing.

I have been hanging around cotton mills, sitting in the houses of mill workers in the mill villages down here, and, on the whole, rather enjoying myself. I wrote a long novel in the fall, and it was announced, but one night in Chicago I tore it up. It wasn't much good.

Hemingway wrote a fine novel.[1] It got everyone over here. I'm sorry to hear he gets on the glums too. What's the good being hard-boiled if it doesn't steer you around that? He's just about the big shot over here now and should be sitting on top [of] the world. Lewis,[2] over in London, wrote a book proving the decay of the whole Western civilization by Lawrence and me. I thought he made us cover too much territory myself.

Occasionally I write a pretty good short story. The book you mention[3] was just a compilation of stuff out of my little weekly country newspapers.

I keep pretty well and on the whole enjoy myself. What are you going to do when you get the job done over there? You aren't going to stay in Europe, are you?

I've a hunch there are going to be things rather doing over here the next twenty years. Wish to God I were thirty rather than fifty. The industrialists are pushing the thing to the limit. Every year there are more people thrown out of work by the perfection of the machines. It's beginning to bite in and will bite in more and more. It is going eventually to make a situation full of possibilities. Now everyone goes rather gaily on — "After us the deluge," etc. I'm trying to sense it as a story. The mills and factories are amazing places, and I've a notion that half the people who work at the machines are half in love with them.

---

[1] Presumably *A Farewell to Arms* (1929).

[2] Wyndham Lewis, *Paleface: The Philosophy of the "Melting-Pot,"* Chatto and Windus, 1929.

[3] *Hello Towns!*

The situation wants a poet, and you know, Ralph, a man at fifty — Well.

Anyway it is the most interesting situation in the world, I suppose.

Write me from time to time. Did you get stuck for that article on Gertie?[4] What did you do with it? With regards to Mrs. Church — and your mother

170.   [?MACON, GEORGIA, ?LATE JANUARY, 1930]

To ROGER AND RUTH SERGEL

Dear Roger & Ruth: The drinks sound marvelous. Come to Ripshin — if I don't sell it, a faint possibility — and we will make them all and consume them under the moon.

I think I am more or less straightened out. Have been in a more or less unhealthy state of mind for 2 or 3 years.

In all my early writing and until my last marriage I wrote pretty much what I damn pleased when I pleased.

Then I became, I think now, very decidedly middle-class. I do not mean by doing what you are, but do mean by writing for money.

It is perhaps only when we try to bend the arts to serve our damn middle-class purposes that we become unclean.

So I tore my novel up and severed my connection with *Vanity Fair*. And here I am.

I have decided that, as I came originally out of the laboring classes, and as the laboring people are and always have been my first loves, I am going to try a year or two of more or less living with them. The most interesting place in America now is the South.

A great class down here, the poor whites, have been brought into the industrial world in the last twenty years. The Southern towns are full of little mill girls, living in mill villages in the shadow of cotton mills.

I am going to try living among them and telling their story. It is anyway an exciting adventure.

I have decided that, for me, the story of sex, what man does to woman and woman to man, what marriage does, etc., is no longer my story. I have said my say on it, I suppose.

This doesn't mean I don't like holding fair females in these arms.

I've just a hunch, a feeling, that the story of labor and the growing industrial[ism] is the great, big story of America.

---

[4] See Letter 153.

I'm not planning to go into the Communist Party or anything. I am only taking it as an adventure, the sweetest one I know of to go into.

I love you both. Write me again some day at Marion. Luck to you and Ruth both in your own adventures.

171. [GREENVILLE, SOUTH CAROLINA] FEBRUARY 20, 1930

To NELSON ANTRIM CRAWFORD [1]

My dear Crawford: Your letter to me at Marion, coming through George Daugherty, just reached me down here.

I would be very glad to do something for you, but, to tell the truth, am rather worked out on the small-town lay.

My going to Marion and running the local papers there rather got the editors after me for small town stuff, and I have done several things.

Just now I am terribly interested in factories and am spending a lot of time in them, looking at them inside, talking to factory owners, workers, etc.

I could probably work out about what you want from this angle and at the same time fit it in with my own interests now. I would do something better in that way I'm pretty sure.

I wish I could explain to you and Morrow [2] what I am up to. I guess you know that I have been one of the outstanding little protesters against the machine age.

However, it is here, and recently I have had a change of heart. I have been trying recently to go to machinery as a man might go to the mountains and to the forests and rivers. I always have had an idea that writers spend too much time in little groups and in cities. That is one reason that I, after being many years a city man, went back to the small towns.

Then I got the notion that the factories, the machines in them, etc., were about the biggest thing in American life. The idea grew in me. When I saw Morrow in Chicago, I had just completed a long novel, but suddenly I did not like it. I doubt if I will ever publish it.

I wrote a long thing recently, called "Labor and Sinclair Lewis," [3]

[1] Nelson Antrim Crawford, editor of the *Household Magazine*, Topeka, Kansas, on February 11, 1930, wrote Anderson asking for "a little article on small-town life."

[2] Marco Morrow.

[3] "Labor and Sinclair Lewis" became "Cotton Mill," *Scribner's* LXXXVIII, 1–11 (July, 1930).

I would like you both to see. I think it has some of the real hum and
speed of modern machinery in it. Also I have written some poetry, the
first for several years. One long one to the automobile I think is pretty
first class.

The factories are really marvelous places. You know how you feel
when you go into a press room. I am after that feeling in prose.

How big circulation have you? Where is it? I am more interested
nowadays in getting to a lot of people with this new slant than in anything else.

God knows, I have been writing for *Vanity Fair*. You know that is a
whorehouse. There isn't in me, Crawford, any of the kind of snobbish-
ness that wants literary magazines, etc.

I presume your magazine goes pretty much to women. Wouldn't it
be rather fun to give them this new slant? It's pretty much a virgin
field, I think. The biggest thing in America the literary men just aren't
touching.

God, man, if I could get you and Morrow into the loom room of a
big cotton mill at night. Why, it is a Niagara Falls of steel, of dancing
lights, of power.

Well, I would try to write you an article about it here. I wish I had
you here so I could talk to you. I'm leaving here tonight. Write me at
Marion, Virginia, Marion Pub. Co., and the letter will be forwarded.
I'll probably spend March in New Orleans.

Regards to you both.

[P.S.] The "Labor and Lewis" thing is 9,000 to 10,000 words. My New
York agent has it. I'd like $1,000.00 for it, if I can get it. I've been laying
for that bird ever since he wrote *Main Street*. Now he is on the labor
lay, and I wanted to skin him alive. He'll do to the factories what he
did to the small towns, the doctors, preachers, etc. The reason I want
so much for it (don't know whether I'll get it) is that it is costing me
something to do this traveling from town to town, city to city, and
factory to factory. It's a big story.

172.   [AUGUSTA, GEORGIA, ?LATE FEBRUARY, 1930]

To HORACE LIVERIGHT

Dear Horace: Bob and John, my two sons, drove down from Marion
to meet me in North Carolina and brought your letter saying you were
going off to Europe.

I've been in Greenville, the big textile center, for three weeks and now am at Augusta.

Of course, as you will have guessed, I'm feeling around.

I suppose I am looking for the swing, the music, that will set me off. I guess you know I've been pounded a good deal lately by the smart young men, but I can't write my kind of prose without poetic content.

Lately I've been feeling for it in machinery, the inside of modern factories. I told you I was on the labor thing, but that is misleading.

I've had this idea for a long time, that the most exciting thing in modern life is on the inside of factories, where writers so seldom go, the whirl and wonder of modern high-speed machinery and, of course, incidentally, what it is doing to people.

I've an idea I had a kind of sneaking notion I would write a modern love novel and get money to go on with this.

I wrote the novel and then couldn't stomach it.

So I've pushed off into this vast river of modern machine energy, and although I have no money now and hardly know from month to month how I am going on, I do go on.

I wrote one long thing, [which] I sent to Otto, I call "Labor and Sinclair Lewis." He is trying to place it for me, but do get him to let you read it before you go.

I think it has got dance and reality in it.

Incidentally, I'd like your lady to see it. I've a notion it would get her.

Anyway there is something on the inside of factories no one has touched in prose.

It's the biggest thing I've ever tackled and some days shakes me to pieces.

I'm going to stay in the big cotton, silk, and rayon mills another week, go down to New Orleans to rest for 10 days, and then to Birmingham to tackle the inside of steel mills.

By the way, before you go, write me a letter, c/o Hotel Monteleone, New Orleans, saying I am writing on modern machinery and asking manufacturers to let me inside their factories. They are a bit suspicious of all writers, and some of them seem to think I'm Lenin.

It's what Gene O'Neill tried for, I think, in *Dynamo*,[1] only if it comes, it will be more logical and clearer, I believe.

Anyway it's great shooting. I hope you have a good time in Europe.

[1] In *Dynamo* (1929), by Eugene O'Neill, the dynamo replaces God as a deity.

As always to you, Tommy, Maurice, Julius [2] and your lady.
[P.S.] Will be at the Richmond, Augusta, Ga., this week and then to New Orleans.

173.   NEW ORLEANS, MARCH 11, 1930

MISS ANNE BOGUE,[1] PARK AVENUE, NEW YORK

Dear Miss Bogue: I had a note yesterday from my friend, Miss Eleanor Copenhaver,[2] about a matter she spoke to you about some time ago. Here is about the situation. I feel that, inasmuch as Miss Copenhaver has talked to you, an explanation is due you.

As you no doubt know, I have been writing for a good many years and have had some success. On the whole, my success has been what I suppose I might call an artistic success, rather than financial. However, I have had no special reason to quarrel with my fate in that direction either.

Until I was about twenty-five years old, I was a laborer and worked in factories. Later I went into business and was in business for about ten or fifteen years. For the last several years I have done nothing but write.

I have always tried to avoid the necessity of writing hurriedly for the popular magazine.

However, what you might call my fame has grown slowly. My last novel [3] sold very well indeed, and I have no doubt if I were to produce another novel now, it would almost automatically sell well.

I did, indeed, write a novel last fall, which was on the theme of love between men and women, etc., and had even announced it for publication, but afterward destroyed it. This I did, because I felt it had been done rather hurriedly in order to get money to do something else in which I was now more interested.

I have been feeling for the last four or five years that the most interesting thing going on in American life is inside the factories, the

[2] T. R. Smith, Maurice Hanline and (probably) Julian Messner, all editors in the Liveright publishing house.

———

[1] Miss Bogue was apparently connected either with Mrs. Straight or with the *New Republic* group.

[2] Eleanor Copenhaver, of Marion, Virginia; at that time and for many years in charge of the Industrial Department of the National Y.W.C.A. She and Anderson were married in 1933.

[3] *Dark Laughter*, which in six months ending in December, 1925, sold 22,603 copies.

growth of the machine, our new high-speed industrialism, its effect on civilization, etc.

I felt that most of us were writing about this and thinking about it from the outside.

I wanted to go to the factories, not only the cotton mills in the South, but to the steel mills, the automobile factories, and to many other such places.

I have already found out that what I am after is going to take a long time. I wanted to get the beauty and poetry of the machine, but at the same time its significance to labor. I have the feeling that the whole tendency of modern industry has been rather to dehumanize people. I felt that if I could go into the factories and stay long enough, I might begin to write, feeling as one of these people, my whole purpose being to give finally an expression, not about these people, but out of them.

Knowing it was going to be a long, slow job, I spoke to Miss Copenhaver about the possibility of having it financed, and she spoke to you.

Afterward I grew afraid. It seemed to me that there were so many places in modern life where money was more needed. Perhaps I shall come out all right without any help.

One of the things I wanted to do was to publish in the magazines that cannot pay so well. I would like to have the things I may do published in labor papers, many of which cannot pay anything.

As a sort of explanation of my occasional fright about finances, I might explain that I have three children. I went down into Virginia two years ago and bought two small weekly newspapers down there. My oldest son is now running these papers and is doing very well with them. I still owe $7,000.00 on the papers, although we are paying off some every year.

My second son is a young painter and, of course, will probably make no money for several years, and my daughter is still a schoolgirl. My oldest son and I plan to try and make the papers support him and the other two children so that I may be free to work at this job of mine in a more leisurely way and not feel hurried about it.

When I talked to Miss Copenhaver, I had in mind that someone might be interested in helping me get the papers cleared, but afterward I grew doubtful about it. It seems so foolish to ask for help in a thing such as I am undertaking, that may not after all turn out, and in a time when there are so many things on foot that need help.

I think, therefore, that it would be better to drop the whole matter for the time and let me see if I cannot fight it out alone.

I give you this explanation, because I did talk to Miss Copenhaver about it during one of my periods of financial fright, and she wrote me that she had talked to you about interesting Mrs. Straight.[3] She also wrote me recently, saying that you had again made inquiry about it, and naturally I wanted to express my appreciation of your interest. With sincere regards

174.   NEW ORLEANS, MARCH 11, 1930

MR. BURTON EMMETT,[1] 40 EAST 34TH STREET, NEW YORK

Dear Burton Emmett: I have not answered your letter of February 25th, or rather your two letters, as I have been traveling almost constantly, and the letters only recently caught up with me.

After thinking the matter all over, I have almost made up my mind that when I go back to Marion in April, I will return the manuscript to you. It seems to me, when I think it over, that it is nothing but pride on my part that I do not want my failure seen. I do not see, after having given the matter some thought, why you should not have it, merely, as you suggest, making a codicil in your will saying that the manuscript was one of my failures and that I did not want it published. If anyone later wants to be so vulgar as to go ahead and publish it, let them do so.

The job I am on now is turning out to be one of the most interesting things I ever tackled. Some of the shorter things will be appearing soon in the *New Republic*.[2] I have done one long thing that my agent in New York is trying to place, but is having some difficulty on account of its length, it being rather long for serial publication. I call it "Labor and Sinclair Lewis," and it says something pretty definite that I have long wanted to say about the whole school of modern hard-boiled writers. Also I think it has got what I am after about the insides of factories.

Later I want to go to Richmond and spend some time inside cigarette

---

[3] Mrs. Willard Straight, wife of the "angel" of the *New Republic*.

[1] Wealthy New York advertising man and collector of rare books, had in 1927 lent Anderson the money with which he purchased the Marion newspapers. Both Emmett and his wife, Mary, became close friends of Anderson. See also Letter 181.

[2] For example, "Factory Town," *New Republic*, LXII, 143–144 (March 26, 1930); "Loom Dance," LXII, 292–294 (April 30, 1930).

factories. Do you think there will be any difficulty about this, and if there will be, can you help me out? I am not writing these things from the Socialistic or Communistic angle, but am trying merely to get at high-speed, modern machinery, a sense of its beauty, and naturally the effect of high speed and nervous tension on workmen. Like most artists, my sympathies lie pretty much with the workmen, the man down under the machine, operating it, rather than with the man who owns it, although I think he is also caught in the same net with the rest of us.

All of this has been very exciting to me, and I am having a grand time with it.

As regards the manuscript of this new matter, here is the way I am handling it. There is a former secretary of mine,[3] now living in Maryland, who is an expert at reading my script. I am writing all of these new things in longhand and sending them to her to be typed. She is saving the original manuscript[s] as they come in and will later get them all together and send them to you. I think this is much better than having them come in piecemeal.

My whole purpose in this new venture is to try to humanize modern industry somewhat by making everybody more aware of the man in the factory. It is going to take a long time and a lot of traveling. It may never prove to be anything out of which I can make much money. I would like very much to give these articles, without cost, to the labor papers.

As regards financing myself in this venture, this is what I have in mind. At the end of this year, my son, Bob, will have paid off all we owe on the papers at Marion except the $5,000.00 I got from you. My second son, John, is studying to be a painter, so will not make much money. I would like to help him out for the next few years and also send my little girl through college. My scheme is to sell the papers to Bob for $10,000.00, letting him pay $5,000.00 each to John and Miss Marion. As the papers are easily worth more than $15,000.00, this will be a start of $5,000.00 for each of them.

This will leave the $5,000.00 to you yet to be paid. I have been trying to sell Ripshin and make it into a club. My scheme was to get five men at $3,000.00 each with myself, making six members of the club. I would take $12,000.00 for the place, leaving $3,000.00 in the treasury. I have already got two or three men interested in this. The idea is to get interesting people so that we can all go down there sometime for a month or two in the summer and have an interesting life together there. The place will be large enough to take care of all of us; it should be a place where we can all rather get away from the world for a time, talk together, and for the time have a comfortable, healthy outdoor life in the mountains. I am tempted to ask you and Mrs. Emmett to go in on this with us, as it would be great fun to have you there sometimes, but of course, you have a country place now.

However, I am going to send you photographs of the place and the prospectus I have written up about it.

I hope I may be in the East sometime in the spring and that I may see you.

With love to you both. Sincerely

175.   NEW ORLEANS, MARCH 11, 1930

BARONESS MARIE KOSKULL, HAMBURG, GERMANY

Dear Hilda: [1] It is too bad about the cigarettes and very stupid of me.

I have about given up the notion of going to Europe this spring, and for a reason. I do not know that you will be in sympathy with what I am now doing. I am sure you are too much the aristocrat. However, it is inevitable.

As I wrote you, I went to Washington in the fall and wrote a new novel. The publisher had announced it. It was another novel about men and women and the tangle of their love for each other. I was about to send it in to be published, but first went out to Chicago to see my little daughter. One night while I was out there, I suddenly threw the novel out of the hotel window. I did this because I had become convinced that I had only written it in order to get some money to do something else I wanted to do. The whole impulse suddenly seemed to me corrupt.

For a long time, Hilda, I have been thinking that the most interesting thing in America is the factories, what goes on in them and the effect of high-speed, modern machinery on people.

America is at the very top of this movement in the world, and to study it America is the best place.

After the incident in Chicago I went down South into an industrial

---

[1] Baroness Marie Louise Koskull, with whom Anderson had become acquainted early in 1929 when she was employed in Washington, D.C., by the German-American Mixed Claims Commission. His nickname for her was "Brunhilde," later shortened to "Hilda."

town and have been spending most of the last three months in factories. The machinery has excited me tremendously, and I have begun to write again, I believe, with real verve and feeling. I have even been writing poetry again and have been very happy.

Of course, I had little or no money to do all this, but I remembered your philosophy and have been going ahead and doing it anyway. Soon I shall be publishing some of these new things. When you get to Germany, and if you stay there for a time, perhaps you will want to translate some of them. They should be really interesting to present-day Germany.

For the last three months I have been doing largely cotton mills, but now I am paying some attention to sugar refineries and expect to go from here to Birmingham in Alabama, to the steel mills. The field is vast and is full of strange poetry and significance. I believe I have got hold of something that will keep me happy and busy the rest of my life.

I am working now on organizing Ripshin into a club in which I will retain [a] share, so that if you come back to America, I can still take you there.

I fell hard for Maurice [2] in Washington and also for Ruth Dove.[3] She seemed to me one of the finest women I have ever met.

Lots of love and luck to you, and don't forget to write to me as soon as you get to Germany and know what your plans are to be. As always

176. [NEW ORLEANS, ABOUT MARCH 18, 1930]

To NELSON ANTRIM CRAWFORD

Dear Crawford: I am really writing this note as a kind of supplement to a hurried letter addressed to you yesterday. It is intended for Morrow and you both. If my agent sends you the "Labor and Lewis" thing, I can't help hoping you will want it.

The idea of 1,800,000 women is really very intriguing. As a matter of fact, I have a notion that American women are much more interested in modern cultural movements than men are. I have even, and very definitely, the notion that we are in a woman's age. Today, if I wanted to fool with a revolution, I would not make the effort among men, but would work among women, who still have some authority.

[2] Maurice Long, wealthy owner of a laundry in Washington, D.C., and one of Anderson's closest friends from 1929 until Long's death in 1931.

[3] A friend of Maurice Long, living in Washington.

Of course, any modern culture that has life in it must take the machine into account, and women respond to the machine much better than men do. They are less afraid of it.

Women are going into the factories more and more everywhere. In some odd way they fit in better. They do not seem in the least out of place there, as men often do.

It would be very, very interesting if we had come into a time when the dominant fact in life is the inadequacy of men and the strength of women.

Of course, it must be obvious to you that women spend the money men make, and how sensible of them. Men are willing to give them the money, hoping thus to blind them to the fact that they cannot give them what women really want.

And I do not mean sex, except as sex symbolizes something else. Men have all along been more interested in sex than women are. Women do want love of course, but what modern man has that to give?

Women obviously know they haven't it to give. That is what makes them so contemptuous.

This is not in the Labor-Lewis thing, but I think you will find in it what I think is a true criticism, not only of Lewis, but of the whole modern Mencken, hard-boiled attitude. It takes strength to be tender, and these men haven't strength. It is too easy to attack individuals.

I was with Jack McClure [1] last night, and he spoke of you with affection. Sincerely

177.   NEW ORLEANS, MARCH 24, 1930

MR. JOHN HALL WHEELOCK, CHARLES SCRIBNER'S SONS, NEW YORK

My dear Mr. Wheelock: Your letter came to me through Marion, Virginia, and has just reached me, but in the meantime I had heard something of how you felt about the Labor-Lewis article, through my agent, Mr. Liveright.[1]

After some searching of my own soul in this matter, I have about concluded that, whereas I was taking Mr. Lewis' hide off for his attitude toward the lady in Baltimore, the small town, etc., I was myself doing something of the same sort of thing to him. Of course, I have no

---

[1] John McClure, one of the editors of the *Double-Dealer*.

[1] March 17, 1930, Otto Liveright cited Wheelock's objection to giving Sinclair Lewis publicity and said it was typical of editorial comments he had received.

personal feeling about Mr. Lewis, but I suppose there is a natural tendency in all of us to occasionally flay some fellow citizen.

I have decided to drop it, and I think you will agree with me. It is much better to do the constructive thing you suggest and let the parallel be drawn by other people.

I therefore think that it would be better to make this whole article entirely constructive by dropping the whole Lewis thing. This will shorten the article a good deal, but will leave in it all the constructive part and what I believe is its real beauty.

I would like to take this opportunity to say something to you and the other editors of *Scribner's* about my scheme. I have been thinking for the last year or two that we writers in America were missing a grand opportunity. Here are these great factories running everywhere. They are increasing in size and importance every year. The machinery is becoming more and more complex.

In the meantime our writers continue to talk of industrialism in an abstract way. Very few people nowadays have any real sense of what is going on inside of the factories. Vast numbers of people in the meantime spend their whole lives inside these factories.

What I want to try to do is to take the readers inside the factory in a new way, to make them really conscious of the insides of factories. To do this I realize that I must go inside the factories myself and spend a lot of time there.

I want to do the job I have in mind without any social theories. When I wrote *Winesburg*, I had no social theories about the small town. I just wanted to get a picture of life in the small town as I felt it, and I would like to do that for the factories now, if I can.

To do this it is going to require a good deal of time and travel. I have spent most of this winter in the cotton mills and I want to go also into steel mills, automobile factories, and, in fact, into all sorts of big, modern industries.

All of this is going to take time and be more or less expensive, and I would like to make a connection with some magazine willing to work with me on it. I do not mean that the magazine will necessarily accept all I write, but they might have at least the first look at everything I write.

It is my present intention to devote myself entirely to this job, and I wonder if you would be willing to advance some money to help defray expenses, on the chance of getting this new slant on American life worked out, very much as you might pay a retainer to some attorney for some investigation in the law.

This I do know, that whether I am able to get hold of it or not, there is wonderful material untouched in this field.

I am returning the Labor-Lewis article to you much shortened and with all the Lewis end of it wiped out entirely. As you will see, I suggest that we call it simply "Cotton Mill."

I think it would be rather gaudy if we could illustrate this article, and I am sending you, enclosed, a catalogue of mill machinery.

Look at figure 4, page 9, and at figure 15, page 14.

Couldn't you make cuts direct from these illustrations or have a mechanical artist make drawings? I think the illustrations would help give the sense of the complex beauty of the machines that I am trying to work out.

I will be at the Hotel Monteleone in New Orleans for at least another ten days, and would like it very much if you would write me on receipt of this letter as to how my ideas for this article strike you, and also, incidentally, tell me whether or not their is any chance of my getting some money from you to help me somewhat in defraying my expenses.

I appreciate very much the fine consideration of your letter. Very sincerely yours

P.S. Please return the machinery catalog to me, if you can, particularly if you decide against the illustration idea.

178.   [TROUTDALE, VIRGINIA, ?LATE MAY, 1930]

To NELSON ANTRIM CRAWFORD

Dear Crawford: I think you are perhaps right about the River thing.[1] Man or woman's magazine, it wasn't so first class.

I sold to *Scribner's* the Machine thing [2] I half promised to send you. Then I wrote a woman thing.[3] They took that too.

Now I have been caught up by the farm. I am trying to do some things having something to do with the people on farms and the domestic animals on farms. The personalities of people as against the personalities of domestic animals, fowls, etc., the dog, the horse, the

---

[1] "Old Mississippi River Men," returned by Crawford as "a man's rather than a woman's story" and therefore unsuitable to the *Household Magazine*.

[2] "Cotton Mill."

[3] "It's a Woman's Age." *Scribner's*, LXXXVIII, 613–618 (December, 1930).

farm boy, myself, the cow, her calf, a guest here who is a painter, etc., etc.

These days I get so many impressions so fast that I am inclined not to complete things begun. I am like a man in love.

I may get one of these farm things completed, in shape so that I like it myself, and if I do, I will send it on to you. They may be slightly long and discursive.

Back of them is the notion that there is a possibility in the land, not quite realized and yet dimly realized by people of the farms, a kind of paganism all farm and small town people feel. Some of the things I may do will be too pagan for you.

For example, the contrast . . . the feeling in the cow, her teats being pulled by the rather dry hands of the farmwoman rather than by the warm, moist mouth of her own calf . . . the feverish desire in her to break away from the farmwoman and go back to the warm satisfying thing. If they come off, all these things will not be that pagan.

I am a bit ashamed of my attitude in sending you the River thing. I really knew it wasn't first class. I'm afraid I simply thought, "There's Crawford. I might buffalo a couple hundred out of him." Give my love to Morrow. Tell him I'm in love. Ask him if he is too old for that to happen to him any more.

179.   [TROUTDALE, VIRGINIA, AFTER JULY 13, 1930]

To FERDINAND AND CLARA SCHEVILL

Dear Man & Woman: I do seem to myself alive again and wish you could see me now, rather than have the memory of me as I was last winter.

It is good to think of you by the yellow sand and the sea. Lake Mich[igan] has always been the sea to me. I have always loved you two. I like to think of you well, working, loving, playing. You are good people in the world. I won't come to you again except sometime when I am as I am now.

I want you to see the thing in the last *Scribner's*. It is called "Cotton Mill." Do get it and read it. I think the machinery of the mill sings and roars and rattles in it a little. Tell me, after you read it, whether or not you feel the belts flying and the looms dancing.

I did right to go the factories. I'm going back to them this winter. In the meantime I'll adventure at the farm. I've got money from the rich for a young painter who is coming to live in the garage. John will probably spend his summers there.

Then I got money from another rich man for a young mountain boy who has some genius at wood carving.[1]

If I don't go broke, I'll spend the summers there.

Of course I'm in love. A little dark-eyed, Italian-looking woman. I dare say I have to love. I can't go out indirectly in work unless, as a relief, I can go out directly to one person.

If I don't do it, nothing sings in me, nothing flames up.

I go stale and limp like an old man's pecker.

So I love again and work, and it seems to me I never loved before; and it is all strangely enough one thing, except that it seemed to me the others lost courage and wouldn't adventure any more.

Wanting to sit secure behind walls.

Odd, isn't it, but that Tennessee came the nearest?

She saw the thing — taking life so, with gusto, to the last drop.

I used to take her sometimes to the very door, put her hand on the doorknob, but she always ran away like a frightened child.

"I'd have to give up everything," she'd say.

"Well, what the hell, why not? What is it so damn precious you are, or have?"

So she didn't do it, and we missed fire.

That's what hurt me so terribly when she died. She always so wanted to, and couldn't.

Well, why review? One of the fine things of my life is my love of you two. I'll come to see you, but I don't know when now.

But I guess I'm on my feet. Lots of love

[P.S.] There is another thing, to be in *Scribner's* soon, to be called "It's a Woman's Age." Watch for it. It will amuse Clara.

180.   [Marion, Virginia] August 7, 1930

Miss Katherine A. White, Studio 671 — 730 South Grand Avenue, (Rare Books and Autographs), Los Angeles

Dear Katherine White: It would take a long letter to explain to you why the artist in prose has within him the kind of resentment, the

---

[1] David Greear, one of the sons in a neighboring mountain family, the first people with whom Anderson became acquainted when he went to Virginia. The expense of a year of David's high school education was paid for by Otto Kahn, who had also bought one of Charles Bockler's paintings. See Letter 155.

value being placed on manuscripts. Many times I have thought of doing an article on the subject. I feel sure that if you were here and I could talk to you, I could make you see the point of view of the author in this matter.

Just the same, money is money, and no one needs it more than the writer who is not working to catch the literary market. I sincerely wish that I had a copy of the manuscript of *Winesburg* to offer for sale. I could find the manuscript of the *Story Teller's Story*, which I turned over to a friend who is also a collector.

The manuscripts to the other stories I have never found, although they may be somewhere among my effects.

The manuscript to *A Story Teller's Story* is intact. When the book is finished, as a gesture I send it to a friend.

Whether or not the friend would want to sell it I do not know, and I have some delicacy about asking.

What would your collector be willing to pay for it? If the collector wants to make an offer and the offer is interesting enough, I might forward your letter to the friend, having in mind that he might want to sell it and perhaps that he would split the proceeds with me.

You might find this out and write me about the matter again. Sincerely

181.   [MARION, VIRGINIA] SEPTEMBER 13, 1930
MRS. BLANCHE CHAPPELL, COLUMBUS, GEORGIA

Dear Blanche: I just got home from driving down to Richmond Fair where I went to see the horse races. It has been cool driving weather here. I guess you know that Virginia had this year the worst drought in forty years, but it has passed now, and the hills are green again, although the crops will be small.

What am I to say, Blanche, in answer to your questions? My whole life has been lived on the trial and error plan. I have tried almost everything, and almost everything I have tried has been an error.

If you want to know frankly what I think, I will speak it out and fight it out with Bemp. He is fine stuff. Do not think he does not love in you those very qualities that he would call queer.

I think that those of us who are what are called intellectuals make a terrible mistake in overvaluing the yen we have for the arts, books, etc. There is a sweet, fine quality in life that has nothing to do with this, and more and more I find myself valuing myself with those people.

To return to Ripshin, the New York club idea may work out and may not, but my original proposal to you would stand.[1] If I got four or five thousand dollars for it with the payment perhaps of a couple thousand dollars, I would let it go. That is to say, if it was to be sold to someone like you and Bemp, I would enjoy the thought of having it.

It isn't, you see, Blanche, a question of values any more, or rather another kind of values. I want to clear my skirts of all kind[s] of property as much as I can.

That doesn't mean that I am going to leave this country. I shall continue to make it my home and my headquarters.

I am planning to leave here about Sept. 24th to drive my daughter to Chicago, will stay out there a week, and may come to New York a week. However, if it was definite that you and Bemp were coming here, I would make it a point to be here at the time.

You understand that the house over there is closed now and that we couldn't live over there at present because during the drought the spring went dry. It probably won't come back until the winter rain. This is the first time this has happened, but springs in Virginia went dry this year that had not for fifty years.

I hate to think of you ill, and frankly, I can't see any great point to the idea of going to New York and getting a job. You would only be keeping somebody else out of a job. If you want to work, why not buy Ripshin and make it a charming place for people to come to in the summer time? Why not be practical about it and make some money out of it? If I had a chance, I could propose a good many ways to do this with that property over there. Why not do something like that rather than go to New York and sit in an office and merely keep some other woman out of a job, the point being that if you want to do something, you should [try] to develop a talent peculiar to yourself.

I could give you a real lecture about this if you were here. With love to both of you

[1] A scheme for turning Ripshin into either a community farm or a New York winter club was once discussed between Anderson and Mrs. Bentley Chappell of Columbus, Georgia. See Letter 174.

182.   [MARION, VIRGINIA, SEPTEMBER 21, 1930]

TO CHARLES BOCKLER

(This was written some time ago. I thought it had been mailed.)

Dear Charles: A man spends his life wavering back and forth between these two impulses.

To go [to] the classic point of view means, it seems to me, a kind of separation from our present-day muddled life that I can't bear.

Such little gracious, amusing, absorbing things do happen among people. I go about, when I am well and strong, with eyes and ears open. So much pride of life in these queer creatures and in myself.

They fascinate me.

Then the other reaction.

My daughter Mimi, Miss Eleanor Copenhaver, and I drove to the state fair at Richmond.

We lived in an upper-middle-class hotel there.

There I saw dead faces about me. There is something about prosperity, the hunger for it, the pretense in all these middle-class Americans, that makes the soul sick.

I presume that is why I keep going back to the workers, poor people with little pretense to them.

They give me, often when they are unaware, honest reactions.

Human nature peeping out. It is like color to you.

You have, I should say, to watch out. You will get that upper-middle-class thing there. It mustn't sour you on people.

Go sometimes, Charles, when you are not working, on solitary walks. If you can do it, stop and talk to Negroes, poor farmers, etc. We, as artists, ought to keep that human love alive in us if we can.

We have to fight for it, I guess, like any love.

I suppose that is why I am always suggesting to you and John that you go in for an occasional portrait.

As a kind of antidote, I presume, for the rather classic thing color can become.

Anyone hurt or twisted by life, to find the wonder in them.

I don't forget that one of the clear, lovely little water colors you did had a shithouse in it.

I don't know whether I am shooting too high with the book or not. There is an epic quality to be got. Perhaps no man should shoot at that.

Still there is so much to be said.

(After I had discovered the above had not been sent.)

I had a letter from John. He had come down from the country and had been in Chicago, where he has seen some paintings.

He seemed in a good mood. He had not been painting, but instead had been helping to build a house.

Still he felt all right — a good feeling about things.

I have been very lonely and restless. It seems to me sometimes that I can no longer bear this town.

This summer it was rather nice. John was with me a long time.

Then Eleanor Copenhaver came home. She is a mature woman and my friend. I am more than half in love with her.

We were together a good deal. We talked. I talked over with her what I wanted to do.

It was someone here who was warm and friendly. That was a terrific help.

Now she is gone.

I am writing you on Sunday the 21st. On Tuesday the 23rd Mimi is having to go back to Chicago. I am going to drive her out there. I will stay, for perhaps 10 days, with my friend Ferdinand Schevill.

Then I will come back here. Perhaps in October I will go to New York to stay a week or two, see people, see paintings, hear some music.

I hope you are at work.

183.   [MARION, VIRGINIA, ABOUT OCTOBER 6, 1930]

To FERDINAND AND CLARA SCHEVILL

Dear Ferdinand and Clara: I came home and went to work. My mind seems clear. It may be that now I am in one of those clear times of straight flow.

It seems horrid to me that when I come to you two I never seem to be able to come when I am not in distress.

My chief distress this time was all unfounded. Perhaps it usually is.

I have put away the machine thing for the time and am at work on a long story. The machine thing must, it seems to me, be let to come as it will. It must have poetic content. It can't be reasoned out or buttressed with facts. It is all in a field where there are no facts.

As you know, poetry — the carrying of conviction to others through feeling through the medium of words — is a complex, difficult thing.

The very color of the words themselves, the feeling in the artist trying to release itself is a part of what must get over to the reader.

As Clara well knows, the notes she sings may be quite perfect at times, but if she cannot get into the song her own inner feeling, nothing happens.

I have been thinking a good deal about Wright.[1] I'll write a story about him someday.

Dear Clara, the things you feel about him are sound enough, and yet . . .

There is something pitiful there, something that should arouse our most tender feeling.

We do have to take intuition in spite of the muddle of fact.

I dare say Wright, when he is alone, does have humble, hurt moments.

Realizing how he has himself killed the chance for a life of beautiful building.

I have done so much at this kind of killing of finer things in myself. My heart bled for Wright when Ferdinand took me to his exhibition.[2]

So many fine projects in myself too — all came to nothing.

Although I am afraid I did not show it much when I was with you two, I did feel love and sympathy in your house. I always feel that. It did something to me. I came away in an odd way better and stronger. I love you both.

184.   [MARION, VIRGINIA, ABOUT NOVEMBER 12, 1930]

To CHARLES BOCKLER

Dear Charles: There is always a temptation to begin writing to you at once after I get one of your letters. There is such a lack of conversational opportunities here. It is the real limitation to country town life. Of course I can go over into the drugstore, but the point of view of the men there is a bit too childish. As for the men here, we

---

[1] Frank Lloyd Wright (1869–), American architect.

[2] An exhibition of architectural designs and models by Wright was held at the Chicago Art Institute from September 25 to October 12, 1930. Anderson is apparently thinking here of the unconventional passages in Wright's personal life.

have set up a ping-pong table in the print shop, and they often come in in the evening and play. They are nicer then.

By the way, I suggest it as one solution of the life there. The table can be made easily, a plain board table, smooth on top and five feet across by nine feet high, the distance from the floor to the table top 30 inches. The little set doesn't cost much. You find yourself quite stupid at the game at first but soon become fast. It is really indoor tennis. I've an idea it would rather solve the Sundays *en* family [*sic*]. After all, none of us play enough.

It is likely, Charles, that no man can have a discussion with another unless they have something like a fellow point of view to begin with.

As for the disturbing thing coming into our lives, I have tried all my life to fight it off and to concentrate on pure storytelling, but for some reason it can't quite be done now. It is like this: the artist is, after all, partly a product of his environment. He can do nothing with nature, cannot draw close unless sensitized. If sensitized, everything beats in on him. He does not escape the general tone and mood of the world in any event. It is antagonistic now. We can't escape that fact. We have to participate, just as a bird has to try at least to build a nest, finding material, etc., before she can lay her eggs.

I think in a sense that is the fate of the artists of our day. One can perhaps do it without quite thinking that what might be called propaganda for better living is an end in itself. The better living is the end.

I can't quite draw away from my fellows no matter how much I try. I draw away and then come back, waver about uncertainly a great deal.

A man cannot love or work, quite. I myself seem to get nothing but fragments done. The sustained thing needs a kind of inner peace that I cannot find.

I can't, however, mourn about it.

There is a book just out by a group of young Southerners. I['ll] *Take My Stand*. Have Mary [1] see if she can't get it in the library. It is an attempt at least to set up a group feeling against industrialism, Communism, etc., and a return to a kind of modified agrarianism. At least it is an expression of something.

I am going to Richmond at the end of this week to introduce the speakers at a debate on the subject, Industrialism vs. Agrarianism — men from the University of Tennessee and Virginia. The biggest daily

[1] Mary Vernon Greear, Bockler's sister-in-law.

there has got it up. At last, anyway, even the so-called big men, men, I presume, of Mr. Peery's [2] type, have begun to realize there is a nigger in the woodpile.

185. [MARION, VIRGINIA, NOVEMBER 26, 1930]

TO CHARLES BOCKLER

Dear Charles: I have a thing in current *Nation* [1] on the Negro in times of industrial depression, an article in current *Scribner's,* [2] and I have just written a new article for *Nation* [3] on the strike at Danville, Va. I seem to be getting into current things more and more, but I do not care much. My situation is a bit absurd. This winter I have had opportunity to make perhaps $3,000 by doing articles for popular magazines, but couldn't do them. It seems to me that I will have to find a way other than writing to make my living.

At that, I do not want much living.

I could be satisfied with running the place here, but have given that job to Bob. If I write for the papers much, people keep referring to what I write, to the detriment of Bob sometimes, and as I am asking him to run this thing, and he wants to do so, I do not feel I should butt in.

A man gets in a queer position. There was that debate at Richmond. [4] Introduced the speakers. There were almost 3,000 people there. I felt I ought to say all I could, put into it all I could.

I did. The result was that I came near stealing the meeting from the others. There was danger of that, as when a man presumed to act a minor part in a play steals the play.

I suppose there is something dominant in my personality. I don't like it.

I have thought up a scheme. Perhaps it will work. I have thought of trying to get money for the idea of devoting myself to the country weeklies in general. I am not so sure, Charles, that we want Socialism and certainly not wholesale Communism.

It seems to me that, for young writing men, the country weeklies

[2] Charles Bockler's father-in-law.

[1] "Look Out, Brown Man!" *Nation,* CXXI, 579–580 (November 26, 1930).
[2] "It's a Woman's Age," *Scribner's* LXXXVIII, 613–618 (December, 1930).
[3] "Danville, Virginia," which was actually published in the *New Republic,* LXV, 266–268 (January 21, 1931).
[4] See Letter 184.

might offer a great field. I'm pretty sure that if we had, for example, 20 or 30 alive country weeklies in Virginia, we could, in five years, raise a lot of hell here. There was a time when country weeklies did have life and influence. What happened was that the kind of young men who used to go into such work got sucked up by the cityward movement and went off to the city dailies.

There is some reaction to all that now, and it might be built up. I could take money from some rich man to do that. I mean to go about, speaking to young university men, etc. about the possibilities, and by writing and working start a drift that way.

I have been sick, with flu, but am better now. It was very difficult reading the Van Gogh letters.[5] I identified myself with the man so closely. You know he has long been one of my real loves. God, how hungry he was and how, more than almost any man I know of, he saw the need of love as an integral part of work.

It has been a queer winter for me. I have stayed here and have made no money. I think, more than ever perhaps in my life, I have felt my own ineffectualness. Eleanor Copenhaver has been partly responsible. She stirred up in me the desire to go where working men were.

Going has, I think, made me feel my middle-classness. That perhaps is the real reason I wanted to sell out at the farm. It has seemed to me that, as so many had to be poor, I'd much rather be poor myself.

Perhaps I have got, in a queer new way, a new sense of God. Well, I do not say "God"; I say "The Thing." I mean a going toward something, first this way and that, as you painters try to do.

But unfortunately with me it is not nature but people, and I feel people disturbed now, thrown off balance. There is little or no peace in me.

That I suppose is the reason I want to be trying to do something now. Sincerely

186.   [MARION, VIRGINIA, EARLY DECEMBER, 1930]

To FERDINAND SCHEVILL

Dear Ferdinand: I have been thinking of Clara almost every day and wish you would write and tell me how she is. I haven't done much work.

It has been an odd year. I am at any rate a good deal amused at

[5] *Further Letters of Vincent Van Gogh to His Brother, 1886–1889* (1929).

myself. This winter I have had opportunity to make three or four thousand dollars, but can't make any of it. I'm becoming a nut. When I am offered money for anything, it becomes spoiled for me. It doesn't matter so much, as I spend little.

I've about concluded that it is wrong for me to go on thinking of myself as an artist at all. I can't be professional, it seems. On the other hand, I can't quite go to work at some commercial thing. I have thought of a scheme. Perhaps it will work. I think I will try to get someone to back me in devoting myself to the country press. It seems, I do believe after three years down here, that the country press offers the biggest opportunity in America for educational work in a real sense. All the big universities now have journalistic schools. Why could I not do a good thing toward directing some of the younger talent and energy away from the cities and to the little weeklies? I would like to go into propaganda work for something of this sort. The country press was once quite a powerful thing, but it has gone to seed. It has got into the hands of the petty bourgeoisie. In a way I think we have proven down here that it doesn't need to be quite that. I believe that I am enough of a figure to attract attention to the idea. I might take it up as a work I could do. If I do, I should get someone with money to put up a fund. It wouldn't need so much. The money would not need to be given, just the interest, for it to keep me going at it, pay a secretary, etc. If I went into it, I would write and lecture on the subject. I wouldn't mind doing that. What I hated about the other kind of lecturing I did was that it had to be devoted to the arts and indirectly to myself, a kind of exhibitionism. I have a kind of growing conviction that these little country papers, once they got into the hands of live young men and women, could do rather wonders. I believe we all believe now that there must come a kind of change in our civilization. The alert, well-educated young man or wom[a]n with a kind of flair — and there must be many such — could get a feeling on a country paper they can never get, buried on the big dailies. Twenty or thirty such people in a state, say, like Illinois or Virginia could do a lot in ten years. They could check a lot of brutality, wipe out a lot of ignorance, and the young men and women doing it might well feel they were going somewhere. At that they could make a living doing it.

I believe it wants but someone of some little prominence pushing the idea. What do you think?

Tell me about Clara and how she is. I'm well. The woman about whom you know and I are all right, but she is very busy and occupied, and I see but little of her. Later in the winter I shall see more.

187. [MARION, VIRGINIA, DECEMBER 13, 1930]

TO CHARLES BOCKLER

Dear Charles: I suspect just the same, Charles, that there is no way for the literary artist to escape. The thing is coming on so fast, the machine is so replacing men, that the situation will have to be met. I myself can't see any way out.

As for that, when it has been done, I can't see any reason why it should affect the artist's life. I am hopeful yet myself that it won't be Communism, but you can't tell. It will depend largely, I'd say, on whether or not those in power now have any sense. Probably they haven't. I think all of this putting men in jail, all that sort of thing, is largely due to fear. Most cruelty must be due to fear really. Why, there is something I also do not like about Shaw. But I think Shaw would be Shaw under any sort of social system. In some way, in the end, doors will have to be opened for the downtrodden ones. If we have to suffer, we have to suffer. It may not come in your lifetime or in mine, but again it may come with a rush. If those in power ease up, take up the slack by shortening hours, without decrease of pay, they may put the thing off a long time. In any event, it will be pretty stupid for a long time when it does come. We can bet on that.

There was a man here yesterday, a keen Jewish man. We walked and talked all afternoon. I showed him your work, and he was enthusiastic. He says that in general the painters have come off better than anyone. They go directly to nature. It's the only thing that I have been able to do here this year. I know of course what you mean. We do need joy, but after all, Charles, we are all wrapped up together. In a time like this, when there is so much depression, so much low spirits, it gets into the air.

The Jewish man had been to Europe. He said there were any number of men there who seemed to think civilization was just hanging by a thread. Germany may go for brutality, black shirts, as in Italy. I suppose that is a stage, don't you?

I had this idea. I went to Danville, Virginia,[1] where there was a bad strike on. The poor strikers are poorly led. On the other hand, when

[1] Anderson addressed a mass meeting at Danville November 17.

you get to know the labor people, your heart is full of sympathy for them also. Poor men, they go from one such place to another. Almost always the men they are trying to lead fail. How can you win a strike with hundreds of unemployed, men with hungry families, walking the streets? The leaders try to keep up the courage of the people, but look at the lives they lead, living in cheap hotels, socially ostracized in the towns into which they go. One said to me, "When we have a conference, we decide nothing. We are so lonely we spend all the time just visiting."

I had an idea. I thought perhaps men like myself, Dreiser, O'Neill, Sandburg, and others might write something for these men, talks to be delivered, some feeling given that artists and writers, some few men they feel have some distinction, were with them, in sympathy anyway. I wrote something myself. I tried to say that the new world of which men sometimes talk was not to be born, but had been born. The machine had made the new world. It was a question of going into the new world, opening doors, going in. Like a new house standing ready.

I am pretty healthy myself. You spoke of something far away about M.[2] It seemed to me as I read your words that you were describing some feeling of my own. Once it was terribly important to me to be producing. Now it is just as important to me to be sitting here, writing to you, as it would be to write what they call a masterpiece. There is a kind of stillness in me. I should be scared. In the mood in which I have written this year I can sell little or nothing. I make no money. It doesn't bother me.

Sometimes I think I am reaching out for something. I don't know. I write and destroy, write and destroy. I don't care at all. I really feel healthy.

There is a way in which I do have to be a man of action too. It doesn't matter. It seems now almost as though I could become one and not at all lose the other thing. If it did not get expressed, what is the difference? It is like love. In a way you can keep loving.

188.   [MARION, VIRGINIA, AFTER DECEMBER 15, 1930]

TO BARONESS MARIE KOSKULL

Dearest Hilda: There has been something heavy in life, but for me it seems to be breaking. The general spirit over here seems to be one

[2] Mary Vernon Greear.

of heavy sadness or of a rotten second-rate cynicism. They both come to the same thing. A little bit, I guess, America is being caught up with. We have gone so terribly far with automatic machinery. This means, of course, more and more men unemployed, while there are more goods than ever being produced.

An artist cannot help being affected by the mood of his time. With every breath he breathes he takes it in. We have now, in our cities, really hard times. From all I hear, France is less affected than almost any country. Perhaps France hasn't depended so much on machinery. Here, in every city we have hordes of unemployed. There are bread lines everywhere.

I have two particular friends in Paris I want you to know. There is Gertrude Stein. I am writing her, giving her your address and asking her to write you. There you will meet Americans.

My friend Ralph Church is at Oxford, where he is an instructor in philosophy, but he is often in Paris. He runs over there at every opportunity. I shall write to him of you and ask him to come see you when he crosses again.

As for writing — my dear, it has been an odd time. I could not do what I had already done, in the tone it had been done. Things are more disturbed. I want a new kind of book. I have written this to hang over my desk.

"They boast of the American sense of humor. They say we've got it. It isn't any good if it can't laugh now. If it cannot laugh at what Americans have done with America, laugh and begin again, then it doesn't matter. If it cannot laugh at the new gods — money, power, imperialism, industrialism — what is it? If it cannot laugh and begin again, what is it, where is it? If it cannot do that, America isn't any good anyway."

In *Dark Laughter* I wrote the laugh of the Negro at the white. Now I want white man's laughter, laughing at others and at self.

I think of a crazy, wild book, half poetry, the jazz of the radios and the talkies, voices, poetry, color — some with warm prose in it, I hope. This I shall strive for now until I get it or die trying.

I have stayed pretty much here in this little town, although I do fly about some, restlessly. Bob, Gil,[1] and the others send love. I am writing by the office stove. It is icy cold with snow outside.

[1] Robert Anderson and Gil Stephenson, the typesetter for the newspapers.

I went to Washington about seven weeks ago, saw Maurice,[2] Ruth Dove, Bubs and Chauncey.[3] I've been broke. I haven't cared much.

We are in for a period of wide discussion, of controversy, like pre-Civil War days here. It's coming.

I want the laugh in all of it, if I can get at it.

All in Wash[ington] spoke of you, as always, with affection. You are loved there.

I am well. My own love goes on and grows. I feel work in my bones. I shall give you a book to laugh and puzzle over one of these days. Love

189.   [MARION, VIRGINIA, DECEMBER 19, 1930]

To RALPH CHURCH

Dear Ralph: I am sitting in my print shop, a great snowstorm raging outside, some 18 inches down now and more coming. It snowed, then rained, then more snow, the limbs of all the trees heavily loaded.

I doubt whether I shall ever return to Paris, Stein's room, Lipp's,[1] etc. Lately I have produced little in the imaginative world.

I work here, and I got interested in modern factories. I spent part of last winter at that and will return to it this winter, some notion of a prose full of machinery.

Things will crack over here presently. The machines throw more and more out of work. Unemployment will grow chronic. The industrial American scheme isn't going to work out.

I look for a time of agitation, new interest in politics, discussions breaking out again. The tired, cynical crowd will have to cough it up.

Right now the reality of life is more fantastic than any imaginary life.

I am agitating to steer, say, hundreds of just such young men as you into country newspaper editorship in America, the best there is. With 20 men in each state we could do wonders. I rather think I will go lecture to the schools and universities on the subject.

I am, at bottom, partly a man of action. I'm having a good time.

God knows, we need prose artists, but the time for what we need now may not have come yet.

[2] Maurice Long.
[3] Mr. and Mrs. Chauncey Hackett, Washington friends of the Baroness.

[1] The Brasserie Lipp had been a favorite of Anderson's on his visits to Paris.

Perhaps there will be a new, gaudy romantic movement. I'd welcome it.

If I start producing again in the imaginative vein, it will be gaudy, fantastic stuff, I'd guess.

Love to Stein, your mother, the Jolas, Maria,[2] anyone you see.

Drink a deep one of Lipp's, thinking of your friend as it goes in cool splendor down your throat.

190.   [MARION, VIRGINIA, DECEMBER 25, 1930]

To CHARLES BOCKLER

Dear Charles: Christmas afternoon, just growing dark. I'm in the print shop, alone. I've been thinking of you, M., and K.[1]

I went out in the car just now toward Wytheville.[2] There has been heavy snow. It is an old snow, now, turning blue.

Do you remember Peter Brueghel the Elder? Was he the man? It is like that — bluish white snow, very cold . . . purple tree trunks . . . a man walking across a field . . . dogs.

I hate Christmas. The last two Christmasses before my mother died,[3] she was ill at Christmas. We were presumed to be a ruined family of some class. We went with middle-class children.

So Christmas came. We were asked by other children to go to their houses and see their things. There was always a flood. We had nothing.

The things didn't matter. My brother said, "Who wants their goddam things?"

He did, though.

Not the things.

He was confused. He thought the things were a sign other children were loved.

It confused. I've always been confused at Christmas.

I went to Pat Collins' new house. They have a 2-year-old child — little pot. Some one, Henry Staley perhaps, ha[d] given him a mechanical toy. He went up to it and kicked it to smithereens.

[2] Eugene Jolas (1894–), experimental poet and one of the editors of *transition;* Maria Jolas, his wife.

---

[1] Mary Vernon Greear and her sister Katharine, Bockler's wife.
[2] In Wythe County, Virginia, 130 miles WSW of Lynchburg.
[3] Emma Anderson died May 10, 1895.

I sat there. I had to hold myself back. I said nothing. I wanted to say, "Kick the goddam thing again."

It seems to me sometimes I am drawing near something. Perhaps I'm not ready yet. My days and nights are full of dreams. I've made no money this six months — a few hundred dollars. I haven't saved. I dream of a book out of the mind of a drunken man —

Comprehending, in a way, all of our civilization.

Poetry, thoughts, little scenes and adventures — passing through a drunken man's mind.

Moist prose, [song?]

The ridiculous physical man. His legs won't work.

It will be a crazy new kind of a book if it ever comes. Love to all

191.   [?DANVILLE, VIRGINIA] DECEMBER 26, 1930

To CLARENCE DARROW [1]

Dear Clarence Darrow: Here we are, four thousand of us, men and women workers, on strike at Danville, Virginia.[2]

People come here and speak to us. They are mostly labor leaders.

We have a feeling that this strike here at Danville is important. The main, the central thing we are fighting for is the right to organize, to have our own workers' union and to have that union organized, respected and honored.

We would like to ask you to come here and speak to us. Perhaps you can't do that. Can you send us a message? Will you write out a speech to be read to us? We feel isolated. Many of us are not educated men and women. We respect you and men like you. If you were here, what would you say to us?

We are writing to well-known American writers, Senators, educators, famous preachers. We are putting it up to them. What would all of you big men out in the big world say to us who have spent most of our lives back of factory walls, if you were here? Write it out so it can be read to us. Please do it now while the struggle is on here. [Spaces indicated for signatures]

[1] Clarence Darrow (1857–1938), famous defense lawyer, especially of criminals and labor agitators.

[2] This strike, of peculiar violence, was inaugurated September 23, 1930 and terminated January 30, 1931. On December 10 many strikers were served with eviction notices, but on December 12 were informed eviction would not take place until after Christmas. Evictions began December 30.

192.   [MARION, VIRGINIA, JANUARY 16, 1931]
To CHARLES BOCKLER

Dear Charles: I am ashamed that I have not written. I have been in a jam.

I went again to Danville and spoke to 2,000 people packed into a big hall, a strange experience. The workers there are going to lose. They have come up, for the moment, out of the queer mantrap they are in, have been in for years, and have seen a little light. They have had the fun of marching and singing and feeling a kind of queer, real fellowship with each other. Now they are being beaten back into the mantrap, starved back into it, Charles.

I had no notion, Charles, I could help them to escape. I thought perhaps I could give them something, some little sense of historic background.

I spoke to them of the coming of Magna Carta in England as a strike, of the French Revolution as a strike, of the American Revolution as a strike.

I wanted them to take back with them, into their mantrap, a little sense of the fact that the battle they have fought down there is just one battle in a long, long war, that they also might be contributing a little something. It was pathetic, Charles, to see the eager light in the eyes of those people.

I can't tell whether or not this sort of thing is worth doing. I have a desire to do it. I spoke at night and went the next morning to the mill gate at dawn to mix with strikers, scabs, and soldier[s]. It was a bleak, cold, black morning. You get the sense of the trap then, rats running in and out. I didn't get slugged or anything, for a wonder.

The letter about the hunt club painting[1] hurt. Don't question, Charles. Don't do it. Don't think about it.

It will have to be carefully explained to the man Joe. He is a kind, good man, I'm sure.

Just the same, it is that kind of man who will have to be jolted out of it. A man can reason himself into it. I did — for a house and a

---

[1] Bockler had been offered a considerable sum to do a painting for a Maryland hunt club. Although attracted by the money, he had been afraid of commercializing his art. Bockler was at this time living on the estate of his father-in-law, Mr. Peery, at Belair, twenty-four miles northeast of Baltimore.

woman, doing things for *Vanity Fair*. The stink of it isn't out of me yet. That's one reason I do things like going to Danville.

I feel sometimes like saying to those poor people, those workers, "Come and smash me in the face, trample on me. See if you can trample the thing out of me."

I wish I could talk to Joe. I'd like to have an hour, two hours, with him.

Don't let them patronize or pity you either, Charles. Of course we can't know we will produce a thing. What does that have to do with it?

What really do they produce, helping some rich man shave down his income tax?

That's the net of it.

I have decided to lecture again next year. I won't mind. I've been offered up to 40 lectures at $100 each on

> Machinery
> Women in Industry
> Newspapers

I won't mind that. I won't have to lecture on writing. I'll see you through, Charles. Don't take the stinking hunt money.

I'm still at the crazy book. Love

193.   [MARION, VIRGINIA] JANUARY 19, 1931

W. COLSTON LEIGH,[1] 521 FIFTH AVENUE, NEW YORK

Dear Leigh: I do not believe that there is any biographical data to be added to what you have except that I have been living for the last four years in this small Virginia town in the Blue Ridge Mountains. I own and publish two weekly newspapers down here. During the four years I have been tremendously interested in the growth of industry in America. I have spent a lot of my time during these years traveling and visiting factories.

I am giving you herewith a sort of synopsis of the lecture subjects proposed.

---

[1] Head of the Leigh Lecture Bureau, which arranged many of Anderson's lecture tours.

WOMEN IN INDUSTRY

Mr. Sherwood Anderson, after years of being an American story teller, has come to the conclusion that the life of the artist in America, standing as the artist does rather aside from life, an onlooker, is no good now.

Mr. Anderson is an American, born and bred, and is intensely interested in American life. Like a great many other men of our day he believes that the coming of the machine and the development of the machine along automatic lines has brought about a tremendous change in all life.

We have, he says, slipped out of an agrarian civilization and into an intensely industrialized civilization.

He believes that the story of life in America now should be told, in part at least, from inside the factory.

He believes that writers should go into the factories and also the painters and the song makers. For the last several years he has himself been spending days inside the factories trying to let himself feel what our modern factory workers feel.

He believes he has found out some things. There are women in factories now, hundreds of thousands of American women.

We tried to get Mr. Anderson to go lecturing about writers and writing. He would not do it. He said, "I don't care to talk to female culture-seekers. I won't."

Mr. Anderson is willing to talk about what he thinks and feels that modern industrial life is doing to American men and women and what it is doing to the relationships of men and women. He believes the machine has already made a new world, a new civilization. We are, he says, in the process of trying to get into this new world, to think and feel and live in a new machine-made world. He is ready to talk on what he thinks may be women's place in this new world.

THE MACHINE

What does the machine do to you? You do not walk nowadays, you ride in a machine. What effect does that have on you?

What has the machine do[ne] to you as a man or as a woman?

How has your whole life and your outlook on life been changed by the machine, and what of the machine itself?

Sherwood Anderson says we are living in a new world. What is this new world he is talking about?

He believes it is a strangely fascinating world.

This lecture is an attempt to at least partly define this new world that he says already exists and of which we as a people are not yet aware.

NEWSPAPERS

What is the situation of the American press?

What are the dailies doing?

What are the country weeklies of the country up to?

Sherwood Anderson believes that there [sic] at present new opportunities opening up in journalism in America. He has himself been in engaged in country journalism for three years and has recently published a book on the subject called *Hello Towns!* He wants to talk to young men and women about the opportunities in journalism.

He believes in the newspapers and what they can do. He wants to talk on this subject to schools or to groups of people anywhere who are interested.

194.   [MARION, VIRGINIA, EARLY FEBRUARY, 1931]

To JOHN W. EDELMAN [1]

Dear Edelman: I feel like writing you, and through you perhaps the *Labor News*,[2] a letter about Danville. This because my own talk to the workers at Danville was published in *Labor News*.

There was a strike down there, and it was lost. When the strike was given up, when it was lost, there was a story spread. It never was very clear. It was about certain ambassadors, presumably from the mill — well, not just from the mill — they were presumed to speak with some kind of half-authority.

If the strikers would go back, they would try to intercede, etc., etc.

Why, I think all of this pretty foolish. I think that confidence in the labor leaders has been hurt by it. I think it would have been so much better to be frank.

I think it would have been better to call the people together down

---

[1] John W. Edelman (1892–), at that time Research Director of the American Federation of Hosiery Workers.

[2] The "house organ" of the Hosiery Workers.

there. They should have been told, "Well here we are. We made a good fight, but we have lost it."

Suppose the leaders at Danville had asked the people there — I saw those strikers at Danville; they were good stuff — suppose they had been asked, "Can you take a licking?"

My God, of course they can. Why, they have never known anything but lickings. Don't think they did not get something out of the strike. They are in a rotten position now, but they were in a rotten position before the strike came. The leaders did not call the strike. The people got a lot out of it. Don't think they didn't. They learned to know each other a bit. For a time, anyway, they had the satisfaction of feeling themselves something other than cogs in a machine.

I think it would be infinitely better in all cases to be perfectly frank with the workers. When they are licked, tell them so. Treat them like grown men and women. Great God, they have been patronized enough. It is the wors[t] form of patronage to think that they cannot take a licking when they have to.

195.   [MARION, VIRGINIA, FEBRUARY 10, 1931]

To CHARLES BOCKLER

Dear Charles: [A] day when I can't work. I couldn't yesterday. The stoppage came suddenly, in the midst of something I thought I had hold of.

I have been trying to build a new philosophy. I say to myself that, as for the general, I have had attention enough, perhaps too much. If a thing breaks, I tell myself that it is because I have not let it work in me long enough.

I do not get much companionship here, so try to make it good by writing you or to Eleanor or someone else I care about.

I have sometimes a queer mystical feeling that, as regards the attitude of people in general, you must be careful. Just as there are physical diseases, so there are diseases of feeling. In a little town like this I feel that on some days everyone goes about hating everyone else. Then something happens and good feeling comes back. I think the whole of mankind must be like that.

I sat with two young lawyers for two hours yesterday while we talked. In the one man there is a kind of contempt. In particular he has contempt for all the underdogs. I think he really believes in a kind of predestination. You are born of the select few, or you are predestined to second-classness. The other man has a kind of openness. Both men are quite sincere.

I think that in myself, Charles, I am prejudiced against the rich. Perhaps I do not feel that they are any worse than the poor, but that they have too great a handicap. It is so difficult, if you are made to stand out a bit from the mass, not to assure yourself that it is all due to some special virtue in yourself. All power of money or place therefore brings a kind of corruption almost inevitably. The poor and the obscure escape, not because of some special merit, but because their chances are better.

This feeling has grown in me. Sometimes I do think that I am foolish in this. I am no longer young and have made no provisions for the future. Sickness or misfortune might well assail me. Still I do not want to make any provision at all for the future. Now I rather live from day to day, a little money always drifting in, enough to keep me afloat. Suppose in ten years it stops.

I used to look with horror, for example, upon the fate of Melville. There were years of his life when he was an old man, as I will presently be, and when he had nothing. He had to live a strange life of obscurity in a little hole, as did also the painter Albert Ryder.

Why, it does not seem any more such a sad fate. I should be able to gather up remembrances on which I can feed. I think of that often in the night.

For example, women. There were hours with Mary, for example, that are shining things. They stay fresh in my mind. They belong to me as surely as any other kind of possession.

I guess, Charles, we can have our own way of gathering riches. There has been no rain for weeks and weeks. The ground is dry lower down than it was even last summer during the great drought. Now in this country the farmers should be plowing, but the ground is too dry. Some go about saying that God is punishing us for our sins. It seems needless cruelty on his part. We get swatted enough.

It has been arranged, through the generosity of some woman in N. Y., that my speech at Danville shall be printed and distributed among the defeated people at Danville. Now that they are licked the Red Cross is going in to feed them. They are still being evicted from their houses by the mill owners. The speech was also pretty generally reprinted everywhere in labor papers. The only hope is that such expressions may give a bit more dignity to the defeat in the minds of the people defeated.

I have plenty of work waiting. There are three or four books that seem to just tremble on the edge of being completed. I suppose you must always have canvases about that are like that. It seems criminal sometimes that a man cannot work more steadily. I guess we ought to thank God that we have something anyway we want to do.

196.   [WINSTON-SALEM, NORTH CAROLINA, FEBRUARY 17, 1931]

TO CHARLES BOCKLER

Dear Charles: Again, as you will see, Charles, restlessness has caught me, and I am wandering about. I had agreed to speak before the State press meeting at Athens, Georgia, on Friday of this week and left home at the end of last week. I have been down here, going again from town to town, walking in the shadows of the factories, and looking at people.

I brought with me Beard's *Rise of American Civilization*[1] and at night in bed have been reading that. What a strange story it all is. So evidently a nation moves much as a man does, not knowing most of the time where he is going — such a queer mixture of good and bad.

I have a hunch now that I will return to my *Perhaps Women*[2] and try to finish it. It would be something behind me. There is something in all this thing not insisted upon enough.

I mean the effect of all this modern mass production thing on the spirit of man.

All of life fallen so into definite patterns.

Why, I know, Charles, that you love your child, come to you out of Kack's body, but my theme is that the child does not mean to you what it does to Kack.

After all, she carried it, created it. It fed out of her body.

Just as I believe that when you really paint you feed out of your own body in a queer, subtle way at your painting.

I believe that all workmen too used to feed themselves into their work as they cannot do now. I used to watch this thing when I was a boy. I am sure that man in general used to have a kind of touch with nature he can't have in a mass production age.

[1] *The Rise of American Civilization* by Charles and Mary Beard appeared in 1927.

[2] *Perhaps Women* was published September, 1931.

The point being that the work of creation in you, when you paint at your best, is not, at bottom, different than the work going on in Kack when she carries a child.

The machine can't touch her in that. It can and does rob [us].

I can't believe we can do away with the machine.

I do not even believe that the great harm our present social structure does is in the form of long hours of work for all of us, low wages, etc. I think all that secondary.

I think we are being robbed in a more subtle way. If it goes on, there will be no ability to fight left in man. It will be worn away.

Then it may have to come to women. They may have to make the fight to get maleness back into the world.

I am predicting that we will have to turn to women so, crying, "Save us. Save us. We cannot save ourselves."

I wonder if you think all this sound. Love

[P.S.] A letter to Marion will reach me.

197.   [MARION, VIRGINIA, MARCH 26, 1931]

To J. J. LANKES [1]

Dear Lankes: I haven't answered your good letter because I've been away and Bob held it here for me until I came back.

I'm not shocked that Burchfield doesn't want to come in.[2] I don't know what he's like. I like his work.

I think he is a bit silly not to trust me, but that's all right. I probably know as much about the machine as he does.

I think American artists ought to be a bit more generous in their attitude toward each other, but I guess they can't be.

There have been so many cheap guys. He may think I was trying to use him. God knows.

Perhaps before the book is published I can see you and talk with you. I might even not publish it.

You may send this letter on to Burchfield if you wish. I'[d] like to

---

[1] J[ulius] J. Lankes (1884–), artist specializing in woodcuts.
[2] Charles Ephraim Burchfield (1893–), American painter. Anderson had written Lankes that he would like Burchfield to make an illustration for *Perhaps Women* symbolizing man's failure and woman's success in withstanding the effects of a machine civilization. When Lankes, acting for Anderson, tried to interest Burchfield in the project, the latter declined to undertake it. Thereupon Lankes himself created the woodcut reproduced as a frontispiece in the book.

be straight with him. I'd like to have him know that I wouldn't give a shit to use him.

And that I admire his work no matter what he thinks of me. Your friend

198.   [ELIZABETH, NEW JERSEY, ?MAY 5, 1931]

To LAURA LOU COPENHAVER

Dear Friend:[1] I drove Eleanor quite rapidly to Philadelphia, but not quite rapidly enough. She missed the train and phoned over. However, another came, and she got to her meeting all right. I think I shall stay here for a time in this hotel and work. It is nice to be buried away so with long, quiet hours. I have already worked today, my first full day here. Here I shall now and then see Eleanor, if only for a few hours at a time. It seems quite necessary to me, and I suppose the whole question of whether or not she should marry me is involved in whether or not it becomes necessary to her.

It might all very well be locked up in what that scientist said about the electrons, something of that sort. It was such a triumph for me when he talked of that discovery. I hope I was not too malicious when the look of triumph came into my eyes.

Your dinner at Baltimore was a delight, one of the nicest I ever sat at, and I surely did like you, sitting there and collecting such great gobs of love and admiration, and just eating it up too. It makes me grin when I think of you talking of going it alone, you being, in your nature, such a born queen bee.

By the way, I have been reading Maeterlinck's *The Life of the Ant*,[2] which I will send you. He seems to think that in bees and ants there is a sense alive that is missing in us. Why, he thinks, as I do, that we will get nowhere until we can begin to not look at all beyond this life. My own notion has always been that to give up everything else, leaving it absolutely to the unknowable, shaking off all false pretense of knowing the unknowable, turning then toward each other, a collective kind of happiness might conceivably result.

It does occur now and then, as at the charming dinner you gave, when everyone is nice. It has happened to me twice on this trip, making the whole thing worth while, aside from the joy of being nearer

[1] Eleanor Copenhaver's mother, one of Anderson's closest friends in Marion.

[2] *The Life of the Ant*, translated by Bernard Miall, New York, The John Day Co., 1930.

Eleanor. There was another evening, very like that, at Maurice's.[3]

I found in the pocket of my coat the enclosed, which I must have rescued from the litter on Sunday morning. It may be of value to you.

I know you will think it silly, but it means everything to me to be near where Eleanor is — I mean the difference in miles — even though I cannot see her often. Electrons again, I presume. With love

[P.S.] I am S. Anderson, not Sherwood, here.

My best to Mr. Copenhaver.

The story on which I am at work gets bigger and bigger in my mind in any event.

199. [ELIZABETH CARTARET HOTEL, ELIZABETH, NEW JERSEY, MAY 16, 1931]

To ROGER AND RUTH SERGEL

Dear Roger & Ruth: A mix-up. I'm not clear. I should have sent that play from home. I had been writing.

I got home & couldn't stay. I was tense & nervous, wanting to work. I forgot everything. I got into the car & came down here.

I might as well tell you I'm also in love. The woman was down here.

I've never been able to work without a woman to love. Perhaps I'm cruel. They are earth and sky and warmth and light to me. I'm like an Irish peasant, taking potatoes out of the ground. I live by the woman loved. I take from her.

I know damn well I don't give enough.

So I ran away from home and came to a town in New Jersey, near N. Y. Now, tomorrow, I have to get on a train & go out again into the Middle West to deliver one more lecture. I don't want to, but I seem to have to get money, some way, as you run that business.

It's the only way I know now. So I'm afraid I'll miss you. I won't be back in Marion until June 2nd or 3rd.

I love you both. I'm sorry. It's bum luck. Is there any chance you might plan your trip to get to Marion about that time? I'd go off with you into a lovely country and loaf with you for a week if you would.

Write me this way —

S. (not Sherwood) Anderson
Hotel Elizabeth Carteret
Elizabeth, New Jersey

[3] Maurice Long.

Could you come here, and be with me here, Sat. or Sunday the 23rd & 24th? Have a letter here for me telling me where I can call you up. I'll be back here by Sat. the 23rd.

Or drive over here and eat & stay at this hotel over the weekend.

200.   [ELIZABETH, NEW JERSEY, MAY] 23 [1931]

To LAURA LOU COPENHAVER

Dear Friend: I saw Eleanor today, and she told me she was afraid you had not been well, also that Mr. Copenhaver had an accident and crippled himself. It's too bad.

I got a very comfortable room here, a half hour from N. Y., and I have really worked. The thing on which I am at work seems to get bigger and bigger. You will remember I told the story of the boy [1] in *Winesburg* by telling the stories of other people whose lives touched his life. This is going to be something of the same thing, if it comes off, only that instead of short stories there will be something perhaps like a series of novels. The first one is about done.

I haven't been able to see much of Eleanor — lunch twice and today a walk in Central Park. It was very lovely. We had two or three hours; then she had to rush off to a meeting. She had been struggling to straighten out a mess at Read[ing], Pa. all week, but I never saw her look so radiantly well.

I had to go out to Purdue University for the big literary event of the year out there, a speech for which I was not prepared. It's the same thing everywhere. Even in this big scientific school, with 4,000 young men learning to be chemists and engineers, there is a hunger for some humanizing thing. It makes you ashamed that you have so little to give.

I told them little stories of common people in towns and in factories, and I guess they liked it. What interested me was this. They seemed most touched by a story of something John once said to me. John had remarked, regarding Ripshin, that it was very nice, but that neither he [n]or I could ever work there. "It sets us too far above all the people around us," John said.

I told them that story and also the story of the old farmwoman who said: "I guess it's nice you being here. I don't think you are an uppity man, but, well, before you came, we were all poor together here."

[1] George Willard.

They got the significance of those two stories. It was interesting to see a queer hush come over the room when I told them.

Eleanor will be driving down with Lois,[2] and do not be surprised if I appear in Marion at about the same time. Karl may possibly drive down with me. It may be too bad, from the family's point of view, but the simple truth is that I grow more and more in love with Eleanor.

I took John to Charles,[3] and he seems to be happy there and to be working well. I was a little afraid. Charles' father-in-law is a rich man and thinks painting rather nonsense. He could so easily make life easy for Charles, but I guess he can't. On everything he uses the terrible money and success standard of measurement.

To go back to the boys at Purdue. They clung to me. You get that sort of thing everywhere now. They seem to think maybe you have the key to the house of God concealed in your pocket somewhere. A young professor came to me and said: "You seem not to be spiritually tired. How does it happen? We have had a lot of men here. They all seem to be tired inside. How does it happen you aren't?"

I couldn't tell them, of course, how much Eleanor had to do with that or how near I was to death and suicide two years ago. Please be careful of yourself. It is all right your saying you do not need other people, but there are a lot of people who need you. With love

201.   [ELIZABETH, NEW JERSEY MAY 29, 1931]

TO ALFRED STIEGLITZ

Dear Alfred: I think I left, near the phone in your place, a small black address book. If I did, will you mail it to me at Marion, Va.?

I got a real, genuine, new love in your place, the yellow and brown Dove.[1] It is absurd of me, of course, to want it. I'll never be able to afford it. I shouldn't have it. It should be where many people can see it.

Perhaps at bottom I'm like Dove, a country man. The warm earth feeling gets me hardest. It's land love, ground love.

Do you know I don't much mind everyone's being broke, myself among them? You too. You have much more energy in you than you

[2] Lois MacDonald, professor of economics at New York University and a friend of Eleanor Copenhaver.

[3] Charles Bockler.

[1] Arthur G. Dove (1880–1946), American painter.

know. You'll swim. If we were all nearer the condition of working people, having to be, we'd be the better for it.

Tell Dove anyway how I feel about his things. I loved the others too. It was just that the one got me as a particular woman gets you, though you know there are other beautiful women about. With love

202.   [?SUMMER, 1931]

To LAURA LOU COPENHAVER

Dear Mrs. Copenhaver: I do think the whole thing hurts — I mean the Daughters of the Revolution, etc.[1] You can't escape the essential setting of yourself apart, because of birth, etc. You know well that it is the essence of the whole thing.

It is this setting of ourselves up as in any way superior to the lowest man or woman in the world that brings evil into the world. It brought it in [in] the first place and keeps it here. Think what Christianity would gain if Christians did not feel themselves superior to non-Christians.

We all do so much of this. The moral man sets himself above the so-called immoral. How does he know what immorality is? In every inch you set yourself above anyone, you hurt that other one.

Love of country, Daughters of the Revolution because of love of country. That is bunk, too. There is little enough love of country. Mr. Copenhaver, in loving his bit of land out on the Walker Mountain road, is loving his bit of the U.S.A. It's the only sort of love of country that is worth a whoop. All the rest is just talk. There you have Marion, a lovely little town really. And how quickly the citizens would rush forward to bring there some dirty factory, making cheap goods of some kind, pouring more cheap, shoddy goods out into the world. And they would call that Love of Their Town. A bit more money brought to a few, the rest degraded, all of us hoping to get up there among the few.

Little groups of THE FEW everywhere. They are essentially evil groups, my dear. I wanted to say something like this the other day.

I have wanted to say so much about my feeling about Eleanor I can't say. The fact that my loving her should hurt others seems horrible to me. I don't want to touch her in her real self, change her. I don't want

---

[1] Anderson and Mrs. Laura Lou Copenhaver, his future mother-in-law, were never able to agree on the merits of the Daughters of the American Revolution, of which Mrs. Copenhaver was a member.

her if it is going to hurt her or you who are dear to her. I'd much rather live the rest of my life alone.

When I came to Marion, I found something in your house. I don't think you and Mr. Copenhaver know how much I have found there. You two made the house what it is; you created the feeling of the house that has meant so much to an essentially lonely man.

I don't want to bring unhappiness into it. I won't. I'd a thousand times rather go on as I am.

You can't very well blame me for loving Eleanor, she being what she is. It doesn't mean that she has to have me.

Bless you people, anyway, for what you are. You are both good. You have been good to me.

203. [MARION, VIRGINIA, ?JULY, 1931]

To EDMUND WILSON

Dear Wilson: I got a wire from Tom Tippett at Charleston [1] — I guess it was after you left there — wanting me to come over and address the strikers from the courthouse steps. I didn't go. I had engaged to go down South.

I might have gone just the same, but was uncertain. I have a queer guilty feeling just now about taking any part in pulling people out on strike. We go and stir them up. Out they come and presently get licked. Then we go comfortably off. It seems to me that [if] we, of what I presume you might call the intelligentsia, are to go in at all with the workers, perhaps we should be ready to go all the way. I mean that we should be willing to go live with them in their way and take it in the neck with them.

I suppose the Negroes are good Communist material, but they will be making a mistake, won't they, if they take that material just because it is easy?

There are no *New Republics* sold here. I have sent a subscription and have asked for the number containing your article on West Virginia.[2]

I sent for the books on Lenin, Stalin, etc. They are interesting, but certainly impersonal. The books make them seem hardly human.

I have had a bad week's slump, but am feeling more like writing

[1] Charleston, West Virginia.
[2] "Frank Keeney's Coal Diggers," *New Republic*, LXVII, 195–199 (July 8, 1931); 229–231 (July 15, 1931).

again. It was great fun seeing you. I hope you will come this way again. Some of these days we'll do that stunt, get in the car and go off bumming together. Love to Mrs. Wilson. As always

204.   [MARION, VIRGINIA, SEPTEMBER 19, 1931]

To EDMUND WILSON

Dear Wilson: I want to thank you for *Axel's Castle*,[1] to me a profound book. Would to God I had your lea[r]ning.

I think that is the way it will all turn out concerning Joyce, Stein, Proust, Valéry, etc.

I presume there is another sort of learning, not always sticking your ear out to the future while you stare into the past.

A walk in any factory town, workers, machines, shop windows, motors in the streets — the machine accepted into life, brought into actual consciousness. I have the feeling most of the time that we live now, mentally and emotionally, in one world, while physically we live in another. If there is sick weariness affecting us all, making it hard to work, wouldn't that account for it?

Axel's Castle is a grand book. Sincerely

205.   [BALTIMORE, MARYLAND, OCTOBER 24, 1931]

To LAURA LOU COPENHAVER

Dear Friend: I came over here from Charlottesville this evening and, I hope, will see Channing, Mazie & Doctor Johnson [1] in the morning.

I thought you might be amused by some account of the writers' meeting.[2]

It opened in a large, rather comfortable room. Ellen Glasgow [3] took charge. She is charming. She is quite old now, but had tremendous vitality. In some way she reminds me of you, I mean in a kind of mental alertness, eagerness and charm.

Her talk was a great success, and then suddenly the meeting got

---

[1] Wilson published this study of symbolist literature in 1931.

---

[1] Mazie, Mrs. Copenhaver's youngest daughter, had married Dr. Channing Wilson of Baltimore. Dr. Johnson was a friend of the Wilsons.

[2] The Southern Writers' Meeting was held at the University of Virginia on October 23 and 24.

[3] Ellen Glasgow (1874–1945), novelist of Virginia life.

bad — long, tiresome speeches from professors. Everyone began to think it was going to be like a dentists' convention.

I was in the home of the acting president and had a whole suite of big rooms, right facing the lovely inner lawn.

As you might suspect, all the writers were looking at each other a bit self-consciously.

There were a good many I knew.

I like Struthers Burt,[4] a small, alert man, with a nice wife. He's a bit dry.

Allen Tate [5] was there with his wife,[6] a fine black-haired, black-eyed creature, who talked intelligently about farming. I liked them.

You know about Cabell.[7] He is placid, 55, face like a baby's in some queer way, clever at retort, always with a sting of maliciousness.

We lunched at a professor's house. I sat with a small woman *****[who] began telling the story of poor Sinclair Lewis['s] effort to give his Nobel Prize medal to Yale.[8] *****

I neglected to say th[at] at the first meeting Cale Young Rice [9] made a long, egotistical, meaningless talk.

At the table with me at the lunch was also Stringfellow Barr.[10] I had met him before, but this time really liked him.

Katharine Anthony [11] — nice. I hadn't seen her for 5 years. She looked old and ill.

There was a charming woman, a Miss Pinckney [12] — The Pinckneys of Charleston — very much Southern family, etc., one of the nicest, simplest persons there. She may be 35, very lovely, really.

Rita Van Doren,[13] Carl Van Doren's wife, editor N.Y. *Herald* book page — very, very charming. She has hair that sticks straight up everywhere — talks brilliantly & intelligently.

[4] Struthers Burt (1882–), novelist.
[5] Allen Tate (1899–), poet and critic.
[6] Caroline Gordon (1895–), novelist.
[7] James Branch Cabell (1879–), novelist.
[8] Lewis received the Nobel Prize in 1930. For the "story" see Harrison Smith, "Sinclair Lewis: Remembrance of the Past," *Saturday Review of Literature,* XXXIV, 7–9, 36–38 (January 27, 1951), pp. 9, 36–37.
[9] Cale Young Rice (1892–1943), poet, husband of Alice Hegan Rice.
[10] Stringfellow Barr (1897–), then associated with the *Virginia Quarterly Review.*
[11] Katharine Anthony (1877–), biographer.
[12] Josephine Pinckney (1895–), poet and novelist.
[13] Irita Van Doren (1891–), literary editor of the *New York Herald Tribune Books.*

I was taken with her and a party of several others to have a drink. There is something terribly tiring about the impact of many personalities.

John Peale Bishop [14] was there. I used to know him in Paris. An intelligent, gentlemanly fellow.

We went to Amélie Rives' [15] place — such a gorgeous place. She was rich and married some prince. She couldn't come out of her room. Many went in to see her, but I didn't. I thought perhaps she was seeing too many people.

There was a big table with many drinks. We strolled about the lawn. I fell in with a Mississippi man I knew. Brickell,[16] now with Houghton Mifflin.

A party of us went off to another big country house. More drinks. I went and sat on the porch — a lovely stretch of country. The man began telling me that he began reading my books at the recommendation of Judge Stone of the U.S. Supreme Court. That pleased me.

We drove to a country club. Small tables. My dinner companions were Rita Van Doren & Mrs. Chapman.[17] She wrote *Happy Valley* [*sic*].

Her husband also a writer. He went about all the time looking frightened, as though the police were after him. He & Mrs. Chapman both rather washed out.

Bill Faulkner had arrived and got drunk. From time to time he appeared, got drunk again immediately, & disappeared. He kept asking everyone for drinks. If they didn't give him any, he drank his own.

Everyone kept running up to everyone else and saying, "Isn't Mr. Cabell nice? Isn't Sherwood Anderson nice, etc?"

Well, everyone was really trying to be nice. After dinner at the club a big crowd gathered about Barr, Ellen Glasgow and myself. We got into an amusing wrangle over some abstract subject, more to hang conversation on than anything else. Presently all joined it. It was the first real thaw-out, fun, going it hot & heavy, good-natured raillery & good talk.

[14] John Peale Bishop (1891–1944), poet and novelist.
[15] Amélie Rives Troubetzkoy (1863–1945), novelist.
[16] Herschel Brickell (1889–1952), on the editorial staff of Henry Holt and Company from 1928 to 1933.
[17] Mary Chapman (1895–), wife of Stanton Chapman. They wrote together, as Maristan Chapman, *Happy Mountain* (1928).

We left there at midnight & went to a professor's house. Mr. Newcomb,[18] my host, came and six or seven men. We drank some more & talked. It was about all the real talking I did. It was just two when I got to bed.

They all went to Monticello this morning, but I didn't go. I slept until ten.

I went to a meeting. I didn't go in. More speeches. I stayed outside. There was too much talk about the South. Presently that Miss Pinckney, Mrs. Chapman, and a writer named Putnam [19] came out. We walked about & talked.

I had gone to see Ham,[20] but he had gone off to a football game at Lexington.

We went to another big country house for lunch. After that I fled.

Mary Johnston [21] — she wears black and has become a spiritualist. She made a long, meaningless speech, about the rhythm of something. I couldn't follow. I didn't make any speeches.

Paul Green [22] is a young man. He looks rather like a football player. He drinks pretty hard. I'm sure they don't all drink like that all the time. They couldn't.

There didn't seem to be any definite thing accomplished. There were a lot of talks I didn't hear. I think the Agrarians [23] were the only ones there trying to put over any definite program.

DuBose Heyward & wife [24] — a bit too soft, I thought. Very gentle, though.

Stark Young didn't show up.

Julia Peterkin [25] "   "   "

Mrs. Stallings came, but not Laurence Stallings.

---

[18] Dr. John Lloyd Newcomb, acting president of the University of Virginia, 1931–1933.

[19] Possibly Phelps Putnam (1894–1948), poet.

[20] John Hamilton Scherer, a cousin of Eleanor Copenhaver then a student in the medical school of the University of Virginia.

[21] Mary Johnston (1870–1936), historical novelist.

[22] Paul Green (1894–), dramatist.

[23] A group of Southern writers, including Allen Tate, who in the early '30's urged that the South return to an agricultural economy and maintain a regional culture.

[24] DuBose Heyward (1885–1940) and his wife, Dorothy, received the 1927 Pulitzer Prize for their dramatic version of Heyward's novel *Porgy* (1925).

[25] Julia Peterkin (1880–), whose *Scarlet Sister Mary* (1928) won the Pulitzer Prize.

Alice Hegan Rice,[26] who wrote *Mrs. Wiggs of the Cabbage Patch,* looks just like Mrs. Wiggs herself should have looked. A suggestion of the refined washwoman.

206.   [ALBANY, NOVEMBER 15, 1931]

TO LAURA LOU COPENHAVER

Dear Friend: I've been flying about, but when I have spoken here tonight and at Dartmouth on Tuesday night, I'll be through for this trip.

However, I intend to give myself a week or ten days in New York before going back to Marion, so I may see you.

On the whole the speaking has gone well. During the time I have been doing it, I have thought of nothing else and have spent the days between working at the talks, changing and, I hope, improving them. At any rate the audiences seem absorbed in the picture as I try to make it for them.

Most of the talks have been about machinery, and I have used, with really quite tremendous effect, the long poem on the automobile from *Perhaps Women.*[1]

I was in Pittsburgh yesterday afternoon and evening with an old friend to Maurice.[2] Went to the International Show of painting.[3] Have just finished a letter to Eleanor about it. What really amazed me was the really tremendous vitality in the Russian room. It seemed to shout and dance, full of joy in life, without weariness, as though the Russian had at least found hope.

I have intended to get and send you Emma Goldman's life story,[4] but haven't had the chance to get near a book store. Perhaps I'll find it in Boston tomorrow.

I hope you and Mr. Copenhaver are both well. My best to you both [P.S.] There is always a whirl of people before and after speaking, usually a dinner to attend, students asking questions. The interest both in my point of view on machinery and on the small-town newspaper is apparently pretty widespread.

[26] Alice Caldwell Hegan Rice (1870–1942), author of numerous popular books, best known for *Mrs. Wiggs of the Cabbage Patch* (1901).

[1] "Machine Song," pp. 9–17 of *Perhaps Women.*

[2] Maurice Long.

[3] The thirtieth Carnegie International Exhibition of Modern Paintings, which was held at Carnegie Institute from October 14 to December 6.

[4] Emma Goldman, *Living My Life* (1931).

207.   [?WASHINGTON, D. C., BEFORE DECEMBER 6, 1931]

To KARL ANDERSON

Dear Karl: I've been about, doing some speaking, and was in New York. I had expected to get there Thursday and have two days, but was delayed and did not get there until late Friday. I spoke to Tom Smith at Liveright's about your novel, and of course he['d] like to see it, if it isn't in someone else's hands. Most places I have been this year are depressed enough. I often remember people's mad enthusiasm for the War, killing Germans, etc., and if people are depressed and low now, I'm rather half glad. It should be good for their goddam childish souls.

Also I think the Depression is good. At least we know the big businessmen and financiers now for what they are — another lot of vain children, they with their eternal dabbling in the arts, etc. Let their sagging asses hang to the ground now.

I'll be back in N. Y. next Sunday, but only for the day. There is to be a protest meeting against the dirty framing of Dreiser,[1] and I am going to speak. I don't know where it is to be. A lot of love, Karl

[P.S.] Would have called you but that I only had the late afternoon & evening in town.

208.   [MARION, VIRGINIA, ?DECEMBER 22, 1931]

To THEODORE DREISER

Dear Dreiser: I received the enclosed. It was on my desk today when I returned from the South. I am not sure who this man is.

I left the lecture in question[1] with the representative of the *New York Times*. I have forgotten his name. At that moment an editor from the *New Republic* came on the platform. There was some talk that they might use it. The *Times* man was to send the ms. over to the *New Republic*. I have heard nothing from *New Republic*. A phone message would discover whether or not they are going to use it.

It is O.K. for any organization to use it that you O.K. I would insist that it not be changed and that I see proofs.

---

[1] At a mass meeting held in New York December 6, 1931, Anderson extolled the outspokenness of Dreiser who had been indicted for criminal syndicalism in Kentucky as a result of his part in an investigation of working conditions in the Harlan County coal fields.

---

[1] Anderson's speech at the mass meeting of December 6. See previous letter.

I am puzzled about Communism, as I am sure you may be. It may be the answer, and then it may only be a new sort of Puritanism, more deadly than the old moral Puritanism, a new kind of Puritanism at last got power in one place to push its rigid Puritanism home.

My central interest in coming to New York was not Communism, but the right of yourself and your associates to speak, and for the Communists to be heard too. You will understand that impulse.

I will be in New York about the second week in January and will phone you. Sincerely

[P.S.] Since writing above I find that my son has printed the speech [2] in our local weekly. I enclose copy.

209   [MARION, VIRGINIA, ?DECEMBER 25, 1931]

TO BURTON AND MARY EMMETT

Dear Burt & Mary: I think you may like "Mill Girls" in the January *Scribner's*. They call it a novel. That was their idea, not mine. I merely intended to make a picture of the girls as a man might paint a landscape.

It was charming of you to send the money as a contribution on the expenses of speaking up for Dreiser. I am enclosing a copy of the speech from our own paper here. Perhaps also the "Travel Note" (enclosed) will amuse you.

It is nice to feel you partners in my sins. I think you would both be interested in something I wrote Dreiser yesterday. (By the way I will enclose a note from him for your Americana.)

I said to him, as regards Communism, "It is probably a new sort of Puritanism, more dreadful than any other sort because having more power."

All the same, dear friends, I go in for their right to be heard, to agitate, etc. I go with Voltaire when he said, "I don't believe a word the man says, but will give my life for his right to say it." [1]

We will discuss all this. I'll be in N. Y. a good deal from Jan. 10 to 20th. We must have an evening, perhaps more, together.

I am happy to have you have the O'Keeffe.

[2] In the Marion newspapers for December 22, 1931, under the title "An Address." In the Anderson mss. these clippings have received extensive editorial alterations by Anderson.

[1] There are various forms of this saying, which has been fathered on Voltaire.

My son Bob married last week.[2]
I'll be telling you all my news when I see you.
I hope you aren't still starving.
Lots of love & good wishes.

210.   [SAN FRANCISCO, CALIFORNIA, AFTER APRIL 8, 1932]

TO LAURA LOU COPENHAVER

Dear Friend: There are several books for you. Wilson's new book
(*The American Jitters*),[1] Williams' book on Russia,[2] and the marvelous
story of the Russian Revolution by Trotsky.[3] This last belongs to
Eleanor. She hasn't had time to read it, so has loaned it to me. Leon
Gelber gave it to her.

Also a rather keen book on Aimee McPherson[4] by a newspaper
woman here who has been taking me about some here, to police stations
and the Barbary Coast — strange, tough little dives, Negroes and whites
and Chinese and Malays and Japs. Often quite fine-looking white girls,
drunk and staggering through the rooms.

I went with several men to hear Lincoln Steffens speak[5] at a big
hotel before a businessmen's club, and he found out I was in the room
and sent for me to the speaker's table. I didn't go but saw him later.

There was a big banquet, and afterward women were admitted to
hear the speech; so I looked across the room, and there, with several
women, was Eleanor.

I didn't like the speech, nor did she. He seems to have the obsession
that some big American businessman, a Ford or an Owen D. Young,
is going to come along and save us. The big, beautiful businessman
idea in a new form, as in his autobiography. He spoke a great deal
about Russia and, without saying the dreadful word, thought Communism had to come, etc., but some big businessman would bring it.

All too flattering [to] the men who filled that room, I thought, and
after the speaking, as he had sent for me, I went and told him so.

---

[2] Robert Anderson married Mary Chryst, a teacher at Marion College.

[1] Edmund Wilson, *The American Jitters* (1932).

[2] Albert Rhys Williams, *Russian Land* (1927).

[3] Presumably *The History of the Russian Revolution*, translated by Max Eastman (1932).

[4] Nancy Marity's *Sister Aimee* (1931) discusses the career and personality of
the evangelist, Aimee Semple McPherson (1890–1944).

[5] Lincoln Steffens (1866–1936), formerly a leading "muckraking" journalist,
had published his *Autobiography* in 1931.

"Were Trotsky, Lenin, Stalin, any of them businessmen?" I asked him, and to my amazement he caved in at once and began to say that I had to come and see him, that I was the one man in America who might help him in his confusion, etc.

So I agreed to go down there to his town on Tuesday. Ted Lilienthal[6] is going to drive me down. We'll take Eleanor if she can get off. There is great vitality in the man, but a queer trickiness in thought.

I'm thinking now that, as soon as I have this novel done and another book to be called *I Accuse* — this already nearly done since I have been out here — an indictment of all our crowd — writers, painters, educators, scientists, intellectuals in general — in a time when the world so needs leadership into revolution, we all such cowards — after all that I want to do a frank book of notes on people, my own relationship to them, notable men, so-called, in America — I have known them nearly all in my time. A book that should be great fun.

Again I am working well, words and ideas flowing pretty freely, not exactly a river but at least a creek of ideas.

I'll leave here when Eleanor does. Why shouldn't I stay near her when I work so well being near her?

211.   [SAN FRANCISCO, MID-APRIL, 1932]

TO VALENTI ANGELO [1]

Dear Valenti Angelo: There is more I wanted to say to you. I think this notion of going to the factories for men's new religious experience is so much the road of the future.

I had the conception myself long ago and tried to express it in *Marching Men*, but later got swept aside from it. I had some success. Perhaps that poisoned me.

The factories and the farms must be the new road.

I think artists, in all fields, must follow this road now and am very happy that your foot is in the stirrup. Keep it there, man. Keep renewing your own close contact with men at work in factories and the machines they handle now. It is the way of the new man.

---

[6] Theodore M. Lilienthal of the bookstore of Gelber, Lilienthal, Inc., in San Francisco.

---

[1] Valenti Angelo (1897–), author and illustrator, was a book designer from 1925 to 1933 at the Grabhorn Press in San Francisco.

There is something personal. There is a woman [2] here with whom I am in love. It is not known that I am in love with her. She is a working woman, concerned now with women and girls in factories. At present she has a job in the industrial department of a philanthropic organization. She is about 35, rather small and dark, with a big head like your own child and with eyes like your child. I would like to have a head made of her for a present to her old father and mother. Would it be possible? How much would it cost? How much time would it be likely to take? I have to ask because she does not have much time away from her work.

I am particularly anxious not to have talk about my being in love with her.

It might actually cause her to lose her job.

We will be married later, but I don't want that known either.

When a man becomes a little what is called famous, there are too many who dabble in his personal life.

Anyway I would like to have you see her and see how you feel about trying to make a head of her. Sincerely

212. [MARION, VIRGINIA] JUNE 18, 1932

MR. ROGER SERGEL, THE DRAMATIC PUBLISHING COMPANY, CHICAGO

Dear Roger: Your letter stirred a lot of emotions in me. Just the same, as soon as the novel comes back from Frederick,[1] send the carbon copy down to me. I want to read it, not only for your sake, but for my own. There remains a certain obligation such men as you and myself have toward each other to know what the other fellow is doing and what he is thinking and feeling. This does affect a man's work, and I want to see the novel for the same reason that I would like to have you down here for a time to walk about and talk with me.

I think we do live in a strange time, but that, whatever happens, we cannot afford to lose courage. We may see it at any moment now pass into an uglier time. I think there is a growing conviction in almost everyone that the new revolution that will have to come must be economic, not politic[al]. The political remedy has failed, and every-

[2] Eleanor Copenhaver, who was attending a Governors' conference on unemployment in San Francisco.

[1] John T. Frederick (1893-), professor of modern letters at Northwestern University, 1930–1944, founder and editor of the *Midland* magazine, 1915–1933.

one in America, in his heart, knows it has failed, but I think every man will hang on to what economic advantage he has to the bitter end.

I think, Roger, that in times like this a man has to force himself out of himself. There is an inclination to draw the circle smaller and smaller. Life grows more bitter. I really believe that I myself, although you give me credit I do not deserve, have been sunk a good deal in the thing you are sunk in. You do get a kind of release, the people you play tennis with in the park, the girls in the office.

I constantly find myself driving in the road down here, and everywhere in the road there are people wanting to be picked up. My inclination is to pass them by. I want to remain sunk in my own thoughts. I have to force myself to make each new contact, but every time I do it there is a kind of reward.

I think I have told you how I went through the whole thing, building my house in the country, retiring from the world, thinking I could live within myself, with my own dreams, in the past. I have had failures I do not believe you have had, Roger. You have not failed with Ruth, but I have failed with women. I found I had to drag myself out of my own little circle, force myself out. We are like swimmers, exhausted and swimming in a sea, and do not know where the land is. There is a constant inclination to give up swimming and sink. All of us pass in and out of this mood, and — I know you will forgive me for saying it — there is an inclination in all of us toward a kind of self-pity that we have to look out for.

The only remedy I know is to be forcing yourself out whenever and however you can with anyone.

However, for the time being, I think it is a good idea for those of us who make any pretentions at all to being a little sensitive, who are trying, at least part of the time, to live the life of the artist, to keep in touch with each other. We ought whenever possible [to] go to visit each other. We ought to write letters. It is a part of a program we must make to force ourselves out of ourself.

When I proposed the pilgrimage to America, I really had something of the kind in mind, always for myself as well as for you. I want to give a little love of man for man as you do. It is the difficulty of doing it that is so upsetting just now. With love

213.   [WASHINGTON, D.C.] AUGUST 10, 1932

PRESIDENT HERBERT HOOVER, THE WHITE HOUSE, WASHINGTON, D.C.

Mr. President: As one of the group of writers, I have come to Washington with some of my fellow writers to protest against the treatment of the Bonus Army in Washington.[1]

, What happened here in Washington looked to me like Tsardom. Are we to look forward to Tsardom? There were ex-soldiers here, certainly demanding nothing they had not been promised. They were destitute. They were driven out like sheep. Is this a sample of what Americans are to expect? This is the center of our Government. Has no American or any group of Americans the right to assemble here, the right to petition, to demand even something like justice be done in times like this? Has he not the right to expect not to be shot down when he comes defenseless to the seat of Government?

All of us are citizens, and some of us have been soldiers. It seems impossible to me that you cannot know what is going on in the country. There is starvation everywhere. It would not make any difference to me if these men coming to Washington and demanding help from the Government were not soldiers. A farmer out of work or a workman out of work is just as important as a soldier; perhaps he is more important.

I understand you are about to tell the country what you are going to do, if re-elected, to help all of us. Life is constantly getting more brutal here. Are you going to reassure us? Will you not tell us what to expect? Is the treatment given the Bonus soldiers in Washington what the unemployed or destitute will have to expect in the future? We have come here to ask you these questions. While you are telling the country about your plans for the next four years if you are re-elected, will you not at the same time answer these questions?

214.   [MARION, VIRGINIA] SEPTEMBER 22, 1932

MR. FERDINAND SCHEVILL, MICHIGAN CITY, INDIANA

Dear Ferdinand: I feel guilty that I have not written you for a long time, and I am anxious to hear from you and all about Clara.

I have just returned to Marion from a hurried trip to Europe. Some

---

[1] President Hoover refused to see this group of writers, August 10. On August 11 Anderson wrote the President a second, open letter, which was published as "Listen, Mr. President," *Nation*, CXXXV, 191–193 (August 31, 1932). See Letter 238.

time ago Romain Rolland sent out a rather despairing call from France, asking organizations of workers and intellectuals to come to Europe to a World's Conference Against War.[1] The matter was taken up over here by an American committee, and a delegation of American workers went. They were very anxious to have the writers of America also represented, and a rich woman of New York came forward and offered to pay my expenses if I would go; so I went.

We had a week at Amsterdam with some thirty million workers represented through their leaders and with a lot of big men of the intellectual and artistic world present. Of course the governments were all against it, and there was even for a time some question as to whether or not we would be allowed into Holland. As a matter of fact, Gorki,[2] who had come from Russia, was stopped at Berlin and was not allowed in. What happened at the meeting, and I think the best thing that happened, was the getting together of four or five hundred French labor leaders, including Communists, Socialists, and trade union men, with four or five hundred of the same sort of men out of Germany. That, I thought, was rather gorgeous.

The whole feeling of the meeting was for direct action against war by way of propaganda on the part of the writers and artists and by way of strikes on the part of the workers. I think it was the first time that the intellectuals and workers of many countries have actually got together in this way. There were thirty-five[3] nations represented. Of course it was a shame that the capitalistic press all over the world remained almost absolutely silent about the meeting, but that was to be expected.

My new novel, *Beyond Desire,* is being published this week, and I see where Laurence Stallings has just given it a grand send-over in the New York *Sun.* I expect to have my own copies in this week and will send you one.

I expect to be here until the 15th or 20th of October, when I expect to go to Russia and spend the winter there. My plan is to go down South to some industrial town, perhaps on the Caspian Sea.

There is something else, Ferdinand, that I wish to speak to you about. I am at work now on a new book that I shall call *A Book of*

[1] For further information on the events of the World's Congress Against War, held in Amsterdam from August 27 to 29, see Letter 221.

[2] Maxim Gorki (1868–1936), the Russian novelist.

[3] Actually twenty-seven.

Days.[4] The plan is to pick out the most adventurous days and their happenings, thoughts, etc., of the last three or four years and make them into a book. I already have all the material necessary and only have to winnow it out and to make selections. My point is that I want to dedicate the book to you and write now to get your consent. Write and tell me all you can about yourself while I am here. With love to you both

215.   [MARION, VIRGINIA] OCTOBER 10, 1932

THE DRAMATIC PUBLISHING COMPANY, CHICAGO, ILLINOIS

Dear Sirs: The little play, *The Triumph of the Egg,* had its New York production with the Provincetown Players.[1] It was put on as a curtain-raiser for Eugene O'Neill's two-act play, *Different.* The play caught the fancy of the audience and was a success.

The Provincetown Players, however, did some things to the play that I rather liked. The scene of the mother and the child was done off stage, in a room opening off the restaurant, the father standing in the doorway and talking to the mother. The audience never did see the stage child and got the sense of him from the mother's talk and from the little voice of the child saying his prayers. One of the New York critics spoke of the child as the most satisfactory stage child ever in the New York theaters. You did not have to look at the child being an actor. Your own imagination — you being of the audience — made the child exist. You — being of the audience — recalled perhaps your own childhood. It was very effective and satisfactory.

At the last, by my friend Mr. Raymond O'Neil's[2] version of the story, you see the two people, the unsuccessful little restaurant keeper and his wife, they having thrown themselves sobbing on the bed. This ending did a little violate my own conception when I wrote the story. To me the whole point of the play should be that the audience stays balanced between laughter and tears. In the Provincetown Players' version and after the outburst of ineffectual anger on the part of the father — his throwing the eggs about the room, etc. — he goes behind the restaurant counter. For a moment he stands there, looking about,

[4] This book was never completed.

[1] Produced February 10, 1925 at the Provincetown Playhouse under the direction of James Light.

[2] The Provincetown production was based on the dramatization made in 1922 by O'Neil and published in 1932 by The Dramatic Publishing Company with this letter as a foreword.

perplexed, his anger dying, hurt. He sits down on a stool, and his head falls into his hands. His elbows are on the counter.

The world, represented by the people passing along the road from the train, goes by the little restaurant. Joe Kane is telling his father about the queer people who run the restaurant. Joe Kane and his father stop a moment by the restaurant door. You hear the voices and the laughter, the talk of other people going up into Bidwell from the train. The poor, befuddled restaurant keeper does not raise his head.

The voices pass and silence comes. The voice of the woman, the mother, is heard — a voice full of sympathy now, all the weariness and irritation gone out of it.

"Father! Father!"

The father is sitting with his head in his hands, half raises his head. Curtain. I do not really know how much of this is from the Provincetown Players' version and how much my own imagination has built up since, but of this I am quite sure: to do the little play in this way will gain tremendous effectualness and will leave the audience, as it should be left, balanced between laughter and tears. Very truly yours

216.   [MARION, VIRGINIA, ?OCTOBER 17, 1932]

TO KARL ANDERSON

Dear Karl: Your letter was a lovely thing. It has done me great good. I knew that *Beyond Desire* [1] was disturbing, and I hoped for beauty. It seemed so far off sometimes.

But your letter was more than a fine reassurance. It was a blood call.

I have thought often, Karl, of your own novel,[2] released at last, as it will be. A man strikes at some inner thing, and then there is this confusion. It is, I fancy, like a woman seeing a child of hers go out into the world, knowing, if she has any sense, what the world is.

The strange feeling, too, that the thing has become something outside yourself. You have resentment at misunderstanding, but it becomes, finally, not personal. All the more bitter a dose for that.

There are the stupid ones, pawing over, not you now, but the thing.

I presume I hate it for other writers — the same thing must happen to painters — because I'm a writer.

[1] *Beyond Desire* appeared in September, 1932.
[2] Karl had finished a novel in the summer of 1932, but it was not printed, despite Sherwood's efforts to find him a publisher.

So to other writers, alas, I sometimes feel almost like calling out, "Don't, don't."

It was a very gorgeous letter, and I love you for it.

[P.S.] I'm going out into the Middle West in my car at the end of the week. I'll be floating some months. The woman with whom I have been in love for several years now will be out there. I am part way in a new novel. I am getting together a book of short stories.

I find I cannot escape, for all my failures, the constant daily need of a woman loved. My life is always too patched and broken without it. Love to all in your house

217.   [MARION, VIRGINIA] OCTOBER 17, 1932

MR. TOM SMITH, LIVERIGHT, INC., PUBLISHERS, NEW YORK

Dear Tom: As regards the book of short stories, I thought of calling it *Death in the Wood*.[1] Since I got your letter yesterday, I have been checking over the stories I would like to have included in this volume. Here's a list of them, not necessarily in the order in which they would go into the book.

1. Death in the Wood
2. There She Is — She Is Taking Her Bath
3. The Return
4. That Sophistication
5. Deputy Pete
6. Why They Got Married
7. Alice
8. The Lost Novel
9. Another Wife
10. In a Strange Town
11. A Jury Case
12. The Fight
13. A Criminal's Christmas
14. A Sentimental Journey

I will send you today enclosed what I suggest as the title story of the book, "Death in the Wood."

I do not know, my dear Tom, how you are [a]ffected by some of the adverse criticism we have had for *Beyond Desire*, but for me, at least, all this talk of its being a confused and muddled book makes me tired. It seems to me that the novel has more real form than any novel I have

[1] Became *Death in the Woods,* published in April, 1933.

written. I have tried to write the story of a confused civilization, and I think the critics have been up to their old trick of thinking that a writer who writes of a confused and puzzled man is necessarily himself confused. You would think, Tom, that some of these critics have found a definite formula for the good life. If they have, I wish to God they would come out with it.

For myself, I know well enough that the book is sound, and I believe it will take its definite place in the story of our American civilization and as a sound piece of work. I am speaking of all this to you, Tom, because I have something else in mind about which I want to speak to you today. Two or three times when we have talked in your office and at your house, I have got a sense of a certain reaction to life that I believe you represent pretty clearly. In fact, you have often said as much to me.

The point of view interests me profoundly and has for a long time; that is to say, the point of the individualist in life, the man who takes the individualist's point of view simply. I think it is a sound point of view.

However, I think that the point of view of the individualist might in the end come to the same thing as that of the Communist; that is to say, Tom, taking the Communist point of view as a philosophy of life. I am not necessarily talking about the Communists as an organization.

I am talking about all this in relation to a new novel. The real reason why I did not want to go off to Russia this winter is that I feel like trying to get this novel down, at least for the first writing. The book of short stories and also the book of days come largely to a matter of selection and of filling in. Both are now detail work. It may be that I will want to add two or three short stories to the book of short stories, two or three stories that have been floating around in my mind for a long time, but that is largely a matter of each one coming clearly forth at one setting. That might not come off. I find I have to wait for stories as I presume a hen must wait for her moment before she can lay an egg.

Now as regards the new novel, I have already launched it. I have got hold of my man and my theme. The man is one who believes absolutely in the development of his own individuality, his own individualistic point of view in life, the development of his own personal life, etc. He is a man somewhere between the age of 37 and 39, the son of an American laboring man, and himself, up to the time he comes into the book, a half-itinerant workman, sometimes a factory hand. His wife has been killed in an accident, and his one child has died. Suddenly the man throws off his old life in a factory town and all hope of the workers' achieving anything through their organizations, and starts out to live his own life. He gets a place in the home of a well-to-do country doctor, working about the house and yard and occasionally driving the doctor's car.

The man is uneducated in the school sense, but has been an eager reader all his life and is full of vitality that expresses itself in his body and also in his mind and in his imagination.

This will bring me into the body of the book, which is to be the study of an American family of the present day, the relationship of the family, father and mother, sons and daughters, to each other and to the outside world. This built up through the mind and imagination of the worker who sees them from the outside, but who, as he goes on living with them, becomes more and more a part of the outside and inside life of the family.

I want to show in the novel, if I can, how this man, living by a purely individualistic philosophy, comes out at about the same place as the man who goes through life struggling to give up individuality.

The story as it lies in my mind is full of intensely dramatic possibilities, and, as suggested, I have already got part of it down.

I agree with you about *The Book of Days*. As I have got it gathered together now, it will want a lot of cutting and trimming, and it will be just as well for me to go through the whole book several times, cutting and trimming each time. Sincerely

P.S. I expect I will leave here in a few days and go out into the Middle West. I am going to keep a few speaking engagements in Middle Western colleges and drift around out there for two or three months while I try to get this novel down for the first writing.

As soon as I have a definite address, I will of course send it to you.

You had better tell me just how soon you will be wanting the complete short story book.

218.   [MARION, VIRGINIA, OCTOBER 21, 1932]

TO LEON GELBER [1]

Dear Leon Gelber: I hear that Valenti Angelo is to have an exhibition of paintings in San Francisco, and I am writing this letter to you to say how much I admire the man and his work.

---

[1] With Theodore M. Lilienthal a partner in the bookstore firm of Gelber, Lilienthal, Inc., San Francisco. In 1925 this firm had published Anderson's *The Modern Writer*.

I was in San Francisco last year and for some weeks lived there, putting the finishing touches on a novel, and it was at that time I first saw Angelo's work. I have very little money, but immediately bought one of his paintings and carried it off to my room. It stayed with me while I worked there, and I brought it home with me to hang over my desk. I have found the painting very warm and living, and as the months have passed, it has grown more alive.

It represents very perfectly what good painting means to me. Valenti has been touched and moved by men at work. These builders and miners and makers he sees with his painter's eyes, connecting them with skies and hills and trees. There is surely here a connection — man in nature, man in the modern world we are making.

To get back the dignity of our living again. This man Valenti seeking that in paint.

Valenti's painting got me, and, as you know, I did try to express my appreciation and my belief in the man and his work in the only sensible, direct way we can express it now, by immediately buying one of the paintings.

I think there is power of feeling in these paintings and that the power goes out of them into a room and returns into them. I think we Americans need this kind of paintings and this kind of painters. I think we need such paintings in our houses. I do. They are reaching for some lost dignity in man and, in reaching, help bring it back.

219.   [MARION, VIRGINIA] NOVEMBER 11, 1932

MR. SERGEI DINAMOV, MOSCOW, U.S.S.R.

Dear Mr. Dinamov: [1] I am in receipt of your very interesting letter and had hoped very much that I would be able to come to Russia this winter, but things have happened concerning my personal life that now make it impossible.

As I read your letter, I couldn't help wishing that you had also at some time known life as lived in America. If you had done so, I believe you would realize with us how confusing life has got here.

America started out, apparently, with so much to offer to the world. In making our offer to the world we have apparently failed. We have

---

[1] The editor-in-chief of the Soviet publication, the *Literary Gazette*, who had sent Anderson a summary of an article he had written, praising Anderson's work but characterizing it as an artistic expression of the psychology of the petty bourgeoisie.

become, as a people, rich in goods and too poor in something else. There are many things here that seem to the American to make the American problem peculiarly difficult.

For one thing, we as a people do not know each other very well, do not draw close together, and I myself, as a writer, have wanted more than anything else to make Americans, in the civilization in which they are compelled to live now, better known to each other.

I am not so sure that simple stories of human beings, caught and held suspended in a civilization, are not better material for the ultimate revolution that must come here than anything else I can do.

You will see from all this that I am not all troubled about what you are doing over there, although I admit that I am sometimes troubled a good deal as to how I may make my own best contribution here. With greetings

220. [MARION, VIRGINIA] NOVEMBER 14, 1932

MR. MOISSAYE J. OLGIN,[1] 35 EAST 12TH STREET, NEW YORK

My dear Moissaye Olgin: You wrote me a letter on October 27th asking me some questions for *Pravda,* and I am very sorry that I did not receive the letter so that it could be answered at once.

What happened was that I was traveling about the country, and the letter was forwarded to me from my home. However, it did not catch me and was sent forward from one place to another and has just been returned here. I am very much afraid that I am too late to answer your questions for the *Pravda.* However, I will make a try at it in the hope that my answers may be of some possible use to you.

1. How has the present economic crisis affected your profession?

A: I understand that in general writers in America have suffered as has everyone else in the present crisis. As a matter of fact, the big capitalistic magazines that paid such high prices to writers in America have suffered rather terribly. In my individual case it happens that these magazines rarely want any of my stories and articles, so that, beginning as a writer without much money, I have simply remained in the same position.

2. How has it affected the development of new, future forces for your profession?

---

[1] The American correspondent for *Pravda.*

A: My own hope is that it will lead to an increased number of our new American writers not having their eyes always fixed on the big successful magazines and upon life as it is actually lived here in America. However, there is something depressing in life here now, not only in the Depression, but in the fact that America does not as yet seem to be thoroughly aroused and eager for a new life.

3. Do you see the possibility of a return to anything like normal condition for your profession without a profound social change?

A: It seems to me that the capitalistic world in America might at least partially recover from this condition and go on for a long time yet. However, I do believe that the older American illusions are slowly dying, and there are signs everywhere that young men of my profession are turning their eyes toward the necessity of the social change you speak of.

4. How do you view the U.S.S.R. in relation to the solution of the above problems?

A: I have not been to Russia and do not know. The stories told in America are very conflicting. I had hoped to go to Russia this fall, but my own personal concerns made it impossible. This naturally was the one thing I wanted to know and had hoped to find out about by a visit.

Very truly yours

221   [MARION, VIRGINIA] NOVEMBER 18, 1932

MISS IDA DAILES, AMERICAN COMMITTEE FOR THE WORLD CONGRESS AGAINST WAR, NEW YORK

Dear Ida Dailes: It is my shame that I cannot promise to be in New York for the meeting,[1] and I am the more ashamed that the meeting held for the return of the delegation had to be held without some of the delegates present. As you know, myself and Mr. Brodsky[2] were held up by a storm at sea which delayed our boat for two days.

At the time I went on this delegation and afterwards, I was compelled to say that, after going for this trip and after the visit to the

---

[1] A symposium on "War and Culture" was being projected for that December in New York under the auspices of the American Committee.

[2] Joseph Brodsky, New York attorney, who represented the International Workers Order on the American delegation to the Congress.

President at Washington in the matter of the soldiers' Bonus,[3] I would have to have personally a vacation to do my own work.

And then besides, I am not a writer who makes much money, and I have no money with which to make these trips and will not take it from any of your organizations. I did take money to go on the European trip, but after all for only a part of my expenses.

The best thing I can possibly see that I can do is to make a statement which can be read at the meeting in New York.

THE STATEMENT

The World's Congress Against War held in Amsterdam in September[4] struck me, as a delegate and observer, as being perhaps the first peace conference ever held that got down to essentials. There were no silk-hatted statesmen staying in expensive hotels, long tables with solemn-looking, frock-coated men having their pictures taken for the newspapers and saying big words and making promises they themselves knew they couldn't fulfill.

If a soldier says, "I will not shoot my fellows who are guilty of nothing but being hungry or out of a job," that means something.

It is, as we all know, the workers and the sons of workers who kill and get killed in the time of war. Generals very seldom get killed, and congressmen never. Businessmen do not get killed. They are much more likely to get rich in a time of war.

I myself remember how, before the World War, I was always reading articles telling me that now, because of the cost of modern war, war could not be carried on by any modern state for more than a few months. There would not be money enough. It was impossible.

And then the great call came, and millions of workmen were killed, killed for no economic or social gain to the world — a few new rich men, that was all. And after ten years the American workmen veterans of this war — over whom there had been so much sentimental weeping, putting of wreaths on graves of unknown soldiers, etc. — these same men were whipped out of Washington like driven sheep.

The point apparently is that so long as the workers of any country refuse to try to acquire real education, so long as they continue to use their hands to make powder, guns, explosives, and poison gas, as

---

[3] See Letter 213.
[4] Actually August 27 to 29.

long as they can carry it to the field of battle, they can go on, money or no money, killing and maiming each other.

Now the essential thing, the really significant thing about the Peace Meeting at Amsterdam last summer, was that it was a workers', sailors', and soldiers' meeting. It is true that the meeting was called by men of my own type, that is to say, writers and intellectuals, but at the meeting in Amsterdam they got quickly submerged, as they should have been. We writers and intellectuals also manage not to do much killing or getting killed in a time of war.

At Amsterdam I thought that even the speeches that really amounted to much all came from the workers, and I myself remember most vividly a sailor from the Italian Navy, a little round-shoulder[ed] French peasant, an American Negro ex-soldier, and certain broad-shouldered German workmen — these standing up before thousands of their fellow workers and soldiers and saying simple strong words, saying them to one another, beginning to know one another.

I remember also how the hall rang with song. I hear it yet sometimes in my dreams.

The meeting at Amsterdam was, I thought, the birth of something, the beginning. What happened there should happen in all countries. This fighting spirit, so sharply opposed to the old ugly kind of wars, should be carried forward now in all countries, not by the intellectuals and the writers, but by workers themselves. What happened at Amsterdam, this getting together of workers from so many countries, plain simple speech, that is what should keep on happening.

America certainly needs it. Often we in America are as separated from one another as are the countries of Europe, at least the workers are so separated. What is wanted is workers of the South [to go] to workers [of] the North, coal miners to transport workers, workers of Chicago and St. Louis to the workers of Pittsburgh and New York, country and small town workers to the city workers.

The beginning of understanding that can keep on growing. There is the eternal conspiracy always to separate, to prevent the growth of understanding among the workers, to build up not only national, but sectional hatreds.

The meeting at Amsterdam was a great beginning. It should be carried on.

Sincerely

222. [MARION, VIRGINIA] NOVEMBER 22, 1932

To CHARLES BOCKLER

Dear Charles: I was very happy to get your letter this morning. On Sunday John, with Dave Greear, went with me for a drive in the late afternoon, and we had two or three hours climbing and going over the hills and through the woods. Dave Greear is a young boy who lives in the house with John now. We got some mushrooms and went home and cooked them for supper. During the afternoon John and I were both thinking of you and talking of you. It is a shame that we can't all live nearer each other. In this confused time if we could have more companionship, between man and man, everything would be sweeter and better for all of us, but as it is, we seem to be condemned to live as we do, more or less separated, in little units.

I do not think there is anything wrong with nature, and surely there is enough here or enough in the view you get from your woodshed to keep all of us or anyone of us busy for a lifetime trying to get hold of a little of its significance.

I guess the attitude of the critics toward *Beyond Desire* was inevitable. Everyone now seems to hunger for a definite statement — Communism, Socialism, the finding of God, the finding of one another, something they can take hold of — and there isn't any doubt that something of the sort is needed. It is wrong and unfair of life that two men capable of giving each other as much as you and I are should not have the rights of a real companionship. I feel this and know you feel it. What to do about it is another matter.

I am constantly sorry that I cannot have the satisfaction of seeing your work from day to day and talking with you about your work and my work. Your letters, when they come, give me a good deal. I wish there were more of them. Please, Charles, do write to me as often as you can and whenever the impulse comes to you. As always

P.S. I was compelled to write a rather severe letter to young Gordon. We took him in here and gave him work for a long time, but he always did his work in a bad, sloven[ly] way. When he was writing for the paper, he spelled everyone's name wrong, and we had to do over everything he did.

After he left, he wrote me and wanted me to give him a recommendation so that some man would loan him money to start a paper of his own, and I felt compelled to write and tell him bluntly that even if there were such a thing as the Communism he dreams of, he would be of no use in it unless he could do his own small portion with some degree of competency.

233.   [MARION, VIRGINIA, DECEMBER 19, 1932]

To FERDINAND SCHEVILL

Dear Ferdinand: The curious indebtedness to you, almost, perhaps quite, above that to anyone who has ever crossed my path.

Naturally it makes me happy that you are coming out from under the nastiness of illness. It belongs so little to you.

I have felt, rather, what you say about the book, but no one else has said it so clearly.

I have been in an odd absorption. I have been getting the book of short things ready and got into another long novel.

In the novel I am going to make the call of American earth come to an American, as it happens to a woman.

There is something to shoot at there — this ground under our feet, how we Americans have been as whoremasters with it, treating the very fields, rivers, and hills as though they were whores.

The deep feminine thing in earth, its wanting the male too, the lover.

❀   ❀   ❀   ❀   ❀

I am very grateful for your letter.
Eleanor is getting well.
My love to Clara.
P.S. I wanted you & Clara to see the enclosed.[1] Do you mind mailing it back?

224.   [MARION, VIRGINIA] JANUARY 9, 1933

MR. OSCAR H. FIDELL,[1] 55 WEST 180TH STREET, NEW YORK

Dear Mr. Fidell: I am in receipt of your letter and should have answered it sooner, but I have been away from town.

I began to write just at a time when there was a sort of renaissance of letters in the Middle West. My first connection of literature was

---

[1] Not now identifiable.

[1] Fidell had written from New York that he was collaborating on a book concerned in part with the history of the *Masses* and its successor, the *Liberator*.

through Margaret Anderson, who started the *Little Review* in Chicago. Floyd Dell was out there at that time, and through him I met Max Eastman, Jack Reed,[2] and others. Jack Reed and I became friends, and after that I saw a good deal of him.

The "old *Masses*" was of tremendous significance to everybody when it appeared. It was bolder and freer than anything we had ever had. I can remember with what eagerness I used to watch for its appearance out in Chicago.

At about the same time I met and became a friend of Art Young's.[3] He and Jack Reed both had a joyous playboy quality that was a very refreshing thing in America.

What I think was the most significant about the "old *Masses*" was this feeling of bold[ness] and joy and life these men managed to get into its pages. Very truly yours

225.   [KANSAS CITY, JANUARY 20, 1933]

To CHARLES BOCKLER

Dear Charles: I am writing from Kansas City, from a little, rather tough hotel, full of little actors, prize fighters, auto salesmen out of work, and whores, also out of work. I stumbled into the place and, to my amazement, got a grand big room, clean, with a bath and an outlook over the city, for $5.50 a week. It's gaudy, and I really love these loose, non-respectable people about, drunk or sober. All I miss is a few of your own or John's painting[s] on the wall. John told me he was coming to Baltimore soon.

❈   ❈   ❈   ❈   ❈

I got into the car and lit out to drift for a time. I had a grand ride, over mountains and rivers and out onto the prairies, crossed the Cumberland, Tennessee, Ohio, Mississippi and Missouri Rivers. It rained, the wind blew & the sun shone. Again I got in love with America. What a land! O, Charles, if we can but begin to love it and treat it decently some day! It is so violent and huge and gorgeous and rich and willing to be loved, like a great, fine wench.

I hardly know what I'll do now. The play has gone off to N.Y. to see if anyone wants to play it, and I've got ready a book of short

---

[2] John Reed (1887–1920), reporter and revolutionary.
[3] Art[hur] Young (1866–1943), cartoonist. Both he and Reed were on the editorial staff of the *Masses*.

stories.[1] Perhaps now I'll go on with the next novel or perhaps another play.

I had a grand letter from Kack. Write me at Marion and tell me what you are doing and thinking.

226.   [KANSAS CITY, ?FEBRUARY, 1933]

To MARCO MORROW

Dear Marco: I really would like to spend some time with you when I get a chance and when you have some leisure. I have come here, to ***** [1] where I am at work and have here a suite, a workroom and a sleeping room. I think I had better explain to you my project, and then you will see what I am driving at.

As I think you know, Marco, I have done a good many books, trying to tell the story of the American small town, of the growth of American industry, of labor, of sex, and of the difficulties of human relations, but there is one side of life here, my own life and yours, I have always left pretty much untouched. As you know, Marco, I myself spent a good many years in advertising, having incidentally got into it largely through you, but I have never used that material. Now I would like to. I would like to do a book, half a story, trying to give a picture of the growth of advertising in America, its vast influence in making our civilization, effect on our newspapers and magazines, our habits of life and thought, and incidentally its tragedies.

Can it be done? It is a job that terribly needs doing.

I am wondering if I am equipped. Am I enough outside to do the thing clearly? Am I too much outside now?

What I would like is opportunity to talk with you from time to time as I go along, perhaps check with you on what I do. You will get the point and the significance. As always

[P.S.] Have recovered from my flu and am at work.

Want you to see my play made from *Winesburg, Ohio*.

227.   [KANSAS CITY, FEBRUARY 4, 1933]

To J. J. LANKES

Dear Lankes: The Troutdale print came like an answer to prayer. I've been on the drift, taking a relook at the Middle West this time,

---

[1] *Death in the Woods.*

---

[1] I.e., to the hotel mentioned in Letter 228.

and am staying at a little hotel in Kansas City, tough but nice. I wanted the feel of a Middle Western city again. Got a workroom and a bedroom for $1.00 a day, but nothing on the walls; so I was just about to write a letter to Bob to send me a couple Lankes[es] and a couple of painting[s].

Then this swell print came, forwarded by Bob.

I took it in to a place called the Alden Galleries.[1] "O[h]," said the man, "a Lanks" (mispronouncing your name).

He looked at it.

"O[h], dedicated to a good writer too," said he.

"You're goddam right," says I.

So he asked who I was, and I told him my name was Beal.

"Do you admire Lankes' work?"

"Tremendously," says he.

So I walked around the room. Not a Lankes. "Why the hell don't you sell it then?" So he spent the rest of the time while I was in there explaining — people weren't educated up to b[lo]ck prints yet, etc. He promised to do better, so I didn't burn his place down. I told him the Beal story as I didn't want to get into the K.C. art or literary world.

You know, Lankes, I've been trying to sell that Ripshin place for three or four years, and now I think I'll go back there to live, perhaps this spring, and if I do, I wish you could come down again and loaf and gab with me for awhile.

I keep hearing of your work more and more. You're beginning to penetrate, I guess. Hope you're pretty well.

My own chief amusement out here is going to working-class dance halls about 3 times a week and dancing my fool head off. As always [P.S.] Haven't your new address.

228.   [KANSAS CITY, MARCH 2, 1933]

To FERDINAND SCHEVILL

Dear Friend: It has been in my mind to write you for weeks. I got the proofs for the new short story book,[1] and they have been returned.

The truth is that when I got the book before me, I was not satisfied

---

[1] The Alden Gallery was at 1026 Baltimore Avenue, Kansas City; the city directory lists its owner as John H. Bender.

[1] Death in the Woods.

with it — two or three very fine stories and several just fair. I threw out two or three.

Then I wrote a new story — the last one in the book, when you see it — called "Brother Death" that I think will make the book. It is, I'm pretty sure, one of the finest stories I've done, and I even dare say one of the finest and most significant anyone has ever done.

Sounds cocky, doesn't it? I did want the book, dedicated to our friendship and my esteem for you and your mind, to have real integrity.

As you will see, I am on one of my jaunts, am in Kansas City, and could anyone find anywhere a more Middle Western city? I am in a rather tough little hotel here — no bedbugs but some cockroaches, but on the whole very clean — where I have a big workroom, bedroom, & bath, all for $1.00 a day.

Poker games in nearby rooms and ladies of the night often laughing in the hallways. What is it that makes me always a bit more comfortable and at home among these folks of the outer rim? I swear, Ferdinand, I never in my life took to my hairy bosom one of these love ladies, & yet —

The drunk woman who met me at the elevator the other night in her pajamas, cigarette hanging from the lip, who told me that her goddam man had run out on her, leaving her with a quart of whiskey and not a cent. (She invited me to go have a drink with her, and I did.)

It may be just a form of the protest in myself against organized society, as now organized, but I do love a kind of defiance in such people.

I picked up in the library here an autobiography by Sir Conan Doyle,[2] and, Ferdinand, the rotten smugness of it. It makes your flesh creep in a way these poor outlaws never do.

I hope Clara[3] is making it through the winter O.K. Write me a line.

> S (not Sherwood) Anderson
> *****, Kansas City, Mo.

＊   ＊   ＊   ＊   ＊

As for work, I am really into the new novel in which I am trying to use the materials got from my years in advertising for the 1st time. I am calling it *Thanksgiving*.

＊   ＊   ＊   ＊   ＊

---

[2] Presumably *Memories and Adventures* (1924).
[3] Mrs. Schevill died in June, 1933, after an illness of several months.

I'm going back to live on Ripshin this summer — can't sell it. Wish you & Clara could come.

I told the publisher to send a copy of the book to you as soon as off the press.

229.   [KANSAS CITY] MARCH 18, 1933

MR. H. S. KRAFT,[1] 140 WEST 69TH STREET, NEW YORK

Dear Kraft: Answering your corking letter of March 14th. I have been ill with a bad chest cold that has kept me laid up in bed. This thought has occurred to me — a combination of the figures of Henry Ford and Abraham Lincoln. Think about the figure of Hugh in *Poor White*, who has something of a Lincoln quality, and then combine him with the figure of Henry Ford. This could be worked out into the factory s[o] that the town of Bidwell in *Poor White* became a place like Ford's Dearborn.

All this contrasted with changing life out of agricultural and into industrial America, the splendor of the machines and the factories contrasted with the growing degradation of the life of the people.

I presume we would have to work out a definite story hung about one man or a family, and above all we must get into it the feeling that it is a transition period into some more splendid America. If we cannot get the story and the figure of one man, I am sure we can do it with a family. Write me again as soon as you have gone through the material I have already suggested.

I am sure I will be on my feet again in a few days. Very truly yours

230.   [KANSAS CITY, BEFORE MARCH 22, 1933]

ADELAIDE WALKER,[1] 176 SULLIVAN ST., NEW YORK, N.Y.

Dear Adelaide: I received your letter today, which came to me through Marion and was therefore a little delayed in getting to me.

I cannot tell you how grateful I am to you for your interest in this

---

[1] On April 5 of the previous year, H. S. Kraft, a free-lance writer in New York, had first written Anderson suggesting working together on a movie or a play. Later this developed into a project for an opera and involved Louis Gruenberg, the composer of the opera, *Emperor Jones*. See Letter 231.

---

[1] Adelaide George Walker and her husband, Charles Rumford Walker, were at this time preparing to establish a workers' theater, later the Theater Union, and had suggested that Anderson apply to the Guggenheim Foundation for financial assistance in order to write labor plays.

matter, which is one of the finest things that has happened to me, and I will reply at once, trying to give you the information you want [for] [2] Mr. Moe.[3]

Several things have happened in the last few weeks which I must tell you about to make the situation clear.

***** * * * *

Recently another matter has come up. Mr. Gruenberg, who made the opera from Eugene O'Neill's play *Emperor Jones,* got excited by some of my machine things and by things of mine touching on the relationship of man and the machine, such things as "Lift Up Thine Eyes," "Loom Dance," and others. I am not sure that you know them. They appeared in a little book of mine last year, a book that did not attract much attention. It was called *Perhaps Women.* Now Gruenberg wants to make an opera founded on these things. He wants to work on this with me this summer. What we have in mind is a kind of march of machinery across American life, the glory and the tragedy of it.

* * * * *

Now as to the Oberlaender Fund.[4] First of all, I must write you frankly how I feel, as I intend this letter also to be seen by Mr. Moe. The truth is that I am very anxious to pick up anything I can from the German or Russian theatre, but I am also anxious not to be out of America for any long period during the next two or three years if it can be avoided. Things are too exciting here, and I do think that we are on the edge of getting hold of something in relation to man and the machine and particularly in relation to America, that might possibly find a grand expression both in plays and in music.

You asked me to give you, for Mr. Moe's benefit, a brief survey of my own life and work, and I will try to do that. I began my life as a laborer, factory hand in America, and for the last two or three years have been renewing my touch. That is what I have been doing this winter, spending my time in factory towns of the Middle West, trying again to get into my bones the feeling of factories and machines in relation to America.

[2] Text reads "from."
[3] Henry Allen Moe (1894–), Secretary General of the Guggenheim Foundation.
[4] The Oberlaender Trust, Philadelphia. The current issue (1948) of *American Foundations and their Fields* lists it among "foundations releasing little or no information." Mr. Moe is one of the trustees.

Now my money is about gone, but it doesn't matter. We will go on with our plans for the summer's work, but if it were possible to get money from the fund for such work, strengthened by travel in Europe, for the next two or three years so that I could give all my energy to production and not have to be constantly haunted by the fear of going broke, it would be wonderful.

Of course I do not know how flexible this fund is. I have, during the last two or three years, got so much from renewing my touch with American life in the factory that I would hate to stay permanently out of America during the few years just ahead.

Now as for my books, my first novel, *Windy McPherson's Son,* appeared when I was well into the thirties. The early part of my life had been spent as farm hand, laborer, soldier, and factory hand. At the age of, say, twenty-six or twenty-seven, I got into business as an advertising man and for a few years was, I think, rather a typical American go-getter. I finally became a manufacturer and was, I believe, on the road to making a good deal of money when I began to write. Evidently the two things do not go together. As I got more and more absorbed in writing, I found myself slipping as a businessman. One day I walked out of my factory and never went back. I have told the story of that part of my life in a book of mine called *A Story Teller's Story.*

During the years I was in business I was writing constantly and wrote several novels before publishing, most of which were afterwards thrown away.

I wrote a labor novel called *Marching Men* that was published and a little book of verse called [*Mid-*] *American Chants.*

Then I went to Chicago and worked there for several years in offices and during that time wrote *Winesburg, Ohio,* a book of short stories, *Poor White,* a novel of the coming of industrialism, and two more books of short stories, *The Triumph of the Egg* and *Horses and Men.*

Then I wrote a novel called *Many Marriages* and the semi-autobiographical book, *A Story Teller's Story.*

There followed another small book of verse called *A New Testament* and my only popular success, a novel called *Dark Laughter.* It was from the proceeds of this book that I got the Virginia farm, and I also used part of the fund to acquire a country newspaper in Virginia. I ran the newspaper for about two years, getting from the experience a book called *Hello Towns,* and then I turned the newspaper over to my son. He is now using it, and it is being used for the support of my three children. During this time I also published a book called *Sherwood Anderson's Notebook*.

It was at about this time that I got the notion that the real story of America should now be told from the inside of the factory. I had the feeling that most of the American writing about our industrial life was being done too much from the outside. I still think so. I think some of our factories are gorgeous institutions. I have myself been a factory man, both as worker and employer, and want[ed] to renew my touch and spent the next few years largely in going to factories, staying inside factories and looking. I have already got from this experience a little book called *Perhaps Women* and a novel, *Beyond Desire*. So you see this is about the story of my life and experience, and of course I am hoping that what I still want to do may fall within the purpose of this fund. Not only would I like to go to German and Russian theatres, but I am also very anxious to go to their factories. All of this tempered by the fact that there is a lot to see and feel here in America that I have [not] got at yet. While I suppose my position in letters is pretty well established in America, I have never made much of any money. It has been hard sledding all along, and I have not wanted to go in for the popular magazines or the movies. On the other hand, I do not want any money at all if my own work can provide me a living, but I believe if I could have a guarantee of say $3,000.00 a year for the next three or four years, we could get some of this material into the theatre in a very effective way. I would like to make my farm down in Virginia a center for work with other men during the summers and do the traveling in the winter. If any of my books or plays begin to sell in a way that makes an allowance from the fund unnecessary, it should be stopped.

This, my dear Adelaide, is about as close as I can get in a letter to my situation, my plans, and my dreams. I am tremendously grateful to you and am grateful to Mr. Moe for his interest. If nothing can be done, I will not stop being grateful. Sincerely

231.   [KANSAS CITY, BEFORE MARCH 31, 1933]

To H. S. KRAFT AND LOUIS GRUENBERG

To Kraft and Gruenberg: I have been ill again, the flu. I am going to leave here today and go back to Virginia. While I have been lying on my back. I have been thinking about the project. G's letter just came, and I believe we can, between the three of us, get what we want. How are you, Kraft, for action? Can you dance, climb trees, leap mountains? I keep wondering if G. in going through my stuff finds anything that makes him want to sing. I've thought, all these years I've been writing, that if I'm any good at all, there should be music at the bottom of my prose. The painters have always liked my stuff. I've never made much money by my writing and haven't been notably successful in personal relationships. I have, however, dreamed all the time that I might be planting song. You know, something like song seeds in prose, I guess.

The American land, its people, towns, cities, farms.

Money and the machine.

When I had a fever, two or three nights ago, the beginning of our piece began to form in my mind. There was, first of all, a grey blanket of sound . . .

(City sounds coming to a sick man in a hotel room.)

Like a theatre curtain of sound.

Not too grey. Let flashes of warm color shoot through the grey monotony of it . . .

Maybe factory whistles on a winter morning, when it is still dark, police sirens, etc. . . .

Then jump to the first scene.

It is a potato field on a cold moonlight night, and people are at work. Everything is cold. The people are poor and ragged.

The cold makes them jump, jump, jump. The ground is icy cold. "We got to get these potatoes out."

It is late fall and getting colder, colder . . .

Their fingers are cold. They are picking up the potatoes and running with them to bags.

They blow on their hands.

They thrash their arms.

They are passing a bottle about, drinking and dancing as they work. They sing and shout and curse.

Then a strange figure appears. The potato field is at the edge of a wood. The figure comes half crawling out of the shadows.

It is Abraham Lincoln, working now, not just to free the blacks, but to free all labor, the heavy, brutal labor that for ages has tied men to the soil.

"Whose was the hand that slanted back this brow?"

This is the American man, tall and uncouth, the dreamer.

He is at the same time practical and shrewd.

He is in the field at night, trying to make his body into a machine. Song of labor. Song of hope.

He crawls grotesquely, writhing, singing, raises arms and legs — the machine being made — drives fist down into the cold ground . . . "See, it goes down so." He arises, feels his arm joints, knee joints. "There will have to be a lever here, a cog wheel here."

Levers, belts, and chains.

He advances upon the potato diggers, unaware of them, absorbed. They are frightened, but fascinated. They run away from him, dance away, dance back, shriek. They think a ghost has come out of the forest.

"But we got to get these potatoes, we got to; they'll freeze, we'll starve."

Now they are clustered at the back against a fence, where the potato bags stand.

The figure on the ground arises and proclaims the machine, the machine that will dig and plant potatoes, make men's shoes, make clothes.

Swing high . . . swing low . . . swing low, sweet chariot . . .

Sweet chariot over seas, under the ground, in the air, under the seas . . .

Swing higher and higher and higher, sweet chariot.

Man is to be free, free, free.

As the man who has been trying to make himself into a machine, in order to understand the machine, dances, a queer, jerky machine dance, proclaiming man's machine dream, the workers huddle against the fence. They are like the potato bags, standing there trembling.

All of this for an opening scene.

Machine man.

Machine dream.

America that was to free the men of an old, tired world.

Don't give up the dream.

Watch.

Wait.

America is to become one vast machine.

Note: With this start might we not go on and develop the whole thing as the story of man's making of the machine, then his struggle with it, the coming victory proclaimed?

✻   ✻   ✻   ✻   ✻

232.   [HOTEL PICCADILLY, NEW YORK, EARLY MAY, 1933]

TO LAURA LOU COPENHAVER

Dear Friend: Things continue to whirl here, and I shall probably not be able to come home until the middle of next week.

1st, Liveright's [1] are on the rock, which is hell, as the book is getting a fine press. It could be sold, but the Liveright mess will probably check it.

Last night E. and I went to see a play by Maxwell Anderson [2] to see a young man for George Willard. His name is Sheppard Strudwick,[3] and he would be swell. They are speaking of Pauline Lord for the mother and Digby Bell for the father.

Barton had his opening of *Man Bites Dog*,[4] and it was pure horrible. Such stuff. It has done him no good, but on the other hand has made him nicer. It's a good thing. Walter Winchell [5] had a headline, "Barton's Dog Won't Bite."

He is, however, really a swell fellow at bottom, and Mrs. B. improves mightily as you know her.

Went to lunch with a nice man from Paramount pictures, and they want a story. That can wait.

In the meantime the Gruenberg thing is on the fire. E. and I are having tea with Mr. and Mrs. G. today, and I am dining with Dreiser. There are a lot of writers caught in this Liveright mess.

As for Gruenberg, when it came right down to it, I found him afraid of the machine theme, fascinated but afraid.

So I gave him another idea, an opera to be called *Mississippi*,[6] the

---

[1] The firm of Horace Liveright, Inc., was in bankruptcy May 4, 1933, but on May 5 decided to contest the petition. Horace Liveright had gone to the hospital January 29, and died September 24.

[2] Maxwell Anderson's *Both Your Houses* won the Pulitzer Prize in May.

[3] A product of the Carolina Playmakers and a graduate of the University of North Carolina.

[4] *Man Bites Dog* by Don Lochbiler and Barton opened in New York April 25 1933.

[5] The columnist in the New York *Mirror*.

[6] Not completed.

story of the Mississippi River set to music. He has jumped at this like a hungry fish, as it gives him colorful opportunities with [Incomplete]

233.   [Marion, Virginia] May 8, 1933

To Burton Emmett

Dear Burt: I am sitting down to dictate a letter to you. It is a confused morning. I have been flying about trying to get arrangements made for life on the farm this summer. How valuable Mary is to you. How quickly and efficiently she would take hold of all these details for me if I had a Mary.

I have been thinking ever since I left New York of yourself and myself as two men, and I do think we are both queerly in the same boat. I think you have come to that time in life where in imagination you always see something around the corner, the end of it, as I do also, Burt.

But also, Burt, it is there around the corner for all the rest of them too.

I'd like to think it doesn't matter. At the same time, Burt, I do realize the difference somewhat, in our two points of view just now. It may be that I am fortunate. It is likely that I shall plunge on to the very end, plans made, the end of a life like the beginning filled with trial and error. Of course I know that it doesn't matter. There is nothing I can do or will do — put down, say or sing — that will not be forgotten, a little sound floating down the wind. However, Burt, it stays in my mind that we also are a part of something, of some incomprehensible thing. If we could understand, we would be gods. We aren't.

There is one thing, Burt, that I would like to have you again to begin to feel, and that is that you remain a part of things. You are a part of my own life and thoughts. You are my friend that I love. Mary loves you. Love goes out to you also from other people.

You must understand, Burt, that I myself have passed time and again through this dark valley, when I felt myself shut out from others and from life, as I have a hunch you now feel yourself shut out.

What can we do when we are in such a pass? All I can do, Burt, is to give you what I can of my own crude formula. What I have always done at such times is to cling persistently to others. I asked them to give to me out of their own warmth and confidence. We can not be afraid or ashamed to ask. When we are in the valley, we must ask.

And after all, Burt, it is surprising and even amazing how much people are willing to give. They want to give. They don't know how to give.

Sometimes we have to be like children, not proud.

You see, I am speaking to you now as another man, and I want you to feel that if there is in you a kind of helplessness, it is in me too. We have an inclination to be proud. We do not want to take this beggar's attitude toward life in others.

But sometimes, Burt, I think we must. It is absolutely essential to us to get away from self. In others life goes on. When I have no more courage, it may be that the person sitting next to me or walking beside me in the street is full of courage. Why shouldn't I ask for it, take it when I can get it? There is a curious contradiction here. Sometimes when I go like a beggar asking warmth, comfort and love from another, knowing I do not deserve it, I begin living a little in others, and thus I get away from self.

As for the end, I have often thought that when it comes, there will be a kind of real comfort in the fact that self will go then. There is some kind of universal thing we will pass into that will in any event give us escape from this disease of self.

I believe, Burt, that it is this universal thing, scattered about in many people, a fragment of it here, a fragment there, this thing we call love that we have to keep on trying to tap. I know that I am being vague in speaking of this, because it is likely that no one of us will ever find it in all its fullness and richness in any one other person, and I know also that I am trying to express the inexpressible.

You know, Burt, how I have always hit at money and positions. The whole subject isn't as important to me as you may think, and the only reason I hit at it is because I think it often gets in the way of understanding. I can't help half wishing that you and I were two penniless tramps, with a loaf of bread between us, sitting perhaps on a railroad embankment and waiting for a train. The only thing about money or the lack of it is that it gets into our thoughts when it shouldn't. If we were the tramps spoken of, perhaps it would be a little easier for each one of us to comprehend the difficulties in the nature of the other.

You see, Burt, I am not saying exactly what I want to say. I want to say that in spite of everything life is a grand show. I don't think we can ever quit. I know that sometimes I myself have had to try and be like a small child learning to walk again. I have walked along streets, saying over and over, to myself, "Now I must look, watch, and listen." I was trying to say to myself that if I could grasp the details of a building, the beauty of a woman's figure, the trouble in another man's eyes, this painting, the street, the stretch of fields and hills —

Why, Burt, do we need to feel that we must always do? Children are not like that. They are very often happy in just being, and I think we have to grasp at that and keep trying and trying, over and over, just to be and always to flee away from self and into others.

Now, Burt, I do not believe that any contribution I can bring amounts to much, but I do believe that I have sincere affection for you, and the fact that I have is also proof that the same kind of affection is coming toward you from many people.

This is the real inner glory of life, Burt, and I believe that all we can do is to try to keep realizing that this thing does exist in others and to try all the time to feed upon it and to go toward it to escape self. Sincerely

234.   [MARION, VIRGINIA] MAY 8, 1933

To PAUL MUNI [1]

Dear Paul Muni: I am in receipt of your letter of May 6th and am bound to say that your handwriting makes me ashamed. I can read every word of your letter without a moment's struggle, and no man on earth has ever succeeded in doing that with mine.

The evening with you and Mrs. Muni remains in my mind as one of the really fine experiences of my trip to New York.

Now, what I think about the story is this: you are going to have a busy summer and so am I. I suggest that you sit down and dictate an outline of the story just as it lies in your mind and send it on to me. If in the fall you still feel that I am the man to work with you, I would make this other suggestion. I think that before tackling a mining story with you, I should go back again for a month or six weeks into the mining country and perhaps to the same country you visited. I should spend a time there going about in the mines and among the men to get myself full of the atmosphere of the place and the life. Then I should come to you wherever you are and spend another month or six weeks in actual work on the story. If you are making a movie,

---

[1] Paul Muni (1895–), movie actor.

I could come to that place, or if you are back on the stage, I could come to where you are. I believe we could work together. I think we should spend an hour or so a day talking about the story as it progresses. I believe there is a chance of getting over a real story and yet having in it a possibility for the movies as they are now. I would not want you to commit yourself to this too hurriedly, as it may be that in thinking the matter over you will light on some other man who might be to your mind better for the proposition.

However, if when the time comes you still feel you want to work with me, I would suggest that you try to get for me $10,000 for my work. I should think the company might also undertake to pay my expenses while I am in the mining town and also the expenses of coming to you wherever you are to do the story. Of the $10,000 I should think $2,000 might be paid to me as an advance and the other when the story is completed to your satisfaction.

I put the figure at $10,000, because I know it would be necessary to pay something to the other man of whom you spoke, and then a deal would have to be made, I should say, with Kraft for his taking the completed story and putting it into form for the director to work with.

I wish it were possible for you and Mrs. Muni to come down here and take a look at this country, and perhaps another season we can make arrangements to do that. If we can make one story that is satisfactory together, we can probably go on to others. Write and tell me what you think of this whole general outline as a working basis. Very sincerely yours

235.   [?June, 1933]

To B. E. Copenhaver

Dear Mr. Copenhaver: I am writing you this little note for two reasons. For weeks and months I have wanted to talk with you, but I have found it very hard. You are not an easy man for me to talk to, and I feel perhaps a lot that you do about the risks Eleanor is taking in marrying me.

Also I am a writer rather than a talker and, I think, can say better what I feel in writing.

As regards Eleanor and myself. We have known each other a long time now. We began as friends and then began to love each other. She has done some wonderful things for me. When I first knew her and we were but friends, I was almost altogether a defeated man.

She gave me new courage, made me see myself, I believe made me a workman again.

As men our two lives have been, I should say, altogether different. I have taken great risks, made mistakes you haven't made. In my own way, I think, Mr. Copenhaver, I have also been a God-seeker. To be the kind of writer I have been and am I had to take risks of misunderstanding. I thought that to understand men and women, get at the inner secret of them, was more important than to gloss over life.

I have been punished for that, misunderstood often. It is, I believe, partly, maybe altogether, the secret of my failure in marriage. I have got in some places the reputation of being what I am not, a sensual man. I do not believe my life would show any such thing.

On the other hand, Mr. Copenhaver, I have got, by the course I have taken, the love and loyalty, I believe, of some of the finest men in America. On the whole I can't apologize. In the end I will stand on my work, and it is because Eleanor has had a real sense of that always, has helped me so much, has stood by me when I was discouraged and defeated that I love her so much, more than I ever thought I could love.

Mr. Copenhaver, I am sorry and hurt that the occasion of our marriage should not be a time of joy and gladness. I wish with all my heart I had found Eleanor earlier. I didn't. I would like to be friends. Even yet, if you can convince her, or if she has any waverings, I will release her from any promise to me.

I am sorry to have been the cause of worry and anxiety to you. Sincerely

236.   [TROUTDALE, VIRGINIA, JULY 7, 1933]

TO FERDINAND SCHEVILL

Dear Ferdinand: I got your letter when I came back here to the farm last night, bringing Eleanor,[1] and I do understand what you mean by the place — the room Clara walked in and loved, things she touched. I myself also loved her, and also, in my own way, I understand a little the half mystic connection between people and things.

As regards you, dear man, I can't avoid also trying to make you remember now that you also belong to the rest of us who love you.

[1] Sherwood Anderson and Eleanor Copenhaver were married July 6, 1933.

You must remember, dear fellow, that once, in *Winesburg*, I wrote a prose poem to the woman "strong to be loved," and I believe there are many men who would say of you that you are a man strong to be loved.

So you must go on letting the rest of us have your company, man. Come when you can and stay as long as you can. If you want to work, we'll make a quiet place for you.

237.   [MARION, VIRGINIA, JULY 14, 1933]

To CHARLES BOCKLER

Dear Charles: Eleanor Copenhaver and I got married a week ago, and we are living on the farm.[1] I have been finishing the play, that is to say, rewriting it. It's rather fun, the whole business of playwriting being different than any other form of art in that it is, all through, a social art — that is to say, an art in which others must participate. You see, a play, even when you have done all you can on it, must yet move through others, a director, actors, etc. Already, of course, I have had experiences, my first collaborator turning out rather second-rate, so that I had to get rid of him.

Well, that is finished. Now I shall tackle something new, and I think it will be *The Mississippi*, with Gruenberg.

In the meantime there is all the fun of really coming back to my own place, house, orchard, fields, and living with them and thinking of them. There is a new feeling of belonging, and it's nice.

We are also lucky. There is a new, big highway being built down to the Lee Highway, and we will not be so out of the world.

I wish I could see and talk with you. Perhaps it can be worked out this fall. Love

238.   MARION, VIRGINIA, JULY 14, 1933

To PAUL ROSENFELD

Dear Paul: Your letter and the article in *Scribner's*,[1] oddly enough perhaps, give me much more pleasure than pain. In particular the letter seems to me a coming toward the rest of us, at least I give

[1] All other letters of this date are headed "Marion, Virginia" rather than "Troutdale."

[1] Paul Rosenfeld, "The Authors and Politics," *Scribner's* XCIII, 318–320 (May, 1933), concerned literature and Communism.

myself the pleasure of thinking of it as a coming toward me. After all, Paul, we are all human. I do not think I have ever wavered in my respect for you. Particularly in the last year I have felt very much the need of the thing about which you are speaking. Something went very wrong with me four or five years ago. I felt myself approaching what was perhaps my own ivory tower. A curious desire for separation, a desire to draw myself away. I think that, for a time, my prose got much attenuated. I give to the woman I just married the credit for taking me out of that, for awakening in me again the desire to participate in life at any cost.

At any rate I did again desire with all my heart to participate. I think I knew that mistakes would be made in such things as manifestoes signed, etc., declarations made that might be a[t] bottom nonsense, but —

Paul, I had rather got on the other side; here in Virginia I was too much respected. I was invited to spend week ends at the Governor's mansion, and word was sent to me by United States Senators asking me to come to their houses. Virginia seemed proud to have me as an adopted son. The trouble with all this, as you well know, is that I am not respectable and do not desire to be.

I knew well enough that I did not belong to all that. I belong much more to the submerged than you ever can or will, Paul, and tried in my own way to get back to the people I feel are at bottom my own.

I think I went through a transition period. I got into my little car and went about to the factories and lived again close to workers. I began again to write. I do think that, although it got practically no recognition, my *Perhaps Women* was a fine and beautiful thing. I think in some places in the book I did really catch the rhythm of modern machinery and put it into a kind of singing prose. I think that *Beyond Desire* comes off, although it also got little recognition, perhaps for the reason that it satisfied neither the Communist nor the capitalist. I do not believe that what you say of it is true. I think the workers in it are as true as the women.

As for the new book [2] of short stories, that you say you have not read, most of them are four or five years old, but at the end of the book there is a story called "Brother Death," written last winter after the rest of the book was in press, that I think does thoroughly refute all you say of me.

[2] *Death in the Woods.*

Now, Paul, as for the matter of the authors' trip [3] to Washington. The manifesto Waldo [4] insisted on handing to the President's secretary I never saw, although I dare say my name was attached to it. I did not write it and had nothing to do with it. It was no doubt somewhat pretentious. You know our Waldo as well as I do. He has a great sweetness in him, but also there is a passionate desire always to represent himself as something big and important. I wish you could have been in the room with us when we were addressing the President's secretary. To that ridiculous man, the President's secretary, Waldo kept insisting, childishly, I thought, that we were an important group of men, and of course that idea amused me. I do not know that I actually pulled at Waldo's coat, but I do know that part of the time I half wanted to laugh, half wanted to cry, knowing, as you, Paul, must know I know, that we were of no more importance than any group that could be picked up anywhere on the streets. I do think we had a right to protest, as any group of citizens would have a right to protest, against the shabby treatment given the ex-soldiers in Washington. As for the fiasco, made a fiasco, I believe, by Waldo's insistence on our importance in the political state, I think that I did later rather give the whole thing some dignity and meaning by my open letter to the President in the *Nation*.[5]

To go back to the manifesto, that you, Paul, take more seriously than I ever did, I have in the last year or two seen a lot of real suffering. On all sides I have seen men's fighting spirits broken down. It may be that I got reckless. After all, Paul, you have to trust someone. I am not a politically-minded man. I think you once said that I was not socially-minded, but I do not think that statement is true. I wrote to Wilson,[6] saying to him that he could sign my name to anything he was willing to sign, and if there were mistakes made, my name signing to things lacking dignity, I certainly do not blame Wilson, taking it for granted he would often be confused as I am.

During the last year I have reached out all I could. I have been writing letters to men all over the country, asking them to try to state for me, as clearly as they could, what they now thought and felt. I wanted to write to you, but felt you withdrawn. After all, isn't it as bad to withdraw as to participate too recklessly? [In] my letters to other men friends I have been pleading for the same kind of comradeship

[3] See Letter 213.   [5] See Letter 213, note 1.
[4] Waldo Frank.   [6] Edmund Wilson.

you speak about. Do not think that I have not missed you. A hundred times I have had the pen in hand to write you, but have not done so because I have felt that you did not want me. I think there is no one at all close to me who has not known all the time that I have loved and respected you and your ability and have wanted from you even an attack rather than silence.

Paul, when I do a thing like "Brother Death" with its real delicacy and strength, and from you and Brooks,[7] the men I have always thought the most sensitive of all our critical minds, no response at all, only the cry that I have inadvertently let my name go on some political manifesto you do not like —

How can I help feeling, Paul, that it is you fellows in your isolation who are failing in the real Communistic spirit?

How, God helping me, can I help feeling that? With love

239. [TROUTDALE, VIRGINIA, AUGUST 10, 1933]

To MAXWELL PERKINS [1]

Dear Maxwell Perkins: I like your letter [2] about my coming with Scribner's, and I know that you must know that I decided to come with your house, not because of any advance you might give me on a particular book, any amount of advertising of my books you might do, etc., but because of a genuine respect I have long had for the position of the house of Scribner's in the publishing world, and also, may I say, because I instinctively liked you, Mr. Perkins.

I do think, however, Mr. Perkins, that there is something in your letter of which I think I should speak. You say that the first book to be put out by your house must be either a novel or a continuous narrative, something after the manner of *A Story Teller's Story*, and in this I think you are right. I know that I myself spoke of this later book. I am calling it tentatively *I Build My House*.[3] It is a book I have long wanted to write. In fact, when I came home from New York last week, having the play temporarily off my hands, I immediately plunged into it.

[7] Van Wyck Brooks.

[1] Maxwell Perkins (1884–1947), from 1914 until his death an editor at Charles Scribner's Sons.

[2] On August 1, 1933, Perkins wrote Anderson suggesting that Scribner's become Anderson's publishers and discussing the possibility of taking over the books by Anderson published by Horace Liveright, Inc.

[3] A second letter, August 14, 1933, from Perkins indicates interest in this project, which eventually became *Sherwood Anderson's Memoirs*.

The general plan of the book is a story of my own experience in the American literary world, people met, what has hurt and what has helped me in my own particular effort to produce beautiful literature here.

I want to write this book now and expect to devote myself to it, but I do think there might be exceptions taken to what seems somewhat a too strong pronouncement. I do not believe you mean it so.

I think I should feel free to come to you from time to time and talk of plans as to a friend. I have a certain conception of what I conceive to be the right relationship between a writer and publisher, a relationship that might be, at its best, a kind of intellectual marriage, and in any such relationship I do not think that either side should be too positive.

I say all of this with no intention of trying to get you to publish anything of mine ahead of the sort of more important things you speak of, but rather to put down a kind of general feeling I have and that I think should at once be made as clear as possible. I am sure you will agree with me. Sincerely

P.S. As I am short of copies, will you return the ms. of the *Winesburg* play as soon as you have had a chance to read it?

240. [TROUTDALE, VIRGINIA, EARLY SEPTEMBER, 1933]

To GERTRUDE STEIN

Dear Gertrude Stein: I have been reading with joy the autobiography as it came along in the magazine [1] — a bit sorry and sad on the night after that number when you took such big patches of skin off Hemmy [2] with your delicately held knife.

But great joy in the whole performance.

I wrote one good story last winter, in a book called *Death in the Woods*. I'd send the book on to you, only the publisher went smash and I haven't any copies. The one story I liked best was called "Brother Death."

❊ ❊ ❊ ❊ ❊

Now I am in a long thing that promises to be fun.

I am in the country, on my farm in the hills of Virginia. Why don't

[1] Sections of *The Autobiography of Alice B. Toklas* appeared serially in the *Atlantic Monthly* from May through August, 1933.

[2] Ernest Hemingway.

you and Alice come to America as a great adventure next summer, Ford around, come see us and others?

And there is something else. There is such a fat, juicy taste to your book. Do another all about people seen and felt, as you see and feel them, all kinds of people, their talks, your talks with them, impressions — well, you'll know.

You ought now to have one big taste, square meal of America again, don't you think?

241.   [?LATE 1933]

To CHARLES BOCKLER

Dear Charles: I must write at once to tell you how happy your letter made me. As for that struggle. It's there, like the storm that sweeps down over the old distillery on the Baltimore road or the disease that attacks a tree or the cloud that changes the light on a landscape.

More and more, Charles, I believe in your painting, because I have lived with some of it. You and John are the two young artists I believe in with all my heart.

I won't say anything about the woman struggle. You know it. I don't know whether or not you are like me. In me the struggle is intense. I had thought you had more reserve than I had. Perhaps you only cover up better. I have to have a woman like I have to breathe. I can't stand aside. I have to kiss, hold, get close to the mystery. At any price in struggle and hurt, I have to.

There is that thing in modern women — my own failures have all been in that — a kind of jealousy springs up. There is something dearer than any woman, dearer than self.

That comes at times like a wall between.

Lately I have thought that our struggle just now in this civilization is beyond that. Plainly, Charles, it is that I must learn to love you and John and Louis Gruenberg and Roger Sergel and other men who I know are lovers, devoted to a thing outside self. I must learn to love them and their drive at the mystery.

A part of all our difficulty with women is that we fail in this. It is America now, the confusion of it. For example, it gives me some essence of new dignity in myself to get this letter that tells me that you, in spite of your difficulties, poverty, humiliations (I know you have had to face) are upright and working. It makes the air sweeter I breathe.

Above all, Charles, I think you and John must keep alive your comradeship. Don't let it get away. Write often to each other. Don't be afraid to love each other.

As for me, you are the two young workers in America closest to my heart.

Isn't it queer — life — it's easier for me to say this to you than to John? Write again soon.

242.   [NEW YORK, EARLY JANUARY, 1934]

TO MR. AND MRS. B. E. COPENHAVER AND MAY SCHERER

Dear Mother, Mr. B.E.,[1] Miss May: I am going to send home some photographs — Dreiser, O'Neill, Nathan,[2] Van Vechten.[3] Put them away for my house.

It was quite hot in the sleeper all night, and E. slept a little restlessly, but was apparently quite O.K. this morning.

I didn't sleep so very much, thinking all night of the book I want to write. If I wasn't very nice at home — and I've half a notion I wasn't — it was, at least partly, because all the time I was reaching for something, a kind of tone, melody, chord — what you will.

I would so like to write, before I die, one joyous book, not at all sentimentally joyous, but having in it a deeper joy, such as I got that day when we all went out to Bob's. (I think it was just the hill before his little house.)

Later in the river below Henry Copenhaver's mill when I went to walk with Eleanor.

You do have to fight so for this elusive joy — just why, in our civilization, I don't know.

Do you suppose it is because of money, and that is the reason why E. and I have to be revolutionists?

These acres that will raise food for people to eat, wheat waving in

---

[1] Although the text reads "Mrs. B. E.," Anderson must have meant to name his father-in-law, B[ascom] E. Copenhaver.

[2] George Jean Nathan (1882–), dramatic critic, was at this time one of the editors of the *American Spectator*.

[3] Carl Van Vechten (1880–), novelist. Anderson carried on an extensive solicitation among his friends for photographs in the middle '30s. See Letter 337.

summer winds, the curious majesty of corn — how can money buy or sell this?

Isn't there a deeper lesson God wants us to know and that we, like perverse children — that's what we are, quite hopelessly children — that we will not know?

I would so like to say it, not as an economist (one of your scientists, Mother), but as some artist, someday, should say it.

I suppose I should be very happy if I get down a few words on the line in a week, but I am terribly impatient.

Anyway, if I do write the book I will dedicate it to you, Mother, and I'll call it *Other Mother,* meaning more than you, of course, as you will understand.

In the sense that a field, a river, a hill, town, city, house is my mother.

Mrs. Miller[4] had hot coffee for us and is having us to dine tonight. E. went off to her office, promising to lie down a part of the day. She probably won't. She looks pretty well.

Mrs. Leach[5] is sick, and the Mary Pickford dinner is called off.

It was cold and grey in the city. I didn't really want to come.

I really wanted to stay in your house where I thought maybe I had begun something.

Tell Mary[6] I am thinking of writing an article for *Spectator* on the Stein thing.[7] I hope May will be careful. Love to you all

243.   JANUARY 5, 1934

RAYMOND MOLEY, 56 WASHINGTON MEWS, NEW YORK

Dear Raymond Moley: There are some ideas I have for possible articles for *Today*.[1] I would like to go to some of the CCC[2] camps, this new venture, young boys, mostly city boys, working in the forest. I would like to try to get the tone of some of these camps, what this

[4] Wife of Ashley Miller, secretary of Stage Relief. Mrs. Miller was a radio actress.
[5] Mrs. Henry Goddard Leach, wife of the editor of the *Forum.*
[6] Mary Chryst Anderson, Robert Anderson's wife.
[7] B. F. Skinner, "Has Gertrude Stein a Secret?" *Atlantic Monthly,* CLIII, 50–57 (January, 1934). Anderson replied in "Gertrude Stein," *American Spectator,* II, 3 (April, 1934).

[1] Raymond Moley (1886–), for a brief period (1933) Assistant Secretary of State, edited *Today,* 1933–1937. Anderson's first contribution, "No Swank," an article on Henry Wallace, appeared in the issue for November 11, 1933.
[2] Civilian Conservation Corps, which set up camps for unemployed youth.

new out-of-doors life is doing to these boys. Is it not a definite move away from the formation of city gangs? The feeling in these camps and the work being accomplished.

I would like to take a look at the Tennessee Valley [3] venture, spend some time down there, talking to men, getting material for an article.

I would like to revisit some of the Southern cotton mill towns. I spent two winters down there before the coming of NRA and would like to go back and look at some of the same towns under the New Deal.

I would really like now to take six weeks or two months for a kind of roving venture, looking and listening. It is a little difficult to tell just what will bring something forth. Do you not think that it would be rather nice to have, for a time, in *Today*, something in the nature of the thing some of the better columnists do for the city newspapers, it to be done, however, for the country and the small towns? [4] I used to enjoy doing this for my country papers, and it was much liked.

My present plan is to start driving about the 20th of this month, and if you will let me know soon, by letter or by phone, what you think of the plan, I will be glad to talk it over with you. I would like now to make my definite arrangements. Sincerely

244.   MARION, VIRGINIA, JANUARY 25, 1934
MR. LEONARD KIRKPATRICK,[1] STANFORD UNIVERSITY, CALIFORNIA

Dear Sir: You must excuse me for the delay in answering your letter of January 1. I am afraid I cannot give a very satisfactory answer to your letter. My mind is not one of the sort that goes in for research. I have always been a great reader and consistently used libraries wherever I go and, I daresay, have been deeply influenced by my reading, but my deepest interest has always been in human beings.

I spend as much time as I can with human beings and really think that this is my library.

I am sorry I cannot give you a more satisfactory answer. Sincerely yours

[3] The TVA (Tennessee Valley Authority) was established May 18, 1933.
[4] See "Explain! Explain! Again Explain!" in *Today*, I, 3 (December 2, 1933), and Moley's comment following the article.

[1] Leonard Kirkpatrick, a member of the library staff at Stanford University, had asked Anderson whether he had done research for any of his novels and, if so, what libraries he had used.

245.   [?NEW YORK, ?LATE JANUARY, 1934]

TO MARY CHRYST ANDERSON

Dear Mary: Regarding the Stein, the *Atlantic* article,[1] it is all possibly true that the Stein thing sprang from unconscious writing. I myself formerly tried this, but of course threw what I had attempted away.

In my own case there was something sought. I think you must know it is entirely possible to be, for example, a fine novelist but a bad writer. I have never wanted that. To me manner is all important.

The truth is that I have always known I was essentially the poet, but I have also always known that the thing least to be desired in this world is to be known as poet. There is, of course, a very difficult and very elusive poetry in all fine prose.

For a good many years I wrote and threw away endlessly. I still do. "Do not too much value the thing done. The joy is in doing." That is the idea.

I have always thought it quite possible to make the habit of writing words with the hand, the arm, so automatic that something within is released. This is surely not automatic writing, and yet I think that all of the more beautiful and clear, the more plangent and radiant writing I have done, has all been done by a kind of secondary personality that at such times takes possession of me.

In this article the writer speaks of the fact that Miss Stein does not know what she is writing, nor do I, whereas while she denies any secondary self, I attribute all to the secondary self.

You can see the advantage of this. The poet thus escaped the nuisance of parading before the world as poet.

And there is something else; the poet lives only as writer. He has no other life, and I can truly say that the person my friends, my own family, etc., know, has nothing to do at all, or at least very little to do, with the second person, the writer as person.

This, I think, might bring me to what Stein did for me. I am always amused by the talk about her. The point is always missed. Suppose she taught me to recognize the second person in myself, the poet-writing person, so that I could occasionally release that one.

And not to blame it for the anxious person, myself as known by others.

[1] See Letter 242, note 7.

You can see the great gain in that to me and why I think that Stein is a genius.

I think that the man in this article also misses it.

246. LYNCHBURG, VIRGINIA, FEBRUARY 21, 1934

MR. BILL STEWART,[1] EDITOR *Today*, NEW YORK

Dear Bill Stewart: I am sending you a piece called "Personalities"[2] that I like very much and believe you will like. I am still hitting rather loosely around the back roads and in some of the Southern industrial cities, picking up impressions and talking to people.

I am going over to Richmond and down to Danville, having this in mind for the next week. I think then I will cut back into Tennessee for another good look at the Tennessee Valley Authority projects.

I am at work on an article I call "Moonstruck,"[3] an article that attempts to bring out the essential and rather pathetic romanticism of the radical.

I dare say a good many of the radicals won't like it, but most of them are essentially such children face to face with the facts.

I am needing some money. Please send me some to the John Marshall Hotel, Richmond, Virginia.

My expenses from Saturday the 10th to the 17th were: $70.95.

247. [NEW YORK] APRIL 5, 1934

MR. JAMES CREELMAN,[1] YALE CLUB, NEW YORK

Dear Jim: I did not get a chance when we talked last night to go much into detail regarding what I had in mind on a possible play to be made of *Dark Laughter*. I do think, Jim, that something striking might be worked out in the theatre in the use of sound. I have had this idea in my mind a long time. I don't see why sound, voices of people, broken sentences, laughter, and things of that kind, could not come

---

[1] William C. Stewart, then managing editor of *Today*.

[2] In an undated note Moley and Stewart express great enthusiasm for "these stories." "Personalities" was apparently broken down into the various sketches of Southern life appearing in *Today*, beginning with "Price of Aristocracy," March 10, 1934. (A previous sketch, "Blue Smoke," printed February 24, could scarcely be part of a manuscript sent from Lynchburg February 21).

[3] This project, apparently, was not finished.

---

[1] James Ashmore Creelman, nephew of Mrs. Karl Anderson.

out of the walls of a theatre during a play, giving the audience the feeling of sitting down in the midst of Life going on busily all around them.

The central idea of the *Dark Laughter* play, if it is ever done, should be as already suggested, the contrast between so-called sophisticated civilized life and the life of the primitive. I do not see why the play could not be played out in, say, the sitting room of a house, just such a story as the story of the two men and a woman in *Dark Laughter*.

Then the same story could be told in the lives of Negro people, servants in the same house, the same problems facing both masters and servants.

I have the idea, Jim, that my own difficulty, as regards playwriting, is and will always be a matter of structure. I believe I could make people live and can build character.

If you are really interested, I believe you should get *Dark Laughter* and read it. Then we should get together and have a real talk about it.

I will be very much interested in the reaction of your friend to the *Winesburg* play, the man you spoke of yesterday. Suppose you let him see the play and see what his reactions are. I presume Courtney Burr,[2] who now has the play and whom I expect to see soon, would have first call, but if I can't agree with him, I will be open to find a producer.

I hope I shall be seeing you again soon.

248.   [NEW YORK] APRIL 5, 1934

MR. BILL STEWART, 152 WEST 42ND STREET, NEW YORK

Dear Bill Stewart: I am sending you today the last of the articles on the South.[1] As I told you, I have tried to make this a sort of general rounding up of the series.

I have been planning to run in to see you and will do so soon. If you have my original manuscripts to all these pieces, I wonder if you would mind getting them together for me. Two or three publishers have spoken to me about making a book of them.

I have another idea in mind that may appeal to you and Mr. Moley. I thought it might be a good idea to pick out some Middle Western industrial city, preferably Cleveland, go out there and spend four or five days and try to get an article on what has happened to some of

[2] A New York play producer with offices at 226 West 42nd Street.

[1] Apparently "New Tyrants of the Land," *Today*, I, 10–11, 20 (May 26, 1934).

the big industrial and banking figures out there, what they have done to the city, and how they have come out in the shuffle.

It is my notion to work out the idea with the period after the War; particularly '25 to '29 was also disastrous to the successful men; that is to say, under the old form of economic individualism the man who won, lost.

I used to live out in Cleveland before the big boom days came; so I am familiar with the old Cleveland. I think Mr. Moley knows this whole story himself, perhaps better than I do. I suggest that you speak of this matter to him. If the idea fits in [with] your editorial plans, I would like to do it sometime perhaps within the next two, three weeks. My most sincere regards

249.   PAOLI, PENNSYLVANIA, MAY 6, 1934

To LAURA LOU COPENHAVER

Dear Mother: I am sending you copy of a letter I have just written to Mr. Lloyd [1] at Courtney Burr's office. It will rather explain itself. Eleanor is in Philadelphia, and I am in the country at Wharton Esherick's house,[2] but we will be back in New York the middle of next week. Write me there.

As you see, I have not worked out this new idea about the play, but it was a very interesting experiment to have it read by Jasper Deeter.[3] It wasn't anything at all like the reading of Barton. The play in this form seemed almost too relentless. By this new plan, if it works out, we can avoid all that business over the money in the last scene. The money will rather pass out of the play as it does in the book. It may take a good deal of writing to get just the quality necessary into this scene, but if it can be done, it might give the play at the end just the thing needed. I had an idea after hearing it read by Deeter that what it needed was a thing you might call horizon — the lives of the people

[1] This letter seems to have disappeared, but on October 25, 1934, writing from Courtney Burr's office, John Lloyd expresses himself as satisfied with conditions laid down by Anderson, and promises to send the first available manuscript of his own play, "In the End." A second letter, undated, says he is at work on an outline of a dramatic version of *Dark Laughter*.

[2] Wharton Esherick (1887–), sculptor and woodcut designer, lived in Paoli.

[3] Deeter, originally with the Provincetown Players, had established the Hedge-row Theatre in 1923 at Moylan-Rose Valley near Media, Pennsylvania. The dramatic version of *Winesburg, Ohio* received its première at this theater on June 30, 1934.

in the play passing into other lives of the town and life going on. After the intense evening a laugh at the end, with Parcival [4] used as a kind of symbol.

I'm seeing very little of Eleanor, but hope she may be able to have dinner in town with Wharton and myself this evening. I have finished the second one-act play and have thought my way at least through the third, to make an evening of one-act small town plays to be called *Small Town Tales*. Lots of love to everyone in the house

250.   MARION, VIRGINIA, JUNE 14, 1934

MR. LAURENCE STALLINGS,[1] YANCEYVILLE, NORTH CAROLINA

Dear Mr. Stallings: I wonder how much in earnest you were in the little talk we had about our doing a play together. I do think there is a play in *Dark Laughter*, and I believe we could do it together if you are interested. I will send you the *Winesburg, Ohio* play to read and let you judge whether or not it has dramatic qualities.

I find my weakness in playwriting to be the structure rather than dialogue, and I believe that if you could bring up the structure of a play out of *Dark Laughter*, perhaps using the Negro voices in somewhat the way you suggested in our talk, we might get at something.

I do not know whether you have *Dark Laughter* or not, but if you haven't, I could send you a copy. If you thought favorably of the idea, I would run down for a day or two with you early in July. Do write and tell me what you think of the scheme.

My regards to Mrs. Stallings. Mrs. Anderson and myself hope to get you up here before the summer is over. As always

251.   [TROUTDALE, VIRGINIA] JULY 9, 1934

JASPER DEETER, HEDGEROW THEATRE, MOYLAN-ROSE VALLEY, PENNSYLVANIA

Dear Jap: We have just got home and have begun to feel a little settled on the farm. This morning we got a log for Wharton [1] so that he can begin to carve his own way to happiness.

---

[4] Doctor Parcival, the central figure in "The Philosopher" in *Winesburg, Ohio*.

[1] Laurence Stallings (1894–), sprang into dramatic prominence with *What Price Glory?* (1924) written with Maxwell Anderson, and in 1930 had dramatized *A Farewell to Arms*.

[1] Wharton Esherick.

All of the depression I am sure you felt in me the last day or two was completely due to weariness, loss of sleep, continual thinking night and day about the play. Now it stays in my mind sharp and clear as a kind of picture that I dreamed of when I began writing it.

All of this, Jap, I do attribute largely to you. I do not believe I am going to strike much of your kind of sensitive, intelligent appreciation.

There are some tentative things that I would like to speak about in order to get your reaction.

First of all, the Parcival. You will remember that when I first gave you the play to read, you said at once that Parcival must come back. I think you sensed, as I did, that the play itself is concerned primarily with no particular person, that the hero of the play is the town.

But you also sensed that in the town life Parcival was something very special. Joe tells Helen about him and his curious religion. Ed Hanby likes him and wants him about his house and his saloon. Reefy, who is himself not a drinker, wants him as his friend.

I think we both felt Parcival in the beginning as mystic and poet, but never obviously so. I think that when he makes his speeches about drinking, he doesn't mean drinking in the sense of drunkenness. It may be that the literature is at fault here. I do not believe it is exactly the quiet and oblivion of drunkenness that he really wants. And I wonder if he shouldn't always be laughing when he makes such speeches. I wonder how it would be to try making him a laughing man. When he speaks saying, "I think too much," let him laugh softly, perhaps pat his belly with his hand when he says it. I am afraid that all through the three performances I saw Harry still inclined to make him a drunk, too sodden.

I wonder if it isn't possible to get an entirely new conception of Parcival with the literature we have. How would it be to suggest to Harry that he think of Parcival in an entirely [?new] way? Let him try thinking of Parcival as a man who wants above everything else closeness to others, human brotherhood. The man is wiser than all the others about him, sees life more clearly than the others, and this is what stands in the way of the closeness he wants. He is in an American small town of the Middle West. He is a doctor, but medicine doesn't interest him much. Jap, I have thought for a long time that one of the most characteristic things about American life is our isolation from one another. We have no common religion, no common love of the land. People are brought close to each other through some common passion. One of the things that made me so happy about your doing of *Winesburg* was the feeling of working with people who had a common passion. You have all sacrificed something for your conception of the theatre but do not feel yourselves as making a sacrifice, but this Parcival of ours is living in no such group. How would it be to think of him as always feeling his isolation and always wanting to break it? The feeling is so intense in him that he identifies himself with a Chicago murderer, with the man who shot Jesse James. The crucifixion of Christ is real to him. He feels it going on and on in people. There is the same identification. "We are all Christs, and we will all be crucified." Jap, I have not spent my time since seeing the play worrying over cuts. There are cuts to be made; I have unnecessary repetitions, even some banalities in the literature. I believe I can get at these, but the tone of the Parcival is something else. It lies rather tremendously in the player.

I would even suggest a physical change. Take the beard away. Let Harry play it physically as close as possible to his own appearance in life. I have been thinking also of this try at making it a laughing part. Every time Parcival makes one of his more thunderous speeches, let him laugh softly. He looks about, hoping to find someone to laugh with him. He might be the kind of man feeling an inner pride, but at the same time ever hungry. Let him be continually putting out a hand, touching, as though about to embrace. He knows too well the cruelty of misunderstanding in people that comes with closeness. He understands the cruelty of love. That is why he insists on the inevitability of crucifixion. He puts out a hand to a man or woman and seems about to embrace, but instead withdraws and laughs. For every noisy speech he makes there is the music of this soft laughter.

I do feel, Jap, that in order to get the poet into Parcival, we have got to get this in, the man both sensitive and rough. In some way you know, as I do, that he is carrying, or should carry, the inner music of our piece.

Jap, when I talk this way I am not talking critically. It may be that the failure of our Parcival to carry his music is due to the literature. If that is true and you feel it, I would like you to say so. I know we both want the same thing.

There is one other character in the piece that I believe is not right yet. I refer to Ferd's Tom Willard. You, Jap, spoke to me once of a performance of the part Ferd did in rehearsal when he got under your skin. I believe that Tom Willard is in some curious way a very typical

American father. I relate him to my father, you to your father, Ferd to his father. How about Ferd's thinking of him in the same way I am referring to when I speak of Parcival? There is the same hunger without wisdom, without the laugh. In spite of everything, Parcival has managed to mature in American life. Willard has not matured.

But he also is always pleading with people. I believe Ferd makes him sometimes too stiff, too withdrawn. I do not believe much in suggesting to men like you and Ferd a way to bring this out. But I do not exactly like it that the audience feels glad when Tom is made to suffer. By the gods, the audience should suffer a little with him. Most of them are so damned much like him.

Jap, the play as a whole stands solid in my mind. I do believe that within a week or two I can do some effective cutting that will not hurt but will help the movement and the music. I shall be very happy if you and your company feel that they want to go on working with me until we get it absolutely right.

In the confusion of getting away I asked someone there to be sure to send playing dates in July and August of the *Winesburg* play to George Jean Nathan, c/o the *Spectator,* 55 Fifth Avenue, New York, and to Joseph Wood Krutch,[2] c/o the *Nation,* 20 Vesey Street, New York. I asked someone to do this, I think but I am not sure. I wish you would also send programs to Stark Young, c/o *New Republic,* 421 W. 21st, Street, New York, to Roger Sergel c/o The Dramatic Publishing Company, 59 East Van Buren Street, Chicago, and also to Paul Rosenfeld, 271 W. 11th Street, New York. Sincerely

252. [TROUTDALE, VIRGINIA, OCTOBER 6, 1934]

To MAXWELL PERKINS

Dear Max Perkins: I have your nice letter of yesterday.[1] I dare say you are quite right about the other things. They are, after all, written in a different mood. I think that perhaps, for a year or two, I did rather go over to something like a Communist outlook. Now again I am rather uncertain about all that. This attempting to touch off the lives

[2] Joseph Wood Krutch (1893–), author and dramatic critic, at that time on the editorial board of the *Nation.*

[1] On October 5, 1934, Maxwell Perkins wrote to say that he liked "Please Let Me Explain," but that the other three pieces sent were too dissimilar to go into the same book with it. They should form a book by themselves. These became *Puzzled America,* published in March, 1935.

of human beings in relation to the world about them is much more healthy for me. I have no solution.

I am going to send you in a day or two another thing, called "The Nationalist." It appeared in the *American Spectator*[2] and was afterwards used in what was called *The Spectator Year Book,* but it was not, the book I mean, much read. You tell me what you think.

I think also that I might write an introduction, saying something in the nature of what I have merely suggested here in the first paragraph of this letter.

When would you like the complete book to be in your hands? Sincerely

253.   MARION, VIRGINIA, DECEMBER 30, 1934

TO RALPH CHURCH

Dear Ralph: Of this thing anyway I am pretty sure: the economists don't begin to get at the half of it. I've an idea now that the big push toward some sort of revolution, if there ever was one, is over for the time. People in general don't want it, dread change of any kind.

What, I've a notion, we'll get is life going on, on a good deal lower plane, the masses of people settling down to cheaper living. They will stand for a lot and at bottom are not revolutionary-minded.

I understand how you feel. I've been about with the revolutionists a good deal, and being with them always intensifies my own individualism.

Then I go with the rich and see how, generally, riches make life ugly.

I've had a kind of idea these last few years, Ralph, but don't myself live up to it very well. It is some sort of notion of a more real man to man relationship. I wrote a little book, called it *Perhaps Women.* If you haven't read it, I wish you would someday. I'd like to know what you think of the idea back of it.

There's something wrong with the whole race of women and us — this connected with the work we're doing — and most of all perhaps with our attitude toward one another.

A curious loneliness, separateness, that dominates lives. Perhaps we want religion.

[2] *American Spectator,* II, 1 (December, 1933), reprinted in the *American Spectator Year Book,* New York, Frederick C. Stokes, 1934, and later became part of *Puzzled America.*

I get a good deal from nature down here, and it may be that I should have been a painter. It is a very beautiful country I have got into here, and I keep going to certain spots I've picked out, a little, I guess, as one might go to church. I never could get anything from going to places — churches, etc. — where people were engaged in the corrupt business of trying to save their souls.

I've been running about, trying to do some things for Moley's magazine, *Today*, not very well satisfied with them when they are done, and for two or three years have not done any long thing. I have a new book out, a special edition thing called *No Swank*,[1] and Scribner's are doing, early in the year, a book of essays.[2]

I did a play out of *Winesburg*, but it has not got to Broadway.

I may be coming to New York toward spring, and if, and when, I do, will write. I'd like you to keep in mind coming down here in the summer if it turns out that you can and want to.

254.   MARION, VIRGINIA, JANUARY 2, 1935

MR. FRED WITTNER, *New York Herald Tribune*, NEW YORK

Dear Fred Wittner: I have your letter of December 10 about the article you are doing for the *New Yorker*[1] and would have answered sooner, but have been ill in bed.

I dare say that my experience with manuscripts is that of most writers. For a good many years it never occurred to me that anyone would want the sheets on which I have scrawled. Naturally I threw them all in the wastepaper basket. Occasionally one does show up. I write both on the typewriter and in longhand. I have certainly never offered my manuscripts for sale. When I discovered that they seem to have some value to some people, that is to say, to collectors, I presented all of them that I could find to a personal friend who happens to be a collector. I do not believe he would want me to give his name. He is a collector and has money, and other writers might get after him. I would myself if I were broke and found I could get money for these discarded sheets.

[1] Published by the Centaur Press, Philadelphia, 1934.
[2] *Puzzled America*.

[1] On December 10, 1934, Fred Wittner of the *New York Herald Tribune* wrote to say he had been assigned by the *New Yorker* to write an article for the "Talk of the Town" in that magazine on how authors dispose of their manuscripts.

Yes, of course I am bothered by collectors. What writer isn't? I never could feel myself much flattered by all this. I have always felt that the so-called admirers of a certain writer who wanted one of his manuscripts was a good deal like a lover who wanted one of his lady's old dresses instead of the lady herself. Surely what there is of a writer should be in his work. Sincerely yours

255.   NEW ORLEANS [?MARCH, 1935]

TO LAURA LOU COPENHAVER

Dear Mother: It has rained for several days, torrential rains. I am very well. Here, when it rains so and as there is and can be so little drainage, the streets become lakes.

Most of the intellectuals and the most entertaining people here are Jews. There are several older Jewish families here with rather high intellectual standards. They came in here after the Civil War, dared to invest every cent when the city was in comparative ruins, and were made rich.

I often wonder what you really think of Eleanor's marriage, particularly as you must often, in your mind at least, go back to my own old record; and I often wish that both you and Mr. Copenhaver knew how successful, at least to me, it is. I guess the truth is that I was never married before. There is to me a new and very definite thing. I think it must be that now, in every little way, I do not live or feel or think alone. Everything in some way has reference to this woman. It is a thing in the blood, and when she is not with me — I am often not so nice when she is with me — life becomes shallow and meaningless.

There is, I think, no doubt that Long [1] dominates this country down here. His strength is not, however, in the city. It is in the country. It lies in that South I am always speaking about, the terrible South that Stark Young and his sort ignore — you often, I think also, my dear — the beaten, ignorant, Bible-ridden, white South. Faulkner occasionally really touches it. It has yet to be paid for.

My hope is that Long can get nothing but just this white South, but the man has — do not doubt it — real power. He isn't, as a lot of people have begun to think, a superman, or superdevil, but he has, hidden away in him, a real feeling, I suspect, for the underdog. He may

[1] Huey Long, governor of Louisiana from 1928 to 1931; U. S. senator from 1931 to 1935, when he was assassinated.

go far in an age of shilly-shally, because he has marvelous audacity.

I am a little sick about Wallace,[2] can't help being. He is making just too many compromises. What is it makes people so want power? What a disease it is.

I must go to work. At least I am working.

256.   New Orleans [March, 1935]

To Karl Anderson

Dear Karl: I have been intending to write you for some time. E. has left me here and has gone to New York. Someday when you are in New York, call her at Nat'l Board, Y.W.C.A.[1] Go to lunch with her. She will be so happy to see you.

We came here after a grand rest and out-of-doors time at Brownsville, Texas, and E. is coming back here early in April. I was in rotten shape when I came down here, but am in great shape now.

I have long wanted to write a book of some sort based on Earl and have got into it, a rather crazy book I call *Brother Earl*, an attempt to get at something in his life, what it meant, etc. I have already, in the last two months, got down some fifty thousand words of it.

And, alas, it has only begun. It is one of those things that, it now seems, may go on forever. Of course, I have given him a new background, different parents, in a different position in life, but yet in some way, I hope, having the essence of his background too. It is the sort of thing in which a man just lets himself go, not thinking: "Will anyone ever care to read this? Will anyone understand what I am driving at if he does read?" Just, you see, letting it flow like water. It is a most satisfactory feeling anyway.

We did have such a grand winter, with the out-of-doors — for me, incidentally, the association with a woman who grows always more and more dear to me — the strangeness of the Texas plains, the sea coast, Mexico just across the border, dining in a Mexican town almost nightly —

And this thing, as one might say, "for better or worse," flowing out of me. I wish I could think you had had anywhere near such a good winter. My love to you

[2] Henry Wallace.

[1] Mrs. Anderson was a member of the Y.W.C.A. staff.

257.   [NEW ORLEANS, LATE MARCH, 1935]

To GERTRUDE STEIN AND ALICE B. TOKLAS

Dear Gertrude and Alice: It is very hot in New Orleans this morning. I just came back here and got your letter. E. went to New York, and I went off to the country. I went to an island, in the Gulf, one of the places among thousands I have wanted you two to see. I think it is because I have felt in you both, with real sincerity, love of seeing, hearing, smelling about America. It's too dead in most people. It does good to feel it in you.

The place to which I went is an island inhabited since before the Revolution — French, Spanish, Indians, and Negroes, all gradually intermarried. They fish. There is no agriculture.

[A] city man owned land on the island and built a ramshackle hotel, putting his mistress in charge, wanted to get rid of her, I guess. It was a crazy place, the landlady always half drunk, crazy plumbing, mostly none, a beautiful beach.

Nights spent on the beach fishing, alone. I hauled out big fish. Don't tell Hemingway. I dare say he would have loved seeing them suffer. It was all moonlight nights and big porpoises swam around me as I walked out into the surf in my hip boots to cast my line. It gets you kinda crazy, the beauty of things sometimes.

Plans hang. I expect E. back here about the 28th. Then she has to go to a lot of places — West Palm Beach, Macon, Ga., Atlanta, etc., etc. — and I'll drive her. We should be back in Virginia by this time next month and then may go East, where I hope we will get one more look at you two. Love

258.   MARION, VIRGINIA, APRIL 20, 1935

MR. EUGENE O'NEILL,[1] SEA ISLAND [GEORGIA]

Dear Gene: Just a note to tell you how much I enjoyed the brief visit I had with you and Mrs. O'Neill.

It was only too short for me. I had a thousand things I wanted to talk with you about, but knew it would take me a long time to get started. I was delighted to find you at work again and in good spirits. I know you are always after something not too easily comprehended

---

[1] Eugene O'Neill (1888–), who in 1934 had produced *Days without End* and was to bring forth *The Iceman Cometh* (1946).

and that you continually have to go through your own little hells. You have always been a man I have looked up to as one of the few great figures of the time, and I am sorry that I cannot see more of you. Sincerely yours

259.   [GREENSBORO, NORTH CAROLINA, APRIL 24, 1935]

TO ROGER SERGEL

Dear Roger: I have made a characteristically stupid blunder. By some slip — I wrote it; it must have got lost somewhere — there is no acknowledgment[1] to *Today* in the book *Puzzled America*. I'll bet it will cost me my job with them, as Moley is terribly sensitive to slights.

Came over here with E., who has to work here a few days. Next weekend at home, and then I'll be going East. I have put the novel temporarily aside, but will go back to it. I want to do the new play.

I got down the first scene and think it is rather corking and have the next scene sketched out. Wish you were nearer at hand so I could show the scenes to you as I go along. I think that I learned this from the *Winesburg*, that I can make the task for the producer easier without sacrificing anything. This play will really be built on *Poor White*, but I am so changing it, scenes, names, etc., that I believe I can get away from Viking.

I have a hunch that this playwriting thing is really my meat. I wonder if I am right. I know all of the difficulties, but in some way love the whole idea, even the stink of the theatre. I do not mean that I have gone back on the novel. I want it to have, perhaps for two or three years, as a big, difficult job to fall back on.

E. said you wanted an autograph letter from Eugene O'Neill. Is that so? I will get you one.

We went to Sea Island Beach, off Brunswick, Ga., to spend a few hours with him on our way North. You know he married the actress Monterey,[2] reputed to be one of the really beautiful women of America. I though her cold, calculating. Certainly she is not one of the women who make a house warm.

Gene is a sick man. He says he is better than he has been for a long time and told me of a vast scheme, a series of eight plays in sequence. I take it they are to be all connected and played night after night, the

---

[1] That is, of the previous appearance of certain items in *Today*.
[2] On July 22, 1929, Eugene O'Neill married Carlotta Monterey.

same characters coming and going through the various plays. God knows, it is [an] ambitious enough scheme, but will he ever pull it off? He is a very, very sweet, fine man, but I did feel death in his big, expensive house. He has drawn himself away, lives in that solitary place, seeing practically no one. He needs his fellow men. I felt him clinging to me rather pitifully.

My best to Ruth and all in your house. Write often. You know my feeling, that we men need each other. I'm sure I'm right.

260.   [MARION, VIRGINIA, ?LATE APRIL, 1935]

To Roy Jansen [1]

Dear Roy Jansen: I think the most absorbingly interesting and exciting moment in any writer's life must come at the moment when he, for the first time, knows that he is a real writer. Any professional writer, any Hemingway, Wolfe, Faulkner, Stein, Dreiser, Lewis — I could name a dozen others, prosemen, I mean — will know what I mean. You begin, of course, being not yourself. We all do. There have been so many great ones. "If I could write as that man does." There is, more than likely, some one man you follow slavishly. How magnificently his sentences march. It is like a field being plowed. You are thinking of the man's style, his way of handling words and sentences.

You read everything the man has written, go from him to others. You read, read, read. You live in the world of books. It is only after a long time that you know that this is a special world, fed out of the world of reality, but not of the world of reality.

You have yourself not yet brought anything up out of the real world into this special world, to make it live there.

And then, if you are ever to be a real writer, your moment comes. I remember mine. I walked along a city street in the snow. I was working at work I hated. Already I had written several long novels. They were not really mine. I was ill, discouraged, broke. I was living in a cheap rooming house. I remember that I went upstairs and into the room. It was very shabby. I had no relatives in the city and few enough friends. I remember how cold the room was. On that afternoon I had heard that I was to lose my job.

I grew desperate, went and threw up a window. I sat by the open window. It began to snow. "I'll catch cold sitting here."

[1] Author and proprietor of a bookstore in Pittsburgh.

"What do I care?" There was some paper on a small kitchen table I had bought and had brought up into the room. I turned on a light and began to write. I wrote, without looking up — I never changed a word of it afterwards — a story called "Hands." It was and is a very beautiful story.

I wrote the story and then got up from the table at which I had been sitting, I do not know how long, and went down into the city street. I thought that the snow had suddenly made the city very beautiful. There were people in the street, all sorts of people, shabby ones, brisk young ones, old discouraged ones. I went along wanting to hug people, to shout.

"I've done it. At last, after all these years I've done something." How did I know I had? I did know. I was drunk with a new drunkenness. I cannot remember all of the absurd, foolish things I did that evening. I had a little money in my pocket and went into saloons. I called men up to the bar. "Drink. Drink to me, men." I remember that a prostitute accosted me and that I threw some money toward her and ran away laughing. It must have been several hours before I got the courage to return to my room and read my own story.

It was all right. It was sound. It was real. I went to sit by my desk. A great many others have had such moments. I wonder what they did. I sat there and cried. For the moment I thought the world very wonderful, and I thought also that there was a great deal of wonder in me.

[P.S.] If you use this, will you see that I get copy?

261.   [MOYLAN-ROSE VALLEY, ?MAY 9, 1935]

To THEODORE DREISER

Dear Ted: I am at Hedgerow working on a new play.[1] Saw *The Tragedy*[2] last night and was bowled over. It's gorgeous, beautiful, direct. It is really much stronger as pure propaganda (I don't mean to say you had that in mind, Ted) than the things the Theatre Union[3] are doing. God, but it's great.

[1] See Letter No. 264.

[2] The Hedgerow Theatre had taken into its repertoire the Dreiser-Piscator dramatization of *An American Tragedy*.

[3] An organization of radical dramatists and actors which produced plays of social protest during the middle 1930's. See Letter No. 230, note 1.

And Ted, the *Winesburg* is a million miles ahead of what it was when you saw it. Jesus, if some producer had the guts to take these two things and put them on in New York, he'd upset the town, and that's a fact.

Hope you are O.K. Love to Helen.[4] Will be out here through June.

262.   [?NEW YORK, MAY 28, 1935]

To CARROW DE VRIES [1]

Dear Carrow De Vries: I have your very charming letter of May 18. Of course it pleased me.

As for your question. Well, as you know, it takes much longer to write than to read all these books. Sincerely

263.   [MEDIA, PENNSYLVANIA, ?LATE MAY, 1935]

To CHARLES H. FUNK [1]

Dear Andy: We came down here, to Media, Pa., on Wednesday to see some plays and tomorrow will go on to Baltimore, returning to New York on Sunday. I have no typewriter with me. I understand that you Tennesseans can read reading but can't read writing.

However, if this be treason, make the most of it.

I have been in a better mood and hope you have. I have begun working again and yesterday, for the 1st time in months, sat at my desk, here in this little country hotel, for hours with no consciousness of time passing, completely lost, the words and sentences with a fine rhy[th]mic flow, ideas coming like flights of birds, for the time, at least, completely happy.

No. Happiness is not the word. To be happy there must be consciousness of self as happy, and in this state there is no self.

---

[4] Who became Mrs. Dreiser.

---

[1] Carrow De Vries (1906–), poet and short story writer.

At the conclusion of his letter to Anderson, De Vries had written: "A few weeks ago I read again all I have of you. It took me about two weeks, as my time is limited. I usually have a desire for women about twice a week but during the two-week period the desire for woman never came to me. It was as though they did not exist. My question is did you when writing the things you have written desire a woman?"

---

[1] Charles H. Funk, lawyer in Marion and one of Anderson's closest friends there. The two men corresponded frequently during the '30's. Andy is Funk's nickname.

I remember the first time this feeling ever came to me. I was living in a rooming house in Chicago. Already I had written and published a novel. It did not come out of my own feeling, my own observation of life. It came, I think, from reading other men's novels.

It may have been that I was born to be a writer. I had perhaps read a lot of novels. "I can do that," I said to myself, and did.

But on this day I had come home from the place where I was employed very tired. My room was small and cheerless enough. I was discouraged and blue, hating the work by which I made a living.

I sat there at my desk and suddenly picked up my pen. I think every man must be filled with a thousand impressions, feelings, impulses that never get expressed.

Suddenly I began to write as I had never written. It did not seem to be me sitting there holding the pen. There was no me. It was as though some mysterious force outside myself had taken possession of me.

There were people everywhere, thousands, millions of people wanting their stories told. They didn't want it glossed over, made glamorous. That, in the end, only hurt and made life more difficult.

"If you knew my story, you might like, even love me a little."

That seemed to be the cry.

It was as though one of these began to speak through me. The pen began to run over the paper. I did not seek for words. They were there. They seemed to leap out from my hand to the paper.

Now there was no such thing as time, no little shabby room, no rainy street outside the window. Life was there on the sheets of paper, word[s] marching, sentences marching.

I don't know how long I sat that day. When my tale was finished, I got up and stood. Tears came. I cried because I was happy. I had written something that was solid and true. There was no fakiness, no false glamour. There was a beauty that perhaps few people would find or understand. I think I must have felt as a woman feels after a birth, when she has her first babe in her arms. I kept saying words to myself. "It's there. It's solid. It will stand there like a rock. If no one else knows, I know."

I was both proud and humble. It was almost as though God had reached a hand down out of the sky and touched me.

It was again a little like that yesterday. It doesn't come often. There are long times of waiting. I tell you all of this to explain why a man can't go to Hollywood.

Anyway such moments, when they do come, are worth all of the waiting.

264.   [TROUTDALE, VIRGINIA, ?MID-JUNE, 1935]

TO ROGER SERGEL

Dear Roger: E. keeps quarreling about you. Seems, when perhaps under the influence of drink, you said you were going to write a sonnet to her. Don't you know, man, that when a fellow makes a crack like that, he's stuck?

I've forgotten what it was about Lucile Cox — used to be a grand little piece of calico, quite pretty once, my sec[retary] for a time and a damned good one.

I think Julius [1] is coming by car with his wife and kids to live in the green house. We rather expect them about the 10th of June [?July].[2]

Paul Rosenfeld's coming about the same time. I got a great slab of country bacon yesterday. We've a big garden.

I wrote half of the new play, some pretty swell scenes, I think.[3] It's the same theme as the novel *Poor White*, but different — new characters, etc. I call it *They Shall Be Free*. Man, I'll tell you what you do. Make an outline for a play. Then let's both hammer away at it.

Aren't you somewhat afraid of *Marching Men?* Not that it couldn't be done. I've been, for some time, hot on the idea of sounds off stage — the threatening thing coming — coming — coming.

Thresh of marching feet, off stage, coming, coming.

This broken and then coming again.

This perhaps against a little inner circle of smug life being played out, in sight.

Fear down underneath —

The thing would be to get a story.

It might be just the story of a man's life, how he lies to his wife, lays up with whores, etc. —

[1] Julius Friend, New Orleans businessman and writer, who had been one of the editors of the *Double-Dealer*.

[2] Friend writes in a letter of this year that he hopes to keep his promise to visit Virginia in July.

[3] This project was not completed.

The drumming sound a kind of cry to some kind of ordered life that drives him crazy.

The sound might be in his imagination. He has in some way sold out the workers.

Begin with a conversation with a friend.

"Do you hear it, what I hear?"

"What?"

"There."

Sound of the feet, low and far away.

Friend: "No. I hear nothing."

"There it is again."

Constant reoccurrence of the sound, growing louder, more threatening.

As though society was calling to the man busy trying to lead his own life.

He might be a big manufacturer, unfair to labor.

It only wants the story.

I can see no reason why this playmaking shouldn't be a social art, two, or even three men engaged in it. Wish you were here now to talk with me about *They Shall Be Free.*

Do go ahead.

Run down, if not for more, for a few days. I feel this playmaking thing may have just begun.

Love to Ruth. Why don't she write?

265.   [?NYACK, NEW YORK, ?AUTUMN, 1935]

To JOHN ANDERSON

Dear John: I think the essential weakness of the ideas suggested by your last letter lies in the supposition that the average man cares for the thing the artist strives for. Probably the average man (if there is any such thing) cannot (life being as it is) go much beyond food, drink, shelter, and the instinct for reproduction. There is, to be sure, always a vague hunger for betterment, an emotional impulse that leads him to worship a vague god, but essentially its energy is spent in trying to get ahead in the material sense.

You simply cannot depend on mass instinct. It is too blind and dumb. Look about you, John. Men can be very decent and yet blind to what you are after. You have to take them as they are, be thankful that life has not brutalized them more than it has. Do you think that enough American men or women would drop nickels, dimes, or quarters in a box at the foot of a painting by Van Gogh? They'd much rather use the money to go to a burlesque show.

You know what they did to Van Gogh in a French village. They howled after him in the streets, tortured him because he was different.

O.K., where are we?

Well, I'm an individualist. I no longer believe in mass good. I believe you have to take the world of men as it is, walk a tightrope.

No use getting angry or ugly about it. It only makes your back ache to get angry.

Hell, I'd take anyone's money if it would permit me to work. If the person giving the money demanded too much in return, I'd tell them to go to hell.

Cézanne was very canny about not letting anyone get their hooks in, but he had a banker father. They'll get their hooks in you, don't fear. You'll just have to pull them out when they hurt too much.

You spend years just striving to find out what you want to do.

Then the problem of doing it.

Why expect men to know as they pass by when it took you so long?

266.   [Marion, Virginia, ?Autumn, 1935]

To Roger Sergel

Dear Roger: After all, it may be that was what I felt wrong about my visit to you and to Ruth.

Not the money.

That confused me a little too. It was my fault. I so wanted to come, but needed so the few hundred I had ahead for some steady work this winter. The truth is that I got your letter today and walked along the street not daring for a long time to read it, thinking, "No, I'm wrong." Thinking you might say, "Fool! Fool!"

And you're but right too. The visit was to me a kind of statement — of what?

Something felt now.

I think Ruth will understand my putting her a bit outside of this as I would put my own woman aside.

My son John, the young painter, and I played together a kind of game a year ago on the farm. I hardly know how it began. We fixed up a little place in a field with boards and with canvas walls and a cot, to which we could both go, during different hours each day, and there lie, naked, nothing to see but the white walls and the sky.

We called it the Karmis [*sic*].

Man's playing place? No. Man's receiving place, aside from all women, even aside from nature, in the form of growing things — all was alive with women to all men.

A common spirit added — the sum, and what? Illimitable space perhaps.

The feeling that men must learn again to renew themselves in other men, as perhaps they did in old days, in battles — hate that became almost love — or —

I grant it might be done in work.

Statement: that is like sand held in the hand. Very well. I had a feeling, regarding the work you are now doing, that if it could be carried forth, say, to the establishing of your own print shop. So that your own boys, for example, might begin to learn, say, to be printers.

It seems to me now that we American men, as men, if we ever are to be men again, have to begin fighting, and keep fighting, for something.

For example, it seems to me that I would like to have you to take your own sons into your business, if they are to come in, not just as future businessmen but as workmen too.

Couldn't something be done in that direction that would also help you? It seems to me now that your business would be strong enough to stand some jolts, and as far as the boys, your sons, are concerned, there is more education to be got from actual work, from materials, with materials, handling materials, than from any education any of us can now get from books.

I have to say to you that I was thinking of all of this when I was there in your house, but — you see, this is also matter of statement, and as you have yourself suggested, statement isn't so easy.

You spoke of my own courage once in throwing a business aside. It wasn't real courage. Real courage, if there ever has been any in me, has come later; it has come rather here, where I am now, in keeping a little business together and making it serve my sons.

I speak of all of this to you because I know that you are puzzled and also for another reason. You have said, and your handling affairs has proven it, that the matter of being a good businessman — a question of having good judgment, I guess — comes naturally to you.

So perhaps you can afford to treat that side of your life with more or less of a passing nonchalant attitude. That, anyway, is a tremendous game.

I think now that we American men, with men children growing up, can't afford to let them depend on the mothers, on the women. There is also our own man's world, rather lost to us now. That is what we are neglecting.

This idea, for example, that you might conceivably extend the business you have to the actual printing — the form of designing the little books, type faces learned, all that, something away from a desk to share with your sons — to give some of your mind and heart to that — the boys, too, in their turn.

Don't trust me too much in this. If I keep talking just now of the advantage of the small town, a kind of renewal of the ground it gives, I admit it is partially because of the sneaking feeling that I may be able to work on you and perhaps even get you down here near me.

And that is natural too; companionship, even love, as between man and man, is a thing most of all wanted now. I myself came near getting it a few years ago after I came down here, with an Irishman [1] who lived in Washington, a man met quite accidentally, a man [who] came here often as I went often to him. He is the man to whom I dedicated the book *Perhaps Women*, but this man went and died on me.

You see, in fancy, at least, I dare sometimes take the thing I am trying here to express, as between man and man, out a little beyond the casual thing we now call friendship.

What is really wanted is something like tenderness, that dares to go [on] and on.

Not, as it just happens now, as is the case of man with woman — the going to the flesh, delicious, as in nature, and entirely authentic — but in this case — necessary now, I think — outside flesh, as in nature or woman, an attempt at the very core of the thing is [*sic*] the mystery of life itself.

EXAMPLE

A man might make a thousand examples. How easy for you to make them. Last evening after a day's work I got into my car and went out

[1] Maurice Long.

over the hills to a certain little wood. I was gathering brick-top mush-rooms — *Hypholoma sublateritium* — whew!

It was just night, and the little mushrooms here thick in the wood as I presumed they would be — cold and tender, masted, from light straw-yellow to deep orange to the edge of red.

The silence of the wood at that hour — the sky to the west — the low hills — just watching the growth on the ground — a sudden quick recognition of something.

What? Words get to be such damn things, as you have yourself said.

You want simply, suddenly, a comrade who feels as you do, sees what you see. There was the town below, to the north, lying in a blue haze.

We try, it's true, in words, in paint. That helps. It never did quite suffice.

There's woman. We American men now, your type of man and my type, are asking too much of women now.

It isn't that they are not entirely capable of the comradeship I am hinting at here, but toward woman just now we men, lacking this balancing thing I have come to believe men should get from each other, we go now toward women wanting too much.

We ask too much. The tremendous confusion of sex expressing itself comes in. We have now — I am sure of it — to try at least to begin to build a reserve among men — outside women now — as perhaps they have to have also to begin building a reserve.

It may be the historic role of women — waiting.

For manhood to come back into men.

I know, for example, that if I dared do it, I could not say things to Ruth touching a conception of womanhood. I don't dare just now. I haven't security enough in myself yet. Wanting now so much this thing that for some reason lies outside our relationship with women now. I am a little trying to get at it. You ask for a statement.

I know that we American men are not doing a damn thing to American women now. I see them all about now everywhere, of all ages, with something defeated in them. I think they will admit it fast enough.

To try again to take it into [the] conception of men and work hinted at in your letter. You called it Work and Love. I am a little afraid of that word "Love" now. I'd rather think of it simply as tender-ness.

SECOND ATTEMPT

In this matter of comradeship. Is it as it is in the matter of women? With the American man of sensibility and the woman doesn't this always happen — we men feel starved? There is for each of us a long starving time.

Then the woman appears. How eagerly we go toward her — how hungrily we go toward her — how hungrily.

There is, however, now — and I think must be now — always in it somewhere, in this relationship, intimacy [*sic:* ?intimacy].

Half a notion about that too, and it concerns all such men as yourself and myself. Men like myself or yourself are likely to pick fine-grained women. The woman is to such a man two things — the flesh becomes beauty, all of these vague, unorganized dreams that have been in us so long now pointed toward a fact.

No woman could ever be in herself what we want, or think we want. Why should we ask her to be?

And then, also, men like you and me have the gift of words, and words, as you know, are tricky things. Often enough we express more than we feel because expression itself creates feeling. How often have I made myself drunk with words as I know you have.

The woman, knowing in her heart that we are asking too much of her, resents the fact. She should resent.

But the attempt at a comradeship, outside the relationship between men and women, is very difficult [for] us now. Now[a]days it is very difficult to find the [co]mrade who dares try to go where you want to go. Any thinking is disturbing to men. Thinking is always a challenge.

There is this to be said: our country is so huge and we American men are always being separated from one another. If you live with a comrade in the city, your meetings tend to become more and more casual. It is difficult to have common experiences, experiences that fall outside the field of words, such experiences as I have already mentioned, the man on the hill where the mushrooms grew, the habits of thought formed by two men who are seeing each other constantly.

I give another example. It is a man, such a man as yourself or myself, who lives in a small town. It may be two or three men in the town the man knows quite well. We will take one of them as an example of what I am trying to get at, and for this man our man — for convenience let us call him Smith — has a kind of tenderness.

A part of it, for Smith, is the fact that he sees the other man constantly, incidentally, in the flesh, quite casually, day after day. Often he doesn't want especially to be with the other man.

Smith is standing in the street in his town, and his friend passes along the other side of the street. It is dark night, let us say. The friend is on the lookout for Smith. They have formed the habit of occasionally taking evening walks together.

But on this particular evening Smith doesn't want to walk with his friend. Why, he is fond of the man. He likes the kind of downright honesty in the man. He likes him physically.

Now you see, this is something men do not yet understand, or perhaps do not dare quite understand concerning their relationships. A man, to be my friend, must attract me physically, not as a woman does, in a special way. We modern men are afraid of facing that fact.

I must like something about my friend's eyes, the way he carries himself as he walks along, something in the temper of the man that fits into my own temper. It is a thing distinct from the tenderness a man feels for his woman.

It may very well be that my friend has a woman of his own. He should have, and also I half have her with him. If she is beautiful to him, she becomes beautiful to me.

Surely you yourself have noticed something, that any woman for whom some man has real tenderness always at once becomes more and more attractive and desirable to all other men, and I suspect that is the basic reason women so hate losing even a second-rate man who has some tenderness for her. Tenderness is the food on which a woman's beauty feeds.

And now to check back again — I also speak of the man Smith and of his friend seen by Smith on the street on an evening when Smith didn't want to walk with his friend. Between Smith and his friend there is physical pull, and it isn't the immediate physical pull as is with woman, toward whom Smith might feel tenderness. Smith's spirit would feed upon the tenderness felt on him by a woman as her beauty would feed on his tenderness. Even to be with her, when he did not want to talk with her, exchange ideas and thoughts with her, receive her common impressions — even then being with her would be satisfying to him.

It is quite so with a man so [sic] — with the comrade.

There the comrade goes along the street. The man Smith, seeing him, is near to him but at the same time far away. As the friend goes along the street in the darkness, Smith stops and steps into a stairway. The friend is looking for him, but he does not want to be seen. The friend is saying to himself: "Where is my comrade? I want to walk with him."

"But not tonight," says Smith. He goes off along a side street to walk alone. Why?

The comradeship the man Smith has formed with another man of his town is not rich enough. It is a half comradeship. Smith's mind is intimately more settled and powerful than that of his friend. He doesn't blame his friend for that and doesn't think of it as a lack of quality in the friend, but it happens — perhaps only because of the different nature of his own life, perhaps greater risks taken with life — Smith has traveled more, he has read widely, he hasn't fallen into the American trick of shutting his mind to new impressions.

As least that charge might be made against his friend, but he doesn't bring charges.

You are to bear in mind that the sort of half comradeship here described, about the only kind men now find in America, is better than no comradeship at all.

But there is Smith now walking in the night alone. He didn't want to be with his friend on that particular evening. However, he was in danger. As he walked, he began to be absorbed in himself, thinking as men do of the difficulties he has in life. He was at the edge of self-pity. We all know well enough that state.

But just the fact of Smith having seen his friend on the street looking for him, knowing the friend wanted his company, began as he walked to take Smith more and more away from self.

Why had he not wanted on that evening to go and walk with his friend?

Men also become sensitive to each other. Perhaps Smith knew that, had he joined his friend on that evening, he would have spent the evening talking all himself.

Now having seen the friend on the street and having for him masculine tenderness, he goes off to walk alone, but having the tenderness for another man, he being at least a half-comrade, Smith has a healthy and good evening alone.

In the past the friend has at least somewhat revealed himself to

Smith. There have been many little fragmentary stories out of another life told.

So, you see, Smith, as he walks along, begins living, not in his own life, but in his friend's life. He escapes from self. He goes in fancy with his friend into his friend's house. He is even a part of his friend as the friend sits in his own house talking to his wife. The friend's wife suddenly becomes lovely to the friend, and something of her loveliness comes through the friend to Smith.

There are enough little things in the friend's life that annoy and irritate him, little qualities in the friend that he himself hates. Once the friend told Smith of the mean act he did to another man, and at another time he told of how he had been a beast with a certain woman. She was a woman depending on him for money and did not care for him, but he took her. She let him because she was afraid. Smith knows these things about his friend, but knows also little flashes of nobility in him.

Well, you see, we are talking of male comradeship. If it had been a woman about whom Smith felt as he felt toward his friend on the evening when he took a walk alone, this comradeship, like all comradeships modern men try to make with women, [would] have lacked something.

There was even something lacking in the comradeship I am describing because of a lack in Smith's friend. Although comradeship has the flesh in it faintly, it is predominantly in the mind, the spirit. It needs for food common experiences — books, feeling for nature, feeling for what we call heart. Most comradeships are too full of blank spaces.

Often Smith's friend bores him, and the friend knows it. The friend has a habit often of going on all evening drearily concerned with minor things in his life. On some evenings the friend spends the hours they have together getting off phrases gotten from newspaper reading. Smith's friend is a great newspaper reader. It is about all he does read. He is a pretty typical American.

You see, Smith would like often to talk with his comrade about Van Gogh, Hardy, or Henry James, or George Moore.

Had the person to whom Smith felt as close as he does to his half-comrade, had the person been a woman — he is in an ordinary way attracted to Smith, but the attraction stays out [of] the world of fact — had the person been a woman, Smith had even this much physical feeling, and [there] would have been the temptation to disregard everything and go to her.

Now you see Smith, and he has touched her body. It begins. Something creeps into his voice. As I have suggested above, words with word meant, paint with painters, can make a man drunk. Smith is saying to the woman, "You are beautiful." It's a lie.

The sense of beauty a man gets from a woman no man perhaps ever gets fully, in its real purity, but from one woman.

I am suggesting how men are attempting to sell themselves out and how they sell out women. You, I know, have done it time and again, and so have I. Is there something that could conceivably be got from male comradeship that would prevent it, that would stand like a wall between man and a tendency to sell himself out and in doing so to sell out others?

I think there is.

267.   [Nyack, New York, early October, 1935]

To Laura Lou Copenhaver

Dear Mother: E. tells me you are silly enough to be ill again. Don't. I'm glad Mazie is there.

I think you'll find me quite out of the novel, as a personality, in the revision. As you know, I waded right on through while writing.

I don't know about the harness, Mother, so let it stand.[1] Of course Scribner's may not want it. It's a bit obvious, but sometimes I want to be obvious.

I went to Jap for 3 days and saw a truly marvelous performance of Shaw's *Doctor's Dilemma*. There was one boy, Bud, who did, I thought, the best piece of acting I ever saw on any stage. They were all very, very sweet. Jap is planning, for next year, to do a new version of *Winesburg*, a more stylized version.

I had a letter from a friend about Pirandello, the Italian writer and playwriter. You'll remember he wrote *Six Characters in Search of an Author*. He said to the friend that a story of mine, "The Man Who Became a Woman," he read in French, was the greatest story he ever read.

---

[1] Mrs. Copenhaver had objected to an episode in the manuscript of *Kit Brandon* (1936), the novel on which Anderson was working.

I wrote, for *New Republic*,[2] an article on Lee Masters' biography of Vachel Lindsay. It's a stirring book. I'll send it later. Mary & E. want to read it.

Puzzled America, the first six months, made us $536.00. Not bad for a book of essays.

I've a rotten bad case of poison ivy, all over my hands and arms. It's an annoyance.

E. is well, and I'm more in love with her than ever.

I'll put in postage for enclosed. Will you ask one of the girls to mail it?

Do get well, my dear. Love to Mazie, Miss May, and Mr. C. It's very beautiful here in the country now.

[P.S.] We are going, E., Mary [3] & I, to the A. F. of L. convention, Atlantic City, next Sunday.[4] May be there a week. I have a commission, *Today*, for an article.[5]

268.   [NYACK, NEW YORK, ?NOVEMBER, 1935]

To LAURA LOU COPENHAVER

Dear Mother: There was a woman out here, friend of Mary's, who reads character by the face. She got at me and spoke of a certain brutality in me. I think you also have it. Look at that remark about the clothes, your natural wrath that moths had been introduced into your home, the perfidy of the Copenhaver cousin, your delight in entertaining Randolph's moths, fury about the ones you attribute to me.

Of course a false accusation. I am too soaked with tobacco smoke for moths to venture near me. It was someone of your own blood, I'll bet.

But that isn't the point. What a chance for a little sane brutality here, saying to them simply: "Look here. I rented you the barn, not this house. I can't be bothered. Either stay out of here or get off the place." That is the sort of thing, Mother, I could do, and you'd be surprised how it would work out. It's foolish to think of all people as sensitive or too easily hurt. If they were that sort, they wouldn't be bothering you. If you can't do it, I'll do it for you when I come,

---

[2] "Lindsay and Masters," *New Republic*, LXXXV, 194–195 (December 25, 1935).

[3] Mary Emmett, at whose country house the Andersons were staying.

[4] The American Federation of Labor met in Atlantic City, October 7–19.

[5] "Boardwalk Fireworks," *Today*, V, 6–7, 19 (November 9, 1935).

if you want me to. You'll find a growing respect in them for you. Saying it would be best, but if you can't, say it in plain terms in a note. We can't be bothered with people like that. There are people who simply need a kick in the behind. It is so often wonderfully salutary.

CAREERS FOR DAUGHTERS

This part of your grand letter — which, by the way, made me very proud, that you should have taken the time — I don't know, Mother. I do perhaps think that you and your daughters are distinctly a part of something. It is hard to put into words. Well, I have been trying for a long time. I have felt that women did not and could not understand the problem of present-day men. I think even that we men of our day have got, and perhaps rightly, a kind of contempt from women. Are we too soft? Are we too puzzled? Apart from E. and you and a few, a very few, other women, women in general bore me. It is, I think, due to this other thing, the idea that men are in a curiously difficult position and that women do not understand what it is and often, often take advantage of it.

There might be a deeper education, Mother, a deeper aspiration for your own female children than that set forth in your grand letter — if I may say so.

But is there possibility of understanding, warm closeness as occasionally? Yes.

You would have been interested anyway in something the woman, so-called expert character reader, said: "You have never really been interested in sex, except in its social implication." She said: "You have a curiously deep social sense, but it never quite alights on another individual. It concerns social principles."

But never mind the truth or falseness of that. I [am] trying to say that one deeply feels, as one matures, a wanting [of] relationships that have as bases mutual principles held to, something not personal.

Oh, it's too hard to say. But it means something very vital to me. Put it bluntly, just between us: sometimes I feel I would go further to help, or stand by, some man of talent than I ever would any woman, as woman. I think men have been caught and partly destroyed by not feeling so, I mean as men.

John — an experiment. Please don't speak of it to him. I have thought it important that he grow to communicate with others openly and freely. The thought may have come with reading the Van Gogh letters, the man to man relationship between two men in them, the feeling also that the development of any one form of expression helps also all other forms. I have been putting on a campaign to get closer to him, not as a personality, but to make him, by communication with me, for example, help me more and of course with the hope that I may help him a little too, as artist, I mean.

My best to everyone. John plans to be here Dec. 9th. You could come with him, you know.

269. [NYACK, NEW YORK, NOVEMBER 8, 1935]

To MAXWELL PERKINS

Dear Maxwell Perkins: It is swell of you to have in mind the books,[1] any books that touch on the Civil War or the period. I'll eat them up later. Perhaps, if you send any more, you'd better send them to 56 Washington Mews, as I will go down to town as soon as the weather gets really bad, and now I do no reading.

It is because I am really absorbed in this novel. It doesn't go so fast. A friend recently said to me, as regards my novel writing, "The trouble with you, Sherwood," said he, "as regards novels is that you chase moods as most men chase women."

He did except one novel of mine — by the way, the only one that ever had a big sale — that is to say, *Dark Laughter.*

And he may be right. I already had something the same idea — that is to say, to try a new approach. I have, almost always, tried to work out of pure feeling, having the conviction that if I got the feeling straight and pure enough, the form I wanted would follow. I am trying to make this job more objective, keep the whole story definitely on two or three people, the whole centering upon one — in other words, being more objective, trying, you see, to use mind as well as feeling. The man of whom I spoke thought also I had been inclined to crowd my canvases too much. I am trying not to do that this time. It is an absorbing job anyway. I like the book.

By the way, I had something in the last *Today,*[2] issue Nov. 9th, that might interest you.

[1] Maxwell Perkins wrote August 5, 1935 that he was sending "the Lee," on November 6 "Grant and Lee" and the "Irrepressible Conflict," on December 26, John Thomason's *Jeb Stuart.*
[2] "Boardwalk Fireworks."

Also I did for *New Republic* [3] a review, really an article, on the Masters book on Lindsay. I liked that book.

As soon as I get down to town, I'll call you. Perhaps I can begin to be more definite about a time for the delivery of the novel. Sincerely

270.   [?NYACK, NEW YORK, ?NOVEMBER 14, 1935]

To CHARLES H. FUNK

Dear Andy: It seems that by my article in *Liberty* I kicked up quite a row in Franklin. That's good. As every statement I made is backed up by the testimony, I don't mind their being sore.

Of course it isn't the kind of writing I care for. A little journalism is all right, but much of it is n.g. It is always taking the cream off your thoughts before it has a chance to rise.

You yourself are always speaking of writing; so I think I will give you a little sermon. I think that, first of all, you have never read much real writing, for there hasn't been much of it done in this country. The truth probably is that my *Winesburg* is the one American book that has become already a classic.[1] I think you, like a lot of Americans who think of writing someday, do not think of it very seriously. You have read O. Henry. You have read the magazines. Of course you know that, in general, O. Henry is the father of most magazine story writing in this country. That's one reason, of course, why it is in general so bad, so false, so tricky.

I don't think I have ever talked to you very seriously about this, as I always took your statement that you were interested in writing rather as bunk. If you had been really interested, as you are, for example, in bird hunting, you would have been seeking and reading good work. I think that you look toward writing sometimes as an easy way to make some money — an utterly false notion. I lectured about this, that is to say, this false notion, twice at Columbia this fall and am to speak on it in Chicago in January.

I don't know how to put it to you. Writing, or any art for that matter, concerns the world of the imagination. Few enough people realize the importance of that world. I think perhaps I could explain it in this way. You also are always living in imagination. The artist tries to bring this world over into life.

---

[3] See Letter 267, note 2.

[1] It should be understood that Funk and Anderson carried on a steady game of boasting to each other.

But you can betray, sell out, the imaginative world as you can the real world, be false to it. This should be elaborated, and I haven't time.

You see, however, what our writers do — build up the idea, in fiction, that to be rich, have success, etc., is happiness. They pervert all the channels of existence. Look at how deeply the false idea that success was the result of merit was built up, whereas any sensible man knows that success, in the money-making sense, is almost always due to the overdevelopment of the acquisitive instinct, to trickery, and often to sheer luck.

Well enough. This endeth the first lesson.

I am offered, tentatively — I would rather you did not speak of this — a professorship at Columbia, one lecture a week. I do not think it will come off.

I have worked better and harder this fall than for years, but it will not show for a time yet. Will be at home for Christmas and will stay until I go to speak in Chicago in January.

Then I think of going down into the Southwest, perhaps to the New Mexico–Old Mexico border. I can live as cheaply. My program of work is made. I might as well be where I can be out of doors.

If I do that, I will come back in the very early spring for some time in Washington.

In the meantime write when you feel in the mood — 54 Washington Mews.

P.S. I had the impulse to write you the above because I think of you as, with the exception of Mrs. Copenhaver, the only real friend I've made down there.

And sometimes I feel like showing you my serious side too.

271.   [NEW YORK, ?DECEMBER, 1935]

To ROGER SERGEL

Dear Roger: Your nice, long, crazy letter came. You speak, old man, as though I were a woman who needed courting or flattery. Of course, what you say of my novel writing is just right and a thing I have been realizing. It is what I meant when I wrote that I was trying to bring in more mind and not depend so much on pure feeling. Did I write that to you?

Let's see, let me count up. There is John, one of my sons, Julius [1]

---

[1] Julius Friend.

sometimes, Charles Bockler, a painter, Mother Copenhaver — she the only woman — Paul Rosenfeld, Jap Deeter, to whom I like to write about work. There might be two or three others. You know that a year or two ago I began writing about something. The idea never got very definite. It was an attempt at expression of a need, not just my own, for a kind of male, if you will, getting together. The muddle of which you speak in this letter when you let yourself go is so damned general. I think we are all bitten by this notion that understanding of the problem and of what we need has to be general; that is to say, that we have to connect with that terrible thing called "the public" — to be a success, in other words — this in the face of the fact that success so obviously does destroy. If we did anything, it would be so slow, slow in percolating anyway, wouldn't it?

You speak of yourself writing these long letters, as a kind of relief, to men friends, among them myself, and then not sending them, so obviously doing an injustice to me. For example, that you, with so obviously a better mind than my own, have perhaps known for a long time just what you now say about my novel writing. Can't you see that it would have been a help to me for you to have said it long ago?

Was it that you thought I might think your opinion unimportant? Now there, have you also got it, the thing so upsetting, a kind of inferiority bug? Jesus.

A kind of man-to-man give and take in a world so much given over to feminine rule, eh?

Or a notion that a man must have recognition, in that big, not understood, outside mass, be some big shot or something, to have value — surely a childish enough notion.

You bet we'll come to your house.

I won't write any more today although I'd like to. I have this goddam sinus trouble every winter. This winter I have given up drinking and am trying diet to keep me up to work. It may be, after all, that I may have to run off to a warm, dry climate, to keep working, I mean. I take letter writing partly as a substitute for drink, I guess.

I wonder if you will do something I tell you to. Go spend the money for the three volumes of Van Gogh's letters. Then you, Ruth, and Chris [2] read them, the other boys later. They will cost maybe twenty dollars or more. A dealer here let me have mine at his cost out of goodness of heart, I guess. For this morning, so long.

[2] Mrs. Sergel and Christopher, the Sergels' eldest son.

272. [New York, December 1, 1935]

To Theodore Dreiser

Dear Ted: For some reason I have recently been a good deal haunted by thoughts of you. How are you? What are you doing and thinking?

I came East about Oct. 1st and went to stay up the Hudson some thirty miles from town on the farm of a friend. Have been at work on a novel. Oh, I know, Ted, that you think the novel is not my field, but I may make it yet. I am trying, this time, to get a bit more outside, not quite so much surrender to pure feeling, more observation — more mind, if I have it.

I haven't been seeing many people. Came into the city about ten days ago and am at that same place, 54 Washington Mews, until Dec. 15th and then to Marion, Virginia until about Jan. 15th. After that I think I'll hit off south and west — I'm thinking of Tucson, Arizona, near the Mex[ican] line — probably for Feb. and March.

Are you at work on a novel, or play, or what are you up to?

I remember once speaking to you of one of my favorite books of yours and said *A Traveler at Forty* when I meant, *A Hoosier Holiday.* I recently reread it with joy.

Ted, don't fail to write that part of your own life having to do with Street and Smith, the *Delineator,* etc.

And we should have also from you a book of people, pictures as in *Twelve Men,* but more general, wider, many sketches put down as you can do it.

Do you write letters? I'd like to hear from you more often, your thoughts, etc. I've had a notion recently that we men, of our time, do not communicate directly often enough. Often during a walk I find myself thinking of you or some other man loved and respected, feeling lost from them. My best to Helen. I like that woman.

[P.S.] Did you know about X., gone clear off, out to shoot people, etc.? Poor cuss, he's now in Bloomingdale.[1]

273. [New York, after December 6, 1935]

To Theodore Dreiser

Dear Teddy: I think that when we are together, there is a natural shyness, and then we are both writers who have written a great deal

[1] A mental hospital in New York State.

and for a long time. In time thoughts flow more freely through the fingers than through the lips.

I am interested in your thinking and in some way will get to see you before I leave. Will phone. I want also to see Helen.

Here is something that may interest you. Some years ago I published a little book, an attempt to get at something about men, women, and machines. Perhaps I should have called it *Men, Women, and Machines*. I called it *Perhaps Women*. It fell flat.

Recently, however, it has begun to come to life, and what may interest you is that letters I get about it seem to come mostly from philosophers.

I have this feeling, that we men of our time have depended too much on women — as I tried to say before, some communication that should go on between us as males, not personal as with women, too much neglected.

You will see my point if you grant me that the machine, in separating men from tools and materials, does make for male impotence.

We are too close to a matriarchy.

Recently I found out something about a man friend in Chicago. For two or three years he had been writing me long letters which he never mailed. His wife told me afterwards that he wrote them to clarify his own thinking and didn't send them because he was shy.

And because men have got this habit of not communicating.

Dreiser, if you haven't it, do get Van Gogh's letters, in three volumes. They cost $22.50 but Weyhe [1] let me have them for $17.50. They are worth it. They are really great literature.

There is a new book by a young man, *Free For All* by Evan Shipman,[2] Scribner's. I'm going to see that you get it. Let me know what you think.

274.   [NEW YORK, ?DECEMBER 8, 1935]

To CHARLES BOCKLER

Dear Charles: It seems to me that I began closer to Gauguin but have come around until I am closer Van Gogh. I hit out, trying to save myself from stupidity in people. Most people shit all over in houses and in streets. I think that man must have offended you because he

---

[1] Proprietor of the Weyhe Galleries in New York.
[2] Published in 1935. Cf. Letter 276.

was shitting on canvas, out there, in the face of nature. There's a lot of that done.

I can't make out about people, why they want to be as they are. Mostly I sympathize with them. Maybe I have an air of superiority with a lot of people, like Gauguin. That offends.

All the time, of course, I want love.

I began like Gauguin, in business. I understood it fairly well. I could handle people. I came to hate the quality in myself. I was ashamed of it. It never brought me to anything but dirty ends.

What purity I have got has come from the contempt of what is called being competent in life. Why should I feel that way — that is to say, that competence is anything?

It is all too cheap, too easy.

This naturally led me over to my present attitude. I presume I got tired and gave it up. The woman I had wanted things, security in life and all that.

I thought I could perhaps be fairly prosperous and that it wouldn't matter. I did. I came nearer and nearer the middle class.

These people, with their houses, lands, automobiles. It makes me sick to think how near I came to going over to them.

You will guess I have been reading the Van Gogh book again. It has become a kind of Bible to me.

What fools to think that man a fool. He was shrewd and real. He had this sense of going into nature and growing out of nature. He must have loved nature as a man would love a woman.

John will be here tomorrow. I do not think it will be more than 2 weeks before he comes. We have so much to talk about. He seems almost like a stranger to me now.

I presume we have to put up with this feeling of people as going far away and then coming back again.

Nature does the same thing.

But people have often so little dignity.

It is O.K. with the young man. When you have a smaller thing you feel like letting go, let me know. I shall take the water colors with me and one oil when I go away to work.

They continue to live. Just now the little bathers is much alive. It glows in the room.

[Approximately twenty words scratched out and erased, evidently not by Anderson.] I fancy life at home is very, very hard and annoying after this summer. Just now I cannot even write to her. I write little notes and put them away.

For me there must be this sense of people dear to me — men and women, drawn close, in fancy at least, sometimes.

I am not worrying about the novel. Something in me is growing stronger. I get a bit nearer all the time — I think.

I send love to you and Kack. I wish I could see you both.

275.   [NEW YORK, ?AFTER DECEMBER 9, 1935]

To GEORGIA O'KEEFFE

Dear Georgia: I wanted to quarrel with you a little last night. You spoke of a story of mine called *Many Marriages,* saying, as you had said once before, that you thought, as you read it, that in it, more, I take it, than in other things of mine, you felt me.

I didn't think it was true, more in that than in any other thing.

How can you know what I am? How can I know?

I wanted to quarrel with you because I thought you had missed the point of the book. It was a book written to bring flesh, the feel of flesh, as far as I could go with it, into prose.

I am always making marriages. We all are. There is a particular man or woman we see. Something happens. Marriages are not necessarily made in beds, although beds are nice too. There is in people a curious sense of dirt. God knows what put it in them.

In my book I wanted to represent a man simply as struggling to escape that feel of dirt. To do it he had, he felt, to go to rather extreme lengths. He wanted not only to free himself but his daughter. He knew his wife past freeing. He sacrificed her.

I think I am particularly touchy on the subject of this book because it was terribly misunderstood. It was a book written in purity and in innocence, and I am neither pure nor innocent; so it is not me.

We ha[d] a good time.

276.   [?NEW YORK, MID-DECEMBER, 1935]

To MAXWELL PERKINS

Dear Max Perkins: Excuse desk paper. I wanted to write a note to tell you that yesterday you gave me a grand thrill, the same sort I got when I first read a Hemingway, a Ring Lardner, a Bill Faulkner story. This Evan Shipman,[1] he's got it.

Lordy, Perkins, it's fine stuff. He sure knows his little old race tracks and all that ever went with them. He's got and put down the very smell of them.

It makes you realize again, as sharp as a good biting wind, what went out of our little old American world with the grand old, once almost universal, horse feeling. I wonder if they'll be saying this guy has too much nost[al]gia for the past. I'll bet they do.

And the running horse crowd won't get it either. That's a gambling instinct. That's what that is. Lord, the Freds, old Tommy, the dancers, the Wills, the horses, the game old sons of bitches like his Stamina. Tell Shipman we always had some niggers around out in the Middle West, and ask if he knows that little book on Pop Geers;[2] I'll try to find it for him if he hasn't it.

You know, Max, there used to be Freds in every little town and druggists, saloonkeepers, town photographers, etc., etc., even preachers, whose great dream was to someday own maybe just one fast one.

Do beg Shipman to keep it up. He might bring some people back to real horses and to a pretty damn sweet male world. You tell him I said this, if it means anything to him. As always

[P.S.] Tell him I said to hell with the saddle horse crowd and the millionaires with their stables of [missing word]. He'll know what I mean.

277.   [MARION, VIRGINIA, DECEMBER 22, 1935]

To THEODORE DREISER

Dear Teddy: I have an idea I wish we could have spoken of. Also I'm sorry we didn't have a chance to talk. I presume you must be trying to get at and perhaps formulate some kind of definite thinking for all of us.

There are two ideas definite in my mind — that the machine, for all it brings in the way of benefits, brings at least an almost equal hurt. You see, definitely my idea has been, for a long time, that all this

---

[1] Author of *Free For All*. The "Freds" and "Wills" in a later paragraph of the text refer to characters in this novel.

[2] E[dward] Franklin Geers, *Ed. Geers' Experience with the Trotters and Pacers*, Matthews-Northrup Company, Buffalo, New York, 1901.

talk of men and women being the same except for a slight physical difference is the purest nonsense. You are never in a room with a woman or with women but that you feel the impulse TO BE. They want beauty of person, and I do not think any man at all male ever thinks of that. Man does want the thing outside self. I want it in this book, in the building I am making, in a stone wall. I want always to do something to materials in nature. Any such impulse in a woman who is really feminine has been put into her by man or to try to compensate for lack of maleness in men.

And another idea — so-called pure science. I think it time to proclaim the end of the period of science. All the damned nonsense of thinking it wonderful, for example, that on the radio I can get the Fiji Islands or Hong Kong or Seattle. It [is] time now to begin thinking, "What will I say to Seattle or Mars when the connection is made?" I think there is a terrific cultural lag in all this talk that suggests that any new physical discovery is advancement. Have you, Teddy, some such belief? I even think that the real war coming is not first of all between Communism and capitalism, but between this obsession with fact and the other conception of in some way recreating the pathway between men. It is hard to say what I mean without using the word "spiritual," a word so damnably corrupted that it is no use at all any more. Sincerely

[P.S.] Greeting of the season to Helen and that grand little gal we saw there.

Will be here at Marion, Va. until about Jan. 15.

278.   MARION, VIRGINIA, DECEMBER 23, 1935

L. CHERNIASKY, SOCIETY FOR CULTURAL RELATIONS [MOSCOW]

Dear Sir: I have your letter, a form, I dare say, addressed to Americans. It was mailed from you Dec. 15th. There are five questions asked.

#1. (I am attaching questionnaire.) It is a pretty big question. We are curiously isolated in America. Working artists here do not often see each other, except in New York. There is a good deal of talk about New York being a cultural center. I doubt if it is. I do, however, have the feeling that the revolutionists here have broadened the bases upon which they work. There seems to be less inclination to be didactic; we do not quite so much romanticize the proletariat.

I do hope this inclination grows, for I feel that the workers themselves are not benefited by the inclination to romanticize.

As for Soviet art, why I do not know enough to speak. You are a vast country, as we are. I cannot accept any work of art because it is done by one who declares himself a revolutionist as great for that reason. I do not think it that easy. I wish I knew more of what you in Russia are doing and trying to do. That is all I can say.

And after all, I feel that what I have said does answer all five of your questions as well as I can answer them. Sincerely

279.   [?1936]
To Frank Fuller [1]

Dear Frank Fuller: I do not believe people change very rapidly. Well, there can be no doubt that the things you mention — the machine, modern industry, etc. — has [sic] profoundly changed life outwardly. You speak of *Winesburg*. Why, I do think that the stories of the book apply as well today as when written, perhaps twenty years ago.

The twists of finance, legislation and its effect, all the mysteries of government. My dear Fuller, do not blame the people of small towns and the farmers that they do not understand.

Do you, do I, did the big men, so-called, who made the peace after the World War know what they were doing? I think not. I think most of what Abe Lincoln called "common people" must be as I am. When I talk to most radicals, I'm strong for capitalism and individualism; but when I talk to most capitalists, I'm hot for the radicals.

I do think that a hundred years from now men may look back on this age as a dark age in human thought, when men tried to explain all of the mystery of existence by the laws of economics.

I think that the average man still goes for the individual and depends on leadership. For example, I do not believe that the President has lost nearly as much ground as is generally supposed.

Men are a good deal lost in our time. They have lost the sense of being a part of the big complex thing in which we seem to be caught. They want that, to feel a part of something big going on. Until the turn of the century there was such a feeling. Read the histories written

[1] The letter from Fuller to which this is a reply is not in the Anderson Collection.

up to that time. There was apparently the belief that we were all marching onward, upward. I do think that feeling is lost.

Men do, I think, want daring, bold leadership. God grant it won't be cheap.

A new Lincoln may be the thing most needed. Sincerely

280.   [PEARLY 1936]

To LAURA LOU COPENHAVER

Dear Mother: In regard to Kit,[1] Mother, I do appreciate your suggestion. I think, however, that there is a certain difficulty. You have spoken several times of the Virginia boy, and I am a little afraid that you overestimate his importance in the story.

True, I have changed somewhat his tone and the tone of Kit toward him. I am using him as the force that finally drove Kit out of bootlegging. What happened to him was too much for her.

But as regards his mother, as another Anabelle, etc. You see, Mother, to really develop that theme would be to write another book. In my present version [2] I am rather leaving the boy's mother out of it. She died when he was a child. There was a rather didactic aunt, a father who drank secretly but was under the thumb of Bishop Cannon [3] — that is to say, politically, as at one time most politicians in Virginia were. He was influenced by his grandfather, a Mosby [4] man in the Civil War, a rather fine sort.

The name of the family was Weathersmythe, and they were a Valley family, insistent, as all you Virginians are — and I have always thought, as you know, absurdly — on family. There were tendencies that made the boy feel, being himself the son of a poor mountain white girl, that he was illegitimate. He was irritated by the fraud in his father. I think it more important to strike in passing at this hurtful notion of aristocracy than to show up an Anabelle.

And anyway, Kit and prohibition is my story. As always

---

[1] The leading character in Anderson's novel, *Kit Brandon,* published in October, 1936.

[2] For the details mentioned in the following two paragraphs see Chapter XV of *Kit Brandon.*

[3] Bishop James Cannon, Jr. (1864–1924) of the Methodist Episcopal Church South, prohibition leader.

[4] John S. Mosby (1833–1916), Confederate guerrilla leader.

281. Marion, Virginia, January 2, 1936

Mr. Alan Calmer, *Partisan Review,* New York

Dear Mr. Calmer: I am not familiar with the magazine [1] you speak of in your letter of December 22. Lately I have been hard at work and have not done much reading. I can say in general that I think it is a basic mistake to limit writing in any way.

I really do not know what is meant by "proletariat writers." If it means that blacksmiths and railroad mail clerks suddenly begin to write, all I can say is that the same thing has always happened. If, on the other hand, it means writing with understanding about workers, farm hands, etc., what in hell has Dreiser been doing all his life? What have I been doing all my life? What did Turgenev do when he wrote *Annals of a Sportsman?*

To tell the truth, I think that all artists, intellectuals, and scientists have their o[w]n job to do. I think it is a kind of seeking of reality and maturity. Something in me resents this kind of classification. Sincerely yours

282. Marion, Virginia, January 2, 1936

Mr. Maxwell Perkins, Charles Scribner's Sons, New York

Dear Maxwell Perkins: Many, many thanks for the thousand advance on the novel.[1] I have been for the last week or ten days rather absorbed in the Christmas thing and haven't made the advance I would like, but have got down some 30 or 40 additional pages, which I am having copied. I am going to North Carolina for a week or ten days, leaving in the morning, and expect I will get some more work done. Then I'll come back here and go to Chicago on January 23. After that I am going South somewhere and will give you an address later. I am going to return to you the part of the novel that is put down, having transferred the corrections to the yellow sheets, which I will keep.

I do not know whether or not I wrote you very definitely about my ambitions as regards this novel, but probably I have. I have thought, Max, that one of the things that has betrayed me as a novelist is the

---

[1] Alan Calmer, one of the editors of the *Partisan Review,* wrote December 22, 1935, that he hoped Anderson was familiar with "*Anvil* and *Partisan Review,* two proletarian magazines that have just combined to publish a new literary monthly," and asking for a contribution.

---

[1] *Kit Brandon.*

inclination to surrender too much to passing moods, a fact that has perhaps made my novels in the past too diffused. I want to avoid this in this novel, and I want you to help me.

I do not think that it is important, with all the other things you have to do, to give much attention to the matter now. Let's hold the novel for early fall publication. When I have got the complete script into your hands, I do wish that you would take a day or two to go through it. Whenever you think that I have got too far away from the main drive of the novel, I want you to say so. I really should get through with it in the next two months, and this would give you plenty of leisure to do this, and I only mention it now because I want you to have it in mind. With the advance you have given me and the amount earned on the previous book, I can see my way clear to devote myself for the next several months to work. With sincere personal regards

283.   [MARION, VIRGINIA, JANUARY 12, 1936]

To THEODORE DREISER

Dear Ted: Had a grand evening with Jap[1] and his gang at Bristol, Va., here about a week ago. They were on their way South to do a tour. We got a big room in the hotel and had a case of beer. Some grand talk. I guess, Ted, he's about the best thing we've got in the theatre.

I am leaving here Sunday, going to Baltimore and then to Chicago. I am to speak in both places, in Chicago to "The Friends of American Authors." What do you think of that?

Hot dickity dog!

Ted, I think you're wet in part, won't say what part. I think the general notion of the writer being also thinker, philosopher, etc., is the wet part — perhaps.

For I do think that the work of men like you and me sometimes, when we are on our real jobs, you in so many respects — Jennie, Sister Carrie, the boy in the *Tragedy* — I mean, when we are simply telling, as we should really always be trying to tell, the simple story of lives, we are doing our best service.

In any one of such stories you break so much ground. You understand I'm not putting this on you. I'm guilty often enough, God knows. There is this terrible loneliness of people in America. You see, I live pretty much in a small town. I go and come a lot. In a way the small

[1] Jasper Deeter.

town is like a goldfish bowl. You can look and see. And I do see often the most sensitive ones breaking down, becoming drunkards, going all to pieces because of the terrible dullness. This goddam science and mechanical development you talk of doesn't help all this, while the other part of your work, the telling of the story, always does.

Am I wrong? Challenge me if I am.

[P.S.] Say, Ted, write a nice little note to Gene O'Neill. I've a hunch he is just now a down pin. Love to Helen.

284.   [MARION, VIRGINIA, JANUARY 13, 1936]

To RALPH CHURCH

Dear Ralph: I began reading Hemmy's *Green Hills of Africa*[1] and thinking of him and a lot of things you said. It's really a lousy book, and the god awful thing is that he doesn't know it and never will.

I rather wonder, Ralph, if it isn't like this. You see, he's got this notion in his head, that you get there by chucking the imaginative world. He got it, of course, because it isn't his world. He can't feel his way around in it, can't get it; so he gets out of it by saying, "The hell with it."

And then you see what he does. He romanticizes what he calls the real world, gets ecstatic about shooting and killing, guts and dung.

There's the whole world of men he can't get at all; so he proclaims his own superiority to it and them.

And then, too, he's too concerned with writing, thinks of it too much like the eternal amateur he is and always will be, the small bad boy. "Kiss my ass," he crie[s] in ecstasy and then is heartbroken because we don't see any sense to it and won't.

I think it's rather like this, Ralph. Of course every man has a hell of a time. First he has to work to get someone else, usually some woman, out from between him and his canvas. That's a fight. Then he has to try to get himself out. That's the thing Hemmy can't do.

I wonder if I'm right.

285.   [TUCSON, ARIZONA, ?FEBRUARY 13, 1936]

To LAURA LOU COPENHAVER

Dear Mother: I have had two or three days of not working well, that is to say, on the novel, but am sure I will soon get back to it. I do know

[1] *The Green Hills of Africa* by Ernest Hemingway, Scribner's, 1935.

where I want to go, but on certain days the sentences will not march. There are too many stragglers among the words. They won't stay in ranks.

The little white truck is a joy, at least to me. We must send you a picture of it. E. pretends she is as pleased with it as I am, but that may only be to please me. When she left us, M.[1] left a check, in an envelope, to pay for it.

[Did] E. tell you of the Sunday at Nogales in old Mex[ico] with the college professor and wife, our sitting in what was called "The Cave," a place cut out of a hillside, wild duck to eat and good wine? They had what they called a "floor show," much good Spanish dancing and some good singing.

Immediately you drive out of town here you are in the desolation of the desert, which isn't desolation at all. There is such a grand sense of privacy in wide spaces, curious cactus growth, beautiful skies.

E. has got to the Van Gogh, and I have, from the library here, some Adams letters,[2] young Charles Francis, Jr. with the Army of the Potomac and his father, Charles Francis, Sr., in London as our ambassador, young Henry Adams with him and all writing letters. It's grand stuff. They are all so intelligent, so absolutely Adamses, and all with such extraordinary good heads. I do wish we could steal the books and send them on to you.

E. wants me to tell you to go on to Florida and get out of that weather.

Report from the sale of old books by Viking unexpectedly good. It is quite extraordinary, I think, that *Winesburg* goes on year after year, about 5,000 a year. What a shame I make such a pittance from it. Love to Mr. C. and Aunt May and lots for yourself

286.   [St. Paul Hotel, Tucson, Arizona, ?February 23, 1936]

To William C. Stewart [1]

Dear Bill: I have been thinking of something, an idea that might possibly be of value to you, or at any rate to your boss.

---

[1] Mary Emmett.

[2] W. C. Ford [Ed.], *A Cycle of Adams Letters, 1861–1865*, 2 vols., Boston, 1920.

---

[1] The text of this letter is that of a copy furnished by Mr. Stewart, the original not now being available. Mr. Stewart was at this time doing editorial work with the McNaught Syndicate in New York.

There is this tourist thing in America; it goes on so tremendously, takes in at some time or other almost everyone.

The growth of road camps, curiosity of Americans about other parts of America. Those who are not tourists dream of being. Why couldn't your boss get some good man to do a column, "The Tourist"? Such a one might travel all over America; he might even have one of those little houses attached to a car, stay in towns, in hotels sometimes, in camps — the people met, characters of the road, the places seen, mountains, deserts, rivers — different modes of agriculture, mining countries, farming countries, industrial towns. I do think we as a people are tremendously curious about each other and of course all towns [?do] cater to the tourists.

I should think the thing I have in mind might be a running story of the life and adventures of such a one, the confirmed tourist, all the things that happen to him, to people he meets, the places seen, no[w] at Palm Beach, now in some little Georgia town, Iowa, Texas, Minnesota — you get the idea. It may not be worth anything. It might interest your boss as a thing to be tried. I'd say you and Bern [2] could do it. Would you think it fun?

It's great out here. You'd love it, but perhaps you already know the deserts, Indians, Mexicans, etc. We live in a little hotel opposite the Catholic cathedral, the Mex[ican] section of town just a few blocks away, the deserts and mountains everywhere about. I am getting to the end of the job of rewriting the novel. I think we'll be here until about March 15th and then to New Orleans for a time before we go North. Our best love to you both

287.   [BIRMINGHAM, ALABAMA, APRIL 1, 1936]

To LAURA LOU COPENHAVER

Dear Mother: I guess I'd better send this home. E. is out shopping. She has been peculiarly lovely this winter. She is really a marvelous woman.

I am myself, at least temporarily, discouraged. It is about the Civil War thing. Mother, there's one thing sure. You do not know the South, its terrible side, the raw brutality of it, separation from earthiness, pretensions, cheapness. I wonder if any of you Southerners would ever dare face it.

2 Stewart's wife, Bernadette.

Really, what is wanted and terribly needed is a devastating indictment. You have been so terribly cheap.

Oh, Mother, if you knew, could dare to face the cheapness of Birmingham, Atlanta, the Natchez Stark Young ***** wrote about, of so many Southern cities.

It all made so much more cheap because of this lousy pretension to culture.

Culture.

Sacred word.

It must, must, must be based on honesty, and there is none here.

Someone should write — shall I? — a blast.

Begone with you, stinking hypocrites. There will be no health in you until you strip clean at last to utter poverty.

Face the land you have destroyed because you never knew it, never dared know it.

I don't mean you, Mother dear, really a worker.

I do mean The South.

Some day someone will do it, blast it utterly.

That's what gets my goat. I'd like to. I wouldn't like to.

288.   MARION, VIRGINIA, APRIL 16, 1936

MR. CLARENCE GOHDES, DURHAM, NORTH CAROLINA

Dear Clarence Gohdes: [1] Your letter of April 1st has been neglected because I have just returned from a winter of wandering. I will do the best I can to help you out. In the first place, there is a question as to what is the best article on myself written by some other person. This is a little difficult, as I presume any writer likes best those articles about himself that are most laudatory. I think we all have that weakness. To tell the truth, there is a pretty big literature of this kind now. There is a book of Paul Rosenfeld's called *Port of New York*, one by Stuart Sherman called *Critical Woodcuts*, and I have seen recently a book by Harlan Hatcher of Ohio State University called *Creating the Modern American Novel*. Then there are several books of opinions regarding American writers by European critics. I should think, however, that you might be able to get all you wanted from the above.

Referring to your second question, I think there were two or three

---

[1] Clarence Gohdes (1901–), a professor in the English Department of Duke University.

quite conventional short stories published in more or less popular magazines before the time of which you speak. While I was running the factory in Ohio, I would, as a matter of fact, write a great deal and probably did a great deal of writing for ten years before publishing.

I have always thought that I came into writing rather through the back door, as my primary object in the beginning was not publication, but rather, if possible, to clear up things about myself and others in my own mind.

I can't remember when I first came across Stephen Crane, but do remember an earlier enthusiasm for [The] Red Badge of Courage, also for a little colorful book of his verse [2] I found one time in the Public Library in Chicago.

I have a notion that the answer to your fourth question as to when I actually started writing is pretty much given by the answer to the second question above.

I am sorry, as you say you are, that we cannot sit down and talk, as I am really interested in what motivates writers, as I know you are. If you are ever up this way in the summer, you stop and see me. I have a summer home in the mountains near Marion, Virginia and would be glad to welcome you there if you come this way at any time during the summer months. Sincerely yours

289. [MOYLAN-ROSE VALLEY, PENNSYLVANIA, MAY 2, 1936]

TO ROGER SERGEL

Dear Roger: It would be swell if you could come here. You could stay at this inn where I have a room, comfortable enough, about five minutes drive from the theatre. I am uncertain now about my own plans, but will be here or near here most of May, as E. will be tied up in New York until about that time. If I am in New York, I can run over here to spend the time with you and Ruth. It is only a three hours' drive.

For better or worse I have finished off the play, and Jap will very likely do it this year. Now, if I attempt another, it must be a comedy. I think of a play about Southern aristocracy.

I couldn't resist showing Jap your letter. It started a long discussion, nothing of course settled. It ended by his saying, "Well, it may all be

---

[2] Either *The Black Riders* (1895) or *War Is Kind* (1899).

true, but, on the other hand, it may be that you can make a new form for us." So there you are.

I have been reading Chekhov's letters. How much letters tell. It is not said to back up my own convictions, I'm quite sure, not absolutely, but it is true that he was accused, when he went as a story teller into the theatre, of almost this same thing. I spoke to Jap of this. "Was Chekhov a real playwriter?"

"Yes. He brought something new in. Half the mss. I get show the Chekhov influence."

This sounds, I know, as though I were trying to build up something, a defense. I wonder if I am?

Or setting myself up. I think I am very uncertain. I like the idea of playmaking. As to my being able to do it, that puzzles me.

Jap is making a new version of the *Winesburg*. It is much simpler. He is trying to so simplify the sets that it can be run off fast, giving the scenes rapidly as pictures out of small town life.

I wrote a short story called "Nice Girl." [1] The girl really wasn't nice. She was a bitch, but I think the story was nice.

Jap is doing rehearsals of the *Egg*, himself as the restaurant keeper. I think he may do it with O'Neill's *Jones,* or he may do three one-acters. He will be amazingly fine in the role.

The comedy, if I can get into it, will be something to play with this summer. When I have extra copies made after I go home, I'll send it to you.

But it would be more fun to have you here. We could walk about and talk.

I had a cryptic wire from E., at Colorado Springs. Mary was driving East from California. Evidently she got as far as Colorado Springs. The wire simply said, "Mary here. Car wrecked. Mary slightly." Lots of love to Ruth and the lads

290.   [MOYLAN-ROSE VALLEY, PENNSYLVANIA, MAY 4, 1936]

TO LAURA LOU COPENHAVER

Dear Mother: As you see, I have a new typewriter ribbon. The novel is sent to the publisher. I am handing the play [1] over to Jap. It is too

[1] In the *New Yorker*, XII, 15–17 (July 25, 1936).

[1] Anderson had just completed a dramatization of "Hands" from *Winesburg, Ohio.*

early to start on the Civil War. E. is not coming until Thursday, and even after she comes, she will be here but a few days. I must have something short to do. As long as I am here, near the theatre, seeing plays constantly, going to rehearsal, I will be unable to think except in terms of the theatre.

It is time now to write a comedy. Suppose, Mother, I do one on the Southern Aristocracy? What say?

I think vaguely of the outlines. There is a man named Grubb. He is fifty, very successful in life, really a shy man but always putting up a bluff. His sister Effileane (made up the name; I may change that and name her after some flower), she is married to a hard working but unsuccessful doctor. They have four children, three daughters and a son. The son is something like the man in my story "Nice Girl." (By the way, no word has come from that.) He drinks, is a problem.

Uncle Alfred makes money hand over fist. He is a little ashamed of his success. Doctor Merriweather, his sister's husband, is of ONE OF THE BEST SOUTHERN FAMILIES. When Alfred Grubb was a young man, he fell in love with a Miss Hunter, also of one of the best families, but, because of the lowly position in life of his own family, did not dare ask for her hand. She married a drunken rowdy, had a child that died, and then she died.

In the meantime everything Alfred Grubb touched turned to gold. He bought and sold houses and farms, always making more and more money.

He lives with his sister and her husband, owns the house in which the Merriweather family lives. He paid his sister's way through college, helped her young husband get established as a doctor. (The husband, by the way, is a tactless man. He is always saying things he doesn't mean and offending people.)

The wife of the doctor is trying to make her way socially against the handicap of the name Grubb borne by her brother. He is necessary but terribly inconvenient.

The uncle is really a good man, big-hearted, essentially religious, somewhat profane, talkative, often absurd, a great getter off of high-sounding phrases, devoted to the radio and the movies; whereas the Merriwell [sic] family, except the son and one daughter, want terribly the social distinction given by a name and so desirable to most Southerners.

The uncle, Alf, is one who goes about with a heartbreak, but he drinks, talks loudly, and has the reputation of associating with loose women. He has really been devoted, all his life, to the Miss Hunter he loved in boyhood. When she was hard up, before she died, he ached to help her, but did not dare.

A sister of this Miss Hunter comes to town, and he finds out she has no money; so he engages her as housekeeper in the Merriweather household, and it is taken for granted she has become his mistress. The relationship between the two is purely sentimental on his part, but no one in the family believes this.

This Miss Hunter, who ran away with a man, a farm hand, when she was a young girl, has had a rough life. Her husband was killed in a shooting affair. She is cool-headed, shrewd, sound at bottom. Thinking she is something she isn't, the son of the house tries one night to break into her room and is caught at it by a sister. Uncle Alf stands by her, as does one of the daughters. The family do not dare throw her out because of Uncle Alf's money.

This is the bare outlines of the situation, the uncle and the woman to win the respect of the others in the end. I think of many situations. What do you think?

I see you have put the college girls on the play. O.K., let them finish as first suggested and send with bill. Tell Aunt May to write Mr. Sullivan [2] for anything she wants done for the holiday and by all means to drop him a card telling him just the date. Lots of love to all

291.   [VALLEY COTTAGE, NEW YORK, MAY 26, 1936]

To ROGER SERGEL

Dear Roger: It seems to me I have not written you for some time. I saw a notice that Perry [1] had got the Guggenheim and thought it was your friend. It turns out to be another Perry.

I have been over at Jap's for some time, but now am at Mary's farm up on the Hudson. I am doing a profile of Jap for the *New Yorker.* Recently sold them a story. [2]

It may be you are in large part right about the play and me as playwriter. But at that I do not think you got at the real fault. I think

[2] John Sullivan, who for many years managed Anderson's farm.

[1] Guggenheim Fellowships were awarded in 1936 to Perry G. E. Miller, literary historian, and Perry William Wilson, bacteriologist. Actually Sergel's friend was the philosopher, Charles Perry.
[2] "Nice Girl."

I discovered it the other day. Paul [3] came out here, and I read it to him and in reading got my own notion of the great fault.

Which is in the theme, the handling of it. I have been trying to tell, in the play, the story of the creative inventive man, working in the fact, that is to say machinery, and realizing how his creativeness, intended to be a help for others, has ended in what seems to be hurt.

My difficulty is that I have been trying to find the answer. That got me muddled, because, as yet, no one, least of all yours truly, knows the answer.

Now I am going to attack in a new way, simply making the play tell, in action, the story, making it a simple tragedy.

In the meantime I did get, out of an attempt that failed, a very beautiful one-act play. So that's that. I'll begin again. If it can be born, it will be born. I've been through abortions before.

I think now that I will go down to the city this week end, spend a week there, and then go on to Ripshin. E. cannot come until about the 15th, but Mary will go down with me and get me settled. Scribner's seem enthused about the novel. I'll be having proof sheets of that.

We are going to be expecting you and Ruth. With love

292.   [?TROUTDALE, VIRGINIA, AFTER JUNE 16, 1936]

To HENRY GODDARD LEACH

Dear Leach: I have read with interest the discussion between Dr. Harry Laidler and Eustace Seligman.[1] I am afraid it only adds to my confusion. The difficulty with me is that when I hear anything that seems like a defense of capitalism, I become Communistic, and when I hear Communistic arguments, I become somewhat tender toward capitalism.

I don't believe anyone quite knows what makes wars.

I don't believe anyone can really think clearly on any subject involving whole peoples.

I do think that our present passion for getting at everything through economics is a little insane. When again, if ever, we can all being to at least try to think small, in little circles, a family, a few acquaintances,

[3] Paul Rosenfeld.

[1] On June 16, Henry Goddard Leach, editor of the *Forum*, sent Anderson proof of a debate between Eustace A. Seligman and Dr. Henry Laidler of the League for Industrial Democracy on "Can Capitalism Keep the Peace?" and asked for comment.

getting at what makes wars there, not forever jumping off into these huge pronouncements (God help me, I'm always doing it too) —

When as individuals we can learn more of the ways of peace, we will have taken a great step toward universal peace.

293.   [TROUTDALE, VIRGINIA, JUNE 18, 1936]

To MAXWELL PERKINS

Dear Max Perkins: It seems to me now that I have begun something mu[ch] more interesting to me than the proposed Civil War [book] so that will have to wait. I am calling the thing tentatively *Rudolph's Book of Days*. It is in a way autobiographic, but very unlike my *Story Teller's Story*. It seems to me, Perkins, that I, as an American writer, have had a peculiar experience. I began life as a young laborer, was soldier, factory hand, wandering worker, then advertising writer, company promotor, manufacturer — all of this before thirty.

As you know, I came into writing in a curious period, just before the World War. There was a kind of Robin's Egg Renaissance that produced Lewis, Dreiser, Sandburg, O'Neill, the *Little Review, New Republic, Seven Arts* magazine, the crowd about the old *Masses*, etc., etc.

All the figures of that time I came to know personally. I imagine this Rudolph, myself really, come in among these men as I came, with just such a background, working for years among them, knowing personally the New York crowd of the time, Mencken, Nathan and the others, at the same time carrying on for years my connection with the business world, myself unable to live by my writing, while at the same time being recognized as one of the significant figures.

I would, you see, have a point of view quite different, I think, than the other figures involved. I would want to write the book without absolute time sequence, partly as history, but most of all as one man's impression of a world of publishers, artists, actors, painters, musicians, sculptors, etc. I think, Perkins, that my life, so looked at, has been a peculiarly rich one in those impressions and contacts. My persistent wandering has taken me all over America. I believe I can make the book big and rich.

For there is also a connection with the radicals, impressions of figures in that world got from contacts too. I would ask you, there at Scribner's, not to reveal that it is so frankly autobiographic. Let them say so if they wish when the book is a fact. It is very rich material, and I am loaded with it. What do you think?

In the meantime I will have finished a book of plays, the dramatization of *Winesburg* and several one-act plays, that I think I'd rather like to make into a book in the spring.

Am going for a day with Ham Basso [1] next week. Mrs. Anderson said she wrote you about coming down to see our place sometime this summer. I hope you will.

I shall be expecting the proof sheets to *Kit* any time now. Sincerely [P.S.] Will be at Troutdale, Va., until October.

I appreciate the books you occasionally send me.

Just now there is a kind of flair for my stories, etc., in England. They are being published in magazines over there and also syndicated in newspapers. Do you have any connections in London that might be interested in doing *Kit Brandon?* Curtis Brown is my London agent.

If you come down, we'll take you over to see the T.V.A.

294.   MARION, VIRGINIA, JUNE 18, 1936

TASS AGENCY,[1] 383 MADISON AVENUE, NEW YORK

In the death of Maxim Gorki the world, as well as Russia, has lost a great human, one of the world's great writers and a leader. With what excitement I, as a young factory hand in America, read his tales of defeated people. I lived among them and knew them. How I hungered to have stories told of these lives that did not sentimentalize, that [had] the sort of tender understanding so characteristic of Gorki, and with what happiness I found the tales told by this great master.

295.   [TROUTDALE, VIRGINIA, ?LATE JUNE, 1936]

TO ROGER SERGEL

Dear Roger: You mustn't be tired, old dear, and that's what your letter a little sounded like. Read Edmund Wilson's new book.[1]

Not that this has anything to do with tiredness, but I do think Wilson manages to give out of himself to all of us.

About the play, I have for the time forgotten it.

---

[1] Hamilton Basso (1909–), novelist.

[1] Anderson dispatched a virtually identical note to *Soviet Russia Today* on the same date.

[1] *Travels in Two Democracies* (1936).

Paul's new book is good.[2]

As usual I have many things to talk of with you, but there you are and here I am.

Of a sudden, for some unknown reason my stories begin to sell in England.

I did a new short story and a profile of Jasper Deeter for the *New Yorker*.[3]

As regards this matter of suggestion. Why, Roger, I don't suppose any man working in the arts really takes them. He has to remain, if he can, in a certain receptive mood. As you well know, an incident in a restaurant or something seen in the street may influence him more than anything any of his comrades may say.

That doesn't mean that the rubbing of mind against mind isn't good.

Between ourselves I have given up the Civil War idea and also the idea that I can take financial aid from Mary Emmett.

I don't know why, but it won't work.

And perhaps the continual struggle for leisure to work and live always a bit on the edge is better.

I have been a little ill, but am better now.

I wonder if I'd better ask you to send the cat or bring it. I think I'd better wait & have you bring it. It may be the best way to insure that you two are actually coming.

We count on that.

296.   [TROUTDALE, VIRGINIA] JULY 16, 1936

To JOHN ANDERSON

Dear John: I am sorry we did not have more time to talk at Hedgerow, but I am sure you had a swell time seeing *Liliom*.[1]

I got your last letter just before I left home to go to Hedgerow, and yesterday afternoon when Paul and I were out in the woods, we talked about it.

I used to think that the thing sought by the painter o[r] the sculptor was already in the stone or on the canvas, that something stood be-

---

[2] Paul Rosenfeld, *Discoveries of a Music Critic* (1936).

[3] Anderson published nothing in the *New Yorker* after "Nice Girl," July 25, 1936. The profile of Deeter was not accepted.

---

[1] Ferenc Molnar's play was in the repertory of the Hedgerow Theatre.

tween it and the artist. There was what I thought of as the disease of individuality. I don't think this any more.

This I have found out: there is in me, as in you, or any working artist, always the danger of a kind of statement. It may be that this only comes because we ourselves, as individuals, get between ourselves and the thing sought. Of course, others thrust themselves in there too, but that is not what I am thinking about now.

This I have found out from experience, that these floating ideas, always drifting through the mind, if given free play by action, seem to become definite and alive.

As the painter might make an infinite number of sketches, often rapidly, but nevertheless making them, as a writer puts down on paper the same kind of passing things, something does often result.

Often a sudden realization of beauty.

Don't you think, John, that the same thing is in all of living, for example, in relationships?

It seems to me that I have felt a growth in you through a new and growing freedom, in yourself, in making contacts with people.

Paul entirely agrees with you that, for the painter, painting is certainly an idea and not something that comes from an idea.

It seems to me that I could carry over your idea of gesture into my own experience. Stories do not come to me as definite facts. I remember once being on a train in a day coach and seeing a man run across a field. The gesture stayed with me and resulted years afterward in a story called "The Untold Lie" in *Winesburg*. This one of many such experiences.

Certainly in what we call love between people the real thing does not come with any declaration of love. I see a man or woman, perhaps walking across a room. Something happens of which the person may be unconscious. I wonder if they are unconscious. They suddenly become beautiful. I would give anything to know whether or not they know when the thing happens.

When I walk here in the country and see a man ploughing, say, on a hillside field, I hunger to have the man know the beauty of the gesture, in himself and his horses, involved in the act of ploughing. I want him to know this in relation to earth, sky, trees, river, etc.

It may be that is all we are after — that he shall know. As always

297.   [TROUTDALE, VIRGINIA] AUGUST 14, 1936

MR. PAUL ROSENFELD, YORK VILLAGE, MAINE

Dear Paul: [1] When you have something constantly on your mind in regard to a friend, there isn't perhaps any health in just letting it go, to let it fester within you.

The truth is, Paul, that I have got something on my mind that has no direct relationship to our friendship. I have hesitated about writing you what is in my mind.

I have wanted to do it and at the same time have not wanted to do it. There has been an effort to justify myself in doing it.

After you left here, I thought a good deal about this matter and even wrote you a letter I didn't send. The letter was a kind of attempt, I guess, to rather put you on the spot. At first I justified my desire to do this by saying to myself, "Well he did not hesitate that time I signed the manifesto [2] to call me to time, rather taking it for granted that by signing I had become a sort of renegade."

I didn't like the first letter I wrote. I didn't want to justify saying what it seemed to me I should say because you had once put me on the spot. Well, here it is.

When you were here with us, there was almost constantly talk of Fascism and Communism, and it seemed to me that you had got hold of something, an idea difficult to put into words.

It had to do with the obligation of the artist, let's say to the tradition. At any rate, Paul, I gave myself credit with having known always what you were talking about.

But, Paul, as you talked, as you made little remarks, I kept thinking of a story I once wrote. I called it "Paper Pills."

You will remember that a year or two ago you took me to task because, in carelessly signing a certain manifesto, I betrayed the central meaning of the artist's life. I probably deserved what I got for signing something without reading it, largely through trust in the political and social keenness of Edmund Wilson.

Paul, I have been wondering this summer if you do not go pretty far the other way, and I have even, from many remarks dropped, got at times the impression that your fear and dread of Fascism springs

---

[1] A note on this letter in Anderson's handwriting states: "Not sent. Too smug." The letter is included, however, because of its intrinsic interest.

[2] *Culture and the Crisis,* a pamphlet issued in 1932 by the League of Professional Groups for Foster and Ford, calling for the election of the Communist presidential candidates.

sometimes almost altogether from the fear of what may happen to you as Jew and have even sometimes thought that you might almost welcome Fascism if it suppressed the troublesome workers and gave you security in your own way of living.

There have been so many things to help build this impression. I remember that once on a former visit Eleanor and I took you on a trip to a little mill town and that afterwards, during the trip home — the place having suggested to Eleanor and myself something like a rather clean and outwardly orderly prison, both of us in a reaction against the place — you came, almost eagerly I thought, to the defense of the system that had created it.

The implications of the place were very sharp in my mind and in Eleanor's mind. Every little house in the town was owned by the mill; the stores were so owned. The police and even, perhaps, the preachers owned by the mill. The houses were not dirty. They were physically liveable enough, and there did seem in you at the time an eagerness to declare that this physical side of the picture was all that it was necessary to think about.

It was as though this other thing of which we who call ourselves artists sometimes speak — let's say the right of the artist to give himself freely and without restriction to the exercise of his art —

It did seem to me that at the moment you were unwilling to give to workers the same right. It was a little as though you thought that the worker could not also feel the sacredness of his tools and his materials.

It seemed to me at the time that you were not asking yourself about the quality of goods made in the particular mill, as though there were not many great and prosperous mills that paid big dividends by making shoddy.

And as though this fact did not go down into the lives of the workers as truly as the doing of cheap work goes down into the lives of what we call the artists' class.

There seemed to me, Paul, a kind of continual insistence, as though it would give you a kind of pleasure to believe that there exists a whole body of people, for convenience' sake called the proletariat, and that these people were really a sullen and ugly folk, existing, as it were, in darkness down below us. I remember a kind of insistent cry from you: "They hate us. They hate us." There was this insistence on hatred that you seemed to want to make to cover the impulses of a great world of people.

Then one day when we were walking, you suddenly said, "There is one good thing about Fascism. It ends strikes," appearing thus to welcome the existence of a civilization that would clamp down whole bodies of people into a mold, holding them there for the comfort and security of a few.

I remember you sitting on your porch before your tent on the morning after Doris left our kitchen to go off and get married.

"It's the proletariat. You can see what they are like," you cried.

Again, Paul, there was no looking into the life of the particular woman, apparently no realization of her puzzle in life, of the fact that she was taking a step that would influence her entire life. You appeared willing to throw her thus blindly into a class, to make a kind of nothingness of her, and I, hearing you say the words, "It's the proletariat. It's the way they always do. They hate us," etc., was profoundly shocked.

As you know, it must have been a terribly important moment in the life of another human being. You may say that you did not know she had gone off to get married, but certainly you had no way of knowing why she had gone. It seemed to me that at the moment nothing mattered to you but our own breakfast and having our beds made, and I couldn't help thinking of how I had written all my life to make it clear that just such human beings as Doris did have existence. On the whole I think I would be very proud to have her, for example, as a sister.

And there also near by was John Sullivan, who has been working on my place for ten years and who has done so much to help make it beautiful. I cannnot help knowing that he is as sensitive a man and as easily hurt as you or me.

I admit, Paul, that you have always recognized the value of all this in my work, but why should it lose value in life, in actual contact with other human beings?

Is it the famous ivory tower? In so many of your remarks there is so much suggestion of the tower.

Paul, I do not believe that any man can interpret American life now and remain so aloof. I do forgive you a lot of all this because of the difference in our background.

You said while you were here — I do not remember your exact words, but there was the implication — that you could not take into your consciousness the sufferings of people, and I did suppose from many other things said that you meant workers, servants — really, after all, the people who create most of the wealth of the world.

I have a kind of passionate desire to get all this clear because, as friend, I do not want to sail under false colors with you.

You must remember that I saw my own mother sicken and die from overwork. I have myself been through the mill. I have worked month after month in factories, for long hours daily, have known the hopelessness of trying to escape. I have seen my own mother stand all day over a washtub, washing the dirty linen of pretentious middle-class women not fit to tie her shoelaces, this just to get her sons enough food to keep them alive, and I presume I shall never in my life see a working woman without identifying her with my mother.

At any rate, I know that there are among workers men and women as sensitive and as easily hurt as you and me.

I have the feeling sometimes, Paul, that if the fight came and the matter of nationalities were not in it, you might line up on the side of those who have against those who have not, perhaps escaping by convincing yourself that it was for the sake of some higher thing, and I want you to know that I would be on the other side.

And so, Paul, you see me going along. I have possessions. I do not definitely line up with the revolutionists or join a revolutionist party. Naturally I have found that among revolutionists there is often the same attitude toward all who have possessions that I have felt in you towards those who have not; that is to say, an insistence that there is in them, as you so often seem to insist in all workers, little but hatred. I do feel that keeping at the task of telling the story of the common man, trying to see clearly, I can best help and can best explain my love. If you were to go through all my writing, I think you would find this impulse in all I have done, and I do think it but fair to our relationship that you know that you have a little shocked me. I did not say all this to you when you were here, because I felt it might upset your work on the novel; but I keep remembering that you are also proposing a study of the American artist, and I feel that I am an American artist and that as such I cannot be the real friend without putting down for you to read and think about these thoughts I have been having.

All of the above, you should know, I could not put down if my own affection for you were not a reality. As always

298.   [TROUTDALE, VIRGINIA] AUGUST 27, 1936

To JOHN ANDERSON

Dear John: I think the impulse is the same. I think the two ways may both come to the same end.

I think perhaps we go for the same thing.

There is in me perhaps sometimes too much desire to influence. I am always trying to escape it.

It is both good and bad. I see a man here, playing in a field. Then I want to be a painter. Someone once said that I often wrote from a painter's impulse.

The man is there in the field with his horses, and sometimes everything is fused.

The field is in the man and his horses. The man is in his horses. The horses are in the man.

There is something lovely, a fact.

But I am closest related to the man. I know no way to tell the horses or the fields. It seems to me that I do want the man to feel as I at the moment feel.

There is at least a faint hope that I may tell him in a poem or a painting.

This the more virtuous, purer side of myself. All the other things that come in, desire for admiration in others, vanity that I can feel and sometimes see — these in there too.

They partly, too, often make it all grotesque.

This matter of having it all, also, up in the head, thought through, as it were.

I'll tell you, John, that I sometimes feel as regards you that there is too much inclination that way. I would have you more reckless sometimes, as I have seen you on several occasions when you have been drinking — this I mean in work, more and more drunken giving, in perhaps just a half-mad thrust at the moment.

One of the best and most thorough artists I have known in my life is Katherine, who at Hedgerow does the Elizabeth in my play *Winesburg, Ohio*. She is in an art that is curiously a woman's art.

But I have seen her also tighten, begin to think her way, absolutely, through a part.

A curious thing, hers being a social art. It was as though some hard thing came out of her destroying all around.

It seemed to me that she had thought so hard, trying to work out a kind of technique of perfection, that all herself had gone up into her head.

There was no energy left, let's say, in bodily warmth, whatever is the instrument in ourselves by which we embrace, kiss, make many marriages with others.

In the self-portrait here and in the portrait of the woman, from whom I got my Kate [1] of the novel, and in the portrait of Zeb's brother, I got this thing, not cold, not mental, very warm, that I didn't get in the work you brought home.

It was in the little alive drawing of the boy's head and very rich in the drawing of the woman in the chair Bob has.

That particularly, to me, a very beautiful thing.

Wouldn't it be a curious twist if, in the end, it should turn out that your road lies along the road of people?

I said something about the possibility of your perhaps some winter coming here. Well, I had something in mind.

This may again be an effort to thrust another's impulse on you, but you can throw that aside.

It shouldn't hurt for me to reveal my thoughts.

That you might live here among these people, say for a winter, trying perhaps even to share a little their lives, not, for the time, trying to earn any money.

There is undoubtedly something here, a people living in a civilization that is not a money civilization.

You might get something very rich from it. I don't know.

You do seem to imply that the associations there have not enriched you.

As Joe Welling in *Winesburg* says, "It's an idea." Love
P.S. If you should decide to do it, I should leave the truck here. I would leave Ranny as a hunting dog for you and Major.[2]

299. [NEW YORK, EARLY OCTOBER, 1936]

TO LAURA LOU COPENHAVER

Dear Mother: It is impossible to tell yet how *Kit* will go. Perkins says that the whole situation, bookselling, has changed since the De-

[1] A character in *Kit Brandon*.
[2] Major (first name, not title) Sullivan, son of Anderson's farm manager, John Sullivan.

pression. Bookstores are cautious. They buy in small quantities, re-order in small quantities. During the worst of the Depression they practically all went broke. Before the Depression you could load them up, force them to make sales.

Criticism is as usual — generous, mean, personal, smart-alecky, often penetrating. We have few big critics, Mother, but, on the other hand, criticism in America is never venal, as in Europe.

There is a sick time, unavoidable. There are these people of your book. You have been so close to them, so long feeling with them.

They are out in the world, public characters, more or less. How you hate & are hurt by mean or smarty things said of them.

You have to remember that many of these poor wretches, news-paper critics, try to cover a new book every day. Ye gods!

About the movies, I'll be sensible, I guess, take any money that may come.

Yesterday Mr. Freedman,[1] my play & movie agent, was in; we talked for a half hour.

He's a really cultured, capable man, probably the best there is. He says it [is] mostly an odd chance, some star, or a director, suddenly wanting, or not wanting.

If, for example, you, who go often to the movies, see a star that you think might like to do Kit, write her a note, say, "There's a part I'd love to see you in, etc."

Any little thing might do it.

Freedman knows so much more than I do. I'm leaving it all to him. Love

300.   [NEW YORK, OCTOBER 13, 1936] AFTER READING FAMILY LETTER

To LAURA LOU COPENHAVER

Dear Mother: I have an extra $1,000.00, just acquired. Write Mazie that if she has to use check before Dec. 1st, to notify you or wire me. I will send you check for $1,000 to cover it.

Do not think my own or E.['s] name on anti-Fascist lists will lead to war. It is, Mother, the one thing I would go to any lengths for, to de-feat dictatorship, either Communist or Fascist.

I got a wire Saturday asking me to go to Los Angeles for an anti-

[1] Harold Freedman, who was attempting to find a producer to put on *Winesburg, Ohio* in New York.

Fascist speech, expenses paid, and, but that I had just acquired a new head cold, think I would have gone.

As for reviews, E. will answer that. I have already quit looking at them. It's better for me. The job is done. The book [1] is between covers. The bird is out of the nest.

However, I am going to write a thing, "The Writer to the Critic." [2] New Yorker has asked me to for a department they call "Upward with the Arts."

After 2 days the head cold is gone — benzedrine and a new infrared ray lamp Mary has brought us.

I'd say, Mother, that that particular relationship is about as right now as it was wrong before.

And, amazingly, Mary is so much more happy. Ain't life amazing?

You see, all the time she knew it was all wrong as well as we did. The jolt (blow, we thought it) has worked an amazing transformation.

No more Hay.[3]

No quibbling.

It has become real fun to be with her. E. and she are going to dine together tonight & go to the movies, while I dine with Geo. Nathan and go with him to an opening.

Had a long talk yesterday with Ben Hecht, who has gone sour on the movies. You know we were once great friends in Chicago. His old mother was killed in an automobile accident in Los Angeles, and the last thing she said to him before dying was that he should have stuck to me and gone with me on my road.

Both he and Nathan are interested in *Winesburg*, not as producers, but as saying the right word at the right time, to the right producer.

Mother, this family letter of yours is the grandest, in its whole tone, the sweetest, and most moving of any of them I ever read. I only hope your own blood children are as really stirred by it as I was. Love

301.   [NEW YORK, NOVEMBER 4, 1936]

To LAURA LOU COPENHAVER

Dear Mother: Well, that's settled. John Emerson, my old boyhood friend, arrived from California, and we had breakfast with him at the

---

[1] *Kit Brandon* was published in October, 1936.

[2] Not accepted by the *New Yorker*.

[3] The Hay Diet, currently popular health regimen, which Mrs. Emmett had been unsuccessfully attempting to persuade Anderson to adopt.

Algonquin. John, although very successful & rich again, a hot Roosevelt man. Jane Grey,[1] the actress I knew long ago, was with us. Anita Loos didn't come with John.

E. went to the office, & I wrote until 3. We went to see *Boy Meets Girl*,[2] a very funny satire on the pictures.

We dined at the Barbison-Plaza and went to see *The Follies*.[3] Very bad.

Returns were coming in from dinnertime on, also in theatre. John very high. We left E. & Jane & went to the Lambs Club, where John talked to Anita in California. She was at Charlie Chaplin's house. Charlie very excited, shouting over the phone.

John: "He's got all but 2 states."

Charlie: "Damn, that's two too many."

In Times Square and for blocks a dense mass of people, all apparently happy, shouting and singing. We sat drinking until two.

Mother, I think the best thing was the huge registration. To me it was a sweet and comforting sign that people are not at all tired of democracy.

Max Perkins just phoned that there are two offers from English publishers.

Will see him this P.M. to decide.

The book keeps moving, but not big. Guess it will make its way. Lots of love

302.   [TAMPA, FLORIDA, NOVEMBER 27, 1936]

To ROGER SERGEL

Dear Roger: You will have to stand for a longhand letter. We are here at the winding up of this annual meeting, A.F. of L., official American labor.

God save labor! E. had to come, and I came along as chauffeur, for education, I guess. It may be, as Henry Adams seemed to think, that there is nothing else to be got, a little education.

This a K.K.K. town — tourists, the lovely sea, some shipping, a curious backwash of ugliness.

A.F. of L. just nothing, Roger, frightened old men hanging on. They

---

[1] Jane Grey (1883–1944), stage actress.

[2] *Boy Meets Girl* opened November 18, 1935, and enjoyed a long run.

[3] This "edition" of the Ziegfeld Follies, starring Fanny Brice, opened in New York January 31, 1936, under the management of Billie Burke (Mrs. Florenz Ziegfeld) after Ziegfeld's death.

sit. They pass resolutions. They are as far away from the actuality of labor as Mars. The whole thing was dominated by Hutcheson, of the carpenters, Landon's labor spokesman, a racketeer. Green is a stuffed shirt, of no importance.

At the same time, all around these dead men marvelous demonstrations of life.

I went one day with some newspapermen to call on some 20 sailors thrown into jail for picketing during a strike. We sat there in the prison, and they talked, labor really speaking, something alive & fine.

I tell you, Roger, more and more one feels that if there is ever anything done to make a better society, it will have to come from the dispossessed.

There has been a woman here from the Spanish Loyalists. She came as representative of Spanish labor, but A.F. of L., dominated by Catholics, wouldn't let her speak. She did, however, speak in a football field before some 5,000 workers, mostly Spanish cigar makers, the greatest speech I've ever heard. I sat with tears running down my cheeks, thinking, as one does, I was the only one so moved. Later several hard-boiled newspapermen told me they did the same. The woman, one Isabella Palencia,[1] is on her way to be Spanish ambassador to Sweden. She has a childlike faith that before Madrid the whole matter between Fascism & democracy may be settled and that democracy will win.

So much to tell you. Why does a man not live nearer his friend? We are leaving here in the morning, and I'll go to Marion to try to work.

Did you see Lovett['s] summing up of my work in *New Republic*[2] last week? Get it. It is, I think, about what you, as my friend, would have liked said.

Lots of love to all the house.

Address me at Marion. Mail is forwarded.

303.   DURHAM, NORTH CAROLINA, DECEMBER 6, 1936

To LAURA LOU COPENHAVER

Dear Mother: I am pretty steadily at work on the new novel, of which I had better say little until it is further along. We went on

---

[1] Isabel de Palencia (1881–) of the Spanish Loyalist Government, whose autobiography, *I Must Have Liberty*, was published in 1940.

[2] Robert Morss Lovett, "Sherwood Anderson," *New Republic*, LXXXIX, 103–105 (November 25, 1936).

Saturday to Howard Odum[1] at Chapel Hill and there met Paul Green, both E. and I taking an instant liking to both Green and wife, as, evidently, they did to us. Green is evidently puzzled. He has had offers of as high as $100,000 a year from the movies. He is the son of a poor N. C. farmer, a playwriter of real promise, a promise that hasn't yet been fulfilled. He is quite a strong athletic-looking man of, say, thirty-eight, and the wife very lovely and at least semi-intellectual. They have built a very lovely house, set back in a deep pine woods between Durham and Chapel Hill. I think Green is in a period of disgust with the movies and determined, at least for the time, to try hard to live by the stage.

That, of course, putting him up against the New York theatre managers, not so essentially different from the Hollywood gang.

We dined there last night, and James Boyd[2] came over from Southern Pines. It is about sixty miles from here, and we are planning to go over there to dine tonight. Boyd, born in N.C. [sic] with a N.C. grandfather, was born in Pennsylvania, his father having gone there and got rich in coal. He married one of the New York Lamonts and lives down here among the rich, is very fond of horses and hunts to hounds.

At the same time a true artist, at bottom perhaps also puzzled. A queer three we made. Boyd is very gentle and fine. He came over last evening, Green having told him I was here, specially to tell me something.

He was in New York, he said, and in hospital after an operation when Tom Wolfe came to see him. Wolfe is a big man, six-foot-five and weighing over three hundred and with a big, booming voice, and Boyd says he sat beside his bed in the hospital and, in a voice to be heard all over the hospital, began to proclaim me.

"So, I see," Boyd says he roared, "that the smart boys are after Sherwood Anderson. Ha! He is the only man in America who ever taught me anything. Anything I know of writing I have from him. He is our one sophisticate. He knows life, all of its ugly and [its] sweet side, better than any of us, but he is not soured. He takes life as it is and loves it, and they will be reading him long after all these smart boys are forgotten."

[1] Howard Odum (1884–), professor of sociology at the University of North Carolina.

[2] James Boyd (1888–1944), novelist, whose *Roll River* had appeared in 1935. It is set in Harrisburg, Pennsylvania.

It was certainly fine of Boyd to come, most of all to tell me this, and, coming from Wolfe, it gave me new courage, a thing rather needed just now when I have the feeling that as fine a thing as *Kit* seems to have fallen pretty much unnoticed. Lots of love

304. [NEW ORLEANS, JANUARY 19, 1937]

To JAMES BOYD

Dear Jim: All sorts of things in the head, dancing about. A man becomes, outwardly, stolid, middle-aged, and remains a colt inside. I'm thinking of things I wish I had talked over with you, but, as suggested, too many ideas. Sometimes I wish I were like a Brisbane,[1] talking, talking, all sorts of wisdom, into a Graphophone.[2]

It was rather a longer drive than I thought, but we got into New Orleans at four Sunday, all hotel rooms taken, prices up, the outlook for any prolonged stay here thin. We get off tomorrow morning (Wednesday) for Corpus Christi, Tex.

Tom Wolfe had just been here, evidently being made much a hero and social lion. Wish I had seen him. I tried to call him, hearing he had holed up at Pass Christian, but he had left there, they said, for N.C. From [what] all my friends here say he is evidently troubled, rather distraught and upset. Ain't it hell? You keep thinking of the other fellow as going on, eating, drinking, perpetually working and happy. I have been having a grand time thinking of Wolfe in that way, a kind of roll river man, and now to find that he also gets upset, perhaps even discouraged — it's disillusioning. Perhaps you'd better write him. If I had found him here, I'd have taken him off to Texas where, as far as I know, no one is literary.

After tonight we will have had three evenings here — too much drinking, talk until two or three, etc. — and will be glad to consort with Kansas wheat farmers down on the coast in their trailers. Wish you and Mrs. Boyd (am tempted to write "Kate")[3] were along.

We had such a good and satisfying time there.

I took Paul's *Rising Sun*[4] play as well as the Virginia Woolf[5] and will return them later in one package.

My idea of the letters I wrote you and Paul and didn't send, after

[1] Albert Brisbane (1864–1936), columnist of the Hearst newspapers after 1897.
[2] That is, a dictaphone.
[3] Boyd's name for his wife, Katharine.
[4] *Hymn to the Rising Sun* (1935).
[5] Virginia Woolf's *The Common Reader* (1925).

my first visit, was, I guess, a kind of confessional letter writing, as between several of us, working now, trying each in his own way to outline to the others his own difficulties, always of course in respect to work and living.

The two being so damned inseparable.

Such ideas seem so far reaching and all right often until you try to explain definitely to another just what you mean. I presume I seek a feeling of some sort of more or less compact body of us with some sense, not only of working together to hold onto something, but also of keeping each other alive.

It may all be silly. If you do see Wolfe and if I have suggested anything at all to you by these words, talk it over with him.

You are very, very fine people. It seems so foolish that I have not known you both longer. Anyway I'm grateful to you for being.

305.　　　　　　　　　　CORPUS CHRISTI, TEXAS [JANUARY 27, 1937]

To JAMES BOYD

Dear Jim: We certainly didn't strike very good weather after coming so far South. It was hot & rainy the last days in New Orleans, and as soon as we got here a cold wave struck this coast.

As a result, no fishing and, for me, a rotten cold that has laid me low. It's hell. We all, I guess, make these great plans, work to be done, etc., only to see them blow up.

Am sending back Paul's little book and also Woolf's *Common Reader.* How brutal and terrible we are. Paul's play touches about the absolute in that.

In the Woolf book I was particularly struck by the essay on the Russian writers. It seems to me that she has here said something I hadn't seen said before, one of the sort of things you know in your heart but have never yourself said and are therefore deeply grateful to the one who says it.

It does seem to me, Jim, that the Russians have this thing of which she speaks. They are not scientific, not technical. They seem willing to run the risk of destroying, not only themselves (enough of us do that), but their work, and this to take the long chance of arriving at something we seem never to get.

We got into ecstasies over, say, a Robert Louis Stevenson, his marvelous technique, etc., etc., but, later, how dead it all is.

And take this little play of Paul's, it also a lot too pat, so that we know as soon as it begins all that is to be said and done.

Would one of the Russians have seen it so? I think not. There would have been the same terrible brutality, but, in the end, we would have been given, in some sharp way, the sense of brutality in all, or rather perhaps some flash of goodness in all, of which we are ashamed.

I presume Woolf is right in saying it is "soul" — I mean the thing we are afraid of — and this leading to a kind of determination to find goats, entirely cruel people on whom we can blame things.

Am feeling lousy at the moment with a neuritis in my hips, the result, I guess, of the cold. Oh, how strong and decent Katharine must be, keeping so dignified and cheerful with such pains in her body. Love to you both & thanks for the books

306.   CORPUS CHRISTI, TEXAS, FEBRUARY 3 [1937]

To MAXWELL PERKINS

Dear Max: I have been intending to write you a note since I landed down here. I left home on January 11th and went first for a little visit with James Boyd at Southern Pines, N.C., and then to New Orleans. I took a great liking to Boyd, whom I had met through Paul Green, and he seemed to me absolutely the real thing. Have you ever been down there at his place? I presume the man must be quite rich and, as you know, is married to a Lamont, by the way a very sincere, fine person.

So here is this man, rich, with a big estate, a huge pack of fox hounds, the sort of people about who go in for fox hunting, all rich, decked out in their white pants and red coats, going whooping and tearing across country, over fences, the whole thing seeming in some way so absurd just now, so far away from anything that matters, and yet Jim himself with such a sincere love of horses and dogs and, I'm sure, with a fine mind.

I went down to New Orleans, and Tom Wolfe had just left there. He had been about with a crowd of my own friends, and they were all full of him. I've just missed meeting the man a half dozen times.

It seems, from the tales told there, that he is, just now, in rather a low state of mind, upset and perhaps even a little frantic, and I was terribly sorry I missed him. I think I would have tried to persuade him to come along with us.

I've a notion, Max, that perhaps Tom takes his critics too seriously.

You know how it is here. A new man, like Wolfe, who really has a lot to contribute comes along, and the critics go for him head over heels.

Then, almost immediately, they begin to draw in their horns, wise-crack at his expense. Most of them, after all, have no standards, no sense at all of what writing, in the way it is approached by a man like Wolfe, is all about. I did wish I could have had a talk with Wolfe.

Don't know just how long I'll stick here. The weather has been rotten, and the writing I've done not just tops yet. I seem to know what I want to do with the new book, but guess I haven't yet got the tone I want.

At any rate I'll stick here another ten days, and any mail sent here will be forwarded. I may go into Mexico or down to Brownsville. There is a combination I'm after, good fishing and a really good writing streak. I hope things go O.K. with you

[P.S.] There is one thing I do want you to do. I want to publish, in the spring, a little book of plays, the *Winesburg* full-length play and three one-acters. Is it O.K.? I doubt if they will sell so much. I think they should pay their own way. I can send you the manuscript in a week or ten days.

307.   [CORPUS CHRISTI, TEXAS, FEBRUARY 4, 1937]

To ROGER SERGEL

Dear Roger: As for the *Winesburg*, better hold it. I will wire you a bit later.

Truth is we may pull stakes here. It has been a fiasco — as regards weather, cold, rainy, and dreary. We may, any day now, light out further south, to Brownsville or across into Mexico.

We have really stayed on here for two reasons only: first, that we are expecting Marc & Lucille [1] to join us, and also a change in weather and this place would be ideal.

There is something about fishing — the quiet of it, the expectation of a struggle with a trout that might come at any moment — all very restful and good, and the place here ideal for that. From where I sit writing I could almost spit into the sea, and there is a little dock

---

[1] Marc and Lucille Antony.

going out into the deep water. We fish with live shrimp, strange, wriggling little pop-eyed things, and I keep a pail of them submerged by the front door.

But the sun and the warmth will not come. There has been 2 solid weeks of this grey cold.

My own chronic weakness is sinus that, when bad, poisons the system, & the nose and throat men among doctors are such shabby racketeers. Right now, however, I am working on myself, giving myself treatment, on prescriptions from Doctor Henry,[2] E.'s brother-in-law up in Stillwater, Minn.

I intend to write you more of Jimmy and Julius.[3] For some reason, this time they only made me sad, as though they were only tricking themselves.

There is something terribly provincial in the worst sense.

Can it be that to be a Jew, in our civilization, is to be, inevitably, provincial? They seem to live and move so much in just that little, rather tight New Orleans Jewish circle.

As regards the means and the end, Roger, I think I've always been pretty clear on that, but any and all government is a confused thing. No doubt it was just the dread of brutality in the liberals, belief in free speech, etc., that enabled Hitler & Mussolini to get the upper hand. However, the ends do not justify the means. On the contrary, the means make the ends. You become through means used to become.

Will write home to Mother for the *Harper*[4] article.

Grey skies, a grey sea, and a grey heart. Perhaps by the time this gets to you, we shall even have some sun and warmth, if not here, at the equator.

When I last heard from Ferdinand,[5] he was in California. Am about to write him. Why don't you drop him a note, c/o the University? Am sure it will find him. Love to Ruth & the boys

---

[2] Henry Van Meier, who had married Katharine Copenhaver, younger sister of Eleanor Anderson.

[3] James Feibleman (1904–), philosopher and author; and Julius Friend.

[4] Sergel had urged Anderson to read Max Eastman's article, "The End of Socialism in Russia," *Harper's*, CLXXIV, 302–314 (February, 1937).

[5] Ferdinand Schevill.

308.   Spohn Hospital, Corpus Christi, Texas, February 18, 1937

To E. L. Greever

My dear Mr. Greever: I am interested in your letter,[1] which I am compelled to answer at my wife's hand, being in the hospital with influenza.

O.K., then, perhaps the use of the word "non-violent" may have been stretching it a bit, but I really fear, after reading your letter, that our points of view are different, not because I am a literary man and you a lawyer, but perhaps of a different viewpoint on property and humanity. My dear man, isn't it a bit absurd to grow excited if labor occasionally picks up what weapon it may find at hand if that is the only way it can win the organization rights that property has long had? One smiles at the idea of piles of door hinges, etc. at hand to hurl out windows when one reads testimony regarding labor spies, machine guns, etc., etc. so long used by property.

I agree with you that it is a bitter shame that anything like violence is ever necessary to achieve a little justice — alas, perhaps it is.

I will be delighted to meet and talk with you any time you are ever near Marion. Do look me up. I am sure we could have a delightful quarrel.

I was a great admirer of your mother-in-law [sic], Mrs. Greever, and used to love to stop at her house for a chat. Sincerely

309.   [Marion, Virginia] April 9, 1937

Mr. Roger [Sergel], Dramatic Publishing Company, Chicago

Dear Roger: Since Eleanor's return things have been in a whirl here in the house. I think we told you about her brother[1] coming home from the Philippines. He brought us some grand presents, myself, for example, the swankiest overcoat you ever saw. I am sure it will make a new and better man of me.

As for John, I sent one of his things for Stieglitz to see. After all, the old man knows a lot about painting. I wanted to get his feeling about John's work to check with my own. He says some pretty fine

[1] On February 12, 1937 E. L. Greever, a lawyer in Tazewell, Virginia, wrote to protest against the sit-down strike, defended by Anderson as quoted in the *Literary Digest* of February 13. In Mr. Greever's view both the sit-down strike and peaceful picketing were in fact veiled forms of physical intimidation.
    Anderson's reply is in his wife's handwriting.

[1] Randolph Copenhaver.

things, speaking of his fine color sense and most of all of a kind of boldness and directness. "There is something here, a clean freshness, that I have not seen in the work of our other men."

I really think, Roger, that what is happening to John is O.K. He was in to see Stieglitz about a year ago, and at that time Stieglitz spoke of tightness in his work, and in this later work he seems to feel the tightness is all gone.

For one thing, he is now working very much more rapidly, I believe thinking less of technique and, I hope, more freely letting loose on emotional reactions.

It seems to me that I could write a volume on that part of your letter regarding the modern man and the machine, and there is an interesting development. In this town, for example, I know six or eight men, lawyers, doctors, and businessmen, who have set up workshops in their houses. They are trying to make things, and already there has sprung up a rather huge business in small machines, lathes, saws, etc., regular outfits for these men. I understand that Sears, Roebuck alone sold over 100,000 outfits last year.

I do think that there is a tremendous problem here. Read my own book, *Perhaps Women*. It is odd about that book. Only a few of the thinkers in the country have ever given it any attention. I think it has a lot to say about the threat.

Naturally I do think there is a way out. I think men always could live through what would kill dogs. I do not believe mankind is going down to defeat. I think he will learn to use even our tremendous machines. In my own book on the subject I got around to the very idea of your letter, that women might eventually revolt to get back into the world the manhood they need. They certainly don't get too much of it now. Love

310. [MARION, VIRGINIA] APRIL 14, 1937

MR. KENNETH DAVENPORT, FORT HAYS STATE COLLEGE, KANSAS

Dear Mr. Davenport: The questions you asked me in your letter[1] puzzled me. You must know it is very difficult for anyone to put down his own motives. I dare say if I have any philosophy, it is a rather pagan one, my desire being to feel more, see more, think more, hear more, and taste more — in short, to attempt to live life fully.

As for the theory of the short story, I can only say to you that I am

[1] Mr. Davenport was at work on a master's thesis.

at war with the idea of what is called the plot short story. I do not believe that I have been influenced in any way by Poe, and I do not believe much in his rather mathematical, clear-cut explanations. I have an idea that the American short story was tremendously corrupted by O. Henry, influenced by de Maupassant. Both Chekhov and Turgenev are to my mind infinitely greater masters.

As for your third question, in regard to America, I myself do not think in such gigantic terms. I should think your own opinion of what is going to happen in America would be as good as my own.

It is your first question that has me quite thrown back on my haunches. You speak of the characters in my stories being grotesque. Are you quite sure you are not grotesque, speaking in these terms? I am quite sure I am. It seems to me that in speaking of literary characters you are making some queer separation between people in stories and people in life. I rather think that modern life and, in fact, any life wherein most people are compelled to be driven by the profit motive makes it impossible for all of us to be anything else but grotesque.

In the front of the book of mine called *Winesburg, Ohio* there is a piece called "The Book of the Grotesque." Read that.

I should think that there is a good deal of material you might be able to get through your library. Read Sherman's *Critical Woodcuts* or Paul Rosenfeld's *Port of New York*. Robert Morss Lovett recently had an article on my work, a sort of revaluation of the whole body of my work in the *New Republic* about November 26, 1936.[2]

I would specially recommend that you go through my *Story Teller's Story*.

Of course, every man's work, if the man had done any body of work, should in itself answer all the questions you asked me in your letter. I am very sorry I cannot answer your letter more fully, but as you work along if there are any other questions that bother you, I will be glad to help you as much as I can. Address me at Marion, Virginia. Sincerely

311.   [MARION, VIRGINIA] APRIL 15, 1937

MR. ROGER SERGEL, DRAMATIC PUBLISHING COMPANY, CHICAGO

Dear Roger: Your letters always tempt me to answer them at once. You are wrong about John. I know that your letters stimulate him as they do me.

[2] See Letter 302, note 2.

By the way, John has been having some trouble and is going over to Abingdon to the hospital on Friday. He has been annoyed with hemorrhoids and has to have a minor operation. I do not believe that it will lay him up for more than a week, and having it done should save him a lot of annoyance.

I am tremendously interested in the whole question raised by your letter. I dare say I [am] an old-fashioned male. I do not think that men and women are alike or that they react to life in the same way. I know that saying this often annoys some women, but still I stand my ground. I do not believe that women employees have been hurt by the modern factory as men have. It is possible for the woman to create in her own person in the flesh, and it is not possible for men. It seems to me that to be is as important as to do. Basically, I do believe that the robbing of man of his craft, his touch with tools and materials by modern industry does tend to make him spiritually impotent. I believe that spiritual impotence eventually leads to physical impotence. This belief is basic in me. The darkness is a darkness of the soul.

We American men have failed our women miserably. It is because the American civilization has centered too much on fact. It may have been necessary. It is a tremendous job to settle a continent.

At any rate we have lost out and as a race have lost our women. We have forgotten the power of the imaginative life. What our women should have had from us is a constant recreating of life for them in the imaginative world. Our creative imaginations should illuminate the lives of our women. We do not do it, and they turn upon us. Can we blame them?

There is great talk now of revolution, and I dare say an economic revolution in our whole outlook on life. Our women are pretty bad, and we have made them what they are. The load is on us. With love to all

312. NEW YORK, MAY 4, 1937

MR. ROGER SERGEL, DRAMATIC PUBLISHING COMPANY, CHICAGO

Dear Roger: Your letter excites me, at least that part of it suggesting that you may come here.

I just returned from a weekend at Jap Deeter's theatre and saw two new plays there, and next Saturday, Mary, Eleanor, and I are driving up to Wells College at Aurora, N.Y. I have a friend up there, Lankes, the woodcut man, and he has invited us up to see a production of *Oedipus*. It is a rare chance. Why don't you meet us at Aurora, at the Inn, on Saturday evening, see the show, and drive down with us Sunday evening? Wire me if you can make it.

I got the copy of the magazine put out by the University of Chicago students and certainly understand Chris's interest, but as for writing something that they might want, I am a little doubtful.

The trouble is, Roger, that I am no longer young. I certainly sympathize with and admire the enthusiasm and determination of Chris and his friends, but as to just where they are going, or where any of us is going, I have these dreadful times of doubt. As you get older, and perhaps a bit more sophisticated, you are eternally asking yourself questions that can not be answered. The truth is that we are probably all headed for something, but whether it will be better or worse than what we have I don't know.

All of this applies to the idea of an open letter to college students. It would be more sensible, if I could find something, to try to confine myself to some little story. I don't tread on anyone's toes, so. I will try to find something.

The great difficulty with me in all this matter of going somewhere is that I am not terribly interested in arriving. My chief interest is what happens on the way, and this makes me a bum revolutionist. Perhaps we can talk all this over when I see you down here. Sincerely yours

313.   [TROUTDALE, VIRGINIA] JUNE 2, 1937

MR. ROGER SERGEL, DRAMATIC PUBLISHING COMPANY, CHICAGO

Dear Roger: We are back at Ripshin, having arrived in Marion about noon on Monday. We left New York at noon on Saturday and stopped for an evening with the Hedgerow Players at Media. We saw a very nice *St. Joan*.[1]

Eleanor went to a class meeting at Bryn Mawr on Sunday morning, and then we drove on home.

I never saw the country more lovely down here. Just now the wild azalea and the purple rhododendron are in full bloom, and presently we shall have the laurel and the white rhododendron. It is going to be a big fruit year apparently, with plenty of apples, cherries, straw-

---

[1] George Bernard Shaw's play was in the repertory of the Hedgerow Theatre.

berries, etc. I think it is a shame you do not live nearer so that we could have you here more often during the summer.

In New York I had another bite from the man who talked of doing *Winesburg* in New York, but nothing has come of it yet. Jap is putting it back in the repertoire in August. He is going to do a whole month of Shaw in July, a kind of Shaw festival.

Earlier John talked a good deal about taking a trip in his old car, but now I think he is about decided to spend the summer here. He has some friends who are coming down and who are going to take a little house up the road. Ferdinand Schevill and Mary Emmett will be here, I think, in about a week. Ferdinand promises to spend about two weeks with us, and I think Mary will stay about that long.

I had a letter from Lucille [2] saying that you and Ruth had become archeologists and were planning to go off to Syria. Can this be true?

There is a serious touch in Lucille's letter. Perhaps she has written you about it. It concerns what looks like the breaking up of the theatre group in New Orleans on which Marc has so set his heart.

I am going to try an experiment this summer working with a secretary who will live over here with us. I have been working blindly on the book [3] I suppose I have written you about. It is an attempt to put down, as honestly as possible, the story of my own adventure in living. I don't know how it will turn out. Sometimes it seems pretty much all rot to me, but I plunge right ahead. I already have done nearly two hundred typed pages. I imagine it is a book that, if it turns out at all, will need a terrific lot of editing. I think I shall call on you and Mother for that. What do you think of the idea?

Our present plan is to stay here until the end of July, when, as I think I have written you, I have to spend two weeks at the University of Colorado. If you have not gone off to Syria or Mexico, we will stop and see you either going or coming. As soon as your plans for the summer are more definite, you must let us know, as we feel we must see you somewhere. With love to both of you and the boy

[2] Lucille Antony.
[3] This became *Sherwood Anderson's Memoirs.*

314.   [TROUTDALE, VIRGINIA] JUNE 5, 1937

MR. ULRICO HOEPLI, [1] MILANO, ITALY

Dear Mr. Hoepli: I have your letter of May 17 and will be glad to send you forward a photograph as you request.

It is a little difficult for any writer who has written many books to pick out one of them and to say, "This is the most important of my efforts." It is too much like asking a mother who has many children to say which of her children is her favorite.

A novel of mine called *Dark Laughter* has had the largest immediate sale of any of my work. A book of short stories called *Winesburg, Ohio* is, I believe, the book of mine most often selected by American critics. It was written some twenty years ago and has become more or less an American classic.

I think that I myself am fondest perhaps of another called *Many Marriages*, but this may be only true because the book, when published, was very generally abused by the critics.

You will see how difficult it is for a writer to make a selection. When I was a boy in an American country town, there was in the town an old horse-trader who had a favorite saying: "The best horse I ever owned I own now." I think most any writer would be inclined to say that his best work is the one not yet done. Sincerely yours

315.   [TROUTDALE, VIRGINIA] JUNE 10, 1937

MISS WINIFRED BYLES, WEST 72ND STREET, NEW YORK

Dear Miss Byles: I have your letter of June 1 about the protest.[1] Naturally I am against all atrocities. I think modern war is itself an atrocity. I might as well be frank with you. It is very difficult for me to have any sympathy at all for people who are struggling to establish Fascism in any country. I am a sincere believer in democracy and believe that any form of Fascism is in itself an atrocity. Sincerely

[1] Of the Casa Editrice Libraria Ulrico Hoepli in Milan.

[1] Winifred Byles was secretary of a group of college women, calling themselves "Committee of Protest against Atrocities Committed in Spain by Either Side during this Present Civil War," and wrote from New York City.

316.   [TROUTDALE, VIRGINIA] JUNE 12, 1937

MR. BEN HUEBSCH, THE VIKING PRESS, NEW YORK

Dear Ben: I had a letter yesterday from a New York literary agent who has been in negotiation, for me, for the reproduction of one of my old stories in a popular magazine called *Redbook*.[1] There has been considerable correspondence about this matter, and naturally, Ben, you will, I think, understand the reason. I tried to get the *Redbook* to take for their purpose some story other than one in one of the books published by the Viking Press.

Naturally, Ben, I made this effort for the reason that your house is the only publishing house of the three American publishing houses who have published my books that has ever demanded or taken any part of any monies that have come to me from the reprinting of old stories of mine or for any translations of my books or stories. Neither Liveright or my present publisher, Scribner's, have ever asked any such concessions of me.

You see my position, Ben. You must know, having been my publisher, what a rather tough struggle for existence I have had. For years, while I was writing these stories, some of which are from time to time reprinted, I had to go on being an advertising writer, an occupation I detested. You know what a tough struggle for existence I have had. As a writer I have chosen always what has seemed to me the artist's way. We will say nothing of what ability I may have developed, but this I think I can say — that I have never gone cheap on the art of writing, in the sense of doing cheap or flashy writing. I have at least clung to a certain sincerity of purpose.

And now, after all these years, I do, now and then, have a chance to get in a little much-needed money. Here is a story, out of a book you published years ago and that perhaps not now even is kept in print. This magazine, *Redbook*, is, it seems, willing to pay five hundred dollars to reproduce the story. The check is sent to you, and you keep and use the money for several months. The agent takes his ten per cent, and out of the five hundred dollars I finally get, after several months of waiting, two hundred, twenty-five dollars.

Do you really think this is fair, Ben? I am not a businessman. I am

---

[1] Anderson's agent, Jacques Chambrun, had written that *Redbook* would pay $500 for "I Want to Know Why," included in *The Triumph of the Egg*, which Huebsch had published in 1921.

an artist struggling to live and do my work. I think I may fairly say I have had some influence on writing in America. I may perhaps even have influenced other writers whose books your house now publishes. At least these writers have written me and said so. My struggle has been a long, hard one. I know that technically, and legally, you probably have a right to half [of] any monies paid to me for the reprinting of old stories, some of them only written after years of effort, but do you not really believe, Ben, that in these cases, that is to say, the reprinting of my old stories, it would be fairer for your firm to be satisfied with twenty-five per cent and that I might have the needed money without several months of waiting?

I put this matter up to you and your fellows in your firm. I do think, Ben, that mine is somewhat a special case. I am very grateful for the permission you recently gave me to use materials from my *Winesburg* stories in my book of plays and for the concession you made me some years ago in reducing your share on translations of my works, controlled by you, from fifty per cent to twenty-five per cent, but I do think that, as I have a sore need of any monies my work may earn, that now, after all these years, this other concession might well be made to me.

I write all of this to you, Ben, without bitterness, but certainly with a good deal of hope that you and your fellows there may accept my point of view. Sincerely

317.   [TROUTDALE, VIRGINIA] JUNE 14, 1937

MISS DOROTHY NORMAN,[1] 1160 PARK AVENUE, NEW YORK

Dear Dorothy Norman: I am also very sorry that I did not see and have a talk with you while I was in New York. Paul [2] mentioned the matter covered by your letter in a conversation with me, but the conversation was brief. Someone interrupted.

Certainly I do feel that there is a place for such a magazine as you have in mind. I remember many conversations I had with Paul when he was down here on a visit to our mountain farm last summer. I am afraid that Paul perhaps thought that Mrs. Anderson and myself sometimes rather ragged him. He was rather insistent on the present-day

---

[1] In 1938 Dorothy Norman began editing *Twice a Year,* a "journal of literature, the arts, and civil liberties." This is the proposed magazine which is being discussed in the letter.

[2] Paul Rosenfeld.

starvation of what, for want of a better word, he might call the "spiritual" side of men in our times.

The truth is that I agree with Paul a good deal more than I let him see. I have been thinking for several years that we would presently grow tired of the rather hard-boiled, pessimistic, wisecracking attitude toward life. In fact I have sometimes said to myself that we are again in a dark age that clings to the belief that a good life may be attained through economic readjustment alone. It is pretty hopeless.

I do suppose that such a magazine as you have in mind would have to be subsidized, and here there comes in something that has often been in my mind about the subsidized magazines. I think it was so of the old *Seven Arts*, of the short-lived *Freeman's Magazine*, and I believe it to be true of the *New Republic*. I don't know exactly why it is true, but so many of our writers are terribly up against the problem of making a living. Often these subsidized magazines have seemed to use up most of the subsidy in paying a staff of editors. The writers have been asked to send in what is sometimes their finest work and are paid little or nothing, while often the editors are rather well paid.

Of course, I know this is an old, old problem. The number of people who subsist between the artists and the publisher is always rather tremendous. I do think that if anything can be done to correct this a little, it should be done.

I really do feel sorry that I did not take advantage of the opportunity, when I was in New York, to come and talk with you about this whole matter. I continually thought about it after the brief conversation I had with Paul, but I was hurried and absorbed and did not do it.

We will probably be on the farm, near Marion, Virginia, until the middle of September. If by chance anything takes you through this way during the summer, do stop and see us. If there is any particular way in which I can help you with this project, do call on me. Sincerely yours

318. [Troutdale, Virginia] June 21, 1937

Mr. Marshall A. Best, The Viking Press, Inc., New York

My dear Marshall A. Best: I want to write you at once and thank you for the concession made me in the matter of the story bought for reprinting by *Redbook*. Before I got your letter, I had already written to the literary agent, Jacques Chambrun, 745 Fifth Avenue, New York City, telling him to forward the *Redbook* check to you.

I have been thinking over this matter, and I believe that when you and your associates also think it over, you will be willing to extend this concession, that is, your taking twenty-five per cent rather than fifty per cent, to cover all reprints.

In your letter you speak of the gamble taken by Mr. Huebsch in becoming my publisher, but, really, I do not think there was such a great gamble. Mr. Huebsch was not my first publisher. The first book he published was my *Winesburg, Ohio,* but already, at that time, I had published two novels and a book of verse, and one of these books had had a marked success for a new writer, selling somewhere between ten and fifteen thousand copies.

It is, of course, quite true that when my *Winesburg, Ohio* was published, it was generally looked upon as being somewhat revolutionary in form. The accepted form of the short story in America had been set by Mr. O. Henry. It is true that I had had some difficulty in getting the book published, but I am sure that Mr. Huebsch never spent much money in publishing it.

I say all of this without intending to reflect in any way upon Mr. Huebsch, a man I look upon as my friend and for whom I have an affectionate regard. It may very well be that, at that time, Mr. Huebsch was in no shape to push my work. He and I have often spoken of this, and I think there is a mutual understanding of what the situation was.

The fact, however, remains that I was, all through the years when Mr. Huebsch was my publisher, always in a rather desperate financial situation. Later, and after I went to another publisher, who was able to spend money pushing my books, I did do better. As I have more than once told Mr. Huebsch, had I known of the prospective reorganization of Mr. Huebsch's publishing business, I never would have left him.

The fact remains that my other publishers, who have handled my books since, that is to say, Liveright and Scribner, have asked and have taken nothing for my foreign rights or for reprints. Some time ago you made a concession in the matter of foreign rights, cutting your share of those rights to twenty-five per cent. You have graciously done the same thing in the particular instance about which we are now having this correspondence. Cannot you now go further and make this concession cover all reprints of my work? I do not think that I am being overly greedy or unfair in asking this. I am no longer a young man and have a family. What rights I have in my lifetime of literary efforts is about all I have to leave to my wife and family. I do think, and believe you will agree with me, that in this matter there is something more involved than an ordinary business matter.

I certainly hope you may be able to see things from this point of view. Sincerely yours

319. [TROUTDALE, VIRGINIA] JULY 7, 1937

MISS MARGARET BOURKE-WHITE,[1] 521 FIFTH AVENUE, NEW YORK

Dear Margaret Bourke-White: We have some of your photographs here at our house in the country. They came here to us in a rather roundabout way. Mrs. Anderson is the National Industrial Secretary of the Y.W.C.A. for the South and, last month, held a camp, of industrial girls, down in the mountains of North Carolina.

I think these photographs of yours were loaned to the camp factory girls through [Lillian] Sharpley at the national headquarters of the Y.W.C.A. My wife, Eleanor Anderson, brought them home with her from the camp.

She was about to wrap them up to ship to you, but I asked her to wait until I had written. My own, perhaps foxy, game is to ask you if it would break your heart if I kept them about here for a month or two. They are so very fine.

Looking at them gives me the same pleasure I get from fine paintings.

A year or two ago you gave me one of your photographs. This was of a Hoe printing press, the white newspaper sheets running through. It is very beautiful, and I have it framed in my workshop.

I don't want to be a pig, but if it turns out that it is no great inconvenience to you to have these other photographs remain here for a time, I will certainly be delighted. Very truly yours

320. [BOULDER, COLORADO, AUGUST 2, 1937]

To LAURA LOU COPENHAVER

Dear Mother: One more week of this.[1] Really, some of the young men are pretty decent. There is a pretty big sprinkling of tired-out

[1] Margaret Bourke-White (1906–), photographer, from 1936 associate editor of *Life*.

[1] Anderson was "Visiting Novelist" at the eighth annual Writers' Conference in the Rocky Mountains, held at the University of Colorado.

schoolteachers who just want to pick up sentences they can, afterwards, get off in their classes.

What strikes you most, Mother, is an essential weariness. People do seem to have the world on their shoulders. There are the young radical[s], the fellows who hope to become *Saturday Eve[ning] Post* writers, and then there are the arty ones. Each group seems to resent the other group.

As for talent, it is pretty rare.

But as for Eleanor, she is resting and having, on the whole, I think, a pretty good time; so I'm glad I came.

But, oh, Lord, I wish you were here. I'd take you to all my classes and try to make you run them.

We escaped yesterday and went into Denver to the ball games. Lots of love to all

321.   [TROUTDALE, VIRGINIA, EARLY SEPTEMBER, 1937]

To MAXWELL PERKINS

Dear Max: Tom Wolfe has been here to see us. I'm afraid we didn't have a bed in the house long enough for [him]. The man is a flood, a continent, but he is generous and full of fine feeling.

He seems worried and upset, uncertain about the future. He seems to want so much, marriage among other things. Max, you'd better marry Tom off, get him a shrewd woman who will keep him out of trouble.

The man has tremendous gifts. He only stayed over the night and through most of the next day and then went on to Roanoke.

I have got seventy or eighty thousand words of my novel down, and it keeps prancing along. I think of it as a novel without a purpose, not intended to reform anyone or make any new world, just the story of a rather shy little man and his half-amusing, half-tragic adventures. Most of the time as I write I sit giggling.

I am sorry we did not get you down. You will have to come next summer. What with prize fights going on in your office and Tom to handle you'll be needing the rest.

I think we will come into town about October first. Sincerely

[P.S.] Paul Rosenfeld is here for a week.

322. [TROUTDALE, VIRGINIA, AFTER SEPTEMBER 13, 1937]

To NORMAN HOLMES PEARSON

Dear Pearson: [1] Your fine letter stirs me. It makes me want to write you at length. There is so much to be said, and I am not now thinking of *Death in the Woods* or any of my own works, but rather of writing, or, for that matter, of the practice of any art now in our time.

I presume that we all who begin the practice of an art begin out of a great hunger for order. We want brought into consciousness something that is always there but that gets so terribly lost. I am walking on a country road, and there is a man on a hillside plowing. There is something nice, even beautiful, in the man striding at the plow handles, in the breasts of the horse pulling, in the earth rolling back from the plow, in the newly turned earth below and the sky above.

We want not only to know that beauty but to have him, at the plow handles, know.

You see, Pearson, I have the belief that in this matter of form it is largely a matter of depth of feeling. How deeply do you feel it? Feel it deeply enough, and you will be torn inside and driven on until form comes.

You spoke of the story "Hands" in *Winesburg,* and it just happens that the particular story was the first one I ever wrote that did grow into form. I remember well the thing happening. I had been struggling with it and with other stories, and at last one rainy night — I was living in a little Chicago rooming house — it came clear.

I remember the feeling of exaltation, of happiness, of walking up and down the room with tears flowing from my eyes.

It was a kind of coming out of darkness into light.

And I do not believe that, when it happens so, the feeling that comes is one of pride in achievement. For the moment form is achieved, the thing goes entirely out of you. It no longer exists in you or as a part of you. It is rather like a child, born of a woman, that begins at once to have a life of its own aside from her life.

I think this whole thing must be in some way tied up with something I can find no other word to describe aside from the word

---

[1] Norman Holmes Pearson (1909–), professor of English at Yale. See in this connection the discussion in *The Oxford Anthology of American Literature,* edited by William Rose Benét and Norman Holmes Pearson, New York, 1938, pp. 1672–1673.

"morality." I suppose I think that the artist who doesn't struggle all his life to achieve this form, let it be form, betrays this morality. It is terribly important because, to my way of thinking, this morality may be the only true morality there is in the world.

For — and this is particularly true of the story writer — there are always others involved. The story writer is not in the position of the painter who is seeking form in nature. He brings other people into his stories.

And what is so little understood is that, in distorting the lives of these others — often imagined figures, to be sure — to achieve some tricky effect, you are betraying not only this indefinable thing we call form, but that you are betraying all of life — in short, that it is as dirty and unworthy a thing to betray these imagined figures as it would be to betray or sell out so-called real people in real life.

And so this whole matter of form involves, for the story writer, also this morality. I should think it might very well be made the whole point of the introduction for your book. It is the thing so terribly important to every artist.

And it may well be that, in some way, it is just this artist's point of view, this morality, always to be gone toward, and that occasionally forces him to bring his materials into real form, that is the only thing that may, in the end, pull mankind out of its mess. Sincerely

323.   [TROUTDALE, VIRGINIA, SEPTEMBER 16, 1937]

To JOHN PAUL CULLEN [1]

Dear Cullen: I think your letter one of the most generous and friendly I ever got. It touched me where I live. And I don't intend to pinch or cramp your generosity.

First of all, I think I should tell you, quite frankly, about my finances. For a good many years, excepting only one year — and this would cover my whole career as a writer — I have made practically no money.

I did have one year when I made a good deal, largely, I think, because that year I was with a publisher who plunged on advertising. He went broke later. I guess you know, Cullen, that American people do not buy books. They don't buy anything. Like everything else, books are sold to people.

[1] John Paul Cullen of the Veterans Administration had suggested Anderson's eligibility for a pension as a Spanish-American War veteran.

I had that one fat year and with the money raked in bought me the little farm, here in the Virginia hills, and built the stone house in which I live. You must come down and see me here next summer. I don't stay here in the winter, largely because of the damn sinus that sends me off to seek warmth. The book that paid the bill was the one you like, *Dark Laughter*. I have written others that go deeper and will, in the end, stand up better, but that is another matter.

I was born, Cullen, in 1876, so you can figure how aged I am. On the whole I'm pretty well, except for getting floored about twice a year, but I presume the damn thing does cut down my vitality and my ability to turn out work. It had me in the hospital last winter.

I presume I don't make more money because I won't write the sort of glamorous stuff the popular magazines want, and there have been years, and this since I have been recognized as, well, you know, among American writers, when I haven't made, aside from lecturing, which I detest, two thousand dollars.

So it is a constant struggle, and I am, for that reason, going to take advantage of your offer to help. I'll be here until October 15th, and I'm going to see the doctor and my friend Funk [2] and send you the papers. As a matter of fact, I held off for so long, making an application, out of pride. When that war broke out, I was working as a laborer at damn heavy, disagreeable work, and so the war, Cuba, etc., was rather a holiday to me. You see, I didn't get shot at, nor did I shoot anyone, although I did come near passing out with malaria.

I'll send you the papers, and I'll be along, sometime in October, driving to New York, and we'll have together the food and the drinks coming to us.

As for Whit, [3] I like the cuss, although I think he has a great shortage of the sense of humor that makes life most worth living. Between ourselves, I think the real sour bird out there [4] was Ransom. [5] That one has that thing so aggravating about many Southerners, a wholly unjustified feeling of superiority. He [is] so damned softly and gently superior that it makes me want to shout, "Balls."

There isn't any way of telling you how much I appreciate your letter.

[2] Charles H. Funk.
[3] Whit Burnett (1899–), of the staff of the Writers' Conference in the Rocky Mountains at Boulder, and editor of *Story*.
[4] At the Writers' Conference.
[5] John Crowe Ransom (1888–), poet and critic.

324.   [MARION, VIRGINIA] OCTOBER 12, 1937

MR. GILBERT WILSON,[1] TERRE HAUTE, INDIANA

Dear Gilbert Wilson: I am sending you under separate cover today a few more photographs. I believe my wife considers these photographs of a good deal of value to her because she has no copies. She has asked me to ask you to be careful with them and please return them. I don't feel quite as determined about it as she seems to be.

You see, I am dictating this letter so it will go a little easier for you.

I note that you are going to be in New York a little later, and I expect I will be there on about the 25th of this month and will be staying at 54 Washington Mews, telephone Gramercy 7–4373, until about November 10.

I will then be out of New York until about the 20th and after that will be there at least until Christmas; so if you come to New York, I would be glad to see you there. I am leaving Marion today, but will be wandering for a week or two, but any mail addressed to Marion will be forwarded.

Now as to speaking of some of the characters in my book[s] —

The idea embarrasses me a little. After all, it is a good deal like asking a mother to choose among her children.

I am very fond of the character of Dr. Parcival in the story "The Philosopher" in *Winesburg, Ohio* and also of the character Joe Welling in the story "A Man of Ideas."

There is also the figure of Hugh McVey in *Poor White* and in the same book the figure of the little harness maker, Joe Wainsworth.

I also like very much the Negro, Burt, in the story called "[The] Man Who Became a Woman." The story is in a book called *Horses and Men*.

I like also the old gaffer, Sponge Martin, in the first chapter of the novel *Dark Laughter* and the figure Beaut McGregor in an early novel called *Marching Men*.

I think this will surely be enough for you if you can get ahold of these books, and I think also that you may note that most of the characters in all my stories are working people. Sincerely yours

P.S. Unfortunately [the] *Scribner's*[2] you mention I have not yet received. I'll be on the watch-out for it.

---

[1] Gilbert Wilson, muralist, of Terre Haute and later associated with Antioch College, was assembling photographs of Midwestern literary men for "a kind of mural 'song.'"

[2] F. J. Ringel, "Gilbert Wilson: Mural Painter," *Scribner's*, CI, 45–51 (May, 1937).

325. [NEW YORK, OCTOBER 28, 1937]

To JOHN PAUL CULLEN

Dear Paul: I read half through the book [1] and sat down and made some notes. I wrote:

Dear Paul —

I guess that what most critics would say is that the weakness in your stories lies in the fact that they don't go deep enough.

You do, however, get something that feeds a man; there is a rich, full sense of the town, youth, streets, the river.

I do miss something of the curious sharp sadness and pain of childhood and boyhood.

I wrote as above before I had read the story "Joe-Joe," which seemed to me very mature and fine. It had solidity. It seems to me, Paul, that the one story proves you a writer beyond a doubt. I guess we all have this other, the hunger back into childhood and boyhood, but the Joe-Joe story comes straight into manhood. If my own hand had written it, I would be proud. Sincerely yours

[P.S.] I think, Paul, that if you intend to follow through as a writer, there is but one way.

To write and write and write, until presently the life in you and about you runs more and more naturally down through your hand to the paper.

More and more and more. I know no other way.

326. [NEW YORK, NOVEMBER 2, 1937]

To JOHN PAUL CULLEN

Dear Paul: I think I should write you at once to get something straightened out. It is about my getting it in the neck. You are all wrong there, Paul. It's true that among American writers who have got a lot of attention I've probably made less money than any of them. Well, what of it? I haven't found that the ones who have made a lot of dough have got much fun out of it.

You see, Paul, I have had and am having a damn good life. In some way I have managed to sleep pretty well, have loved some damn fine women, wear good enough clothes, have always had a roof over my head.

[1] Cullen's book of short stories, *Hello Wisconsin!* (1931).

People like you come along and do swell things for me. In my wanderings I've probably covered more of the country than most men. I have known, pretty intimately, practically all the outstanding men in the arts in my time.

It has been a damned good life for me. It is right now. I might very well have got it in the neck a hundred times worse by being a big popular success. People do pretty nasty things to successful men. Don't go wrong on that, Paul.

I just wanted to get this clear with you, Paul.

Last night Eleanor gave a little cocktail party, mostly her radical friends, and Jenkins [1] came. He didn't bring his new wife, because she was working last night. He's O.K. As always, My regards to Mary

327.   [NEW YORK, NOVEMBER 9, 1937]

To LAURA LOU COPENHAVER

Dear Mother: Word has come that Mary is to arrive Thursday, the day I leave. Eleanor will not leave until Friday, joining me in Philadelphia. Last night we had Paul [1] to dinner. He seems to have recovered from the shock of losing the *New Yorker* job.

You are right about the story "Not Sixteen." [2] What happened was that I ran on into the story while writing the adventures in the S[panish] War. I realized what had happened after I got into it, but did not want to stop. Then later I thought I'd better have it copied, to work from, as was.

The typewriter is O.K. I merely work faster with the pen because I have never become expert on the machine.

I presume that it should be made clear that the men pinned the cards on their own coats.

Your letter was grand, Mother. It expressed a lot I feel. I think that, in the case of Hemmy,[3] there is too much talk of style. In the end the style is the man. I keep wondering why the man feels life as he does. It is as though he saw it always as rather ugly. "People have it in for me. All right. I'll go for them." There is the desire always to kill. Stein says that it is because he cannot bear the thought of any other men as artists, that he wants to occupy the entire field.

[1] A New York student who had attended the Boulder Writers' Conference.

[1] Paul Rosenfeld.
[2] "Not Sixteen," *Tomorrow*, V, 28–32 (March, 1946).
[3] Ernest Hemingway.

There is this sharp difference between the man and, say, Wolfe or Faulkner. They may write of terrible happenings, but you feel always an inner sympathy with the fact of life itself. Lots of love

328.   [NEW YORK, ?DECEMBER 4, 1937]

To ROGER SERGEL

Dear Roger: I find myself deep in one of my periods of rebellion against all organization of life. I think it must be because, here in New York, associating a good deal with the intellectuals, I hear so much of it. I get it at the breakfast table, at lunch with some man, in the evening at cocktail parties. Of course it is a part of E.'s job. At night the bed is strewn with *New Republics, Nations, Surveys,* the People's this and that.

So I get this mood. "To hell with all of it," I cry. "What has become of the modest men and women of the world? How do they know that a world they are so busy making will be a better or more livable world?" I shall be glad to go back to the farm, hear the brook chattering by my cabin.

I have been rereading *Annals of a Sportsman,* Turgenev. Do you know it? How much better revolutionary stuff, really.

I think you are wrong to be so troubled. We should have more laughing men. When will just joy in living come back?

You see the mood I am in. It will probably pass. I wish you had come. Damn.

Well, I am going to work. God bless us all.

[P.S.] Pardon the above mood. I am sure it must come often to you. We should see each other more often, laugh more, love more. Ain't it hell?

329.   [NEW YORK, DECEMBER 17, 1937]

To THOMAS WOLFE

Dear Tom: I do hope, Tom, you didn't take seriously the queer row we seemed to have got into that night at Mary's [1] house. I am a bit uncertain yet what it was all about.

We are leaving about the middle of next week, and I don't suppose we will be back here this winter.

I phoned you about the cocktail party Mary Emmett is [giving]

[1] Mary Emmett.

from 5 to 7 next Tuesday afternoon. She is doing it as some kind of scheme to raise money for the Spanish Loyalists; people are going to chip in $2 each.

Dreiser and a lot of others are coming, and I hope you can come, as I'd like to see you again. Sincerely

[P.S.] Why not have dinner with us afterwards at some nearby restaurant?

330.   [NEW YORK, DECEMBER 18, 1937]

To THOMAS WOLFE

Dear Tom: When I wrote you yesterday, suggesting that you have dinner with me Tuesday evening, I had no notion how you felt. As you have expressed such a hearty desire to chuck our acquaintance, why not? Sincerely

331.   [NEW YORK, ABOUT DECEMBER 21, 1937]

To ROGER SERGEL

Dear Roger: There is something very charming about the Jews. Here, in New York, I found myself unable to work in Mary's house. There is too much ringing of phones.

And besides, Mary is too rich. There are too many rare books and art objects about. There is something of the monk in me. I like bare walls.

Also, I adore hotels. They are charmingly impersonal.

I went to a Jewish hotel in the neighborhood. I am quite sure I'm the only Gentile in the hotel.

So, because the proprietor had read my books, I got a big room at ½ price. I think the man would have liked giving it to me. He said:

"I would like my son to meet you. I would like you to talk with him."

The clerk, very Jewish, leaned over his counter.

"In a certain story of yours (he named the story) you used the word 'fantod.' It puzzled me. I could not find it in the dictionary."

I do not sleep here. I came in the morning at nine. I found the Jewish chambermaid reading some of my ms. She was ashamed when I caught her.

"My son is in school. He has one of your books."

Is it not quite amazing? Is it not an amazing race? There is this culture hunger. They have the idea that I am culture.

I am really writing to wish you, Ruth, and the big sons a good holiday season.

I hope there has been and will be a great flood of demands for your plays. I hope you will have to hire more help, build a 20-story building.

The plan for coming there in July is still alive. Lots of love to all

332.   MEXICO CITY, FEBRUARY 24, 1938
To EDWARD H. RISLEY, JR.[1]

Dear Edward Risley: Your letter about the Granville Hicks was sent down to me here, and it amuses me; that is to say, the Hicks point of view amuses. It just happens that I had not read his *Great Tradition*. It is of course nonsense. It is true that in '31 and '32, when I went about a good deal in industrial cities, when I saw American working men eating out of garbage cans, etc., I got pretty wrought up. I think it must have been during those years that I got what of the red label has been pasted on me.

As for Hicks, he wrote me a few years ago about my former friendship with Jack Reed, wanted me to tell him any little facts, etc. I could; so I told him of a talk [I] had one night with Jack in which he said to me that if he could be sure he was a poet, really had the stuff, he would chuck the radicalism. I told Hicks that and was later amused to see the use he made of it, the twist he gave it to serve Communist ends.

Frankly, I don't think you can trust the Communists, and, as for yourself, I would a thousand times rather suggest that you trust your own natural reactions.

Yes, I would stand by the sentence: "All a man is should be found in his work."

As for Hicks, this I know, that Dreiser, one of my real friends, is no more a Communist than I am, and, only a few weeks ago, I had a note from Dos Passos that went a good deal further than I have here in saying, "To hell with them."

I think it much more sane and healthy to just go on your own judgment, whatever it is. Sincerely

[1] Risley, a Harvard undergraduate, who was later killed in World War II, had written Anderson on November 30, 1937, requesting information for a Harvard honors thesis. On February 15, 1938, he wrote that in his *The Great Tradition* Granville Hicks announced that Anderson had been won over, along with Dreiser, to the Communist cause.

[P.S.] And all of this doesn't mean that I am not, heart and soul, for anything that I think will bring to an end the dominance of business in American life. I don't at all mind being canned [?called] "red." I just object to the Communists trying to herd me into their camp.

333.   ACAPULCO, MEXICO, MARCH 18, 1938

To LAURA LOU COPENHAVER

Dear Mother: I have not written home for some days, and I suppose you may be in New York. However, I am not sure, so I send this to Marion. If you are not there, I hope Mr. Copenhaver opens it.

We are in a most wonderful place. The hotel here is perched high up on the rocks above the Pacific and is not, like most hotels, a matter of one big building, but consists of many small one-room or two-room houses, perched about on rocks, with winding paths among the rocks going to your own place, and everywhere dense tropical growth, palms and mango trees, and masses of many other tropical plants and flowers, all growing with tropical abandon.

And there is the Pacific, down below there, the waves beating on rocks, sea birds floating, and always, all day long, the most soft and balmy breeze you ever felt.

Mary came down here with us, and today she and Eleanor are off, in a boat, to visit some of the inner tropical lagoons, while I stay home to work. A Detroit newspaperman, Sam Marshall, came down with us, and he and Mary are going back to Mexico City tomorrow, leaving Eleanor and I alone here, I hope, for two or three weeks and for a grand rest. We will, I think, stay here until we start for home at the end of the month, as it is, by all odds, the most lovely place we have ever been in.

We are high up on the rocks, but there is a road up, and we go down in the car to the town by the seashore to bathe. There are at least a half-dozen marvelous beaches, and the water the softest, the cleanest, and the most satisfying to be in you ever saw.

It was, frankly, one hell of a job getting here, the road, over mountains most of the way, just being built, so that we had to creep along for some two hundred miles, but once here, it is paradise.

And such soft-speaking, soft-footed Mexican servants. How you and Mr. Copenhaver would love it.

The hotel is The Mirador. If you write, air mail, we will get it here in a few days.

It is impossible to describe how restful and grand it is. Lots of love to all

334. [?BROWNSVILLE, TEXAS], APRIL 1, [1938]

To GERTRUDE STEIN

Dear Gertrude: I will have to send this to the old address,[1] because I cannot make out the new one. Your writing, like my own, has a certain mystic quality. It seems strange to think of you two in any place other than the beautiful rooms in the rue de Fleurus.

Eleanor and I have been down into old Mexico. We went clear down, past Mexico City, to the southwest, to the Pacific, in the car, turning back at a place called Acapulco, where we had marvelous bathing on wide beautiful beaches. Most of the trip was over mountains, sometimes ten thousand feet up. It was certainly a new America to us; in the people, for the most part Indians, something very bitter and cruel, something very rhythmic and laughing.

We are on our way home now and got your letter here.

As for John, I haven't heard. He has got a little house in the country and is painting. God knows what will best bring out the poet in such a young painter. It may be that marriage will work for him.

I wish we could come to see you in your new place. It was a satisfaction always to think of you in the place we knew.

Lots of love to you both. I hope you are working away.

335. MARION, VIRGINIA, MAY 18, 1938

To HENRY SCHUMAN [1]

Dear Henry Schuman: I want to add my word of protest against the effort to suppress Ernest Hemingway's novel, *To Have and Have Not*. Mr. Hemingway is a great writer. Nothing he writes will hurt anyone. It would be a thousand times more intelligent to fight the kind of evil he depicts than to fight him.

I hope you win. Sincerely

[1] Gertrude Stein had moved from 27 Rue de Fleurus to 5 Rue Christine, Paris. A letter, undated, from the new address inquires whether John Anderson had received a Guggenheim Fellowship.

[1] Henry Schuman, of Detroit, dealer in rare books. Detroit police authorities tried in May to ban the sale of *To Have and Have Not* in that city. Opposition was led by Alvin C. Hamer (a book dealer), and Henry Schuman. See *Publishers' Weekly* May 14, 1938, p. 1935; and June 25, 1938, p. 2434.

336.   MARION, VIRGINIA, JULY 2, 1938

MR. JACQUES CHAMBRUN, 745 FIFTH AVENUE, NEW YORK

Dear Chambrun: I have your letter about the outline I made for the *Redbook* story. I am not altogether surprised. [The] truth is that, as it has turned out, I would have been unable to deliver. I began working on the story and suddenly realized that the story I wanted to write did not at all follow the outline I had made. I began to be interested. What had happened is that I have been busily writing on the story, which I expect will turn out to be a novel, ever since I sent you the outline. I have already probably written 20 or 25 thousand words. And I, when your letter came, was just about to sit down and write, telling you the situation. The difficulty is that I am at present so absorbed in the story that has come out of the brief outline that for a long time I may not be able to do anything else.

The other evening I was sitting in my home when some friends came. I began telling them a story of a rather strange character. It was about a man I formerly knew. The man had been a crook. He had belonged to a gang of safeblowers. He reformed.

The man got into politics. He became a figure in the city. He fell in love with a young painter. She was at the time engaged to be married to another painter, a German.

At this time I was living in a little town down on Mobile Bay. I knew and was interested in the man who had been a crook. For a time the woman wavered between the two men, and my ex-crook friend advised her to come down and have a talk with me.

She came. She stayed for a time. She lived in a small hotel in the town, and almost every day I saw and talked with her.

However, she did not ask my advice about the two men, but one day suddenly disappeared. She had decided to go to the man who was an ex-crook. They were married. She continued to struggle along as a painter, but had got no recognition.

Some two summers later I was in the North living in a house up on Green Bay, which is an arm of Lake Michigan. My acquaintance, the ex-crook, had, before he became a safeblower, been a mechanic. There was a kind of iron egotism about the man. He thought that anything he built with his own hands was perfect. He built himself a 20-foot boat, put in it an outboard motor, and came up to where I was living that summer.

It happened that when he arrived I had some guests staying for the weekend with me, and he was afraid that I would think he was not married. He arrived in the little bay in which my house stood during a storm and just did manage to get in. The woman, the painter, who had something very refined and ladylike about her, had been horribly frightened. He was afraid I would think that they were not married and that the fact of their not being married might shock my friends; so immediately upon his arrival and before he got into dry clothes, he took me into the kitchen of the house to show me his marriage certificate. The two people stayed about for perhaps a week. There was a small fishing village near by, and some of the fishermen came to me. The fishermen were alarmed about the idea of his taking the woman back down the lake to Chicago in the boat he had built. They asked me to plead with him.

"If the fool wants to venture alone, that is all right, but do not let him take that woman," said the fishermen.

However, and in spite of my protestations, he would insist upon the woman returning with him in the boat. I shall never forget the expression on her face as they set out. There was a look of terror which she was determined to conceal from her man.

What happened was that half way down the lake they ran into a violent storm. The woman was drowned, but after some 18 hours the man was picked up still alive.

The woman had been struggling for years for some recognition as a painter, and that year a painting she had done was pronounced by judges the best painting produced by a living Middle Western painter. She, of course, never received the prize or the recognition. Before it was publicly announced, she was dead.

I did not see this man again for several years, but was very curious when I did see him to see if the tragedy through which he had lived had shaken his egotism. It had not. He still believed just as implicitly in anything his hands had touched. He did not mention the tragedy in the lake, but stood for a long time boasting to me and declaring that any machine constructed by his hands was safe. I have never written this story. I wonder if it was also too tragic. Sincerely yours [1]

[1] Some of the phraseology of this letter was changed by Mrs. Laura Lou Copenhaver, and the letter was sent in revised form on July 5. Anderson's original draft is here reproduced.

337.   [?MILFORD, IOWA, JULY 16, 1938]

To MAXWELL PERKINS

Dear Max Perkins: I have taken a fancy to the idea of having a room in my home decorated with framed photographs of some of my old personal friends. This because, as life runs, you so seldom see the people of whom you are fond. At least a photograph, to bring thoughts of your friends, is something.

Have you a photograph, for framing, that you can send me?[1]

Address it to Troutdale, Virginia.

I will be grateful. Sincerely

Dear Max —

Have been writing my head and arm off on a new long novel I call *A Late Spring*.

338.   [?TROUTDALE, VIRGINIA, AFTER JULY 21, 1938]

To FRIEDA MEREDITH DIETZ

Dear Frieda Meredith Dietz: Your letter[1] is very interesting, but indeed it does arouse in me a desire to comment.

First of all, I think you are very courageous. I am a little sorry that you feel you must limit yourself to Southern writers. You see, I am not enthusiastic about the regional idea. I think any art expression, if it has any importance, becomes important only when it becomes also universal. You will pardon me. You see, I was born a Yank, of a Southern father to be sure, but in Yankee land. I got all my early impressions there, and while I love the South, I shall always feel rather an illegitimate son. It must, I think, have been instinct that led me, when I did settle in the South, to settle among mountain folk, who aren't, you know, very Southern. They are just people, and it is just people, not Yanks or Southerners as such, that interest me.

I remember once going to a dance of Southern cotton mill girls and boys in a cotton mill village in Georgia and, as I sat watching, amusing myself by picking out from among the dancers those who in some odd way suggested to my mind more or less famous people I had known. I

---

[1] This is but one of many such notes sent by Anderson to various friends.

[1] On July 21, 1938, Miss Dietz wrote Anderson, saying that she and her brother, August Dietz, Jr., of The Dietz Press, Richmond, Virginia, were going to revive the *Southern Literary Messenger* and requesting support. It was to be "a revival of the 'Old South.'"

assure you that I found there among the mill people a certain very aristocratic Southern woman poet whom I much admire. I found Theodore Dreiser, Harry Hansen,[2] John Marin, the painter. Please don't tell on me. I found James Branch Cabell. He danced just as Cabell would have danced had he been born a mill hand.

So you see [how] hopeless I am about regional literature.

I shall turn your letter over to Eleanor, who will send you the data, etc., for which you ask. Can't you pay any money for articles, stories, etc.? I do so love money. Sincerely

339.   [TROUTDALE, VIRGINIA, JULY 25, 1938]

To MAXWELL PERKINS

Dear Max: I am delighted to have the picture,[1] which I think is a fine one.

I am thumping away at the novel. I call it *A Late Spring*. It is the story of a man and his adventures in trying to learn to live, to get belief in himself, to feel himself a man with a man's right to live. I started it in the form of letters sent to a boyhood friend, but after writing some thousands of words, one day I suddenly began to wonder why any of us wanted to write. This sent my mind off on a new angle, and as I have got into the habit of thinking on paper, I proceeded to write some twenty or thirty thousand words on that subject.

Then when I went back to the novel, I didn't like the form and began again, telling the story this time straight out, and that is what I am now doing.

It is too bad about Tom.[2] Poor man he must wear himself out. He got suddenly angry at me. Something was said at a dinner party [3] that he took as personal. It wasn't meant so. I didn't say it, but he included me in his anger. Then one day when I was lunching at the Brevoort with a woman who was doing an article on my work for some French magazine, he came in, called me aside, and began to berate me,[4] saying

[2] Harry Hansen (1884–), literary editor of the *Chicago Daily News*, 1920–1926, and in 1938 on the *New York World-Telegram*.

[1] See Letter 337.

[2] On July 20, 1938, Maxwell Perkins wrote that Wolfe had been "mighty ill with pneumonia" in Seattle. On July 29 Perkins replied to Anderson's letter explaining that Wolfe was angry with himself on such occasions as here described and simply "loosing his anger against the nearest target."

[3] See Letter 329.

[4] This luncheon actually occurred on December 17, 1937.

that I was woman-ridden, that I had shot my bolt, was done as a writer, etc., etc. It apparently all happened because of a chance remark made by someone else. God, the poor man must wear himself out with these outbreaks. There is something very real and sweet about him under it all.

I wish we could induce you to come here for a visit with us. As always

340.   [TROUTDALE, VIRGINIA, ?AUGUST 1, 1938]

To ANITA LOOS

Dear Anita: I have for a long time been pounding away at John to bring you and himself for a visit, but not being successful, have asked him for a photograph, which he has promised to have taken. This because I am doing a room in my house with photographs of men friends.

I am also planning to do one of women. Can I have one of yours, and will you please hold John up to having his taken?

There was a little play, made from my story "I'm a Fool," on the radio the other evening, done by Orson Welles,[1] and they tell me it was quite charming. I didn't hear it. Did you?

If John won't come to see us, why don't you come this way when you go East? You came to see me once and, if I am not mistaken, wrote *Gentlemen Prefer Blondes*[2] during your visit. I've got a much better gal now. God knows what you would do. With love

341.   [TROUTDALE, VIRGINIA] AUGUST 6, 1938

To ALFRED STIEGLITZ

Dear Stieglitz:

I have written, asking for the photograph. It is a way to remind myself how rich I am. Already I have some twelve or fifteen men looking down from the wall of the room. It is just possible that the whole thing will be too much for many people. There is such a richness of life, of character.

I was shocked to hear of your illness. It doesn't seem right. Illness in you is too much like a mountain running from the moon.

But I know this, that the life in you is real life. I have made an epitaph for my own grave: "Life not Death is the Adventure."

You shall always mean sweet life to me. As always

[1] Orson Welles (1915–), actor and producer.
[2] Published 1925.

Anderson at Ripshin Farm with a Favorite Dog — 1938

342.   [TROUTDALE, VIRGINIA] AUGUST 27, 1938

TO GEORGE FREITAG [1]

Dear George Freitag: It sometimes seems to me that I should prepare a book designed to be read by other and younger writers. This not because of accomplishment on my own part, but because of the experiences, the particular experiences, I have had.

It is so difficult for most of us to realize how fully and completely commercialism enters into the arts. For example, how are you to know that really the opinion of the publisher or the magazine editor in regard to your work, what is a story and what isn't, means nothing? Some of my own stories, for example, that have now become almost American classics, that are put before students in our schools and colleges as examples of good storytelling, were, when first written, when submitted to editors, and when seen by some of the so-called outstanding American critics, declared not stories at all.

It is true they were not nice little packages, wrapped and labeled in the O. Henry manner. They were obviously written by one who did not know the answers. They were simple little tales of happenings, things observed and felt. There were no cowboys or daring wild game hunters. None of the people in the tales got lost in burning deserts or went seeking the North Pole. In my stories I simply stayed at home, among my own people, wherever I happened to be, people in my own street. I think I must, very early, have realized that this was my milieu, that is to say, common everyday American lives. The ordinary beliefs of the people about me, that love lasted indefinitely, that success meant happiness, simply did not seem true to me.

Things were always happening. My eyes began to see, my ears to hear. Most of our American storytelling at that time had concerned only the rich and the well-to-do. I was a storyteller but not yet a writer of stories. As I came of a poor family, older men were always repeating to me the old saying.

"Get money. Money makes the mare go."

For a time I was a laborer. As I had a passion for fast trotting and pacing horses, I worked about race tracks. I became a soldier, I got into business.

---

[1] George Freitag of Canton, Ohio, entered into correspondence with Anderson in the summer of 1938 on problems of the young writer. He published "The Transaction" in the *Atlantic* for August, 1938.

I knew, often quite intensively, Negro swipes about race tracks, small gamblers, prize fighters, common laboring men and women. There was a violent, dangerous man, said to be a killer. One night he walked and talked to me and became suddenly tender. I was forced to realize that all sorts of emotions went on in all sorts of people. A young man who seemed outwardly a very clod suddenly began to run wildly in the moonlight. Once I was walking in a wood and heard the sound of a man weeping. I stopped, looked, and listened. There was a farmer who, because of ill luck, bad weather, and perhaps even poor management, had lost his farm. He had gone to work in a factory in town, but, having a day off, had returned secretly to the fields he loved. He was on his knees by a low fence, looking across the fields in which he had worked from boyhood. He and I were employed at the time in the same factory, and in the factory he was a quiet, smiling man, seemingly satisfied with his lot.

I began to gather these impressions. There was a thing called happiness toward which men were striving. They never got to it. All of life was amazingly accidental. Love, moments of tenderness and despair, came to the poor and the miserable as to the rich and successful.

It began to seem to me that what was most wanted by all people was love, understanding. Our writers, our storytellers, in wrapping life up into neat little packages were only betraying life. It began to seem to me that what I wanted for myself most of all, rather than so-called success, acclaim, to be praised by publishers and editors, was to try to develop, to the top of my bent, my own capacity to feel, see, taste, smell, hear. I wanted, as all men must want, to be a free man, proud of my own manhood, always more and more aware of earth, people, streets, houses, towns, cities. I wanted to take all into myself, digest what I could.

I could not give the answers, and so for a long time when my stories began to appear, at first only in little highbrow magazines, I was almost universally condemned by the critics. My stories, it seemed, had no definite ends. They were not conclusive and did not give the answers, and so I was called vague. "Groping" was a favorite term. It seems I could not get a formula and stick to it. I could not be smart about life. When I wrote my Winesburg stories — for the whole series I got eighty-five dollars — such critics as Mr. Floyd Dell and Henry Mencken, having read them, declared they were not stories. They were merely, it seemed, sketches. They were too vague, too groping. Some ten or fifteen years after Mr. Mencken told me they were not stories, he wrote, telling of how, when he first saw them, he realized their strength and beauty. An imagined conversation between us, that never took place, was spoken about.

And for this I did not blame Mr. Mencken. He thought he had said what he now thinks he said.

There was a time when Mr. Dell was, in a way, my literary father. He and Mr. Waldo Frank had been the first critics to praise some of my earlier work. He was generous and warm. He, with Mr. Theodore Dreiser, was instrumental in getting my first book published. When he saw the Winesburg stories, he, however, condemned them heartily. He was at that time, I believe, deeply under the influence of Maupassant. He advised me to throw the Winesburg stories away. They had no form. They were not stories. A story, he said, must be sharply definite. There must be a beginning and an end. I remember very clearly our conversation. "If you plan to go somewhere on a train and start for the station, but loiter along the way, so that the train comes into the station, stops to discharge and take on passengers, and then goes on its way, and you miss it, don't blame the locomotive engineer," I said. I daresay it was an arrogant saying, but arrogance is also needed.

And so I had written, let us say, the Winesburg stories. The publisher who had already published two of my early novels refused them, but at last I found a publisher. The stories were called unclean, dirty, filthy, but they did grow into the American consciousness, and presently the same critic who had condemned them began asking why I did not write more Winesburg stories.

I am telling you all of this, I assure you, not out of bitterness. I have had a good life, a full, rich life. I am still having a full, rich life. I tell it only to point out to you, a young writer, filled as I am made aware by your letter to me, of tenderness for life, I tell it simply to suggest to you plainly what you are up against. For ten or fifteen years after I had written and published the Winesburg stories, I was compelled to make my living outside of the field of writing. You will find none of my stories even yet in the great popular magazines that pay high prices to writers.

I do not blame the publishers or the editors. Once I was in the editorial rooms of a great magazine. They had asked me in for an editorial conference.

Would it not be possible for them to begin publishing my stories?

I advised against it. "If I were you, I would let Sherwood Anderson alone."

I had been for a long time an employee of a big advertising agency. I wrote the kind of advertisements on which great magazines live.

But I had no illusions about advertising, could have none. I was an advertising writer too long. The men employed with me, the business-men, many of them successful and even rich, were like the laborers, gamblers, soldiers, race track swipes I had formerly known. Their guards down, often over drinks, they told me the same stories of tangled, thwarted lives.

How could I throw a glamour over such lives? I couldn't.

The Winesburg stories, when first published, were bitterly con-demned. They were thrown out of libraries. In one New England town, where three copies of the book had been bought, they were publicly burned in the public square of the town. I remember a letter I once received from a woman. She had been seated beside me at the table of a friend. "Having sat beside you and having read your stories, I feel that I shall never be clean again," she wrote. I got many such letters.

Then a change came. The book found its way into schools and col-leges. Critics who had ignored or condemned the book now praised it.

"It's Anderson's best work. It is the height of his genius. He will never again do such work."

People constantly came to me, all saying the same thing.

"But what else of mine have you read since?"

A blank look upon faces.

They had read nothing else of mine. For the most part they were simply repeating, over and over, an old phrase picked up.

Now, I do not think all of this matters. I am one of the fortunate ones. In years when I have been unable to make a living with my pen, there have always been friends ready and willing to help me. There was one man who came to me in a year when I felt, when I knew, that I had done some of my best and truest work, but when, no money coming in, I was trying to sell my house to get money to live.

He wanted, he said, one of my manuscripts. "I will lend you five thousand dollars." He did lend it, knowing I could never return his money, but he did not deceive me. He had an affection for me as I had for him. He wanted me to continue to live in freedom. I have found this sort of thing among the rich as well as the poor. My house where I live is filled with beautiful things, all given to me. I live well enough. I have no quarrel with life.

And I am only writing all of this to you to prepare you. In a world controlled by business why should we not expect businessmen to think first of business?

And do bear in mind that publishers of books, of magazines, of newspapers are, first of all, businessmen. They are compelled to be.

And do not blame them when they do not buy your stories. Do not be romantic. There is no golden key that unlocks all doors. There is only the joy of living as richly as you can, always feeling more, absorbing more, and, if you are by nature a teller of tales, the realization that by faking, trying to give people what they think they want, you are in danger of dulling and in the end quite destroying what may be your own road into life.

There will remain for you, to be sure, the matter of making a living, and I am sorry to say to you that in the solution of that problem, for you and other young writers, I am not interested. That, alas, is your own problem. I am interested only in what you may be able to contribute to the advancement of our mutual craft.

But why not call it an art? That is what it is.

Did you ever hear of an artist who had an easy road to travel in life?

343.   TROUTDALE, VIRGINIA, AUGUST 27, 1938

TO GEORGE FREITAG

[No salutation] Note.

Writing can be, like the practice of any other art, a way of life. It is what we all want, to find a way to live. There is this town, the people of the town or of a city street, trees along a street, familiar fields, old houses with children playing in the yard, a fat prosperous-looking man coming out of a big house set far back from the street.

What is he like?

He is rich. He employs a chauffeur to drive his car. He cannot help wondering what his chauffeur thinks of him. Many of our rich people are a little frightened when they think of their wealth.

"I have this security in life. Do I really deserve to have it?"

These eternal questions always rising up from deep down within ourselves. We keep trying to hush the inner voices.

The rich man has a house filled with servants. He would like to think that they all love him. Our so-called Southern aristocrats are always telling of how their ancestors were adored by their black servants. Page Stark Young. He will tell you.

We live in a world in which most of the channels of public expression are ruled by the advertisers, and it is difficult to write of human life, giving yourself to the life immediately about you, without getting upon forbidden ground.

It can be done. Trick writing can be learned. It is a trade, not an art. It may be all right. Formerly I used to grow indignant because so many writers seemed to be selling out. Now I think it doesn't matter. I think every man writes as well as he can. Ordinary people need to be amused, taken away from thought. Life itself is too terribly real for them. We hear of great statesmen, scientists, etc., who spend their leisure hours reading detective stories. Why not? The statesman might begin thinking of how he got to where he is. The scientist had made some great discovery, but he is using his knowledge for his own private ends. He is no better or worse than the rest of us. But above all things he doesn't want to think.

We live, you see, in a thin age. We can't take it. There may have been times, periods in the history of man, when man did face the moral obligation of living. In our age we can't do it. Don't blame us too much.

I have become a veteran among American writers. Where have the years gone? How little I have done.

Young writers, new men among writers, are always writing letters to me. They come to see me. "How can I write as I please and still make a living?" It is a question for which I have no answer. To tell the truth, I am not interested in how you make a living.

I am interested only in what you give me, in how much you extend my own knowledge of life. You came from a different environment. You were born in a rich or a well-to-do family, while I came from a poor one.

What was the tone of life in your house? How did you feel? What made you what you are?

There are a thousand questions I want to ask you. Tell me in your work. Tell me. Tell me. The tales you tell, the way you tell them, the tone, color, form, all of these should reveal yourself to me. Give me a little of yourself. Extend a little my own knowledge, my own capacity for feeling, for understanding. I am a lustful man. I want everything. I knew a painter once who said to me, "I want to make love to a thousand, a hundred thousand women." I understand him. He didn't really want to bed the women. He wanted to go into them, penetrate into the mystery of women. It was because of something he wanted in his art.

It seems to me that we shall have more and more writing. People, it seems to me, are becoming more conscious of thinness. Now[a]days I myself no longer hope or want to be a popular writer. I write for myself and for other writers. It doesn't matter to me now that I am often misunderstood. I have come to realize that I have dreadful limitations. Once I thought, I will write so well, so clearly, will tell my tales so clearly, with such verve and gusto that everyone must accept me, but now I do not care for such acceptance. If you are mine, I cannot lose you. If I am yours, I will remain yours.

It is a way of making love. It is a way of losing self. It must be that the painter, as he paints, becomes always more and more conscious of nature, its moods, of the strange beauty coming unexpectedly out of what seem to others commonplace scenes. Why should I care whether you, the young writer, have had your breakfast, whether or not you have money to pay your rent or buy a car? I care only that you may broaden my own vision, increase my own capacity to feel, add a little to my understanding of others.

344.   [TROUTDALE, VIRGINIA] AUGUST 29, 1938

MR. JACQUES CHAMBRUN, 745 FIFTH AVENUE, NEW YORK

Dear Jacques Chambrun: I have your letter giving a very full report on the stories sent you, and going over it makes me feel very grateful to you. You have been very patient, and I do not know what more could have been done.

The experience you have had with my work has been my own since I began writing. You sold for me a reprint of the story "I Want to Know Why" for $500.00, but when written, none of the magazines would take the story. I had to sell it to some little highbrow magazine for $25.00.[1] So also with such stories as "I'm a Fool" and "Death in the Woods."[2] For several years the man O'Brien[3] selected stories of

---

[1] "I Want to Know Why" first appeared in Smart Set, LX, 35–40 (November, 1919). The "reprint" was in Golden Book, VII, 501–506 (April, 1928).

[2] "I'm a Fool" first appeared in the Dial, LXXII, 119–129 (February, 1922). "Death in the Woods" first appeared in the American Mercury, IX, 7–13 (September, 1926).

[3] Edward J. O'Brien edited the annual Best Short Stories from 1915 to 1940.

mine as the top stories of the year. He wrote me that he did it until he got tired of doing it, but none of the stories so selected brought me any money.

You understand, Chambrun, that I am not blaming the editors. There is involved, I dare say, a certain feeling about life. I was myself, for years, in business. I know also what the businessman is up against. It may be that my eyes see too much, my ears hear too much. For example, the whole Winesburg series, that have become rather American classics, had to be peddled to little art magazines. The whole series, a winter's work, brought me $85.00.

But, Mr. Chambrun, I hope you will not give me up as hopeless. I have tried several literary agents, and you are, far and away, the most intelligent man I have been connected with. I feel a kind of loyalty in you for which I am grateful.

There are other stories, all needing editorial work, but I will presently get at them.

Again accept my gratitude. Sincerely

345.   [TROUTDALE, VIRGINIA, ABOUT SEPTEMBER 12, 1938]

To MAXWELL PERKINS

Dear Max: Alas, the summer is getting to an end. I think we will probably come to New York shortly after October 1st. I thought I would make a kind of report to you on what I have been up to.

As I think I have told you, I have been wrestling with a novel. I have tackled it from two or three angles. Now I am at it again from a new angle. My theme is American men in relation to their women, and now the title I have got for the book is *Men and Their Women.* In getting at this theme I have decided to return to a form I used in *Winesburg, Ohio;* that is to say, taking a related group of people, their lives touching, never quite touching, what they do to each other, the growth of misunderstandings. I think I can bind all of these together, making a whole, as I did with this form in *Winesburg.*

I find myself curiously at ease in the form. It seems to relate itself to life as I feel it.

I have done a lot of work. Some of it will fit, some of it will not. I can't say just when the book will be ready.

And there is something else in my mind. Max, I have been writing now for twenty-five years. I have thought about writing a great deal.

I keep writing essays on the theme. What I have had in mind is the writer's obligations, his attitudes.

There is a lot of confusion.

Would it not be possible to make a textbook for students, say for the English classes in colleges, on the situation of the American writer? Such a book founded on the experiences of a veteran American writer. It would be a frank, but not certainly a bitter book. My idea is to approach the whole subject in a new way. Most of such books are prepared by college professors. They consist of fragments, samples of writing by older writers. It seems to me that the life of the writer, what difficulties the young writer has to face, what the real rewards are for the writer, are not touched on.

Do you think that a new kind of textbook might be built on this plan? Let me know what you think.

Does your house put out textbooks?

Are you in touch with this market?

It is the sort of thing I do constantly as a kind of by-product to my storytelling. I do it often to clear my own mind. It seems to me that it might be valuable.

346.   [TROUTDALE, VIRGINIA] SEPTEMBER 29, 1938

TO MAXWELL PERKINS

Dear Max: I was terribly upset by Tom's illness and death.[1] Such a grand young talent gone. Eleanor thought I should go down to Asheville to his funeral, but hating funerals, I didn't. I did, however, send his mother a wire. It's a bad business. Tom had so much of the thing needed, vitality — a great and rich talent.

To tell the truth, however, Max, when he separated himself from you, I was afraid for him. I had a friend once, strangely like Tom, who, after years of tearing himself to pieces, much as Tom did, ended by driving himself insane. Naturally, Max, I never mentioned this to anyone, a curious likeness in the two men, the same violence, talent, Mississippi River kind of force; and I speak of it to you only because, in spite of everything, you remained, to the end, closer to Tom than

---

[1] On September 14 Maxwell Perkins informed Anderson that Wolfe was seriously ill in the Johns Hopkins Hospital and that he went down there "when they operated." Wolfe died on September 15. On September 23 Perkins wrote to say that he and Mrs. Perkins had attended the funeral.

anyone else. I was often frankly afraid Tom would drive himself into the black hole of insanity as my other friend did, but my saying this is just for you.

The loss to literature is just a bitter fact. It hurts. We don't get many in Tom's class.

As regards the book on writing — Max, it is true that an amazing number of the younger writers have gone out of their way to say practically that I have shown them the way. They have written to tell me so. If it would be in decent taste to use some of the things said for the book on writing, to introduce it, it ought to count. Whether or not it would be in good taste to use these expressions of esteem in private letters, for example from such men as Tom, I a great deal doubt. It is something we could talk about, anyway.

I keep going on with the other book — I have now given [it] the title *Men and Their Women* — in the loose form I have told you about. Anyway, Max, it is the form that seems best fitted to what talent I have.

I wish we had got you down here this summer. I'll not be satisfied until you know this beautiful country. I'm sure if you came once, you would come again.

I'll be in New York sometime in October. As always

347.   [TROUTDALE, VIRGINIA, ?SEPTEMBER 25, 1938]

To ROGER SERGEL

Dear Roger: I didn't mean to suggest that Schevill or Lovett were criticizing Mr. Knight.[1] There was an idea in my own head. Perhaps you had put it there. You have spoken so often of him as one who had the answers. I had got that idea rather fixed, and when, having spoken of him — I was reading to them that portion of your letter outlining your scheme for restoring prosperity, and it included your reference to Knight. I think they both admire him. They didn't seem to think he was infallible. I had hoped he was.

We are all hoping for the god who will lead us out, or rather the Moses. X. seemed to think, when I was there, that Trotsky[2] was it. I didn't agree. You had me sold hard on Knight.

[1] Ferdinand Schevill and Robert Morss Lovett; presumably, Frank H. Knight (1885–), professor of economics at the University of Chicago, 1928–1951.

[2] Leon Trotsky, the Russian revolutionist, was in Mexico in 1938. In December he was to predict a revolution in the United States.

Roger, the suggestion, in your letter, that England may be deliberately building up Germany to see Germany throw itself against Russia does seem plausible. It is the sort of thing England has always done. I suppose it is real statesmanship. Manage so that your own people survive.

No, Roger, I have not lost interest in the man-to-man thing. Have you really found it? So often I can't make out whether I am myself sincere. It may be that I am sincere only in the one thing — in the desire to do good work.

It may be that I don't exist. I have been, in imagination, so many other people.

I have to use people constantly. I presume that I sometimes cry out for a more direct, more objective contact with living people because so much of my time is put in trying to think and feel myself in the body of others.

Did I tell you that Lovett talked of your *Arlie*,[3] saying it was one of the fine novels that had been produced by Americans? Love to all the family

348.   [New York, October 23, 1938]

To Charles H. Funk

Dear Andy: I got into New York a week ago tonight, having stopped over at the Hedgerow Theatre to see some new plays. Eleanor met me over there, and we drove in on Sunday evening, even the big four-way highway into the city so packed with cars that I am sure I must have shifted gears a thousand times in the hundred miles. To tell the truth I didn't want much to come here. There are such vast hordes of people. It has struck me this time more than ever before. I guess I feel that at best a man gets to know but a very few people during a life, and now, after all of these years of coming here, I am still the country boy, a little astonished and frightened. I know it is often lonely there for you, but there is a kind of greater loneliness in crowds.

Often, Andy, I think it is all a mistake. Here in New York, as at home there at Ripshin, I live too much like a rich man. I don't seem to myself to earn it. I keep questioning myself. It may all be due to the fact that all of this summer, as now, I haven't been doing any work I feel is of any importance. Do you sometimes feel that way about your own work

[3] *Arlie Gelston* (1923).

as a lawyer? I suppose you do. That must be what gives you the same kind of depressed feeling I have. We get, I guess, a little relief from playing with women, something of that sort, but it is false too. It would be better, perhaps, if a man could live in a more simple way, earn something with his hands, be a farmer or just a man sweeping dirt out of the street. I don't know.

And then again, at times I feel that it is all due to a kind of sellout. It may have begun with the World War, a new belief in brutality, the rest of the world too brutal with Germany and Germany now, in its turn, being more brutal. Do you not sometimes wish that we could get back to some simple belief, something perhaps like the early Christians may have had?

I presume I'll be more cheerful when, if ever, I begin to really work again. Anyway I wish you'd write. Tell me how it goes with you. Address 54 Washington Mews, N.Y.

349.   [NEW YORK, OCTOBER 30, 1938]

To CHARLES H. FUNK

Dear Andy: I guess the worst of the present low time with me has passed, as I seem to be at work again. I have my suspicions about it all. A man gets older, a certain buoyancy goes out of his body, and this is accompanied by a loss of buoyancy of spirit. And then too, we are probably both men too much absorbed in self, lean men who think too much.

The trouble with the creative impulse of which you speak is that it tends to lift you up too high into a sort of drunkenness and then drop you down too low. There is an artist lurking in every man. The high spots for the creative man come too seldom. He is like a woman who has been put on her back and made pregnant, but even after he gets the seed in him, he has to carry it a long time before anything comes out. We are an impatient lot, we moderns. It may be that life has made us so. Everything about us goes so fast we feel we must also go fast. Our fathers went slower, the horse and buggy, the oxcart way. We pay a lot for the period of invention when men thought they could solve all of life on the mechanical plane. They got the automobile, the flying machine, radio, etc. What of it?

Men still seem to have nothing to say to each other. The old comforting belie[f] in salvation, through Our Lord, has passed and something wanted, as between men and man, has not been found. It may be that what is wanted and so much needed is just more understanding.

I know that you have often been puzzled by a certain attitude in me. You have several times said that you thought I might make a great deal of money by my trade. You have seemed to think me foolish for not trying to do it.

But there's the rub. In my trade the money is made by giving the life you represent in your writing a certain twist — glamour is the word. It seems to me to be but creating new misunderstandings, like the illusion always being built up that there is happiness in getting rich. Occasionally you meet a rich man. Well, he is no more happy than you or I.

Sometimes I think, Andy, that the artist is the only religious man we have left. There was once a kind of religion of good honest work in workingmen, but it has been hurt, destroyed by modern high speed industry. We get cheap chairs, tables, suits of clothes, etc., but with them get a cheapened kind of man. As workman you can't work, day after day, making, for example, [cheap articles] [1] without growing immoral. We lose sense of the value of morality, the kind of morality, for example, that makes us so respect an Abraham Lincoln.

We are all, you see, constantly being rule[d] by a force that i[s] not at all physical. We have imaginations. Nearly all of our intercourse with each other is through the imagination. If I take you as friend, it is because you help feed my imagination. If I get high on some woman, it is because she does that or because I can exercise my own imagination by courting her. The trouble is that so few of us ever get trained imaginations. We play with the imagination like children playing with toys.

The false artist is always putting a false glamour over life. He betrays our imaginations. It is really the great betrayal, and it is being done all the time, in the movies, in the theater, in books and stories, over the radio. It is one of the things that ha[s] most to do with our loneliness, our separation from each other. It does it by killing any real understanding.

You speak of Bob. I have rather fallen out with him. There is a misunderstanding. I think perhaps that he thinks that I would like to hold him down, but I have just not wanted him to waste his young life and

[1] Seven words have here been deleted by the editors and the two in brackets inserted by them to indicate the general sense of the deleted material.

his energy. It seemed to me that getting into politics with no end in view he wanted to serve was a kind of walking on quicksand. Suddenly the ground gives way under him and he sinks. I only wanted Bob to see another thing, that [it] wasn't so damn important to be a big shot, that the human relationships about him were more important, that it was more important to run a really good newspaper in a small town than even to be governor of Virginia. If he wants to understand what I mean, let him go to Wytheville and take a look at Lee Trinkle. By going into politics in the way he has, he has already lost something that had begun to exist between him and you, him and others. I hated to see it happening.

Write when you are in the mood.

350.   [NEW YORK, OCTOBER 31, 1938]

To LAURA LOU COPENHAVER

Dear Mother: It was silly. I have got over the worst of it. It has probably just been one of the well-known times between. It is what George Moore [1] spoke of as the misery of not having a theme. It isn't that you are not well enough. Life simply, for the time, gets away from you, far off. If you are that sort, you simply have to live in others, that is to say, in the imaginative world; and when that seems to fail, you[r] all seems to slip away.

It isn't that a man don't write, but, at such times, he is like a composer who sits, day after day, at the piano, making sound[s] that don't get related.

Then you begin to push yourself too hard, to press. It is impatience. Life seems so short. "I must, I must," you cry. It does no good.

And all the time you realize that what is wanted is a kind of smiling looseness, to let it go through you as it will. You seem to know you are a fool when you can't help being a fool.

It is a crying shame that you are ill and still in bed. I know it is no fun, that it get[s] boring, wearisome. Mother, there must indeed be a devil. Who else could have invented disease, all such evils? The good God couldn't have been up to that.

E. and I leave Tuesday evening for Niagara Falls and, as I understand, will be there for about a week. We hope to make it a kind

---

[1] George Moore (1852–1933), the English novelist.

of delayed honeymoon. I presume she will send you the address. We have had remarkable weather here. Yesterday Mary went off to the country, and E. and I took a long walk up Fifth Ave. in the sun. We went into the Hippodrome and saw three games of a Spanish game, very swift, very beautiful, called "High Lo" [2] — it is pronounced that way — something between baseball and tennis, really marvelous to see.

I wrote to Orson Welles, but have not heard from him. I probably will. He is having a bad time with his new play, *The Death of Danton*,[3] and is putting off the opening. I suspect they have been rehearsing until they are about worn out. I'll probably hear from him later. Lots of love

Mary is really a new person. She is being quite wonderful. [P.S.] Love to Mr. C. & May. Also Leona.[4]

351. [NEW YORK, NOVEMBER 1, 1938]

To LAURA LOU COPENHAVER

Dear Mother: I hope this will find you again out of bed. Your two letters came and were fine. You are of course right. I am right in getting little or no satisfaction out of what I may have done in the past, and what I have been going through is of course inevitable. It is silly to make so much of it.

I think perhaps that a part of it has come from the inclination of others, always about, to try to think and feel nationally and even internationally. I get caught up in it. It won't work, is false for me.

You go about in the crowds here. The crowds are so strange. "So this is the material out of which what we call 'mankind' is made up." It is better when I begin to pick out individuals. I should always be like that, let others do the big, broad thinking that I cannot do. Let me take some little girl, or man, and try to think and feel my way through the one life. I should always be at just that.

Eleanor and I went last night to see the play *Oscar Wilde*,[1] but we did not like it too much. However, there was a packed house. I can't

[2] That is, *jai-alai*, the Spanish national ball game.
[3] *Danton's Death* by Georg Büchner (translated by Geoffrey Dunlop) opened November 2, 1938. It was produced and directed by Welles.
[4] Leona Gross, the Copenhavers' maid.

[1] By Leslie and Sewell Stokes.

quite understand this notion that perversion has in it some beauty and meaning that is not in the natural flow of life. I couldn't accept the notion that Wilde was a great genius. It has always seemed to me that the one notable thing he did was the jail ball[ad].[2] As played he is very womanish.

E. leaves tonight for Niagara, but I think I shall wait until morning and drive up. I like the idea of the drive through the country now, and while she cannot take the time to drive, she can drive back with me.

Speaking of autobiography, you should do your own. Why don't you get at it? Just put down the story, never minding about its being literature, and then someday hand it over to me to see what I could do with it.

We are awaiting word from Baltimore.[3] Love to all and many, many thanks for your letter.

352.   NIAGARA FALLS, NEW YORK [NOVEMBER 7, 1938]

To LAURA LOU COPENHAVER

Dear Mother: We are leaving here Wednesday morning and hoping this fine weather lasts until we get over the road, as much of it is through mountains. It is 450 miles, but as we will start early, we hope to make it in one day. I did alone coming up. We rather thought Mary might come up and drive down with us, as the road goes through very beautiful country, but there is no word from her.

E. is off this morning to interview the head man at the Mathieson.[1] This is their big plant, and, as at home, they are very powerful here. They have, I gather, a good deal to say as to what money, from the Chest, the Y. can have and accuse the Y. of being Communist, too sympathetic to labor, etc., etc. The truth probably is that they realize that labor is going to have its day, but are determined to fight to the last. I looked at some of the reports they have made, and there is the same thing that went on in the days just before the Civil War. They, Calhoun[2] and others, were very determined about the natural superiority of certain classes — God had made them so, etc., some to rule

---

2 "The Ballad of Reading Gaol" (1898).
3 Eleanor Anderson's sister, Mrs. Wilson, was about to have a child.

1 The Mathieson Chemical Corporation.
2 That is, John C. Calhoun (1782–1850).

and others to be servants. The literature of the period, from the Southern angle, was amazingly like the literature now being put out against
the rise of labor. It is an interesting thought, Mother, that what is
really on test now in the world is Christianity itself. I do not think
that Christianity can survive in a world given over to totalitarianism.
(I had a bad time with that word.) [3] What I mean to say is that all
assertion of superiority as natural, as between classes, is at bottom
anti-Christ; for whatever you may say about the failure of Christians
as Christians, there is no doubt that Christianity itself was the first
assertion in the world of the democratic idea.

E. wants to know what you are going to do and, like all of your
children, is ripe with advice. She thinks that, as soon as you are able,
you should go to Randolph.[4]

I really seem to be working, Mother, and, as usual, when I really
work, my gloom passes. I would tell you of what I am up to, but
have a curious superstition that I must not talk, that the taking in of
another, any other, brings in something as between the canvas and
myself. Lots of love, not only to you, but to Mr. C., to May, and to
Leona

353.   [NEW YORK, NOVEMBER 12, 1938]

To CHARLES H. FUNK

Dear Andy: I get your point. The idea is that you go so far in this
matter of giving them what they want, or what they think they want,
and no further, but it sounds to me rather like speaking of "fairly" fresh
eggs. The trouble is that you get this damn thing we call Sophistication. Spoiled eggs become simply spoiled eggs to you. That is really
the hell of education, of real education. In my play, *Winesburg, Ohio*,
I have an old character called Doctor Parcival, an old small-town
drunk, who says: "I am too wise. I know too much. For that I will be
crucified." There is something in it.

For example, I do try to go to the movies now and then. I went the
other night to see one called *The Great Waltz*, a movie pretending to
be written about the figure of Johann Strauss, who wrote that superla-
tive thing, "The Blue Danube," and what did they do with it and with

[3] A good instance of Anderson's uncertainty in spelling. Having crossed out
two unsuccessful attempts to write the word, he ended by writing "totilitarianism."

[4] That is, to the home of Randolph Copenhaver.

him? They made a goddam cheap movie guy of the man. It was sickening. It hurt me as though someone were sticking knives in me, the thought of the figure of such a man so cheapened, his work so cheapened, to make a Roman holiday for a few bum actors and the poor saps who sat looking at it and who never did have a chance in the world of knowing what Strauss and his work were really like.

No, Andy, it won't work.

I was up at Niagara Falls. E. had to go up there on her job, and I went along, lived for a week in a hotel just at the edge of the Falls. After several days of it I got to thinking — the truth is that the grandeur of it got rather boring — I got to thinking how much more interesting were the little, quieter rivers, and I've a notion that it is true, and it may be right there, Andy, that the trouble lies with all of this glamour business. We shouldn't, I presume, let all of the things you speak of in your letter and that I speak of, it may be too much, get us to roaring like a Niagara. I mean the industrial age. I do know that with myself, when I use my imagination, this trick we both have of pretending for the time that we are not ourselves but another, when I use it to try to feel my way, through the imagination, into some other quite common life — if there is such a thing as a common life — imagining myself, let us say, the mail carrier going along the street, o[r] a fellow digging a sewer, trying to think and feel my way into him, feeling in my body his weariness at the end of the day, the way the cop's feet hurt who has to stand for hours at a city street intersection, trying to be that one, living with that one's wife, in that one's house, etc., etc., I don't get so let down afterwards as I do trying to imagine myself some big God almighty thing. In the end it's more interesting too.

I think the election was a good thing all around. If we must be a two-party country, it's better to have two strong ones, and I presume the essence of democracy is that both sides, the capitalistic and the other, have their say. I don't, I admit, know just what you mean by saying that the Republicans must get back to the roots. Do you mean that they should try to tie up with the underdogs, as, apparently, the Democrats have more or less tried to do? If they did that, then wouldn't they be just as the Dems are, that is to say, being compelled to tie to the John Lewises,[1] etc. How could they do that and keep the big boys?

[1] John L. Lewis (1880–), president of the United Mine Workers of America.

Or do you simply mean that they should send more money to the county chairman. I could sure understand that wish. Write soon again [P.S.] You do seem a bit unnecessarily concerned about the law in shipping birds. Can't you imagine yourself a great lawbreaker and so get away from the tender conscience?

354.   [NEW YORK, MID-NOVEMBER, 1938]

To ROGER SERGEL

Dear Roger: I have been trying for several days to answer your letter, which was one of the finest I ever got. It brought you back to me in a queer way. I had for a long time been feeling that some intangible thing had happened to our friendship, but your letter made me realize that the fault was probably in me. I hate to be too sweeping — we are all just now, I am afraid, trying to think too big — but it may be posible that the thing going on now in the world, this new assertion of the power of sheer brutality, the insane new insistence on nationalism, etc., has set up a kind of wall between all individuals. God help the poor Jews. There are so many in the arts and on the edge of the arts. They keep coming to see me. I find them looking at me, as they must now look on all Gentiles, asking, asking, "You too, Brutus?" This suspicion of the individual toward the individual creeping through all life. We become afraid to go out to each other. I think that each of us must feel his own inadequacy. Perhaps we transfer it to other[s]. A kind of poison gets loose.

I have had recently an idea — that there should be started now a new movement for the protection of our democracy. It may be women should do it. Let us organize, outside politics if possible, just for that. It should be a no[n]-Jewish organization, to be spread through the country, in every town, non-Jewish to show the world that all of the feeling against totalitarianism is not directed by Jews. Exclude the Jews. They will get the idea.

Why not get Ruth excited? A kind of world's Gentile committee against totalitarianism. The time is ripe for it.

Here I am thinking big again. Forgive me, but it should be done and now.

I am myself fighting some inner thing, Roger, and don't know, as yet, how it will come out. When it does clear up — I mean this damn cloud of doubt, of myself, of my own ability to live, really live — I will work again, and in the meantime I find myself clinging to all of my old friendships. That is why your letter was so grand and why it was difficult for me to answer. It deserved so much. As always

355.   [NEW YORK, MID-NOVEMBER, 1938]

To ROGER SERGEL

Dear Roger: I am sorry we seemed unable to make the trip to Pittsburgh. It was largely due to E.'s being so tied up. I find myself more and more, I'm afraid, in the position of the man who has no very definite place in the scheme of things, while his wife keeps taking on more and more responsibilities. I was very gloomy about it for a time, but lately have been less so. Have I not long contended that we live in a matriarchy? So what? Lately I have again had offers to go to Hollywood, but although just now I earn nothing, I have not done so. It would be for me a great illness. I find that the trouble with me is that I cannot see life now with the glamour over it, [so] that the magazines from whom money could be got will not take my stories. Again so what?

As regards the woman's organization thing,[1] I wrote to Mrs. Roosevelt. It occurred to me that, although it might not be wise for her to do it, giving it a partisan slant, she might be interested to get some woman who would do it.

In the meantime, Roger, there may, a little, be an awakening. We have, it seems to me, rather been traveling through a desert. For a long time I have been terribly fed up on this business of explaining all life — that is to say, all that life lacks for us now — by economics. For a long time it seems to me that we have been simply fooling ourselves, telling ourselves that we were making progress when we were making only physical progress. It may be good that we be forced to find out, through our Hitlers, that we are still savages.

When you get home, write and tell me what you found at Pittsburgh. Did you drop the picture-selling thing? It seemed to me that the painters themselves did not become convinced. And I do hope you will be getting to N.Y. during the winter.

Will write again soon. Love to Ruth.

[1] See Letter 357.

356.   NEW YORK [?NOVEMBER 17, 1938]

TO RIFKA ANGEL [1]

Dear Rifka Angel: Mrs. Anderson and I recently came to New York and are staying here with our friend, Mrs. Emmett, at the above address. Your letter sent to me at Marion came to me here. Certainly I shall be glad to do as you say. In fact, there have been at least a dozen requests for such action come to my desk in the last few days. Is there any comfort at all to be got from the situation? Yes, a little. It is terrible, but the fact is that Germany has now, I'm sure, over-reached itself. I have now some hope that there will be a real reaction to this horrible anti-Jewish feeling run over the world. That is at least some comfort.

The thing makes it impossible to work. I begin to wonder how long it can go on — I mean this dominance of hate as a motive for action in the world. Is there indeed some horrible power in just hatred? Is it in all of us in some form, balanced there against the other thing in us? There is something sickening in the thought. What has made the whole world so sick?

We tried to find you in the telephone book, wanting you to go out and sit with us and dine with us. Later, I hope. Sincerely

357.   NEW YORK, NOVEMBER 25, 1938

TO THE LEAGUE OF AMERICAN WRITERS [1]

[No salutation] Answering yours addressed to writers, November 21.

Certainly there is danger. Democracy is man's only hope, but it will probably always be inefficient, and the passion for efficiency is strong in us.

I would suggest a nation-wide organization of women in defence of the democratic idea and to educate concerning its historic value to mankind. Women are wonderful organizers. They have tremendous influence upon the young, and that is the place to begin. Totalitarianism must inevitably lead to brutality, and I do not believe our Ameri-

[1] On May 5, 1938, Mrs. Rifka Angel, the painter, had written Anderson, asking his support for unrestricted immigration into the United States for the Jewish people.

[1] An association for American writers formed in 1935 as part of the "Popular Front." Anderson was for some time a member.

can women will want to see their young made into brutes. There is no real strength in brutality. Real strength is gentle.

I have already, in letters and in talk, suggested the beginning of the building of such an organization of women for this purpose to Mrs. Roosevelt and others, suggesting also that it might well be made — its leaders — non-Jewish, simply to show to the world that others beside[s] the Jews are interested in putting down race hatred. I am sure the Jewish people could not object, the object being to circumvent the notion that it is a Jewish movement. The Jews seem to be the point of attack now.

It would certainly interest me to have other writers push this idea. Get the women at it. Sincerely

[P.S.] Let this be my article.[2] In 500 words I could say no more.

358.   [NEW YORK, ?DECEMBER 13, 1938]

To ROBERT SHERWOOD

Robert Sherwood: There is a very American theme about the figure of Abraham Lincoln[1] that has not yet been done into a play and that should be done. It concerns the two men, Lincoln and Seward, his Secretary of State. As you know, Seward was very much the cynic. He was, as I think of him, a good deal the laughing cynic, certainly not much faith in humanity, an educated, cultured man, shrewd and smart, but with none of Lincoln's patient wisdom.

When Lincoln came East to be President he was no doubt pretty much subdued. The speeches he made on his way East were weak. He seemed struck dumb by the realization of what he had to face. His mind seemed clouded.

You know of the impertinent letter Seward wrote him, practically offering to take over the Presidency, letting Lincoln be a figurehead, a stuffed shirt, while he, Seward, cleaned up the mess, and how quietly and with what real dignity Lincoln put him in his place without humiliating him.

I am sure, Sherwood, that Seward, the New Yorker, the cynic, the

---

[2] Over the signature of several American writers, the League had sent out a letter to many of "the country's best authorities," one of them being Anderson, asking for contributions to a book on methods of combatting anti-Semitism.

---

[1] On December 14, 1938, Robert Sherwood thanked Anderson for approving of *Abe Lincoln in Illinois,* but said he would not write another play on the Lincoln theme.

smart Eastern man of the world, was the first of all the Eastern men who realized that in this raw Westerner a man of power had come to town. Douglas would have known. Lincoln had already crossed his path, but I am sure all the others thought Lincoln a fool and a political accident.

Seward got his lesson quickly, and it hit home. Of all the Cabinet he became Lincoln's closest and best personal friend. Each of the two men had something to supplement and strengthen the other. Both men had a literary flare, Lincoln's power lying in his basic tenderness, that of Seward in his cultural knowledge. He was a stylist.

I think the relationship profoundly affected the two men, that out of it two quite different men emerged, Seward building in Lincoln much of his later confidence in himself, helping to make Lincoln the man who in the end quietly and growing [in] power came to dominate his Cabinet and the Congress; while Seward, losing his arrogance, became in the end much more the Lincoln type of man.

Does it not seem to you that there is material for real drama there, in it something that might bring out the curious misunderstanding of the rest of the country by the New Yorker and of the East by the native Westerner?

If you were interested, I would be glad to try to develop the idea for you. Sincerely

359.   NEW YORK [DECEMBER 14, 1938]

To ROGER SERGEL

Dear Roger: I think we will get off for Marion on Saturday. Do let me [know] there how you come out with the man at Cleveland. I guess you feel as I do about organizations, but it seems men must work in them. My own feeling of distrust comes partly, I dare say, from the fact that my own work, when I do work, has to be so entirely an individual matter. I feel so much of the time just a guest in life.

I don't want really to think either of the future or the past, and anything I may have done means nothing to me. There is only out of that the memory of occasional hours of the joy of doing. It seems to me now that I want only to live in the NOW, in myself and others, to the top of my strength.

I dare say that every day a man lives brings him closer to the time of the trembling hands, the lean and slippery pantaloons,[1] etc., and I can't say I don't often think of that, usually at night when I am getting into bed. Hell, another day slipped by, so damn little done — too often nothing done. You know the feeling.

I wish I could say just what I want to say — something about a hope, that someday men may really begin to find each other again, this damn separateness through hate shown up for the nasty fake it is. Man's energy going into that.

Is that just a pipe dream, Roger?

There is some talk of my going to a little college, Olivet, in Michigan, for three or four weeks in Jan. for — well, God knows what — a kind of temporary decoration, I guess, that young men may look at me and again have hope for the race, eh, what?

We will be at Marion at least until the New Year. Write me there. Love to Ruth and the boys

360.   [MARION, VIRGINIA] DECEMBER 19, 1938

MR. DANIEL LERNER,[1] BROOKLYN, NEW YORK

Dear Daniel Lerner: Your letter of December 13 went to me in New York, missed me there, and has been returned to Virginia.

As to the *American Spectator,* I had nothing to do with its beginning. Theodore Dreiser came to me and talked about the magazine, saying that it was too much dominated by Broadway. I am betraying no secret in telling you this, as he said the same thing frankly to the other editors. He begged me to go into it to help him overcome this Broadway influence. I do not think that O'Neill or Cabell had a great deal to do with it. When I got in, it was pretty much dominated by Nathan and Boyd.[2]

I am not saying this as reflecting on either of these men, both of whom I personally like. Their point of view is not my point of view. They are what life has made them, and I would be mighty sorry to say anything to you or anyone else that would hurt them. I don't much

---

[1] Misquoted from the speech of Jacques on the Seven Ages — As You Like It, Scene 7, line 158: ". . . the lean and slipper'd pantaloon. . . ."

[1] Daniel Lerner, at the time a fellow in American literature at New York University, was writing a master's thesis on the American Spectator and had written Anderson for information about the magazine.

[2] George Jean Nathan, and Ernest Boyd (1887–1946), literary critic.

like going around and making cracks about people, and my relations with the two men have always been friendly.

I never went to but one or two editorial meetings of the editorial board, and I am afraid I did not have much to say when I did go. As suggested, I went in after Dreiser plead [*sic*] with me, and a very short time later Dreiser got sore at the others and resigned.[3]

I never heard of any anonymous board.

In answer to your question 5, I don't think there was ever any crying need for the magazine.

I don't think it was concerned with any problems very vital to people. I think Dreiser felt that way. I think he wanted to make it that kind of a magazine and, feeling that he could not, got out.

It was but a short time after this that the magazine folded up and I lost any connection with it. I felt that it had accomplished little or nothing. You speak of the Revolt of the Twenties and seem to feel the potency in American life of any work done in the period is a thing of the past. I think it is difficult to pass such an opinion. We have passed and are passing through the age of the hard-boiled boys. I think that phase will pass too. I think that whatever has real integrity in what you speak of as the Movement of the Twenties has not lost its potency.

You ask me to estimate my own part in all of this, and that I feel incompetent to do. I think that had better be passed on by somebody else.

Your question No. 10 asking me to estimate the parts of other members of the editorial board of the magazine, *American Spectator*, I must also pass up. I have a great deal of reluctance about passing judgment on other men. I do not think it is my job. I have never been much concerned with this question of the value of the work of other men. I think it must be because I am so absorbed in trying to get at and understand a little the lives of so-called ordinary people. I think I am sincere in saying this. It may be that I will be again in New York sometime in February, and if you desire, I would be glad to see you and talk as frankly as I can about all of these things. You are, however, to bear in mind my reluctance about stepping over into a field that I presume belongs to the critics. With most sincere regards

[3] On January 4, 1934.

361.   [?1939]

To LAURA LOU COPENHAVER

Dear Mother: Now that I think back, I am surprised at your kindness and tolerance of me when I once attacked your daughter. I have been thinking about some of the things I said, and, thinking back, it seems to me that in relation to your children you are in very much the same position that I am in relation to the children of my imagination.

There is a woman hidden away in every artist. Like the woman he becomes pregnant. He gives birth. When the children of his world are spoken of rudely or, through stupidity, not understood, there is a hurt that anyone who has not been pregnant, who has not given birth, will never understand.

And that, Mother, is why I think your tolerance toward me has been so very fine. Love

362.   [OLIVET COLLEGE, OLIVET, MICHIGAN, JANUARY 11, 1939]

To LAURA LOU COPENHAVER

Dear Mother: I have finished the Franklin [1] and am mailing it. I take back anything I may have said against it. It is a fine job. When you have finished, you do know your Franklin.

I am having a bit of a fight with your daughter. She keeps getting presents for me constantly — shirts, socks, handkerchiefs, etc. Now I want her to go get a fur coat that I am to pay for.

I'm afraid she won't.

Will you kindly, in some subtle way, help to make her do it, please?

I am finding it not unpleasant here. There is very good male society, good live talk in the evening. The faculty is predominately male and young. There are several bachelors. I have found no yearning females.

As yet I have made no public appearance, but I begin tonight. I will have two classes a week. I do not believe I'll mind it too much.

On my way East I am to go to Antioch College for 3 days. They announce it as a kind of state homecoming & recognition. [2] It sounds nice.

I must say, Mother, that there is something very heartening to me

---

[1] Carl Van Doren, *Benjamin Franklin* (1938).
[2] Anderson spoke at Antioch College on January 31.

I find here. I hope it is not vanity, but my work does seem to have penetrated, and I feel that my influence is constantly growing. As I have been, for a long time, rather down and very doubtful, I do not think a bit of this sort of reassurance will hurt me too much. My love to all of you there

363.   [?OLIVET COLLEGE, OLIVET, MICHIGAN, ?BEFORE JANUARY 24, 1939]

TO ROGER SERGEL

Dear Roger: I have been thinking a good deal about your idea. Do forgive it. I should think you would conclude, "To hell with them." But you can't do that, because, at bottom, you are one of us. When I say, "To hell with them," referring of course to those who would benefit by the plan.

The trouble with my own reactions is an old fear of anything that gets itself organized. There is, for example, the Nobel and the Pulitzer. A man hears constant tales of the influence brought to bear.

How, Roger, for example, can the last Nobel [1] be explained?

The Nat'l Academy, Authors' League,[2] etc., etc. — O.K. I am in both. I dare say they serve a purpose, but in these organization[s] also there is — it seems inevitable — politics and more politics. Would it not soon be inevitable in the bestowal of these annuities? How keep it clear? Those who could would pull wires to get it, and, Roger, sometimes I have the suspicion that your own interest is partially a kind of personal and private interest in your friend S.A. How the hell do we know that he deserves any such consideration?

I guess the old nobility with its power to pension certain favorites was as good as anything.

Would it not be better for a man to simply resolve that, when the time comes, when the old head is emptied, when a man becomes a burden to others — the dinner in Thessaly,[3] the little white pill, eh? The hell is to know when to swallow it. There's the rub.

---

[1] The Nobel Prize for Literature was awarded in 1938 to Pearl Buck.

[2] Anderson became a member of the National Institute of Arts and Letters in January, 1937, and had joined the Authors' League of America some years previously.

[3] A reference to Anderson's article, "The Right to Die: Dinner in Thessaly," *Forum,* XCV, 40–41 (January, 1936).

364.   [OLIVET COLLEGE, OLIVET, MICHIGAN, JANUARY 24, 1939]

To ROGER SERGEL

Dear Roger: It's a shame, but I really won't be able to make it. They have plans for me here up until Saturday, and I am to be at Antioch, Yellow Springs, Ohio, on Sunday evening. It seems beastly to be so near you and not have a visit. I had myself, for a day or two, a touch of something like intestinal flu, but seem to have ridden through it.

I had an idea. It concerns your plans for taking care of us fellows by a kind of annuity. I wonder if this idea couldn't be combined with some educational idea. If, for example, I could come to some such place as this for, say, seven months a year, be here, have a class or two a week, much as you suggest in your letter, I am very sure I wouldn't mind. The touch with youth would probably be fine for me, and in that case we could feel ourselves of some possible use and not objects of charity. At the same time, with some such hookup to your idea it seems to me it would be easier to get money interested. Men are nuts on education, you know.

I have had a good feeling here, a new aliveness. I seem to get on well with the kids. We seem to talk easily together. At times I think that there is something in the idea back of any art that has any integrity that has in it perhaps the only real moral base we have left to us, and surely that is something we all want. It may be the great want of our lives, just a moral base on which to stand.

I find, Roger, and it always surprises me, that there is something I seem to have acquired, in many mind[s], that goes beyond my actual writing — as I find it in many who have not read me. I seem to stand in their minds for something. I am a little puzzled by it.

I wish we might have had a talk.

365.   NEW YORK, FEBRUARY 7, 1939

To JOHN PAUL CULLEN

Dear Paul: I got back to New York on Sunday night and found your letters and also the grand photographs of yourself, Mary, and the babe, all of which, bless you, were very gratefully received. As you know, I have been being a college professor, first at the small school in Michigan, Olivet, and then at Antioch, at Yellow Springs,

Ohio, a town some ten miles from the big industrial town of Springfield, where I spent a part of my late boyhood.[1] I really enjoyed it all and particularly the time spent at Olivet, where I stayed long enough to get rather acquainted with a lot of the kids, and, on the whole, grand kids I found them. There is something disillusioned and pretty swell about these modern kids, they not apparently believing half as much as we of our generation did in the bunk about the happiness to be got from success, work-hard-be-patient-and-industrious-and-rise-in-the-world, all of that sort of thing. I certainly liked the kids and thoroughly enjoyed being with them. They have also a writers' conference up there in the summer, and although I do not think much is accomplished at such conferences, I have agreed to go back to it, largely, I think, because of friends made among the faculty members.

And by the way, a few days after I had agreed to go to Olivet, I had a wire from Ted Davison,[2] wanting me to come back out there, but, having promised Olivet, I couldn't do it.

As you perhaps know, Paul, I have always been a Borrow fan. The old bastard is, I fear, a complete fraud, but he can write, and I love his flamboyancy and gusto. Read the two books *Lavengro* and *The Romany Rye,* but I warn you, Paul, the damn old cuss is a nut on the Church, always putting it in the worst possible light, and you may well hate him for that.

Did I ever recommend to you a book of Turgenev's called *The Annals of a Sportsman?* Do you read Chekhov?

Paul, I am not so clear as to just what is needed to furnish proof of birth. I was born in a small Ohio town named Camden. I never went there until about two years ago when Eleanor and I were driving North and spent part of a Sunday afternoon in the town. My father, at the time I was born, had a small harness shop in the town, but within a very short time after my own birth the family moved to another small Ohio town, named Caledonia, where my father set up another shop.

There is, in Camden, Ohio, a young man, the son of a local doctor, who is, more or less, a fan on my books, and before my visit to the town I had had some correspondence with him; and when E. and I went there, we called on him, and he took us to the house of my birth, a

---

[1] Anderson lived in Springfield for a year after returning from the Spanish-American War.

[2] Edward Davison, then professor of English at the University of Colorado, was in charge of the Writers' Conference held annually in Boulder.

very charming little brick house occupied by a very old woman who remembered my mother and father.

Later there was a woman schoolteacher [3] at Athens, Ohio, who, in working for her master's degree, made quite a study of my background and went also to Camden to make inquiry. I think she met some other men who had known my father.

I have living an older brother, Karl Anderson, a quite well-known American painter, who is, I should say, some three years older than I am.

I give you all of this dope, Paul, hoping you can tell me just how to go about it to get the proof you say I will be needing.

Eleanor will be sending a snap of my mug, or I will order one sent from Marion.

My sincere love to all of you, Paul, and in particular my gratitude to you for all of the interest you have taken in my interest. As always

366.   [NEW YORK, ?FEBRUARY 17, 1939]

To GILBERT WILSON

Dear Wilson: What heels we are! It needed you, going up to Art Young,[1] to make me think of saying through you the few words that you say pleased him. Great God, that such a guy should be pleased that I admire him, this on his record as an American man. What was it old Bill said — "Take him all in all there is a man." [2] I only wish he had health to go on being just what he always has been for another hundred years. We don't get any too many of that kind.

About your letter to me, Gilbert, the one you wrote at Antioch and that I didn't know about, I have thought of this. Why don't you sit down, get at it, put down from time to time facts and impressions out of your boyhood and young manhood down there in that Indiana town? Do it for your own satisfaction. Naturally I'd like to see it. However, I'd probably steal from it.

There is this about it. I tried to say something about it in the public talk at Antioch. Don't know how clear I managed to make it, the idea being that the putting of things down is a kind of healthy unloading.

---

[3] Helen Dinsmoor, whose thesis, *An Inquiry into the Life of Sherwood Anderson as Reflected in His Literary Works,* was accepted for the master's degree at Ohio University in 1939.

[1] The cartoonist.

[2] *Hamlet,* Act I, Scene 2, line 187: "He was a man, take him for all in all."

You get things put down and face them, just as you must yourself face the walls on which you do your murals. An old printer who worked for me when I ran a small weekly paper used to say, praising his craft: "You see, in this trade," he said, "your own mistakes are right there before you in print. You can't laugh or think them off."

I find, Gilbert, that many of the young artists who from time to time come to see me are too full of a kind of self-pity. The cruelty and indifference of so much of life amazes them too much. There is, I guess, a kind of final test, to take it laughing, as Art Young has done so much. There is a kind of maturity in that.

I guess what I think is that if you start to write of your own life experience, you will find yourself more and more, as you go along with it, stopping to think about this or that situation you have been in. This is pretty likely to get you to thinking more and more of others involved with you in the damned difficult business of living, this all the time leading you more and more out of yourself and into others. Damn it, there is something to be said here. I think Art would very much understand, because of all the crowd he was connected with, I always felt him closest to all kind[s] of other humans.

I have thought sometimes that the young painters, for example, of our day are a bit too much inclined to take other humans merely as symbols. There is a lot of "big thinking" going on. It is rather in the air now. I get it from almost everyone. There is a kind of national thinking, international thinking, etc. The Jews are so and so, the Germans, French, English, The American Way, etc., etc., march of armies across the pages of the newspapers every day. It['s] hard to get back from all that — I call it vacuum thinking, vacuum feeling — into, say, a street, a house, just a man walking along a street, a pair of young lovers in a dark doorway on a cold night in a city street.

You see what I am driving at, the thought that perhaps your trying to set down intimate happenings, thoughts, and feeling[s] out of your own life might be a way to save yourself from too much of the BIG-NESS, this whether it had so-called "literary value" or not. That could be something left, I'd think, [on] the well-known knees of the gods. What do you think?

I have a hell of a time reading your script, Gilbert. It's as bad as my own.

Love to Art and you if this gets to you while you are still with him.

367.   NEW ORLEANS, MARCH 19, [1939]

To GILBERT WILSON

Dear Gilbert Wilson: Your letter came to me down here in New Orleans. When I got up from the flu, I felt pretty weak and despondent and wanted to be out of doors, so got in the car and drove, ending the trip down here, where I am in a hotel room overlooking the Mississippi. I have had good luck about weather, warm, sunshiny days and clear skies.

This is what I wonder about the writing. Don't mind if I am frank with you. A good many years ago I started to paint. I think what I wanted was to paint people, more and more of them. I wanted to find out how to do it in my own way, but after a time I gave it up because I grew to feel that one art was enough. It was so damn hard to get at what you wanted in that. I began to feel that if I could get what I was after at all, one art might lead me to it as well as another. All this said not to discourage you, but simply to tell of my own experience.

Naturally I will be interested in White's [1] response to your letter. I doubt anything will come of it. There is dynamite in the idea too. You see, now the question of labor organization has penetrated into more and more of the towns. When I was in Michigan, before I came to Antioch, I was asked to address the state publishers' organization, all the editors of the state, at their convention at Lansing, Michigan, [2] and I found them on the whole pretty stuffy. Little middle-class businessmen for the most part, nothing else. But, Gilbert, that is what the factory owners want them to be, of course.

I think I will leave here about Wednesday, driving slowly north to my place in Virginia. Address Marion, Va. I am still a little floppy, but have managed to work while here. I am not sure where to send this, but as you say you are driving west, will send it to Yellow Springs. You will be back at those walls soon now.

Keep me posted as to how things go with you. As always

---

[1] William Allen White, to whom Wilson had written concerning a project suggested by Anderson. See also Letter 392.

[2] On January 26 Anderson had talked at this convention on his experiences while running the Marion newspapers.

368. [MARION, VIRGINIA, MARCH 31, 1939]

To EDWARD H. RISLEY, JR.

Dear Edward Risley: Your letter has been following me about, and I just got it here. The main point seems to me the Hicks matter,[1] and I have a feeling that I would much rather not make a point of that. It is a kind of raking over of a dead man's bones — I mean Jack Reed's bones.

I presume Hicks is like all men who start out to make a point. They become advocates for a point of view. He might well believe that, in what Reed said to me, he was just pulling my leg, although I do not believe so.

Anyway I do not believe that I would like you to use what I said to start a controversy. The point was spoken of in answer to some question by you. I do not personally know Mr. Hicks and would not want to be put in the position of questioning his intent without being more sure of his understanding of what I said to him. This repeating a conversation — I mean the Reed conversation — after several years is too ticklish a business to stand on. That is the way I feel. Sincerely

369. MARION, VIRGINIA, APRIL 8, 1939

To HENRY T. VOLKENING [1]

Dear Henry T. Volkening: I have been reading with glowing pleasure your piece on Tom Wolfe in the *Virginia Quarterly*.[2] It is a grand job you have done. So much of the real Tom is in it, the often terrible injustice of the man, his outbreaks, absorption in self, all of this not glossed over and yet the reader left with a genuine feeling of respect and affection for Tom. Your piece gives just the feeling Tom gave a friend.

Frankly, the only thing in the piece that didn't ring quite true wasn't yours but Tom's. I mean the quotation regarding death. It struck me as fancy writing. I really think that at bottom Tom felt as I do that Life not Death is the real adventure. I could feel only the damned injustice of the gods when word came of Tom's death.

You did for him a beautiful job. Sincerely

---

[1] Granville Hicks, in collaboration with John Stuart, had published a biography, *John Reed* (1936). See Letter 332.

---

[1] Of the firm of Russell and Volkening, literary agents, New York.

[2] "Tom Wolfe: Penance No More," *Virginia Quarterly Review*, XV, 196–215 (spring, 1939).

370.   [MARION, VIRGINIA] APRIL 10, 1939

To JAMES BOYD

Dear Jim: I just got your letter yesterday. I was mighty sorry not to see you and Katharine when I was on my way South. Southern Pines and particularly your place were so lovely that spring morning. A colored girl came to the door, and I ask[ed] her for a little slip of paper. I wrote my name on the paper, leaning against the nose of my car. Filled with sadness that you weren't there. I knew there were a lot of trotting horses in training over at that track where we once went together. I thought we might have a morning together over there watching them step.

In your letter I like particularly your saying that about the business of writing, that it is the highest business there is, although I wasn't so hot, Jim, on your using the word "business" to get at your meaning; and between us, Jim, I don't think that talent has a great deal to do with it either.

The country and our civilization has lost its morality, and what is man without a morality?

You see, Jim, it is my notion that we American writers, all of us, are pretty lousy. Who among us really takes upon his shoulders the responsibility of what you speak of as the business of writing? We do make a business of it.

I guess it is pretty much my notion that man's real life is lived out there in the imaginative world, and that is where we sell him out. That's what we writers haven't found out. That is what we will someday have to find out if we are really ever to take on the responsibility implied in your saying that writing is the highest business there is.

I know you agree with me, Jim. I am mighty sorry I did not see you. I haven't yet read your new book. Tell Max to send me a copy. With my best to you both

371.   MARION, VIRGINIA, APRIL 17, 1939

To HERBERT FEIS [1]

Dear Herbert: My wife and I are driving to New York next weekend and expect to spend at least a day in Washington, perhaps next

---

[1] Herbert Feis (1893–), an economist, was then an adviser in the State Department on international economic affairs.

Monday. I hope you will be in town, as I would like very much to see you.

A little matter has come up that perhaps you can put me straight on. Yesterday a young man called on me from the Department of Justice. It seems there has been a law passed that any officer or organizer of any organization having international affiliations has to register with the government.

Some years ago I had a letter from Henri Barbusse or Romain Rolland,[2] I do not know which, asking me if my name could be used in some sort of an organization, as I understood it, against Fascism, and I presume I said O.K. I am sending you a copy of a letterhead they use in their literature. As a matter of fact, Herbert, I have never been to a meeting of the organization and know nothing about it except what appears on this letterhead. The letterhead seems to say that I am counselor to the president, who seems to be Romain Rolland; but if I am, he never in any way consulted me, nor did I ever give him any advice.

I presume, however, that I will have to find out whether or not my name appearing thus on the letterhead of this organization makes me any kind of an officer. At any rate, I know I am not an organizer of anything. I really suppose, Herbert, I am just an ordinary old-fashioned liberal Democrat and certainly with the same impulse against Fascism, Communism, or any other sort of dictatorship that most of us feel. I wonder if you could enlighten me about this.

372.   NEW YORK [?MAY, 1939]

To JAMES BOYD

Dear Jim: I have just finished reading your story.[1] Jim, it's a dandy. It [is] such damn good storytelling. I think it's by far the best thing I've ever read about the old West and altogether good, hard writing.

The movement of it makes me jealous. Myself, I'm always so stationary, wanting to go writing forever about some figure as it stands, often not going anywhere, just there.

And Jim, how far, far away that old Western life or anything like it seems now. We've got all of this so-called progress — cars, tele-

---

[2] As a result of receiving this letter, which is not in the Collection, Anderson had agreed to become a member of the Executive Committee of the World Committee Against War and Fascism. See Letter No. 373.

[1] Presumably *Bitter Creek* (1939).

phones, airplanes, radios, machinery, and more and more of it.
And it all ending in guns.

Christ!

I am very, very grateful to you, Jim, for this story that takes me so far from it. As always

373.   [New York] May 1, 1939

M. Romain Rolland, World Committee against War and Fascism, Paris

Dear Monsieur Rolland: Some time ago I must have received a letter from someone connected with the Comité Mondial Contre la Guerre et la Fascisme and, I am sure, must have consented to the use of my name in connection with the organization. I live most of the year in the country and do not speak or read French, and, although I have received from time to time the literature of the organization, I have been unable to read it.

A week or two ago a man from the United States Department of Justice called on me at my home to find out just the position I hold in connection with this organization. The Department of Justice is a part of our State Department.[1] There has been a law passed [2] requiring the registration, as I understand it, of all officers and organizers of such organizations as have international connections.

I do not wish in any way to repudiate the use of my name. However, if I am an officer, I do not know it. I do not wish to register as holding a position of any authority that I do not really hold.

As I am essentially a story teller and usually deeply involved in my own work, and as I am seldom in New York, I have never attended a meeting of this organization, nor do I know anything about its work.

Being recently in Washington, I went into the State Department and tried to get clear in this matter, but they also did not seem able to decide where I stood; so I told them I would write to you, hoping that you would be able to clear the matter up or pass it on to someone else.

I should say, as I have the opportunity, that I have long been your sincere admirer, both as artist and man. Sincerely yours

[1] Anderson's error. The Department of Justice is, of course, a separate branch of the government.
[2] The so-called Foreign Agents Registration Act of 1938, which became law on June 8, 1938.

374.   [NEW YORK, BEFORE MAY 13, 1939]
TO JACQUES CHAMBRUN

Chambrun: In our conversation the other day I made a suggestion to you of something I think I would like doing. As you know, some years ago I became a country editor in a Virginia town near my own Virginia farm. I had settled down to live in that country, had bought a farm and built a house. You know how it is with us writers. A man gets up in the morning and goes to his desk to work. The writer is lucky if he can get in two, three, four hours of real work. There are days and sometimes, alas, weeks when words will not behave for him. He feels useless, no good.

On such days and often in the afternoon when I did work in the morning, I used to drive down into Marion, the nearest county seat town. I began to get acquainted down there.

I always felt, however, that the people were a little suspicious of me. They knew I was a professional writer, and there is a certain attitude people are inclined to have toward professional writers. They feel he is constantly looking for material. They are afraid he wants to use them. Almost every man has some story in his life he would as soon keep hidden.

I was a little irked by all this. I thought I would like to get into some position having some real part in the community life. It was this feeling that led to my becoming for some years a country newspaper editor.

I went down into the county seat town and purchased the two county seat papers, one Democratic, the other Republican, and both published at the time from the same office and by the same man. They were pretty dull.

I became editor and publisher of both papers, getting two men, a local Democrat and a Republican, to handle the political matter that went into the papers. I did everything else, was editor, reporter, advertising man, job printing salesman. The papers were both weeklies. I did all right with them, in three years made them pay for themselves.

I think, Chambrun, that when I became thus a country editor, the people of the community were suspicious of me. I was in a town of four to five thousand people, but the papers circulated more or less throughout the county. There are some twenty-five thousand people in the county. I think the people felt that I might be wanting to reform them, perhaps go highbrow on them.

I hadn't any such notion. I simply wanted to make the papers interesting. Life in a good many of our country towns gets pretty dull. I wanted to liven it up. As I was doing practically all the writing for both of the papers, outside political writing, I didn't want the people to get tired of reading me, and as I couldn't afford to hire other writers, I invented some. I think perhaps I got the idea from the comic strip in our dailies. The county I was in was in the lower Appalachian Mountains, the town being in a broad, rich valley that is an extension of the Shenandoah Valley, and so I invented a young mountain man to come down and be a reporter. I called him Buck Fever.

Then there was an imagined lady of the town interested in public affairs named Mrs. Homing Pigeon, and a Colonel Stardust, and others. The idea was to give the people of a small town and the country people these imagined figures to play with, people out of much the same background, having the same problems, little tragedies, adventures in living.

I found that the people came to love these figures. Later I sold the papers to my son, and he tried to carry the figures on, but couldn't do it. He had to drop it, but, although several years have now passed since I had anything to do with the papers, the people still keep talking about these imagined figures that had become a part of their own imaginary lives. They keep wanting them back.

I speak to you, Mr. Chambrun, about this matter because I believe it is the kind of thing that could be done with fine success by some national publication that has a big circulation in small American towns and on farms. I'd like to do it myself, as it is the sort of thing I love doing, but wouldn't want to try doing it unless I could have at least a year to build it into people's consciousness. I'd much prefer doing it for a monthly. It shouldn't be a monthly piece of more than 1500 words. It should be kept close to everyday life. It should build into the consciousness of readers much as the comic strip men work to build their people into the consciousness of the readers of the dailies. Although the strips done in the newspapers are called "comic strips," the more successful ones are always kept very human.

If you should find an editor interested in this idea, I would be glad to talk it over with him. My notion would be not to make it political or for it to get into economic problems, but simply to enrich a little the ordinary lives of ordinary people, as I believe I was able to do as a country editor. Sincerely

375. [NEW YORK, ?MAY 20, 1939]

To JAMES BOYD

Dear Jim: It is uncertain how long we will be here. It depends largely upon Eleanor, who seems to have got herself tied up here.

How have you escaped? I seem to have become a kind of stuffed shirt for all sorts of things. People keep coming to me, wanting me to sign this or that manifesto, for Cultural Freedom, for Peace and Democracy, for this and that. I do it and find myself involved.

From time to time an impulse comes to me. I would like to write the story of a man during an hour of his life, without physical action, the man sitting or standing or just walking about. All that he is that made him what he is. I have this temptation and at the same time realize that man is best understood by his actions.

Sometimes my feelings about inanimate objects goes, I'm afraid, to too great lengths. I remember a room in which I once lived in Chicago. Some men came to see me one evening, and something vile happened. It was largely stuff going on in the men. It seemed to me to make the room vile. I had worked pretty well there, but after it happened couldn't work. I got the notion they had put something into the very furniture of the room, into the walls and the wallpaper. I carry it too far, I think, sometimes.

Your letter was something fine to me, the quality of the mind back of it so finely shown. We are working in a tough time, Jim. There are so many forces pulling away from the real point. It is good to have you thus unload your mind to me. I am grateful.

376. MARION, VIRGINIA, JUNE 14, 1939

DWIGHT MACDONALD,[1] *Partisan Review*, NEW YORK

Dear Dwight Macdonald: Indeed, Macdonald, I remember you very well and also your review in the Yale magazine,[2] but I remember you

---

[1] At this time one of the editors of the *Partisan Review*.

[2] Ten years previously, on March 4, 1929, Macdonald had sent Anderson an essay on the author's work, which he had contributed to the *Yale Literary Magazine*.

more vividly in connection with the young painter we both knew and where I once saw you.

And now as to the questions.[3] In answer to the first, I would have to say that it is no part of my nature to analyze very closely what influences me and what doesn't. I am interested in storytelling. My mind is likely to stay on the street in which I happen to be walking rather than on America as a whole. I just don't think that way, and in thinking that way it is impossible for me to say whether either Henry James's or Walt Whitman's work is more relevant to the present and future of American writing, etc., etc.

Nor do I think that I have any audience in view when I am writing. I have a notion that at the present time many people who otherwise might be more interested in the human side of people have gone off into their effort to solve life through economics. They may be right. From my angle they are all wrong.

The third question again pitches me outside my own world. When it comes to criticism, I like praise and dislike blame. In regard to question No. 4, God knows how I have managed to make a living, but in some way I have.

However, for twelve or fifteen years after I began publishing I had to make my living as an advertising writer. Now after some twenty or twenty-five years enough usually leaks in to keep me going.

No. 5. To the first part of this question I would answer no. To the second part, yes.

Question No. 6. I have a notion that in all of the arts there is a thing called "the great tradition." I think it goes on and on in spite of all the things you mention. The difficulty is to keep it straight. All the morality of the artist is involved in it.

And now a[s] to question No. 7. This again gets me outside the house in which I sit, the street in which I walk. It plunges me off into a world of thinking that in some queer way does not belong to me. I believe that my own responsibility is to those immediately about me. I frankly do not understand world movements. They seem to me queerly accidental. Outside any possibility of any clear thinking on my part. I want my own job, and while these things may have a tremendous influence on my job, I try to keep my own mind on the job itself. I am not and do not pretend to be a world thinker, a national thinker, or a political thinker. You see, Macdonald, this is about all I

[3] The nature of the questions is clear from Anderson's answers.

can say on the subject. To me all such words as "the people," "the masses," "nations," etc., etc., are rather empty words. I don't like attempts at big thinking. I suppose there are men who can do it, and I am satisfied to leave the job to them. To me the world is simply filled with individuals some few of whom I would like to come to understand a little.

I am not returning the postcard, because it seems to me that all I can say on the subject is in the letter. Very truly yours

377.   OLIVET, MICHIGAN [JULY 26, 1939]

To ROGER SERGEL

Dear Roger: I'll hang the tie up in the house at Ripshin, the idea being that you may begin to long for it and come down. We'll be there straight on now, at least until September 15th. Do try, you and Ruth, to run down. Ripshin was never so beautiful.

You are right about Ferd.[1] He is the steadfast one. Not only do you love the man, but year after year your feeling doesn't change.

As for Wilson,[2] how can you blame him? The revolution, after Stalin, got so lost. I agree with him that now there is no other position except that of the isolationist you can take. I feel that way, although Eleanor does not. Of course, she isn't a Stalinist. She does, however, still dream of a real revolution.

For myself I feel that it is a good thing to give it up. It at least brings us back to individuals, and, after all, it may be a bit absurd, this trying to think nationally or internationally. More and more when I am anywhere and the conversation drifts off to nations, statesmen, etc., etc., I go away, I mean my mind goes away.

So I find myself clinging to an old thing, the man or woman. It feels better anyway, doesn't leave quite the same emptiness.

Do come to us before the summer ends.

378.   [TROUTDALE, VIRGINIA] AUGUST 2, 1939

MR. PAUL CULLEN, WEST LOS ANGELES, CALIFORNIA

Dear Paul: I have your grand letter of July 25th but as it has suddenly happened that I will probably be in Los Angeles about No-

[1] Ferdinand Schevill.
[2] Edmund Wilson's position may be gleaned from his *To the Finland Station* (1940).

vember 15 to 30 and can see you there, I believe I will just let the matter rest until then. Do you think this is the best plan?

I am a little confused when you speak of copies of Karl Anderson's painting. I believe that you refer to the painting of three brothers.[1] I dare say I could get a photograph of the painting for you if that would be of any satisfaction to you. The painting was made here on my farm at Troutdale, Virginia.

I am glad that you got ahold of the *Sportsman's Sketches.* I guess the Garnett translation is about the best there is.[2] You note, Paul, that there was quite a joke about myself and the Russians. Most of the critics spoke of the influence the Russians had had upon me when my stories first began to appear. As a matter of fact, I had read none of the Russians at the time this criticism was made and cannot now remember just when I began to read them. I wonder if you know that it was largely because of the *Sportsman's Sketches* that Tzar Alexander freed the Russian serfs?

As regards the manuscript of *Winesburg, Ohio,* it is in the college library at Dartmouth. It, however, does not belong to them; and I have only left it there at their suggestion for sa[f]ekeeping, they having agreed to keep it heavily insured.

The name of the young man at Camden, Ohio, is Steve Coombs. There is a very interesting story about him which I shall tell you and Mary when I see you in the fall. The woman who is doing her thesis on my work is Miss Helen Dinsmoor at Athens, Ohio. I have not her address as I write this, but will add it at the foot of this letter.

I am very much interested in what you say about Jack London. The trouble with Jack, as you of course know, Paul, is that he became merely a romancer and, I think, has not had any very definite influence on the march of literature. Such men, while their work is very fine in some respects, are outside the great tradition. They are, I presume, romancers rather than artists.

I was delighted to get the clippings of my old friend, Dreiser. I will write immediately to my brother and get the information about birth that he can give, also to the bureau in Washington for the forms, and will keep you in touch with anything I do in the matter.

Both Eleanor and I expect to be on the coast in October and No-

---

[1] Karl's portrait of three of his brothers, entitled "Earl, Sherwood and Irwin."
[2] Constance Garnett's translation of Turgenev's *A Sportsman's Sketches* was published in 1895 and has been frequently reprinted.

vember, and we are both looking forward to seeing you and Mary. Sincerely

[P.S.] The woman, Miss Dinsmoor, is going to have the thesis printed & bound.[3] If you wish, I can send it to you later. Miss Dinsmoor's address is 26 Fern St., Athens, O.

379.   MARION, VIRGINIA, AUGUST 9, 1939

CARROW DE VRIES, WYANDOTTE, MICHIGAN

Dear Carrow De Vries: I think looseness is but a part of it. The free flow wanted comes, I've a notion, from unconsciousness of the act of writing.

It is true that as a man walks along a street or sits, often with friends, he hears bits of conversation or the sounds of the street, while at the same time his thoughts go wandering, doing many strange things.

A certain amount of control is, of course, possible, or there would be no work done at all.

You sit with a group of people, and there is a conversation going on, words and sentences being made. At the same time there is an unspoken conversation. A man may be in such a group speaking of literature or painting. There is a woman present he has a sudden desire to lie with. She may be the wife of some other man in the group. Naturally he says nothing of his sudden desire aloud.

Nevertheless he says it and she answers. She would also rather like it, or she would like it not.

Someone in the group is lying. No one questions aloud what he is saying, but we do question. "He is lying now," the under voices cry back and forth. Always this under, unspoken communication between people, a constant flow. Often I think no man really ever succeeds in lying to another.

It is possible at times, I think, to get into the flow, the under voices becoming audible. It may even be that this is what the mind, when it is wandering, running, leaping, as described by Verga,[1] is really seeking, to connect itself with the flow.

No one ha[s] ever been able to entirely control this flow. It is undoubtedly controlled at times, even for long periods, in the consumma-

[3] See Letter 365, note 3.

[1] De Vries's letter, to which this is an answer, quotes from "*Cavalleria Rusticana*, by Giovanni Verga" in *Phoenix: The Posthumous Papers of D. H. Lawrence*, edited by Edward D. Macdonald (New York, The Viking Press, 1936).

tion of some work of art. When I was at Olivet and had looked at some work turned in by one of the students and it was time for me to talk with the student, I took him or her into my car. I refused to quibble over words and sentences put down. That did not interest me. In all of the stories, novels, etc., I saw there was the same lack of respect for the characters in the imagined world they were trying to create.

People pushed here and there in the imagined world. There was a constant violence being done these people. Some scheme for a story or novel had come into the writer's mind. They were making the characters of the story or novel do this or that to fit into the scheme thought out. Something false there. Often horrible violence done to these people. As though I, a writer, had a right to do as I pleased with people carried into an imagined life.

The thing never understood was the sacredness of that life too.

The obligation to that life, to my mind, is greater than to the characters in what we call real life. If there is any such thing as real life, reality. I often doubt there is. In real life the character you see can at least fight back. He can deny the lie you tell about him.

Have you not often read a story where a character has been made by the storyteller to do something you knew the character could not do? We call it bad art. It is more than that. It is a display of immorality.

What is needed among so-called artists is moral men who will not do this violence to people in their imagined world. That is what the world is seeking, a morality. To my mind the place to find it is in an attitude, first of all, to this imagined life. Sincerely yours

380.   [TROUTDALE, VIRGINIA] SEPTEMBER 6, 1939

TO EDWARD H. RISLEY, JR.

Dear Edward H. Risley, Jr.: I did not until last night read your thesis. It was a bad evening. My wife had gone from our farm into town and came back full of war news.[1] I do not know whether or not America will get into it, but it will get into America. There will be the strange fake excitement in the voices of radio announcers, the newspapers shrieking. Everything real will have to sing low.

After the news came, I left the house and went down by a bridge over a creek. It was a black night. I don't know what happened down

[1] The German invasion of Poland began September 1, 1939. On September 3, France and Great Britain declared war on Germany.

there, but something in the voice of the creek in the darkness helped. I went home and read your thesis.

I have to be grateful to you. You have sensed something, something I would like a little to stand for. I don't think it matters much, all this calling a man "muddler," "groping," etc.; the very man who throws such words as these knows in his heart that he is also facing the wall.

I hope the war won't come to America or into American minds too strongly and that, if it actually comes here, it will escape you. In any event it is going to be a struggle just to keep a part of the mind free for some of the significance of everyday life. Sincerely

381. [TROUTDALE, VIRGINIA] SEPTEMBER 19, 1939

MRS. HARRIET MARTIN, COLLINSVILLE, ILLINOIS

Dear Mrs. Harriet Martin: When your brother Mike was over here last Sunday, I told him that while I would be very glad to read your stories, I felt that the probabilities were strong that I could be of very little help to you. I rather got it from Mike that what you are after principally was to do what is called "crashing the magazine market," and I have never much had this aim, nor have I ever been to much extent a magazine writer. I rather came into writing by the back door. Writing seemed to give me more satisfaction than anything else I could do, and what reputation I have got is rather, I think, a literary rather than a popular one.

I will not try to go into a detailed discussion of your stories, because I feel I am incapable of doing so, but it does seem to me, from my point of view, that yours is wrong.

I have read with a good deal of interest the letters to you from the man Uzzell,[1] and it seems to me that when the characters of stories are taken from this point of view — a character in one of your stories, for example, who is a farmer, suddenly turned into a lawyer, a doctor, or something else in order to fit into some plot — there isn't much left of the character. It does not seem to me that it is right or fair to people to push them about in this way. A farmer is a farmer, a lawyer a lawyer, a doctor a doctor. It seems to me that the duty of the storyteller is to study people as they are and try to find the real drama of life just as people live and experience it. In other words, I feel that the obligation

---

[1] Thomas H. Uzzell (1884–), "professional adviser and instructor of American writers since 1920."

to imagined characters is exactly the same as the obligation to real characters in real life.

If I were advising a young writer who really wanted to get any satisfaction out of writing and who was willing to rather give up the idea of immediate success, I would certainly tell them to spend their time studying people and in not trying to think out plots. It seems to me that the stories and the drama of the stories should come out of the real lives of people, and that there is something false and wrong in this shoving imagined people around in this way; but, as I tried to tell Mike, any success coming to a writer out of this kind of work is likely to come slowly. You will have to get what satisfaction you get out of the work itself.

Now, I am very sorry that I cannot go at your stories as a Mr. Uzzell would do, for to tell you the truth, I do not much believe in the Uzzells of the writing world. I tried to tell Mike that, but am afraid I did not make myself very clear, and perhaps I am not making myself clear to you.

If I were a young writer, also it seems to me I would study, not the work of the tricky, flashy magazine writers, but of the masters of the craft. I would read the stories of Chekhov, such books as [Turgenev's] *Annals of a Sportsman,* and books of that kind. If you are interested in my own work, read *Winesburg, Ohio, Triumph of the Egg,* etc.

As suggested, I realize that the suggestions I am giving are not suggestions likely to lead you to any quick success, but they are the only kind of suggestions I feel able to make you. I am sorry that I cannot be of more definite help. Very truly yours

[P.S.] Stories returned under separate cover.

382.   MARION, VIRGINIA, OCTOBER 5, 1939

TO CARROW DE VRIES

Dear Carrow De Vries: That was a very fine letter. The very instant you speak of, the woman remembering a scene in the kitchen, is the whole end a man is working for.

Light in darkness.

Your own scene in the drugstore, holding the pencil and pad of paper, arises to what seems a kind of glorious clearness.

You write so freely of this scene, so that I see you, the man in the store, the street outside. To make me see something so vividly, the intensity of life in you at the moment, makes new life in me. So that I am for the moment no longer blind.

Isn't that the object of all so-called art?

How many such moments can we crowd into a life? So much of life being so dark.

We are such curiously lonely creatures.

Such flashes open doors, but I think that when you wrote to me of the scene in the drugstore, you did not quite know it was then you were writing well. It may have been because you had forgotten you were writing and were thinking only of the moment. Sincerely

383.   [NEW YORK, ?OCTOBER 9, 1939]

To MARGARET BARTLETT [1]

My dear Monte: The imagination plays a queer trick. If I see you, and I hope I shall, I am sure I shall expect to see you as you were when I saw you last. A long time ago that, surely.

Remembrances come by way of little pictures — your father coming out of his bathroom where he had been washing his socks — woolens, I presume — his saying something about the advisability of leaving a little soap in the socks, not washing it all out.

Then on a golf ground. There was a tall, dark girl, or woman, your father's friend. I have forgotten her name. I see you, your father, and the tall, dark one walking toward me.

Monte, I don't know what to say about the things you have sent. I am no critic. It seems fragmentary to me. You are having thoughts about the stars, the way the earth moves, have read Fabre and Jeans.[2] You seem, my dear, a bit awestruck by your own thoughts. I am afraid you are writing sentences. The sentence should fairly tear itself out of you because it must. It is, it seems to me, a terrible mistake to think in sentences.

To be sure I have got, from these fragments, little enough sense of your journey. You seem, Monte, to be floating off somewhere in the air. Didn't you ever have a bellyache or headache or an ingrowing

---

[1] Margaret Bartlett was one of the daughters of Judge George A. Bartlett of Reno who had presided over the case when Anderson obtained his divorce from Tennessee Mitchell Anderson in 1924. She had sent Anderson the manuscript of a travel book which she had completed.

[2] Presumably *The Heavens* by J. H. Fabre, translated by E. E. Fournier d'Albe, Philadelphia, 1925; and *Man and the Stars* by Sir James H. Jeans, New York, 1931. Miss Bartlett's book was dedicated to Jeans and Rainer Maria Rilke.

toenail? It is so rarified. A man want[s] the smells, lusts, hurts, annoyances, surprises of strange places, and intimacy, self-revelation. You get so far away, in the stars, the moon, the moving earth.

No, I don't believe you have got to writing yet. If you do it, you'll have to get more in it, more of your own smallnesses, bignesses, secret lusts, a lot of stuff that will make it all less floating. Is this severe? Forgive me. I don't know what else to say.

Indeed I hope we may see you. We should be along in early November. Then you may pummel me, scorn me, spit at me.

But no great thought[s], Monte dear, no great thoughts.

What [a] bastard I am to speak so.

Do remember me to your father.

Love to you both.

384.   [DENVER, COLORADO] OCTOBER 26, 1939

MR. GILBERT WILSON, TERRA HAUTE, INDIANA

Dear Gilbert Wilson: Your letter reached me only yesterday at Denver, Colorado. I have been wandering around since you left our place, and mail has been following me from place to place in the meantime. Your letter puzzles me, and of course I do not know how to answer it, nor can I tell you what to do. In the first place, however, let me say that the letter from Alexander seems to me very fair and sympathetic. It seems a shame to let them down, and the first thought that occurred to me when I read that you were living with Art and going off by yourself was to wonder why instead you didn't go to Antioch and sit down before that mural and do your thinking about it rather than about yourself.

Of course, I know that you are terribly puzzled, and it seems to me also that all of those who accepted as a kind of mission the changing of human beings through some big national movement have been let down most terribly by recent events.

I expect this has upset you. My own theory as to the position of the working artist that I expounded to you when you were with me may be also a dodging of the issue, but at least in the absorption in other individuals you are not let down so terribly as you are in these big attempts that take in great masses of people.

I do not know whether or not, when you were at my place, you took much note of the man who runs my farm and who, with his son, was building the barn. He is a simple countryman and can barely read and write, but I must say gives me more satisfaction as a companion and friend than most of the artists who come to me and who are so terribly concerned about their genius and their missions.

Frankly, I do not believe this sort of thing concerns me at all. I have no feeling of being a public figure and do not want to be one, and often I think that my own interest in the lives of people about me has at bottom more integrity than this ambitious effort to think of masses of people, where they are going and what is best for them.

The problem you suggest in relation to the college professor with whom you are so close and which came to nothing apparently is not a new one. You would be surprised, Wilson, to know how many other young men have written me similar letters. It may be something in my work that makes them feel that they can tell me things that are very intimate to them.

However, alas, I have no solution to offer. I think most people in life are pretty lonely. I think there is a tendency to live on this loneliness, make it something precious and personal.

You speak of this man, and you have talked to me a great deal of what Art means to you. You come to me and to Dreiser. I do not think we can really help. The truth is that we are probably wanting what you say you want, but have had experience enough to know that few men get it. I really think there is some danger of surrender to self-pity and also perhaps too much clutching at others. There is too much emphasis on what you can get from others and not enough on giving. This may sound like preaching, but it is pretty sound.

The truth is all I can see for you, if you play fair, is to return to Antioch and face your problem there.

I am sorry not to be more helpful. I do not know what else to say. As always

385. HOTEL CANTERBURY, SAN FRANCISCO [NOVEMBER 6, 1939]

To ROGER SERGEL

Dear Roger: I got your letter here. We were about a week in Denver, and I went out to Boulder and made a talk. I'm doing just enough of that to pay my way, but don't mind it as I once did.

As for the War, I try to keep my mind off it. It doesn't make sense to me any way I look at it and only takes my mind off the fellow I'm passing in the street or sitting near in a restaurant. Still, I don't believe democracy is on the way out. It's crude, sure, but these one-party states have, I'm sure, no way to correct their own evils. You can't throw out the party in power without a revolution, and revolutions are, apparently, N.G., just as war is.

I try to keep [o]n the little side, constantly saying to myself, "Little man, don't be trying to think big."

We had a gorgeous trip out here. From Denver we swung far south, taking in the Grand Canyon, a bit of Death Valley, and then Boulder Dam. That's something. It takes your breath, grander and gaudier, I think, than the Grand Canyon, I guess because you feel the human in it, man struggling with a really gigantic thing and bringing it off, something outside of the bigness of big guns and big battleships, real achievement. It got me in a big way.

I got a divorce once in Reno, and when we got there, the little judge, hearing we were in town, came and hauled us out of our hotel, taking us to his house, where he had two amazingly charming daughters.

Then on Sunday morning we drove over the High Sierras — more and more magnificence. All of this, to say nothing of the drive up through Nevada from down near Needles to Goldfield and Tonopah, often fifty miles without meeting another car. The next time you and Ruth set out on a trip, there's one for you. Love to the lads

386.   [SAN FRANCISCO, NOVEMBER 10, 1939]

To LAURA LOU COPENHAVER

Dear Mother: I have just been reading your family letter and like best the picture of you sitting under a tree and talking to Saint Paul. Please remember that George Moore says he was a bald, sweaty old man with blotches on his face and that a bad smell arose from him.[1]

You do not speak of anyone's weeping on Abraham's bosom — no grapefruits — but Mark Twain says that if a lot of people think they are going up there and get Father Abraham all wet like that, they are mighty mistaken.[2]

You speak of Stalin's stupidity, but I guess, Mother, it all depends upon the point of view. Statesmen, it seems, are like that — us, under

---

[1] See the characterization of Paul in the last third of George Moore's *The Book Kerith* (1916).

[2] See *Extract from Captain Storfield's Visit to Heaven* (New York, Harper & Brothers, 1909), p. 83.

the first Roosevelt, grabbing the Canal Zone, browbeating South American countries; England's generations of grabbing; the French the same. The devil, he's evidently been smart anyway, making Hitler pull his chestnuts out of the fire, as England made us pull them out in the last war.

But we'll stay out of this one, I'll bet on it.

And as for Communism, as Communism it's gone. There isn't any such thing, and all the excited little children of the economic field, many of them with fine enough impulses, are let down hard.

Any minute now I'm expecting the honorable Jim Scherer [3] to lunch with me. From his phone voice I'd say he'll turn out a bore. We'll see. Eleanor won't be in on it, but we are going to their house on Sunday afternoon for tea.

We'll go somewhere else later for cocktails.

Anita Loos phone[d] from Los Angeles and offered us a furnished house there on the beach, but I'm afraid we can't take it. It may be too far from E.'s work.

E. in fine form, coming home after one of her speeches and telling me how rotten she was, but wearing flowers they gave her. She sure looks swell in the fur coat.

Had to stop here. Jim Scherer came and [we] went down to dine together at the sea front. Far from being a bore, he turned out to be very charming, although, I must say, most of the conversation concerned your honorable self. He evidently has a great love and respect for you. Love to all

387.   [SAN FRANCISCO, CALIFORNIA, ?NOVEMBER 11, 1939]
To MARGARET BARTLETT

Dear Monte: I think you'd better not, Monte. I guess it would be all right for the poets, but I don't fancy standing up and trying to say wise things.

There is a stupid picture of me in the *Chronicle* today with a stupid interview.

I was really quite sincere in saying I didn't like being played up. That night at your house I much admired Don Caples,[1] no one taking anything he said so seriously, he giving himself very much to the feeling of the room and the people sitting about.

[3] James Scherer, cousin to Mrs. Copenhaver.

[1] A doctor practising in Reno and an "old friend" of Anderson's.

I very much don't want to be a public figure. In America it just happens to do something very strange to a man. Let yourself be taken up, made a public figure, and they do something terrible to you. I've seen so much of it.

I've been told sometimes that my writing has had a pretty deep effect on other and younger writers in the country. A good many of the better young writers have told me so. That's better. You throw a stone in the pool, and the circles spread far out.

Not that I've ever had any idea of being an influence. I like best to think that I'm just a storyteller and a pretty good liver. To me it's like this: there are people everywhere you go. They talk. The voices go on endlessly.

But they are not saying what they think, what they feel. Very well. If you can keep something quiet and a little relaxed in yourself, you can, sometimes, hear the unspoken words people are saying. That's better. It seems to get you a little way along.

For people are very lonely, terribly so.

I used to think I wanted to change everything, smash it. I don't now. I guess I really began writing because I wanted to get off self and found that, sometimes, I could by absorbing myself in others.

That's why I objected to having your letters filled with ME. I thought it would be nicer if, when you wrote to me, you'd tell me of others. That's why I don't want to be any radio man, except casually, if it fell out so, for a few minutes — not something prepared, to be thought out.

I guess you'll realize all I mean.

I got a real love of your house, the Judge, Dorothy,[2] you running about.

Remember, we will be at the Figueroa Hotel in Los Angeles. I think we'll probably get there about a week from today.

[P.S.] In the newspaper I am very heavy and stupid, and am often so. I perhaps live only in affection, when I can get it, and if I was at all nice in your house, then all of you made me nice. That's why Eleanor is so terribly important to me.

We both went to Robert Caples[3] house. What a lovely woman he has got. She seemed very fine and beautiful to us both.

[2] Margaret's sister.
[3] A young painter, son of Dr. Don Caples of Reno.

And what a beautiful woman Dorothy is. She stays so very sharply in my mind.

I am glad you are launched in the book. If you can think and write just about the people who have come and gone there, it will be wonderful. Again love to you all

388.   [SAN FRANCISCO, NOVEMBER 12, 1939]
To MARGARET BARTLETT

Dear Monte: I think the poem very beautiful and also think it absurd that I should have wanted you to write the book of prose. It's better, I'm sure, to stay there with the moon and stars.

Just the same, I think, if you don't do it, Dorothy should. It should be such a tale, of life there, people coming and going, so few staying, the strange state people are so often in, just little personal stories.

I guess it's all America too, in its way, none of our roots so very deep down as yet.

You get such a strange sense of the country, its terrible vastness, on the drive up through Nevada.

And then Reno, old hopes dying, new ones being born there. For a long time, you know, I have been thinking that we Americans are the loneliest people on earth. We keep feeling for each other and so seldom finding. I guess I think that's what made Reno so significant. It's there before your eyes, the feeling, in half darkness, one for the other.

Yes, Eleanor is like that. She's never assertive, as I am and as I suppose I like being. We've always been good for each other. When we are not together, often I try and try to find out something personal about her. I can't. She'll give me all the news I want of the doings of everyone about, none of herself, while with me everything is personal. It may be the real reason I write, to occasionally escape out of myself and into others in that way. The truth is that I think the Judge and I are a great deal alike. Both of us would like, really, to make love to all the world.

It's the not being able to do it that baffles.

Don't get too idealistic a picture, Monte darling. In my book a man is only of any account when he is just something going along, not wanting to be anything special, knowing, in his guts, he isn't and not resenting the fact too much.

Anyway it's what makes the sun shine and the laugh come.

So I laugh gaily over the idea that anything I may have said or any-thing I am or can be should have been blown up [s]o grandly b[y] such a stargazer as you are.

We do count on seeing the three of you down South.

Again love to you all.

[P.S.] I wrote a note to Robert Caples, and he called last night, but I was out. I expect I'll be seeing hi[m] today.

389.   [LYNCHBURG, VIRGINIA] JANUARY 6, 1940

TO MAURY MAVERICK [1]

Dear Maury Maverick: An idea came into my head. It concerns that theatre you are building down by the river. Paul Green, as you per-haps know, wrote a play [2] about early life on an island down on the Virginia coast. I think he got the Rockefeller Foundation to put up the money and that the state helped some. But wait. It wasn't Virginia. It was North Carolina, about the first settlement on Roanoke Island, the little group of adventurers who all disappeared. Anyway the thing is done annually in an outdoor theatre they have built down there, and thousands of people come to see it. It's a sort of Oberammergau idea, but tied up to the drama of an American scene.

Think, Maury, what a drama could be written about early San Antonio, the lovely little Spanish town you are restoring. The Alamo, Santa Anna, figures of early Texas, the great setting you have already created for it. I think of a play bringing back that early life, the crea-tion of a state, done by local people, native Americans and Mexicans, trained there, played, say, for two weeks each year or even longer, the thing properly publicized. Where is there another city in America that has such grand dramatic material?

Get some rich man who has made a lot of dough in oil to put up for it. Get a good man to do the play, someone like Paul Green or Sherwood Anderson, [to] write it and train the players. It would stand on its own feet after the first year. It could be local and at the same time all Texas, all the Southwest — cowboys, Indians, early gold seekers, Spanish priests, Kit Carson — boy, what material — a play built out of

[1] Maury Maverick (1895–), lawyer, U.S. Congressman, and at this time mayor of San Antonio.
[2] *The Lost Colony* (1937), originally written to commemorate the 350th an-niversary of the birth of Virginia Dare.

the actual material at hand. You'll get the idea, Maury. What do you think? Why wouldn't it be a thousand times better and more significant than, say, to get some little theatre company to do worn-out Broadway successes or even Shakespeare? It could, it seems to me, so easily be built up into an institution, an annual affair, a real part of the city's life.

Eleanor and I are on the way to New York. We will be at Hotel Royalton, 44 West 44th Street.

Write and tell me what you think of the idea. Don't take too seriously the idea that I would be the man to do it. That's just thrown in, Maury. Sincerely

P.S. At that I'd like to try it. Maybe because I like San Antonio and get excited every time I think of the dramatic material right at hand there.

390.   [NEW YORK] FEBRUARY 1, 1940

To LAURA LOU COPENHAVER

Dear Mother: What I tried to convey in the Ford piece [1] is that it is entirely possible for the imagined world to become, for the time, real. I do think that, without drunkenness, the houses were real to Ford.

Anyway, to my mind there is to every person a reality outside any conception they may have of themselves.

Always the imagined world is more important than what we call "reality."

I keep addressing you care of R.,[2] because I do not know when you will be moving to his house.

I presume Mr. C. has left.

E. and [I] are going over to Princeton on Saturday to spend the night with the Centenos,[3] the delightful Spaniard who came down last summer. We will go to Washington, the Hotel Washington, on Sunday afternoon and be there Monday & Tuesday. Back here on Wednesday.

I go to Oklahoma City on the night of Feb. 13th. Back here about the 18th.

[1] "Legacies of Ford Madox Ford," *Coronet*, VIII, 135–136 (August, 1940), and in *Memoirs*, pp. 479–480.

[2] Randolph Copenhaver.

[3] Augusto Centeno (1901–), professor of Spanish at Princeton University, who made the Spanish translation of *Dark Laughter*.

There is a most delightful place here, in the Rockefeller Center. There is a sunken skating pond.[4]

We dined in one of the restaurants the other night. There are some gorgeous skaters. I think some of the professionals practice there. Sonja Henie did when she was here. You sit back of a plate-glass window dining, and there is this very beautiful thing going on so near you can almost touch the skaters.

Karl came in to dine with us last night. He looked fine. We went to a beautiful French movie called the *Harvest*. Why can't our people do some of these simple things? It was like one of my own best stories.

I sold the thing on Maury Maverick to *New Republic*.[5]

Eleanor is well and busy. She is to speak at the meeting of prominent women in the White House.[6] Love to you & R.

391.   [NEW YORK, ?EARLY FEBRUARY, 1940]

TO ROGER SERGEL

Dear Roger: I guess that what I mean when I speak of trying to confine thinking to the more immediate and personal is an avoidance of a kind of looseness and gumminess, to which I am myself so often addicted. It is really amazing how much better life goes when I do not do it. For example, sometimes when I am at Ripshin, weeks pass when I do not look at the newspapers or listen to the radio. I seem to lose so little. It seems to me that we all try to live too much both in the future and in the past.

Here in New York, with the people with whom we seemed destined to associate here, the intelligentsia, I suppose, it's really terrible. Oh, the eternal flow of loose words.

"The Russians are so and so."

People want this or they want that.

The Chinese, the Japs, the Spanish, the Italians, the English, the Germans are so and so. Words like "the people," "the masses," "the proletariat," "the capitalists" so happily and freely thrown about, everyone so grouped. There are times when I devoutly wish Karl Marx had never lived. A man has to work so hard to pull himself away from this indulgence.

[4] Anderson here draws a rough sketch of the skating rink in the Plaza at Rockefeller Center.

[5] "Maury Maverick in San Antonio," *New Republic*, CII, 398–400 (March 25, 1940).

[6] This meeting was concerned with national defense production.

Yes, in spirit anyway I go for the individual, the present as against the past or the future. What else can a man do?

We are looking forward eagerly to seeing you all. Love to all

392.   [NEW YORK] MARCH 20, 1940

MR. GILBERT WILSON, ANTIOCH COLLEGE, OHIO

Dear Gilbert Wilson: The other day I received a copy of the little magazine *Unquote*,[1] containing the correspondence between you and White.[2] It is certainly revealing.

However, I do not wonder that the man is puzzled. Who isn't nowadays? Have the Communists really hooked up with the Fascists? It makes a sick-looking picture.

Am I right in thinking that every effort we make to think our way through these big world movements [is] bound to come to nothing just now, so that a man must work in his own back yard, hoping that these big, power-hungry ones will kill each other off and a little sanity come back into life?

Anyway you know what I mean when we talked of a man working in the small, trying to save a little of the feeling of man for man. Sincerely

393.   [NEW YORK] APRIL 26, 1940

To JOHN ANDERSON

Dear John: I have been thinking a good deal about the letter you wrote me in relation to the father and son problem, and which I got before I saw you in Marion. I didn't speak of it at that time, because I do not know the answer. I am going to try to write something about it later. As a matter of fact, in talking to others I find this same problem exists with all fathers and sons. There is something about the relationship that it is pretty difficult to put your finger on. I think fathers realize this and have it on their minds a good deal more than the sons realize. If you later have sons of your own, you may be up against the same problems one of these days.

In my own case, and as regards you in particular, I simply try to think of you as a workman, perhaps going through some of the same

---

[1] *Unquote* was published irregularly in mimeograph form at Antioch College, Yellow Springs, Ohio, beginning in 1940. Wilson was on the editorial board.

[2] On this matter see Letter 367.

difficulties and facing the same problems that I met at your age and still meet. In regard to a man's work, the whole thing is sort of timeless. The solution never comes quite clear, and the same thing may be true of the relationship. For that matter it may be true of all relationships, not only between fathers and sons, but between men and women. Nothing seems fixed. Everything is always changing. We seem to have very little control over our emotional life.

However, as regards the particular relationship, I am thinking about it a good deal and plan to try to write something about it. Often in writing it is possible to get things clearer than it is by word of mouth. With love to all in the house

394.   [NEW YORK] MAY 22, 1940

To TRILENA WHITE [1]

Dear Friend: I have been going through a siege of flu, and your letter coming in when I was in bed gave me real pleasure. I certainly understand how you feel about people who come and stay indefinitely when you are not up to receiving them. It continually happens to me. You do not want to be rude, but the one thing you most wish is that they would go away.

I am afraid you are entirely mistaken about Carl Sandburg. He is really very shrewd and is well fixed. It is true that for years poor old Carl had to go around the country putting on his show to make a living, but I am told that the *Woman's Home Companion* paid him $30,000 for the portion of the Lincoln they published a few years ago.[2] The other day I had lunch with one of his publishers, who told me they had already sold forty thousand of the complete Lincolns [3] at $20 each. At 15 per cent you can figure that out yourself. As a matter of fact, any book on Lincoln is pretty near sure fire. It can't miss. He remains in our minds and in our imaginations the ideal ruler, and I sincerely believe that his figure will loom larger and larger as the world gets more into a mess.

The mess now is simply inconceivable, and I am not sure that it is not

[1] Miss White, one of Anderson's teachers at Wittenberg Academy, had been "the first woman who introduced [him] to real writers." Anderson corresponded with her regularly until her death after a long illness.

[2] Sandburg's "Mary Todd Lincoln" ran serially in the *Woman's Home Companion* from September to December, 1932.

[3] *Abraham Lincoln: The War Years,* four volumes (1939).

the cause of my own illness. I fought and fought, but cannot get it out of my mind. I keep thinking of friends I have in England, France, and Holland, some of them very dear to me. It fills my dreams at night. I shall be glad to escape to the country where at any rate I can look again at the trees and the streams. I wish I could take you there with me. Much love to you

395. [NEW YORK] MAY 23, 1940

MR. DEWITT WALLACE, *Reader's Digest,* PLEASANTVILLE

Dear DeWitt Wallace: [1] I just received your wire forwarded from Troutdale, Virginia. Here is a story that I hope may be both amusing and the sort of thing you want.

I had returned to my native Ohio small town after twenty-five years. I had written perhaps twenty books. I needed a haircut.

I went into a barbershop, and there I was in the chair of a man who had been one of my closest boyhood friends.

His name was, let's say, Tom Mann. He had been the pitcher on the town ball team when I played in right field. I wasn't much good, couldn't hit, wasn't so good on fly balls. They let me play on the team because they liked me.

Tom was giving me a haircut. We had both, at one time, been in the Army together. I presume that I had rather hoped that, in coming back to my native town, I would be recognized as a sort of genius.

I do not mean that I wanted a band to meet me at the railroad station, nothing like that. But, you know, now and then a citizen coming up to me.

"I read such and such a book of yours. You sure can tell a story."

Something of that sort.

It hadn't happened.

So there I was in Tom Mann's chair in the barbershop. He had almost finished his job. He walked out in front of me and stood facing me.

"Look here," he said, "did I hear that you had become a writer, that you wrote books?"

There seemed to be an accusing look in his eyes. I swallowed hard. "Why no, Tom," I said.

[1] DeWitt Wallace (1889–), founder (1921) and editor of the *Reader's Digest.* On May 23, 1940, he requested a brief humorous story or an amusing true anecdote for a symposium in the next issue. On May 29 he wrote that he liked the autobiographical fragment but that it did not fit "this particular collection."

A look of relief spread over his face. He went back to his job. For a moment our old friendship had been apparently threatened.

"Well, I heard the story," he said, "but I never believed it. I never thought that you would turn out to be that kind of a guy."

I am leaving here early next week to return to Troutdale, Virginia. I hope you may find this little anecdote what you want. Sincerely

396.   [TROUTDALE, VIRGINIA] JULY 12, 1940

MR. JUAN ADOLFO VAZQUEZ, LA PLATA, ARGENTINA

Dear Juan Adolfo Vazquez: Your letter sent to the hotel in New York was late coming to me in the country. I have a small farm in the hills in the state of Virginia, U.S.A., where I have built my house. It is three thousand feet up from the sea, cool and pleasant in the summer; and I shall be here until late fall.

The address is Troutdale, Virginia, U.S.A.

Now I am going for two weeks to teach in a college in Michigan, and then I will return here to stay for the rest of the summer.

At best I shall not again be so stupid as to address you as anything but friend.

I think we must all hope now that something real will begin to build up between the countries of North and South America. I wonder if it can be done. I have always, whenever opportunity afforded, urged publishers to publish more books by South Americans.

If real understanding is to grow, it cannot be done by politicians and businessmen. There must be, instead, a flow of ideas back and forth, a flow of feeling. What I, with many other ordinary North Americans, fear is the growth of imperialism in the United States of America. We, as a nation, have been so powerful, so rich.

Perhaps, with the world shaken as it is, we shall not be so rich. It may be better.

It is very dangerous to be too rich, too powerful.

I cannot tell you in words how much and how sincerely I appreciate your own friendliness and generosity to me. You must someday tell me more of your own life.

Has any of your own work been translated? Gratefully

397. [TROUTDALE, VIRGINIA] AUGUST 16, 1940

To MAXWELL PERKINS

Dear Max: Your letter touched me. It had in it the note I have always felt in you and liked in you.

At the same time, Max, I can't live by merely being thought of as a sometime master of my craft.

It is, Max, my own pretty firm belief that the American people do not buy books. Books are sold to them. Pretty much everything is sold to Americans.

When I began publishing, I began with Ben Huebsch, who had a curious reluctance about selling books. I stayed with him a long time, for years. I was, at the time, strong enough to work, often at work I hated, to make a living and support my children and do my writing at night. I had finally to quit him or starve.

I went to Horace Liveright, and while he lived, Horace did sell my books. He took a gamble on me, and he won and I won. Horace had, as we both know, a lot of unpleasant things about him, but he did put a roof over my head and free me from having to sit day after day in a damn advertising office.

Which convinced me that my books could be sold.

I think it takes a personal interest, a willingness to gamble a little on me, go back of my books.

I had a feeling, Max, when I went to Scribner's, that I might get this kind of interest. I have a suspicion that perhaps I didn't get it because Mr. Scribner thought of me as a man too old to spend money on.

I understood that. It was all right with me, but I did, frankly, expect a better job of selling my books than I got.

And I do know from experience that it can be done.

And I haven't really blamed you, Max. I just figured your real interest was in other men.

It may take a long time, a year or two, to get down all I want to put down in this book on which I am now at work. I have had pretty damn good offers on it. I think I can make it an important book that can be sold by a house that is willing to go back of it.

I don't believe you can blame me for feeling as I do, Max.

Whatever I do, I want you as a friend. Sincerely

398.   [NEW YORK, ?NOVEMBER 24, 1940]

To LAURA LOU COPENHAVER

Dear Mother: I have consulted several people high up in radio about the proposed radio program, and they are all enthusiastic, but after thinking it over, I am less and [less] enthusiastic. It seems to me, Mother, that up to now I have gained a good deal by never becoming a public figure. The big money in these radio programs comes from a sponsor. It would be indirectly plunging me back into at least a loose connection with that advertising world from which I once escaped.

It is true there is big money in it — a thousand a week would not be an unusual mark to shoot at — but what do I need of a thousand a week?

It would all put me into a new, strange world, the temptation always there to play up to the audience.

I'd better stay in my own groove, Mother. I think I'll just forget it. Lots of love to all

[P.S.] We have a Spanish teacher now, a delightful woman, who will come in for an hour and a half three times a week.

Am afraid E. cannot get much of it, as she comes in the afternoon.

I am enclosing an editorial sent out by the syndicate here that handles South American stuff, the syndicate directed by Davila.[1] The teacher made a rough translation that Eleanor will send. It is for the files.

399.   [NEW YORK] NOVEMBER 28, 1940

MR. CARROW DE VRIES, WYANDOTTE, MICHIGAN

Dear Carrow De Vries: I think that after reading your letter I understand exactly how you feel. I believe sincerely that your writing may pull you out of it. The disease we all have and that we have to fight against all our lives is, of course, the disease of self.

I am pretty sure that writing may be a way of life in itself. It can be that, because it continually forces us away from self towards others. Let any man, or woman, look too much upon his own life, and everything becomes a mess. I think the whole glory of writing lies in the fact that it forces us out of ourselves and into the lives of others. In the end the real writer becomes a lover.

---

[1] Carlos Davila, director of the Editors' Press Service, New York City.

Just now I think the thing for you to concentrate upon is to do a lot of writing. Go to your desk every day. Write down things you have felt and sensed in others. Do not, for the present, think too much about success. The real point is to have your own thoughts and feelings get the habit of running down through your arm and fingers to the paper.

In your letter to me today you speak of not having all clearly in your head before you started to write to me and of not having made what you wanted to say clear in your letter. That is again self-consciousness. In reality your letter is simple and direct and tells me plainly what you are up against.

Do not be buffaloed by it. Write and write and write. I am pretty sure that presently things will clear up, and you will do what you are intended to do. Sincerely yours

400.   [NEW YORK] DECEMBER 5, 1940

MR. ROBERT LITTELL,[1] CARE OF *Reader's Digest,* PLEASANTVILLE

Dear Robert Littell: I think it might be well to attempt to put down, as clearly as I can, what is in my mind in connection with the proposed trip in South America.

This, in a broad way, is what is back of the proposal that I have discussed with you. I have no notion that I could do anything in either the economic or the political field. There are too many other and better trained men at that job right now.

What I would like to do is to get up into some South American town, say of five to ten thousand people, settle there for a time and try to get to know the people of such a town; that is to say, not public figures but the people such as a man might get to know in any one of our own towns, as far as possible getting to understand a little their way of thinking and feeling, and trying to pick up the little comedies and tragedies of their lives, much as I have always tried to do in relation to life in our own North American towns.

I do think it may well be quite possible to find for the *Reader's Digest* stories of everyday life in such a town which would be well worth while for your North American readers and that might possibly also strengthen your South American edition.

My notion is that I should not ask you to gamble much on such a

---

[1] Associate Editor of the *Reader's Digest,* who, in his reply to this letter, offered as an alternative plan that the *Digest* pay Anderson $2,000 for the first of his contributions to be accepted.

venture. It would possibly be several months before I could send you anything. I do think it might not be unreasonable to ask you to venture, say, $2,000 or even $2,500. I am pretty sure that I can bring out of such a stay in some town down there enough of the feeling of the everyday life of the people, stories out of their lives and their way of life, to make it worth your while.

This is about the whole of what I have in mind, that is to say, not to shoot for the big stories, but for the more intimate stories down nearer where people actually live.

I certainly appreciate the friendly attitude you have taken toward this venture, and naturally I hope it may be one that will appeal to your editors. Sincerely yours

401.   MARION, VIRGINIA, DECEMBER 27, 1940

MRS. WILLIAM BROWN MELONEY,[1] WALDORF–ASTORIA, NEW YORK

Dear Mrs. Meloney: I read your little book on Christmas morning — a good time to read it — and it seemed to me, dear Mrs. Meloney, a very fine and clear assertion of the basic faith by which the coming America must stand if it is to stand.

And it surely will. I have lived long enough, traveled widely enough, and have known the so-called common people enough in the United States to believe that there is, at bottom, a great store of good common sense and of belief in democracy in our American people.

As for the dictatorships, isn't it obvious, Mrs. Meloney, that they create their own disease, that of bureaucracy, and isn't it also an obvious truth that all bureaucracies must become corrupt? Under a dictatorship people cannot criticize. It is death to criticize, and therefore the dictatorship with its bureaucracy cannot create the remedy that might cure its disease.

There is, to be sure, a kind of temporary efficiency under a dictatorship, but what of this efficiency? It has simply become an efficiency that maintains itself by brutality.

As for our own democracy, why I dare say it will always be a somewhat blundering thing, but it can always cure itself. Men here dare think and speak. Under our democracy we do not need to go about

---

[1] Marie Mattingly Meloney (d. 1943), journalist, editor of *This Week Magazine*, 1934–1943. As her Christmas card for December, 1940, Mrs. Meloney had privately printed a "little book" entitled *What Man Can Not Destroy*, a copy of which had been sent to Anderson.

always under a cloud of suspicion les[t] we be not worshipful enough to some monster of a dictator. All of this, Mrs. Meloney, I have read into your little book, and it was a good book to read, as I was saddened by the death of a very great woman, my mother-in-law, Mrs. Copenhaver.

Many thanks and a fine year to you. Very truly yours

P.S. Where do you women get it? I have been very fortunate. A surprising number of very great people I have known have been women, not young, inexperienced women, but women who have been through the mill, who have been ground by life and fate into something very shining and beautiful.

Index

Index